THE UNITED STATES AND THE HAWAIIAN KINGDOM

A POLITICAL HISTORY

THE UNITED STATES AND
THE HAWAIIAN KINGDOM

A POLITICAL HISTORY · BY MERZE TATE

YALE UNIVERSITY PRESS   NEW HAVEN AND LONDON

Copyright © 1965 by Yale University.
Second printing, February 1967.
Designed by Sally Hargrove,
set in Caledonia type,
and printed in the United States of America by
The Murray Printing Company,
Forge Village, Massachusetts.
All rights reserved. This book may not be
reproduced, in whole or in part, in any form
(except by reviewers for the public press),
without written permission from the publishers.
Library of Congress catalog card number: 65–22342
Published with assistance from
the Bureau of International Research of
Harvard University and Radcliffe College.

PREFACE

This book is designed to provide for the general reader and the
scholar a treatment in depth and breadth of the relationship of the
United States and Americans, in both official and unofficial capacities, to the decline and eventual fall of the Hawaiian kingdom.
The underlying or indirect causes of that decline are treated as
thoroughly as the alleged immediate cause of the overthrow of
Queen Liliuokalani, namely the attempt to promulgate a new constitution.

Since the major portion of the archival material used is preserved
in the Archives of the United States and of Hawaii, I am much indebted to the staff of the Diplomatic, Legal, and Fiscal Branch and
Central Search Room of the former, and to Miss Agnes C. Conrad,
archivist, and the staff of the latter for the courteous and efficient
assistance always given me. I am similarly indebted to the staff of
the Hawaiian Room of the University of Hawaii Library, especially
to Miss Janet Bell; to Mrs. Willodean Handy, formerly director of
the Hawaiian Historical Society Library; and Miss Bernice Judd,
formerly in charge of the Hawaiian Mission Children's Society
Library (both collections now housed together as the Mission-Historical Library in Honolulu); as well as to the staff of the Library
of Congress, particularly to those in the Manuscript, the Newspaper, and the Thomas Jefferson Reading Rooms of the Annex.

I am grateful to the *Washington Evening Star* and the Rocke-
feller Foundation for grants in aid of research on the Pacific area,
some of which financial assistance was used in the preparation of
this study, and especially to Dr. James M. Nabrit, Jr., President of
Howard University, who provided grants which made possible the
condensation of a much longer manuscript, the typing of this one,
and of twelve articles dealing with Hawaii. Efficient secretarial
help was rendered by Miss Gloria Nelson, Mrs. Vivian E. Taylor,
Mrs. Yvonne Roberts, and Miss Dorothy Claude.

My deepest gratitude goes to Vice President Emeritus Bernice Brown Cronkhite of Radcliffe College, and to Professor Emeritus Sydney B. Fay of Harvard University for their continued interest in my research and for a publication subvention from the Bureau of International Research of Harvard University and Radcliffe College. None of the above-mentioned persons, however, is responsible for any errors of fact or interpretation that may appear in the book.

M.T.

Howard University
December 1964

CONTENTS

Preface   v

Abbreviations   xi

1. EARLY AMERICAN INTEREST   1
   A Cultural Frontier   4
   The Role of Americans   10
   Diminishing Influence   18
   Constitutional Change   22

2. AMERICAN CONCERN, 1864–1882   27
   The Succession and Annexation   28
   Reciprocity Consummated   38
   Decadence   43
   Cabinets and the Legislature   49
   "Wild" Proposals   53
   Disaffection of the Propertied Class   58

3. THE BLOODLESS REVOLUTION OF 1887   60
   Reaction in Washington   71
   Primacy in Polynesia   75
   The Hawaiian League   81
   The Bloodless Revolution   86
   The Constitution of 1887   91
   Status of American Residents   94
   The Insurrection of 1889   95
   Fall of the Reform Ministry   101
   Proposals for a New Constitution   102
   Growing British Influence   105
   Kalakaua's Last Visit   107

4. LILIUOKALANI'S REIGN   111
   The Annexation Club   115
   Thurston's Mission   116
   New Prospects of Annexation   121

The Queen Regains Control 129
Preparing for Annexation 135
An Overture from Washington 146
Stevens Presses Hard 148

5. THE REVOLUTION OF 1893: FOUR DAYS 155
January 14 155
January 15 167
January 16 171
January 17 182
The Aftermath 191

6. AMERICAN REACTION 194
Official Reaction 196
The Treaty 199
Early Reaction 205
A Protectorate 209
Ratification Delayed 213
Individual Influence 218
The Strategists' Point of View 224

7. CLEVELAND'S POLICY 228
The Initial Approach 231
The Blount Investigation 234
Gresham's Position 237
Willis' Mission 242
Cleveland's Message to Congress 246
Congressional Action 251
Uncertainty 258

8. SUCCESS OF THE ANNEXATIONISTS 269
A Second Treaty 269
Americanists and Strategists 273
To and from Annexation 281
Reaction of American Labor 288
Opposition of the Sugar Interests 291
Abandonment of the Treaty 292
Annexation through Joint Resolution 294
Formal Transfer of Sovereignty 306

9. SUMMARY AND CONCLUSION 308

Appendix I: Biographical Notes 317

Appendix II: Taxation, 1881 340

Appendix III: Native Monarchs of Hawaii   342

Sources   344

Index   349

Four nineteenth-century maps from Library of Congress collections
appear on:

page   5   Sandwich Islands
page   127   Honolulu and Pearl Harbors
page   177   Downtown Honolulu
page   343   Pacific Naval Stations

ABBREVIATIONS

ABCFM	American Board of Commissioners for Foreign Missions.
AH	Public Archives of the State of Hawaii.
CO	Colonial Office Archives, in the British Public Record Office.
FO	Foreign Office Archives, in the same repository.
FO Ex.	Foreign Office and Executive File, Archives of Hawaii.
For. Rels.	*Papers Relating to the Foreign Relations of the United States.*
HHS	Hawaiian Historical Society.
HMCS	Hawaiian Mission Children's Society.
JL	Journals of the Legislature.
LAB	Letters to the American Board.
MH	*Missionary Herald,* official organ of the ABCFM, published in Boston.
RLA	Resolutions of the Legislative Assembly.
USDS	United States Department of State Archives.

EARLY AMERICAN INTEREST

Probably the earliest American contact with the Hawaiian Islands
was made in 1789 by a small Boston trading craft, the *Columbia*,
under the command of Captain Robert Gray in the course of his
voyage from the Pacific Northwest coast to China and his circum-
navigation of the world. The *Columbia* arrived on August 24 and
remained twenty-four days at the islands, "salted down five pun-
cheons of pork, and sailed with one hundred and fifty live hogs on
deck." [1] Captain Gray's visit established a precedent for vessels sailing between Oregon and Canton. Practically every ship that visited
the North Pacific in the closing years of the eighteenth century put
in at "the Islands," which proved a delightful and glamorous refreshment and rest station. By 1800 the trans-Pacific fur trade was
almost a monopoly of New England craft seeking the midocean
haven.

The sandalwood (*sandalum album*) trade that flourished in the
Sandwich Islands between 1812 and 1829 was a monopoly of three
Bostonians, Captains Nathan Winship, Jonathan Winship, and William Heath Davis, during the first ten of these years.[2] Although the
avaricious traffic in this product, which was highly prized in China
as incense and in the making of delicate pieces of furniture, caused

1. Samuel E. Morison, "Boston Traders in the Hawaiian Islands, 1794,"
Massachusetts Historical Society, *Proceedings, 54* (1920–21), 11.
2. Ibid., p. 16.

the island population to wither and the sandalwood forests to disappear, "it represented the beginning of American interest in the Islands and of American concern for the fate of the archipelago." [3] A small but influential group in the United States became concerned over the location, inhabitants, and commercial advantages of the mid-Pacific kingdom.

Honolulu's significance as a trading center increased when, in 1804, Kamehameha I took up residence in Waikiki, whence produce from other islands was transshipped. When the War of 1812 broke out, complications were envisaged in Honolulu if the Hawaiian Islands were to continue to fly the Union Jack, which, after Captain George Vancouver left in 1794, replaced Kamehameha's original pennant. A new flag—a compromise between the emblems of the warring nations—was adopted. The crosses on the blue field in the corner retained the friendship of Great Britain, while the eight red, white, and blue strips recognized the United States and, at the same time, represented the eight larger islands of the Hawaiian group.[4]

After the war, various American trading houses regularly stationed as their representatives one or more agents at Honolulu. James Hunnewell of Boston conducted a regular retail store there for about ten months in 1817–18. Five years later there were four American mercantile establishments, of Hunnewell; John C. Jones, agent for Marshall and Wildes; "Nor'west John" De Wolf, from Rhode Island; and one from New York, probably that of John Ebbets, who represented the house of John Jacob Astor and Son.

The outcome of the Anglo-American contest spelled the eclipse of British pelagic whaling, and after the contest Americans extended their search for new grounds in the Pacific. In 1818, after increased numbers of Europeans had entered the whaling industry, causing a depletion of the aquatic mammal in the North Atlantic and the regular grounds of the South Pacific, Captain George W. Garner, in the *Globe* of Nantucket, steering west from the old tracts, discovered what he called the "Off-shore Ground" in 5° to 10° south latitude and 105° to 125° west longitude, where whales teemed in almost countless numbers. Within ten years, more than fifty ships were whaling in this same locality.[5] The crews of two whale ships,

3. Harold Whitman Bradley, *The American Frontier in Hawaii: The Pioneers, 1789–1843* (Palo Alto, 1942), pp. 119–20.

4. W. D. Westervelt, "Kamehameha's Method of Government," HHS Thirtieth *Report,* 1921 (Honolulu, 1922), p. 36.

5. Alexander Starbuck, *History of the American Whale Fishery from Its Earliest Inception to the Year 1876* (Waltham, Mass., 1878), p. 96.

the *Balaena* of New Bedford and the *Equator* of Nantucket, killed a whale off Kealakekua Bay, Hawaii, in September 1819, and the next month two whalers visited the islands, the vanguard of a vast fleet to use the ports.[6]

During the latter 1820s the whaling industry replaced the traffic in sandalwood as the chief commercial activity in the Pacific. Six-sevenths of the world's whaling fleet operated in that ocean, and the majority of the ships engaged in the business hailed from New England. Another impetus to the industry was given by the opening of the Arctic fishery. The recurrent visits of large fleets of whaleships to Hawaiian ports were a significant factor in shaping the history of the islands and people, and the results were mixed: great pecuniary gain and equally great moral loss. Water and fresh provisions were the ship's principal requirements; whereas the crew's need was diversion after many days at sea. Favorite ports of call were Honolulu, on Oahu; Lahaina, on Maui; Hilo, on Hawaii; and Waimea, on Kauai—with a preponderant preference for the first-named port. During the twenty-year period 1824–43 approximately 1700 whaling ships arrived at Honolulu, or an average of about 85 annually, nearly 1400 of which were American, while slightly more than 300 were British.[7]

The long reign of Kamehameha III, 1825–54, coincided with the period of greatest activity in the American whale fishery, most of which was conducted in the Pacific on newly discovered grounds. This was the golden age—when the Hawaiian kingdom enjoyed its greatest prosperity from the visit of whalers. The average number of vessels stopping at the islands annually from 1843 to 1855 was 419, the great majority being American.[8] A zenith was reached in the whaling industry between 1840 and 1860, the climax occurring in the late fifties. A combination of circumstances caused the business to decline after 1860,[9] with the consequent transfer of capital and crews to more attractive commercial enterprises. As the whaling industry replaced the traffic in sandalwood in the late 1820s, the cultivation of sugar, with its concomitant activities, superseded whaling in the 1860s, and in this new field of economic endeavor Americans were and remained predominant.

6. Ibid.

7. Ralph S. Kuykendall, "American Interests and American Influence in Hawaii in 1842," HHS Thirty-Ninth *Report*, 1930 (Honolulu, 1931), p. 49.

8. Raymond A. Rydell, *Cape Horn to the Pacific* (Berkeley and Los Angeles, 1952), p. 70.

9. Ibid., p. 73.

Thus in the early nineteenth century "sandalwood, geography, and fresh provisions made the islands a vital link in a closely articulated trade route, between Boston, the Northwest Coast, and Canton." [10] American fishers of whales and fishers of men had, by the 1840s, created in the Sandwich Islands an economic, commercial, and religious frontier. Although remote from the Atlantic seaboard— separated from it yet linked by thousands of miles of water requiring five to six months to traverse—Hawaii had become an outpost of New England. Besides the Hudson's Bay Company's agency, there were in Honolulu six houses of business. Of these, four were American, one British, and one French.[11] The little community might not have been quite as Yankee as a suburb of Boston, but the town was certainly more American than European.

A Cultural Frontier

Missionary endeavors and influence were a significant, if not a preponderant, magnet in drawing Hawaii from the British into the United States' sphere of influence. Although the missionaries' primary interest was nonpolitical, their direct and intimate association with both the highborn and the lowly gave them a personal ascendency over the Hawaiian mind, and consciously or unconsciously presented to it an American point of view.

Aside from conversions, the most notable and noble achievements of the Congregational and Presbyterian missionaries, who journeyed to the Sandwich Islands under the auspices of the American Board of Commissioners for Foreign Missions, were the systematization of the Hawaiian language, the preparation of literature to be used in the churches and schools, and the development of an educational system. Evangelism was the primary function of the mission, but teaching and printing, although auxiliary to the main function, played a large and significant role in the Christianizing process. Through the printed word, the missionaries gained access to the hearts and minds of their pupils: religious concepts and ideas were incorporated in the reading material, and teachers converted as they taught.

The members of Reverend Hiram Bingham's pioneer band, before leaving Boston in the autumn of 1819, were instructed "to obtain an adequate knowledge of the language of the people; to make

10. Morison, "Boston Traders," *Proceedings, 54,* 14.
11. *MH, 28* (1831), 113.

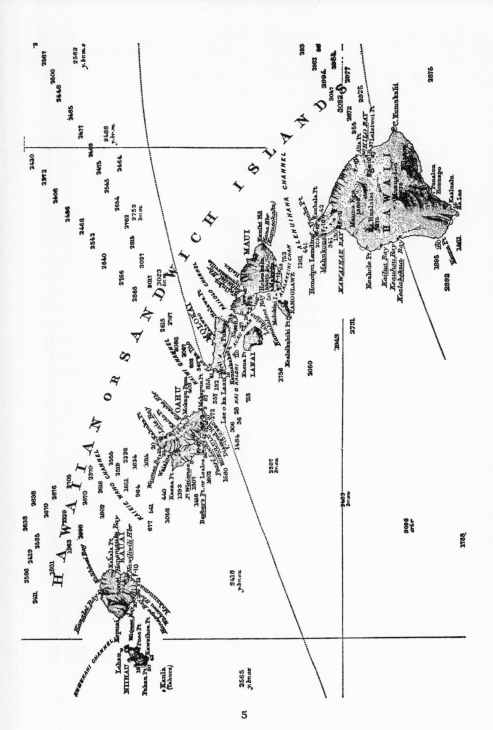

HAWAIIAN OR SANDWICH ISLAND

NIIHAU

KAUAI

OAHU

MOLOKAI

MAUI

LANAI

KAHOOLAWE

HAWAII

them acquainted with letters"; and "to give them the Bible with skill to read it." [1] Since the Hawaiian language had never been reduced to a practical written form, one of the first tasks of the missionaries on their arrival in the islands was to learn the tongue, to invent a system of transcribing it in Roman characters, to translate the Bible and textbooks into this form, and then to print them.

Printing of necessity involved the establishment of an alphabet, which required considerable time and study to perfect. Undaunted, the missionaries proceeded to print simple teaching materials while they settled the orthography of the vernacular. Assisted by the Reverend William Ellis, who had labored for six years in the Society Islands under the auspices of the London Missionary Society, where he had acquired a facility with and an intimate knowledge of the Tahitian language, the frugal Puritans chose a simple and fairly consistent phonetic system, making use of only twelve letters of the Roman alphabet to represent the sounds of the Hawaiian language.[2] After a definite alphabet was adopted in July 1826, every Hawaiian word was spelled precisely as it was pronounced, which made spelling and reading much simpler than in English.

The achievements of the mission press in the first two decades of its existence were impressive. Laboring under the handicaps of meager resources, over-age second-hand Ramage presses, inadequate fonts of print without accents, and a shortage of trained assistants, the printers practically performed miracles. The missionaries prepared and printed nearly 1,500,000 pages in 1825 and 5,000,000 in 1830; two presses were then inadequate to supply the demand for *palapala*.[3] The mission printed nearly 18,000,000 pages in 1837; it had three presses in operation by 1840 and had printed in all 100,-000,000 pages, covering perhaps fifty different works. Two years later more than 12,000,000 pages in the Hawaiian language had issued from the press. The entire Bible had been printed in the Hawaiian language by May 10, 1839.[4]

Thirteen separate works in the Hawaiian language were published

1. ABCFM, *Instructions of the Prudential Committee of the ABCFM* to the Sandwich Islands Mission (Lahainaluna, 1838), p. 27.

2. Thomas Marshall Spaulding, *The Adoption of the Hawaiian Alphabet,* HHS, *Papers,* No. 17 (Honolulu, 1930), p. 30.

3. Characters made on *kapa,* or paper—hence, writing. Later the word was popularly employed to designate the system of education introduced by the missionaries.

4. MH, 35 (1839), 145–46; 37 (1841), 145.

by the Oahu Mission press in Honolulu and six others by the press at Lahainaluna during the year ending May 1840.[5] The volumes written or translated and printed by that year embraced a wider range of literature than that which constituted the library of many children and youth in progressive New England in the 1830s, to say nothing of the less fortunate parts of the United States and the world.[6] By 1873 not less than 150 different works, as well as thirteen magazines and an *Almanac, 1834–1862,* had been prepared and printed, and the printing exceeded 220 million pages.[7] Credit must be given the Sandwich Island missionaries for making a substantial beginning in the development of a printed Hawaiian literature.[8]

The educational work of the missionaries, initiated first among the chiefs, their children, and the advisers, developed through several stages. Simple grass-hut schools—in which the curriculum consisted primarily of learning the alphabet, spelling, and simple reading— were followed by substantial and permanent schoolhouses, with suitable textbook materials outside the field of pure religion. A high school was established at Lahainaluna, or Upper Lahaina, on Maui, to "instruct men of piety and promising talents" in order that they might become assistant teachers. At the request of the chiefs, a family or boarding school was opened in Honolulu in 1839 for the education of their children, and remained under mission supervision until 1846, when it was placed under the ministry of public instruction and designated the "Royal School." Panahou School, later known as Oahu College, developed into a preparatory school, elementary and secondary, and performed a distinctive service through the education of a significant proportion of Hawaii's business and professional leaders. The missionaries, in instituting several manual-labor schools, were forty years ahead of their contemporaries in the United States. Select schools, or boarding schools, for Hawaiian children, along with station schools, were the missionaries' pride and stronghold. Through their instrumentality the mission raised up and influenced an intelligent and somewhat educated people. We

5. Ibid., 37 (1841), 145.

6. Laura Fish Judd, *Honolulu: Sketches of Life, Social, Political and Religious in the Hawaiian Islands from 1828 to 1861* (New York, 1880), p. 68.

7. Rufus Anderson, *History of the Sandwich Islands Mission* (Boston, 1870), pp. 390–97. Anderson, *The Hawaiian Islands: Their Progress and Condition under Missionary Labors* (Boston and New York, 1864), pp. 262–68.

8. See my "The Sandwich Islands Missionaries Create a Literature," *Church History,* 21 (1962), 182–202, for a catalogue of publications.

may conclude that the educational work of the Sandwich Islands Mission up to 1840, when it surrendered the administration of the common schools to the government, was of incalculable value in disseminating knowledge to all classes of people in the kingdom, in planting and nurturing religious concepts and some of the better features of Western civilization, and in laying the foundation for a system of public instruction in the English language.[9]

In the technical, mechanical, and industrial field, the efforts and performance of the missionaries, often overlooked, were commendable. The pioneer company—which included a printer by trade, a teacher and skilled mechanic, and a prosperous Massachusetts farmer—carried a supply of seeds and agricultural implements, including axes, plows, hoes, and shovels, the most important tools of various mechanical arts, surgical instruments, and a twenty-year-old Ramage printing press and apparatus. These Puritans were the first in Hawaii to yoke oxen. In the introduction of foreign plants, in the milling of sugar and molasses, and in making spinning and weaving a cottage industry, they demonstrated their interest in teaching Hawaiians new trades. In the construction of stone churches and schoolhouses to supplant the native grass structures, from the time the first stone was cut until the last finishing touch, missionaries laid out the plans and superintended the work. Even when the people built houses for themselves, unless they used grass, they called upon their teachers for instruction and for assistance in the planning and execution of the building. If a wheel or a loom or a piece of furniture was to be made, they were sought out to see it done.

Realizing their limited resources and numbers, the missionaries appealed, in a memorial drafted in July 1836, to the American Board or some society formed on similar principles to send to Hawaii agricultural and industrial teachers. Thus, 113 years before President Truman's "bold new program" for making the benefits of American scientific know-how and industrial progress available for the advancement of undeveloped areas of the world, the Sandwich Island missionaries demonstrated a genuine and prophetic acquaintance with the requirements of a humble people lacking skill, enterprise, and industry. The missionaries' schools served as the first American technical mission overseas; their tireless labors and simple instruc-

9. See my "The Sandwich Islands Missionaries Lay the Foundation for a System of Public Instruction in Hawaii," *Journal of Negro Education, 30* (1961), 396–405.

tion in the agricultural, mechanical, and manual fields represented the first chapter in the prelude to Point Four.[10]

The unique achievements and moral victories of the Sandwich Islands Mission were possible because its members, as a whole, were men and women of superior ability and training. Even more important were their intense convictions, their profound altruistic enthusiasm, and a triumphant certainty of success in their divine task. Out of the seventy-seven married couples who sojourned in the islands, forty-two families continued to be represented by descendants. Among them the grandson of Reverend Asa Thurston, the son of Reverend Daniel Dole, the son of Reverend William P. Alexander, and the sons of two secular agents of the mission, Amos Starr Cooke and Samuel N. Castle, became powerful in the economic and political life of Hawaii and influenced tremendously its destiny.

For the first quarter of a century after its advent in 1820, this Christian mission was by far the predominating white influence in the islands, and for another twenty-five years "it so assimilated and moulded the other growing white elements as to secure their practical cooperation." In the words of the Reverend Sereno E. Bishop, son of the Reverend Artemas Bishop of the first reinforcement, "the whole community, both native and foreign, became subject to their controlling moral and social influence. With the natives the yielding was trustful and willing. With the restive and violent whites it was quite otherwise, yet conclusive and effectual." [11]

The homeward current of a number of missionary couples who felt it a duty to their children in the late 1840s to remove them to the United States for their education, combined with the movement of population toward California and Oregon and the swing of world interest into the Pacific region, created in 1848 a "grand crisis" for the Sandwich Islands Mission. The problem was finally resolved by the American Board revising its original policies concerning secular pursuits, the acquisition of property, and citizenship. Mission property, including herds, was divided, and the missionaries were encouraged to become naturalized Hawaiians and remain in the islands. As a further inducement, provision was made for the college education of Mission children at Punahou, and the Hawaiian government agreed to grant adequate lands in suitable

10. See my "Sandwich Islands Missionaries: The First American Point Four Agents," HHS, Seventieth *Report*, 1961 (Honolulu, 1962), pp. 7–23.

11. S. E. Bishop, "The American Missionaries Here," *Pacific Commercial Advertiser* (July 2, 1906), p. 81.

situations. The "real object" of the American Board in its 1848 decision was "to get the institutions of the gospel fast rooted in the soil of the Sandwich Islands," for the benefit of whatever community that was "to occupy and possess those Islands in all times to come." There would be an Anglo-Saxon community at the islands, and the Board considered it the duty and the privilege of the missionaries to see that it was a "religious community." [12]

The old Sandwich Islands Mission ceased to exist as an organization accountable to the Board on May 23, 1854, when it was superseded by the Hawaiian Evangelical Association, composed of missionaries of the American Board who were residents in the islands, together with other resident ministers of foreign birth in sympathy with them. Early in their sojourn the missionaries, hesitatingly but very gradually, trained a native pastorate who for a time served as assistants and belatedly were licensed as ordained ministers with their own charge.[13]

The Role of Americans

The major credit for the predominating political influence of the United States in Hawaii "is almost universally given to the missionaries—and rightly so." [1] In the beginning the members of the mission were in a strict sense *amici curiae*, remaining in the background, prompting, teaching, and guiding the rulers. From the peculiar nature and structure of the government, and the fact that the dominant chiefs were members of the church and, after 1824, zealous for the newly adopted religion, "it came to pass that church and state were actively for a time united." The churches, schools, teachers, and the whole system of religious order and influence depended in no small degree upon the support and sanction of the

12. Rufus Anderson to the Sandwich Islands Mission, July 19, 1848, and May 8, 1850, *General Letters of the ABCFM* (Honolulu, 1834–59), pp. 30, 9–10. Printed as leaflets, leaves, or broadsides for circulation among members of the mission. Pages refer to each letter, not to the volume. See my "The 'Grand Crisis' for the Sandwich Islands Mission and the Year of Decision," *Journal of Religious Thought, 20* (1963), 43–52.

13. See my "The Sandwich Islands Missionaries Train a Native Pastorate," ibid., *17* (1960), 33–39.

1. Kuykendall, *Report,* p. 55. For a general treatment of the subject see my "The Early Political Influence of the Sandwich Islands Missionaries," *Journal of Religious Thought, 17* (1960), 117–32.

government.[2] The premature death of King Liholiho in 1824 and the consequent continuation of the regency during the minority of Kauikeaouli (Kamehameha III) gave the mission a considerable period of influence at court, during which time church and state drew closely together. During the 1820s and early 1830s no missionaries held official positions and were prohibited by the American Board from doing so; nevertheless, they were convinced that the government should foster education, religion, and private virtue; that they should encourage and advise the rulers along these lines; and that they "ought not be indifferent to the kind and nature of the laws about to be promulgated." As teachers of the chiefs and people, they felt a duty "to give information and advice . . . when asked to do so by the proper authorities." If necessary, they might also translate for the chiefs' use such of the laws of foreign nations as might be applicable to the conditions of the Hawaiian people, and "render them any other such assistance when requested as shall be consistent with our profession as Christian teachers." [3]

Efforts of the converted chiefs to have five laws interdicting murder, theft, prostitution, gambling, and the retailing of ardent spirits ran into the opposition of Chief Boki, governor of Oahu, no doubt influenced by the antimissionary element led by the British consul, Richard Charlton. As a result, on December 8, 1827, only the first (prohibiting murder on penalty of death), the second (prohibiting theft on penalty of confinement in irons), and the third (prohibiting adultery, the penalty being the same as for theft) were promulgated, in a great concourse of people assembled under a grove of coconut trees near the sea.[4] The Puritans rejoiced over their partial success. A good start had been made.

The confusion following Kaahumanu's death, and the desultory and disorderly course of Kauikeaouli, led the chiefs in January 1834 to prepare a little penal code, in five chapters or divisions, providing graduated penalties for five major groups of crimes: (1) murder and lesser degrees of homicide, (2) theft, (3) unlawful sexual intercourse and divorce, (4) fraud and perjury, and (5) drunkenness and offenses committed while intoxicated. Although the code

2. Sheldon Dibble, *History of the Sandwich Islands* (Lahainaluna, 1843), p. 203.

3. Extracts from Minutes of General Meeting of the Mission 1826, Archives of the Hawaiian Board, Honolulu. Transcript in the archives of HHS.

4. *MH, 24* (1828), 209.

was prepared by the chiefs and proclaimed by the young King on January 5, 1835, there is little doubt that they were encouraged by their teachers. Four years later a declaration of rights and a code of laws provided something like a civil code for the kingdom. The former document plainly showed the influence of both the Bible and the American Declaration of Independence.

Negotiations and often complications with foreign traders and captains of visiting men-of-war pointed up the importance of the king and chiefs being "enlightened on points of civil policy and the laws of nations—that they might know how to meet public officers and how to advocate their own cause and maintain their own rights." [5] The chiefs, cognizant of the advantages foreigners took of them, the importance of acquiring knowledge on their part, and the significance of putting their own government on a firmer foundation, invited Reverend Lorrin Andrews, principal of the Mission Seminary at Lahainaluna, to become their teacher and assistant in political affairs. Although Andrews gave his assent, his colleagues on Maui and Molokai opposed the change, with the result that the clergyman continued in his "appropriate business" [6] as principal of Lahainaluna until 1842, when he terminated his services with the American Board.

Decidedly against the ancient system of government by 1838, the missionaries, especially those who had recently arrived at the islands, spoke out sharply in the *Kuma Hawaii* (*Hawaiian Teacher*). The *Hawaiian Spectator*, among whose founders and first contributors were several missionaries, had as one of its avowed aims to emphasize the "importance and bearing of other efforts for converting the world, besides such as are generally termed missionary efforts; such as gradual change of their laws and political institutions." [7] Thus the evangelists, while not officially advising the chiefs, resorted to the press as a medium of instituting needed reforms.

When Reverend William Richards, who went to the United States in the summer of 1836, returned to Honolulu in the spring of 1838

5. Ralph S. Kuykendall, *The Hawaiian Kingdom 1778–1854* (Honolulu, 1947), p. 154, quoting Peter A. Brinsmade.

6. Andrews to Rufus Anderson, Nov. 13, 1837, LAB, *135*, No. 175, Harvard College Library (ABC:19.1–9).

7. *Hawaiian Spectator*, 1 (1838), frontispiece. See the first issue of Jan. 1838, pp. 55–57, for a considered view of conditions in Hawaii written by Rev. Artemas Bishop. These early issues of the *Hawaiian Spectator* are in the Spaulding Collection, University of Michigan Library, but not in the Library of Congress.

without the teachers the King and chiefs had requested and had hoped the American Board would send, they prevailed upon him to accept an appointment as "chaplain, teacher and translator" to the King.[8] During his first year with the government the clergyman devoted a little less than three months' time to the King and chiefs and continued to do "a large share of the native preaching in the church which he had served for so many years." [9] Eventually, Dr. Gerrit P. Judd, Richard Armstrong, and Lorrin Andrews followed Richards' example in entering a new sphere of labor which bid fair to increase their usefulness and in which they hoped to enjoy the same confidence as if they were under the immediate direction of the American Board.

Judd was in effect a prime minister, performing the duties of head of the Treasury, secretary of state for foreign affairs, and minister of the interior. Under the first organic act, "to Organize the Executive Ministry," April 13, 1846, the King commissioned Judd minister of finance, Robert Crichton Wyllie as minister of foreign relations, William Richards minister of public instruction, and John Ricord, a young American lawyer who had just arrived in Honolulu, attorney general. Judd devised a policy whose fundamental principle was a union of Hawaiians and foreigners as subjects and supporters of the independent native monarchy, which should be organized on a constitutional basis, so as to gain for the kingdom the benefits of foreign intercourse, without allowing the indigenous race to be overwhelmed by a flood of aliens.[10]

John Ricord was the first American layman with legal background to enter the service of the Hawaiian government. Appointed attorney general of the kingdom on March 9, 1844, he helped to interpret the constitution of 1840 and prepared drafts of the three organic acts, providing for the privy council, the executive department, and the judiciary. He brought into existence the courts of chancery, probate, and admiralty, and provided with them, a body of law by which their adjudication ought to be governed. This was accomplished by adopting the common and civil law as administered especially in Great Britain and the United States, and in attempting

8. Richards to Anderson, Aug. 1, 1838, LAB, *135*, No. 83.

9. William Richards, "Report to the Sandwich Islands Mission on His First Year in Government Service, 1838–1839," HHS Fifty-First *Report*, 1942 (Honolulu, 1943), p. 68.

10. *Friend*, 20 (1862), 67, See Gerrit P. Judd, IV, *Dr. Judd*, Hawaii's Friend. *A Biography of Gerrit Parmele Judd (1830–1873)* (Honolulu, 1960).

to make court decisions conform to practices and precedents in these countries. Often records were sent to jurists in England and America for their decisions. Ricord also contributed his legal and literary talents to the initial work of the land commission. In interpreting and reforming the constitution to meet the exigencies of a small kingdom having intercourse with the great powers and their citizens, he adopted so far as possible the principles of the British constitution and attempted to assimilate Hawaiian laws, influenced by American practices, to British models. Although his sojourn at the islands was comparatively brief, the domineering and ostentatious John Ricord made a permanent contribution of the highest value to the country and one which entitles him to be numbered among the builders of Hawaii.[11]

The second man with legal training to visit the Sandwich Islands was William Little Lee, who, on a stopover en route to Oregon in 1846, was persuaded to remain in the kingdom to head the prospective judicial system. Pending the passage of an act reorganizing the courts, he was offered a position as one of the judges of Oahu, an appointment intended to be coordinate and concurrent with that of Lorrin Andrews, who had entered the service of the King. The Hawaiian Records begin in January 1847 with the recorded decisions of Judge Lee.[12]

At the age of twenty-six, and only seven weeks after placing foot on Hawaiian soil, Lee became one of the leading men of the kingdom. Before his premature death on May 28, 1857 he was reported "to control almost every important action of the government." [13] He was duly selected as chief justice of the newly created superior court; under his capable, dignified and unostentatious guidance, emphasis was placed upon the interpretation and enforcement of law. His abilities were still further recognized by appointment to the privy council and to membership on the land commission. Fur-

11. W. R. Castle, "Sketch of Constitutional History of Hawaii," HHS Twenty-Third *Report*, 1914 (Honolulu, 1915), p. 16. For further information on Ricord see the pamphlet *Motion in the Hawaiian Parliament, Made by R. C. Wyllie . . . To Release John Ricord . . . from a Debt Standing against Him in the Books of the King's Treasury . . .* (Honolulu, 1853), and a manuscript title on John Ricord by A. F. Judd, II, read before the Bar Association of Hawaii, June 20, 1923, HMCS Library.

12. Thomas M. Spaulding, "Chief Justice William Little Lee," *Honolulu Mercury*, 2 (1930), 346–47. Thomas M. Spaulding, "William Little Lee," *Dictionary of American Biography, 11*, 135.

13. Gregg to Marcy, March 9, 1857, No. 207, USDS, Dispatches, Hawaii, 8.

ther, the legislative council requested him to draft civil and criminal codes. Drawing liberally from the proposed penal codes of Massachusetts and Louisiana, Lee drafted one which remained the permanent basis of Hawaiian criminal law.[14] He also participated in the preparation of the civil code, which was not completed until after his death. He was elected a member of the house of representatives, from which judges were not excluded until the adoption of the constitution of 1864, and he served ably as the speaker of that chamber.

Judge Lee, representing the house of representatives on the three-member commission which drafted the constitution of 1852, did much of the preparation, and the instrument represents his democratic point of view. Two of its articles, differing from practice in the States, bear unmistakably his mark. Article 12 of the declaration of rights, which declares: "Slavery shall under no circumstances whatever be tolerated in the Hawaiian Islands; whenever a slave shall enter Hawaiian territory he shall be free," reflects his bitterness on the antislavery question. Article 88 of the constitution reads: "The King, His Minister, and each branch of the Legislature shall have authority to require the opinions of the Justices of the Supreme Court, upon important questions of law, and upon solemn occasions." Although the right to call upon the justices for advisory opinions was rarely used until the stormy reigns of King Kalakaua and Queen Liliuokalani, all later Hawaiian constitutions, monarchical or republican, contained a similar provision.

After the constitution of 1852 was adopted, Judge Lee was appointed chief justice of a reconstituted supreme court and held this position, as well as that of chancellor of the kingdom, until his death. When he planned to visit his homeland in 1855 to relieve himself for a time of the immense burden that had shattered his health, he was appointed plenipotentiary to the United States, Great Britain, France, and Russia to negotiate a quadripartite treaty with those nations for the preservation of the king's sovereignty, and a reciprocity convention with the United States.[15] The envoy failed to secure a joint guarantee of the independence of the kingdom, but he ne-

14. *Penal Code of the Hawaiian Islands, Passed by the House of Nobles and Representatives on the 21st of June, A.D. 1850; to which Are Appended the Other Acts Passed by the House of Nobles and Representatives during Their General Session for 1850* (Honolulu, 1850). Cf. pp. iii–iv for Lee's report on the preparation of the code, and the *Polynesian*, Aug. 3, 10, 17, 1850, for "an Act Establishing a Penal Code."

15. Privy Council Records, 9, Minutes of Nov. 20, 1855, AH.

gotiated without difficulty a reciprocity treaty with Secretary of State William L. Marcy. This American served both Kamehameha III and Kamehameha IV "with a talent, integrity, and devotion" to Their Majesties' "interest and the cause of justice, never surpassed." [16]

Elisha H. Allen of Maine and Massachusetts, a former United States consul in Honolulu, after serving as minister of finance for both Kamehamehas, succeeded Lee as chief justice and chancellor of the kingdom, and was held in high esteem by the young King. Allen's greater period of service and contribution to Hawaii came, however, in the mid-1860s, when with Minister Wyllie he controlled the course of government policy.

It was Lorrin Andrews' integrity and his facility with the Hawaiian language—not his evangelism—that recommended him to the King and chiefs, who by 1845 were in urgent need of an honest person to handle the ever-mounting legal complications between Hawaiians and aliens. The missionary educator was appointed by Kekuanaoa, the progressive governor of Oahu, in September of that year to act as his substitute in his court in Honolulu in all cases between or affecting the interests of foreigners, whether alien or naturalized. The mild yet firm manner in which Andrews administered the duties of his office not only created a favorable impression upon the public but won the esteem of even the convicted themselves. Under an act to organize the judiciary, passed in April 1846, he was officially designated a judge of original and appellate jurisdiction. When the superior court of law and equity was created the following year, Andrews, along with John Ii, was appointed associate justice of a tribunal that was substantially a supreme court in all but name, and whose chief justice was William L. Lee.[17] Andrews served his adopted country honestly and diligently in the position of associate justice until the end of 1854, when he was appointed a judge of probate, who should have concurrent jurisdiction with the judges of the supreme court in hearing and determining probate and divorce cases in which native Hawaiians were involved. The former missionary's "correct knowledge of the native language" rendered "him particularly fitted" to fill this post.[18] In the privy council, to which he was appointed in 1846, Andrews

16. Wyllie to Ricord, Dec. 1854, AH. FOEx., Misc. Foreign file.
17. See the *Polynesian*, Sept. 20, Oct. 18, 1845; June 27, 1846; Jan. 15, 1848.
18. King Kamehameha IV to Privy Council, Dec. 25, 1854, AH, Local Officials.

served for several years as secretary, and to him we are indebted for the early records of that body kept in both English and Hawaiian.[19]

On the death of William Richards, the King's councilors were of the opinion that since the mission had done so much for the nation, a missionary should be appointed to the vacancy in the ministry of public instruction. Richard Armstrong's fifteen years' acquaintance with Hawaiian life, language, and customs, his deep concern for the welfare of the nation, his editorship of two native-language newspapers, and his zeal for the cause of education all combined to make him the natural choice for the vacant post. Moreover, fears were expressed that if he declined the position, the then existing public instruction system would probably be abolished for want of a suitable man.[20] Recognizing the need for establishing a thorough common-school system, Armstrong accepted, in 1848, the position of minister of public instruction, notwithstanding the disapproval of some of his associates. He was vigilant in his defense of the common schools, which he considered the "poor man's college," for "the little education he gets is there." [21] Instruction of boys in the elements of agriculture and of girls in homemaking he viewed as fundamental,[22] and he made strenuous efforts to have some sort of manual labor connected with every school. His general plan was to "aim at the improvement of the heart, the head and the body, at once." [23] Through extensive tours of inspection, Armstrong kept in touch with the grass roots. He encouraged the teaching of English insofar as possible with the limited sources available, and he recommended an appropriation to aid in the support of English-language schools. He also favored and promoted the expansion of

19. J.C.A., "Lorrin Andrews," *Dictionary of American Biography, 1*, 296.

20. Armstrong to Chapman, Dec. 8, 1847, Armstrong-Chapman Papers, Library of Congress. Armstrong's concern and anxiety for the future of the Hawaiian Kingdom runs through his correspondence with his brother-in-law, Judge Chapman of Massachusetts. See especially his letters of March 3, 1843; Sept. 18, 1844; Oct. 5, 1846; and Oct. 11, 1847.

21. *Report of the Minister of Public Instruction, 1855* (Honolulu, 1855), p. 4. Also in LAB, *224*, No. 172 (ABC:19.1–13).

22. Benjamin O. Wist, *A Century of Public Education in Hawaii* (Honolulu, 1940), p. 60.

23. Armstrong to Chapman, Sept. 8, 1848, Armstrong-Chapman Papers. Cf. *Report of President of Board of Education, 1856* (Honolulu, 1856), p. 5. This plan was carried by Armstrong's son, Gen. Samuel C. Armstrong, to Hampton Institute, whence Booker T. Washington went to train the head, the hand, and the heart of Negroes at Tuskegee Institute. The idea was borrowed by Mahatma Gandhi for his basic education of the masses of India.

Punahou School into Oahu College, considering the transformation important from the national point of view, for it would save the expense and risk of sending youth in pursuit of a liberal education to the Americas or Europe, and would create a class of learned men on the islands.[24] During Armstrong's tenure as minister of education the privy council set apart one-twentieth of all unappropriated government lands, the income from which was to be expended upon public education, available to all.[25] The legislation enacted between 1848 and 1855 recognized the principle that public schools should be conducted at public expense, which was in line with American practice.

Armstrong's services to his adopted country extended beyond the field of education and morality to include matters of land distribution and utilization. He, along with Judd, Lee, and Wyllie, realized that the first steps toward democracy should be the granting to the Hawaiian people undisputed right in the soil—fee-simple title to the land they had lived on or occupied. After many interviews with the King and chiefs, the advisers demonstrated the justice of their views, and Kamehameha III, in 1848, granted the *Mahele,* or division of the lands of the kingdom.

Of the eight outstanding foreign officials who served Kamehameha III—Richards, Judd, Wyllie, Ricord, Andrews, Lee, Armstrong, and Allen—all but Wyllie were Americans and four had previously been connected with the Sandwich Islands Mission. Undeniably, missionary personnel provided the leadership in the formative days of the Hawaiian constitutional monarchy. Richards, Judd, Armstrong, and, to a lesser extent, Andrews, were instrumental in bringing about a new political and economic organization in the Hawaiian kingdom, having played a vital role in the modifications in government by the declaration of rights, the Constitution of 1840, the Mahele, financial and juridical reforms, and the school laws, all of which were definitely influenced by American ideals and practice. Thus missionary work which began with proclaiming the gospel eventually led to the reorganization of the national polity.

Diminishing Influence

In spite of the preponderance of American commercial and business interests and investments in the Hawaiian kingdom, the ubiquitous

24. Ibid.
25. Wist, pp. 60–61.

moral and social influence of the puritan missionaries, and the predominance of Americans in government, certain factors tended to
militate against American prestige in the islands. One was the lack
of unity within the ranks of Americans themselves. There was a
division, from 1824 on, between the missionary and antimissionary
parties, who at times waged outright war on each other. Hawaiians
observed the unedifying spectacle of American citizens attacking
the person and homes of revered clergymen. Petitions and memorials prepared and sponsored by American malcontents and directed
against their countrymen in official positions were not uncommon.
In addition, certain members of the British diplomatic corps ex-
ploited American racial prejudice and slavery in order to stir up
antipathy against "Yankees."

This was not difficult. En route to London in 1849–50 the two
impressionable teen-age royal princes had been subjected to offensive racial prejudice when they visited the United States with
Dr. Judd. In contrast, on the Continent and in England they were
accorded the courtesies and honors befitting royal visitors.[1] The re-
actions of the youths to their English welcome were reflected in
subsequent events in the islands. Liholiho, especially, became an
admirer of British institutions and people. The violent slavery controversy on the mainland, the "bleeding Kansas" episode, and the
Civil War, which appeared to demonstrate the weakness and vulner-
ability of the American democratic system, did not add to the esteem
and admiration of the United States in the islands. Moreover, the
behavior of irresponsible residents provided a basis for British and
French contentions that Americans were hostile to the Hawaiian
race.[2] The English and French were more careful or less fastidious
on this point and did not commit themselves.

Kamehameha III, throughout his reign of thirty years, generally
relied on the advice and counsel of American missionaries for problems of state. There was no serious political conflict between him
and the missionaries or those associated with them. The only differences were on moral points. The missionaries were the King's most
loyal subjects and staunch supporters. Prince Alexander Liholiho,
who ascended the throne as Kamehameha IV on December 15,
1854, had definitely antimissionary feelings. The new King im-

1. George B. Merrill, "Hawaiian Civilization," *Overland Monthly,* 1 (1868),
80. Cf. Ralph S. Kuykendall and Herbert E. Gregory, *A History of Hawaii*
(New York, 1926), p. 209; Wist, p. 75.
2. Gregg to Marcy, July 24, 1855, No. 111, USDS, Dispatches, Hawaii, 4.

mediately reappointed all the ministers who were in office when his predecessor died. However, by an act of the legislature the following year, the office of minister of public instruction was abolished and for it was substituted a board of education consisting of a president and two other directors, Prince Lot Kamehameha and Elisha H. Allen. Richard Armstrong, as president of the board, continued as head of the school system, but ceased to be a member of the cabinet. Ostensibly this change was made to enable Armstrong to devote all his time and energy to the public schools, but the ulterior motive prompting it appeared to be the desire to remove missionary influence from the inner circle of government. This influence waned after 1855, and never again did American missionaries—or those of any other nationality—hold high cabinet positions or wield the power of a William Richards or a Gerrit Judd. In the summer of that year no member of the cabinet had ever been connected with the American mission, and an Englishman, Charles Gordon Hopkins, replaced Edwin O. Hall, a former secular agent of the Sandwich Islands Mission, as editor of the *Polynesian*, the official organ of the government. Thereafter, that journal, both by omission and commission, constantly sought to depress American and elevate British character. The effect of the new management of this newspaper was to diminish the good opinion of the Hawaiian people for the United States.[3] Finally, when David L. Gregg—who, after the expiration of his term as United States commissioner, became Hawaiian minister of finance—was forced to resign his post in late August, 1862, the King's cabinet contained not a single American. The veteran Robert Wyllie was the commanding figure in government.

Annexation of the Pacific archipelago to the United States was seldom mentioned and never officially considered in the first half of the nineteenth century; after 1850, the subject was frequently discussed both in Hawaii and on the mainland. The United States government made no official propositions providing for union before 1854, but it was determined to resist strenuously any attempt on the part of Great Britain or France to obtain possession of the islands and refused to enter with the governments of those countries into a tripartite agreement regarding Hawaii. In the spring and summer of that year a treaty of annexation was laboriously negotiated and thoroughly considered by the privy council for nearly three months, but was not signed and ratified by the ailing Kamehameha III, and was withdrawn by his successor. During the period of negotiations

3. Gregg to Marcy, May 3, 1856, No. 163, ibid.

British Consul General William Miller repeatedly raised the twin bogies of American racial prejudice and slavery to frighten and deter the Hawaiian chiefs, the Crown Prince, and the King.[4] The treaty's statehood article, insisted upon by Foreign Minister Wyllie and Judge Lee in an effort to shield from slavery the inhabitants of the Hawaiian Islands, which lay south of the Missouri Compromise line of 36° 30′, made the treaty unacceptable to President Franklin Pierce.[5] Even with statehood, Prince Alexander Liholiho did not contemplate with pleasure the union of Hawaii with the United States, and at the beginning of his reign several Americans who were known to have been active in or to have shown sympathy for the annexation movement were removed from office. Thereafter, numerous suggestions for annexation emanated from various sources, but never from a Hawaiian sovereign.

The brilliant young Alexander Liholiho, two years after his accession, married the accomplished Emma Naea Rooke, great-granddaughter of the younger brother of Kamehameha I, granddaughter of John Young and adopted daughter of Dr. T. C. B. Rooke, an English physician who had long resided in the kingdom and had wedded a sister of Emma's mother. The tragic death of the heir to the throne, the beloved four-year-old Prince of Hawaii, on August 27, 1862, was a staggering blow from which the young King never recovered. His demise on November 30, 1863, brought to the throne the less sensitive royal brother, Lot Kamehameha.

An important reason for the antimissionary policy of Kamehameha IV and his brother, which was often misconstrued as being anti-American, was their fear that the great preponderance of American interests, including missionary, would lead to the overthrow of the monarchy, annexation to the United States, and ultimate extinction of the Hawaiian race. For this and personal reasons—including a preference for English institutions, a partiality for British aristocracy, a desire to make Queen Victoria a model in all official matters, and a wish to have the little Prince of Hawaii educated by an Anglican bishop—the royal brothers and Queen Emma encouraged the introduction into Hawaii of the Episcopal Church, with a bishopric connected with the Church of England. When the Anglican Church mission was inaugurated in 1862, Americans vigorously opposed the step, believing it was a move on the part of the British

4. See my "Slavery and Racism as Deterrents to the Annexation of Hawaii, 1854–1855," *Journal of Negro History*, 47 (1962), 7–8, 11–13.
5. Ibid., pp. 10–11, 17–18.

government to strengthen its influence in the islands and perhaps to annex them. Although this was not the case, the establishment of the Anglican Church certainly brought to the Hawaiian kingdom "a new political force extremely pro-royal and anti-American." [6] The influence of Bishop Thomas N. Staley and British Consul General William W. F. Synge over Kamehameha V was a significant factor in bringing about a diminution of American control over political and educational affairs. The Church enjoyed the high patronage of the Hawaiian royal family and leading members of the government, who were convinced it would bring closer ties of friendship with England and thus strengthen the Hawaiian monarchy.[7]

Constitutional Change

Concurrent with the diminution of the Americans' influence at court and in government was their growing dissatisfaction with the constitutional arrangements in the kingdom. In the Constitution of 1840 granted Hawaii by Kamehameha III, the legislative power was vested in the House of Nobles, composed of fourteen hereditary nobles, together with the king and premier, and certain representatives (later fixed at seven) elected by the people. This instrument was modified in 1852 so as to extend the principles of representative government. A House of Representatives, composed of not less than twenty-four or more than forty members elected annually by universal manhood suffrage, was to originate all money bills. The king was declared the supreme executive magistrate of the kingdom, his person "inviolate and sacred," his ministers "responsible." All laws that had passed both houses of the legislature had to be signed by him and the *kuhina-nui*.[1] All his other official acts had to be approved by the privy council, countersigned by the kuhina-nui and the minister to whose department such an act belonged. The sovereign was designated commander-in-chief of the army and navy, but he could never declare or proclaim war without the consent of his privy council. The supreme court was remodeled to consist hence-

6. Wist, *A Century*, p. 75.

7. Ralph S. Kuykendall, *The Hawaiian Kingdom, 1854–1874, Twenty Critical Years* (Honolulu, 1953), p. 96. Cf. pp. 202–07; McBride to Seward, Aug. 12, 1965, No. 50, USDS, Dispatches, Hawaii, *11*.

1. A co-ruler more powerful than a premier. The first kuhina-nui, the Dowager Queen Kaahumanu, was a royal woman, and in the routine administration of the government, more active than the young King, who was the highest officer in the state.

forth of a chief justice and two associate justices to hold office for life, subject to removal upon impeachment.[2]

These reforms, which curtailed the power of the sovereign and instituted parliamentary government, together with the decline in number and influence of the Polynesian stock, increased the confidence of the mercantile class in the regime. The United States extended quasi recognition to Hawaii in 1843 and signed a commercial treaty with her in 1849.

For twelve years the constitution of 1852 worked fairly well. Although the sovereign had practically an absolute veto on legislation, this and other theoretical powers were exercised only in accordance with English precedents. He had always in his cabinet men of ability and integrity, and no minister was arbitrarily dismissed from office. There were no serious political conflicts—except for one on moral points—between Kamehameha III and the missionaries, for they were the sovereign's most staunch and loyal subjects. The memory of this ruler, called "Kamehameha the Good," is cherished with gratitude for the liberal constitution and the gift to the people of land in fee simple, which together formed the glory of his reign.

Neither of the royal princes approved the radical constitutional changes made in 1852, believing them—especially the universal manhood suffrage provision—unsuited to the Hawaiian people. They were also displeased with the independent spirit shown by the lower house in its investigating committee.[3]

On Kamehameha IV's sudden and unexpected death, a small but influential section of American missionaries raised the question whether Prince Lot's title to the throne was sufficiently clear, or whether, according to the constitution, the regency of the kingdom should not be placed in the hands of Princess Victoria Kamamalu (sometimes spelled Kaamamalu), as kuhina-nui. The privy council, however, acted promptly and declared the late King's brother to be his successor. Kamehameha V appointed as kuhina-nui his father, Kekuanaoa, who had served for years as governor of Oahu, in place of his sister Princess Victoria, who was considered not only anti-

2. These early constitutions are analyzed in Ralph S. Kuykendall, *Constitutions of the Hawaiian Kingdom: A Brief History and Analysis*, HHS, *Papers*, No. 21 (Honolulu, 1940), pp. 8–22. A treatment is also found in Sworn Statement of William DeWitt Alexander, in which is incorporated a constitutional history of Hawaii, *Sen. Reps.*, 53 Cong., 2 sess., No. 227, pp. 316–19. Hereafter referred to as Alexander Statement, *Morgan Report*.

3. Ibid., p. 300.

British but pro-American and under the influence of the Protestant missionaries.

The strong-willed and shrewd Prince Lot was proclaimed king without taking the oath to support the Constitution of 1852, which he had resolved never to swear to maintain and at the earliest opportunity to make such changes in it as would increase the power of the crown. He placed in his cabinet able men who were in sympathy with his views, and at the same time was careful not to convene the regular legislature of 1862, but issued a proclamation for the election of a constitutional convention. Meanwhile, accompanied by his minister for foreign affairs, Robert C. Wyllie, Prince David Kalakaua, and other officials, the King toured the islands, explaining and defending the changes he desired to make in the constitution. The royal progress was only partially satisfying, for by mid-June it was apparent that a majority of responsible people were hostile to the proposal of revising the constitution.[4]

Composed of sixteen nobles and twenty-seven elected delegates, presided over by the King, the convention met on July 7, 1862. The question was hotly debated whether it had the right to draft a new constitution. Some strongly argued that the "only legal method in which the constitution can be referred back to the constituting power is prescribed in that instrument itself. Any other method is revolution, and revolutions do not generally claim to be constitutional."[5] The constitution of 1852 stated that amendments had to be approved by a majority of one legislature, published for three months previous to the next election, finally passed by two-thirds of both houses, and signed by the king. When the question was decided in the affirmative, four delegates resigned their seats. The convention continued with the revision of the constitution, but it became deadlocked on the subject of property or income qualifications for voters, which the King wanted. Therefore, he dissolved the assemblage in a speech on August 13, stating that those "who possess property are the proper persons to advise their Representatives in regard to the necessities of the Government." It was clear to Kamehameha that if universal suffrage was permitted, the government would soon lose its monarchical character.[6]

4. Charles de Varigny, *Quatorze Ans aux Iles Sandwich* (Paris, 1874), p. 217.
5. Alexander Statement, *Morgan Report*, p. 320.
6. For accounts of the convention see Hawaiian government official publication, the *Convention;* the *Pacific Commercial Advertiser* issues for the period; Varigny, pp. 219–26; Kuykendall, *Constitutions*, pp. 33–36; and Kuykendall, *Hawaiian Kingdom, 1854–1874*, pp. 127–34.

For seven days the kingdom was without a constitution, the government being "an Oligarchy, ruled by a Ministerial Cabinet of four." [7] The King and his ministers, assisted by Judge George M. Robertson, in sessions held on the three consecutive days of August 15, 16, and 17, went over the draft of a new instrument, quickly modifying the old as seemed desirable and including several amendments adopted by the convention.[8] Kamehameha V—in the presence of his ministers, the council of state, foreign representatives, and other dignitaries assembled in the throne room of the palace—at 3:00 P.M. on Saturday, August 20, 1864, took the oath to maintain the new constitution. The same evening the instrument was promulgated as the fundamental law of the land. There were not so many radical changes in it as had been expected and no public demonstrations against it.[9]

The office of kuhina-nui was abolished and provision made for a regency in case of the minority of the heir to the throne or in the absence of the king from the kingdom. The nobles and the representatives of the people were to sit together in one chamber and be known collectively as the legislative assembly, thus effectively checking the independent action of the house of representatives. Minister McBride considered this Article 45 the most important revision of all, for by such an arrangement the king could "use great influence if not control all measures of importance." [10] The powers and prerogatives of the sovereign were substantially increased, and the position of the cabinet as an administrative body was strengthened. Consequently, the king and cabinet became the dominant elements in government. There was a requirement of a property qualification both for representatives, and for voters, and an educational qualification for voters born after 1840.[11]

Article 22 of the new constitution provided that the succession to the throne should be to the direct heirs of Kamehameha V; in the absence of such heirs, to his sister Victoria and her direct heirs; in

7. *Pacific Commercial Advertiser*, Aug. 20, 1864.

8. AH, Cabinet Council Minute Book, Aug. 15, 16, 17, 1864. Kuykendall, *Constitutions*, p. 36.

9. Varigny, p. 246. McBride to Seward, Aug. 24, 1864, No. 34, USDS, Dispatches, Hawaii, *11*.

10. McBride to Seward, Aug. 13, 1864, ibid. No. 33.

11. The Constitution was published in the *Pacific Commercial Advertiser*, Extra, Aug. 20, 1864, and is to be found in *Laws, 1864–1865*, pp. 85–97; Lorrin A. Thurston, ed., *Fundamental Law of Hawaii* (Honolulu, 1904), pp. 169–79; Robert C. Lydecker, *Roster Legislatures of Hawaii*, pp. 88–97; Kuykendall, *Constitutions*, pp. 38–40.

default of these, "the successor shall be the person whom the Sovereign shall appoint with the consent of the Nobles, and publicly proclaim as such during the King's life"; if there were no heirs and no appointed successor, then the cabinet council, immediately after the occurrence of a vacancy on the throne, had to call a meeting of the legislative assembly who would elect by ballot some native *alli* (high chief) as successor to the throne, the successor so elected becoming a "new *Stirps* for a Royal Family."

By the promulgation of the Constitution of 1864—his so-called coup d'état—Kamehameha V accomplished his purpose to make "the influence of the Crown" pervade "every function of the government," and it continued to do so throughout the remaining eight years of his reign. This "last great chief of the olden type" believed that he inherited the right to lead his people firmly along the proper path. Although his thoughts and actions were despotic, his nine-year reign was a benevolent despotism. His Constitution continued in force for twenty-three years, longer than any other of the Hawaiian kingdom.

AMERICAN CONCERN, 1864-1882

The United States minister in Hawaii, James McBride, concerned over the rights and duties of Americans under the new constitutional arrangements, wrote the Secretary of State for instructions.[1] William H. Seward, referring to the obligations of Americans under the circumstances of the changed constitution, responded: "I view the subject as a domestic question, with which this Government has no duty to interfere. Americans, who have renounced allegiance here and have been naturalized there, cannot in any case be regarded as citizens of the United States, entitled to the protection of this Government."[2]

In another communication containing instructions to follow in case of further alterations in the form of government, Seward observed:

> This government has no right or disposition to interfere in the changes of the Hawaiian Constitution . . . Citizens of the United States, who have gone to that country for the purpose of remaining, and have been naturalized there, must expect to incur the risks as well as enjoy the advantages from their migration.

1. McBride to Seward, Aug. 13, 14, 1864, Nos. 83, 84, USDS, Dispatches, Hawaii, *11*.
2. Seward to McBride, Oct. 12, 1864, No. 22, USDS, Instructions, Hawaii, *2*. Seward's stand is similar to the position taken by Daniel Webster but in contrast to the later aggressive attitude of Thomas F. Bayard and James G. Blaine.

The flag of the United States has no other privileges there than those which are stipulated by the treaty or are secured by public law. If there should be alterations, either in the form of the Hawaiian Government, or in its administration, so far as they may affect the interests of the United States as in your opinion to make the expediency of continuing formal diplomatic intercourse with the Government questionable, you will desist from such intercourse until you shall have received the information of the Department, after presenting a full statement of the case. Such informal correspondence, however, as may be made indispensable by events may nevertheless meanwhile be carried on.[3]

The Succession and Annexation

Agitated over the growing British influence at court promoted by Commissioner William W. F. Synge and the Reverend Thomas Nettleship Staley, bishop of Honolulu, McBride made suggestions to Secretary Seward "toward forming a new and more decided policy in reference to the islands." The Minister observed that Kamehameha IV had died at the age of thirty "really from the effects of most depraved appetites, stimulated and kept to their full tension by a set of English parasites about him." His thirty-five-year-old brother, following the same course, was liable at any time to go as suddenly as his predecessor. "When this occurs," McBride counseled, "by giving me power to act, and the means to back me, I will venture in one week's time to restore things to their original constitution, fill the Ministry with Americans, or foreigners with American principles, and have upon the throne a Queen entirely in our favor."

The heir presumptive to the throne was the Princess Victoria Kamamalu, a woman of "considerable mind," whose predilections were for Americans; for this reason she was kept in the background. McBride's proposal was that on the moment of the King's death his sister should ascend the throne with a new ministry—"the Ministry of course vacates at the King's death." [1] There were good and competent Americans in Honolulu, some of whom had formerly held office. Were they installed, "in one week's time, the entire machinery

3. Seward to McBride, Oct. 16, 1864, No. 23, ibid.
1. On the death of King Kalakaua, in January 1891, this was a debatable and politically explosive question.

of the government could be in working order under the old constitution precisely as before." This could be accomplished without the least fear of outbreak or serious trouble, for both chiefs and people would readily yield "to decided action on the part of foreign powers." All that would be required would be the presence of two good American men-of-war in the harbor, the moral effect of which would be sufficient to prevent the existing government party from committing an overt act.[2]

Kamehameha V managed, however, to reign for nine years. Anxiety over the succession increased with the death of the unmarried Princess Victoria on May 29, 1866, with the disinclination of the King, in spite of promptings from several sources, to name a successor[3] or to marry,[4] and with his continued physical deterioration. The political situation was further complicated by serious resentment against the protracted sojourn of the U.S.S. *Lackawanna* in Hawaiian waters, which many believed was detained in order to take advantage of the sovereign's expected demise. Furthermore, the monarch harbored a personal dislike of the ship's captain, William Reynolds, for his advocacy of union with the United States and his campaign against reciprocity on the ground that it would defeat annexation.[5]

Kamehameha V died on December 11, 1872. Governor Nahaolelua of Maui refused to appoint a successor, and High Chiefess Bernice Pauahi (Mrs. Charles Reed Bishop), present in the death chamber, declined the crown,[6] Minister Henry A. Peirce heard "influential men speak of annexation to the U[nited] States as being the most preferable measure for the future prosperity and security of these

2. McBride to Seward, Aug. 12, 1865, No. 54, USDS, Dispatches, Hawaii, *11*. Cf. Synge to Russell, Dec. 12, 1863, No. 32, FO 58/98.

3. *Pacific Commercial Advertiser,* June 2, 16, 23 (editorial), 1866.

4. Charles de Varigny, "Emma Reine des Iles Havai," *Revue des Deux Mondes,* 72 (1885), 101–02. Varigny, *Quatorze Ans,* p. 270. James Wodehouse to Secretary of State Earl Granville, Jan. 7, 1873, FO 58/136.

5. San Francisco *Bulletin,* Sept. 21, 1868. For the long diplomatic correspondence concerning the *Lackawanna* see Varigny to Harris, June 1, 18, July 12, Aug. 24, Sept. 24, Oct. 18, Dec. 9, 1867, AH, FOEx., file box No. 58, folder "C. C. Harris Mission to Washington," Nos. 6–10, 12, 13; Harris to Varigny, July 23, 1867–Feb. 27, 1868, Nos. 12–23, ibid.; Wodehouse to FO, Dec. 26, 1867, FO 58/136.

6. "Correspondence Relating to the Last Hours of Kamehameha V," HHS, Sixth *Report,* 1898 (Honolulu, 1898), pp. 11–16. For the obituary of Kamehameha V see the *Hawaiian Gazette,* Dec. 18, 1872. Cf. *Pacific Commercial Advertiser,* Dec. 17, 1872. For Mrs. Bishop's candidacy see New York *Herald,* Jan. 9, 1873, and New York *Commercial Advertiser,* Jan. 8, 1873 (editorial).

Islands." A moment so favorable for a canvass to obtain the sense of the whole people in regard to the transfer of the sovereignty of the islands was not likely to occur again. Peirce strongly urged that a war vessel be dispatched from San Francisco "*as soon as possible,* and that one shall hereafter be kept in these waters constantly under a system of relief." [7]

Edward M. McCook, who had formerly represented the United States in Honolulu, confided to President Grant his belief that Charles C. Harris, minister of foreign affairs, Stephen H. Phillips, attorney general, Judge Elisha H. Allen, chancellor, and General Alfred S. Hartwell, vice-chancellor, could, if they so desired and were assured of support, "control matters in an emergency like the present, so as to shape them in accordance with your policy." McCook presumed that these gentlemen would have to be "taken care of" in order to secure their cordial support and assistance.[8]

In the meantime, Admiral A. M. Pennock, commander of the United States North Pacific squadron, received orders to proceed to Honolulu as soon as possible, and, in concert with Minister Peirce, to "use all your influence and all proper means to direct and maintain feeling in favor of United States, and at least to secure selection of successor favorable to our interests." [9] Pennock carried with him a telegram from Secretary of State Hamilton Fish to the Minister Resident, directing him to confer and consult with the Admiral and "endeavour to make the good offices of the United States useful to both Governments, and to give such directions to the events to take place so far as you can without objectionable interference, as will promote the influence and advance the interests of the Government and People." Inasmuch as detailed instruction could not be given, the Secretary observed, "much must be left to your discretion and his." [10]

The anticipated crisis did not materialize. This was due to the fact that there was no apparent opposition to the election of the people's candidate, Prince William C. Lunalilo. The popular declaration for him became so great that all the other candidates, except Prince David Ekamae Kamaeanaia Naloiaehu Kalakaua, withdrew.

7. Peirce to Fish, Dec. 11, 1872, No. 174, USDS, Dispatches, Hawaii, 15. All of Peirce's dispatches for 1873 are in this volume.

8. McCook to Grant, Jan. 4, 1873, USDS, Misc. Letters, Jan. 1873, Pt. I.

9. Secretary of the Navy George M. Robeson to Pennock, Dec. 25, 1872, U.S. Navy Dept., Letters to Flag Officers and Commandants of Vessels, 7, 256.

10. Fish to Peirce (telegram), Dec. 25, 1872, USDS, Instructions, Hawaii, 2.

In the legislative assembly, on January 8, 1873, the vote for Prince William was unanimous, with Governor John O. Dominis, as the brother-in-law of Prince David, declining to cast his ballot.[11] There is some ground for the allegation that the American missionary party, definitely opposed to Kalakaua, coalesced with the Hawaiian nationalists in urging the people to strong measures in favor of Lunalilo, in case of necessity.[12] Sanford Ballard Dole and Peter Cushman Jones, who twenty years later played a significant role in the provisional government after the overthrow of Queen Liliuokalani, promised their support to the popular Prince if the election went against him.[13] The presence of the U.S.S. *Benicia* relieved the public mind and gave assurance "that the peace and good order of the town would be preserved."

The succession problem, however, was by no means settled. Peirce observed shortly after the election that Lunalilo was "in danger of dying of intemperate drinking." In that event the Minister foresaw "every probability that a republic would succeed the present government; or if the United States desires to annex the Islands the measure can then be accomplished if proper instructions are given to the Minister Resident here in season to shape the desired purpose." He believed that late events had advanced American interests very considerably, but concluded that the annexation of the islands to the United States would never be adopted or presented as a government measure, "however much the people as a whole may desire it." Should the great interest of the country "demand that 'annexation' shall be attempted, the planters, merchants, and foreigners generally will induce the people to overthrow the Government, establish a republic, and then ask the U.S. for admittance into its Union." [14]

Several events of 1873, including the weighing anchor in Honolulu harbor for extended periods of American battleships; the presence of Major General John M. Schofield and Brevet General B. S. Alexander, prying and probing about Pearl River lagoon;[15] the

11. *Hawaiian Gazette*, Jan. 8, 9, 1873, Extras. Cf. *Pacific Commercial Advertiser*, Jan. 11, 1873; Peirce to Fish, Jan. 10, 15, 1873, Nos. 182, 184, USDS, Dispatches, Hawaii, 15.

12. Davies to Granville, Jan. 13, 1873, FO 58/136.

13. Kuykendall, *Hawaiian Kingdom, 1854–1874*, p. 244, citing Dole's diary for Jan. 8, 1873.

14. Peirce to Fish, Jan. 21, Feb. 17, 1873, Nos. 186, 191, USDS, Dispatches.

15. These military officers, armed with secret orders to examine and report upon Pearl Harbor, arrived in Honolulu as tourists on board the U.S.S. *California*, Jan. 16, 1873.

publication in the New York *Evangelist* of April 17 of Samuel N. Castle's letter advocating annexation of the islands to the United States under certain circumstances;[16] the airing in the Hawaiian and American press of questions concerning the succession to the throne and reciprocity with the cession to the United States of Pearl Harbor as a *quid pro quo* crystallized sentiment among native Hawaiians against the idea of union with, or even the lease of territory to, the United States. Theo. H. Davies, acting British commissioner, perceived in August 1873 that "within the last six months the United States has lost ground here which it can never regain— that is in the hearts of the people. It is commonly believed that if Great Britain were to ask for Pearl River, or even one of the Islands, the natives would grant it at once." [17] An unfortunate breach developed between the indigenous population and resident Americans, and a definite antiforeign disposition could be detected.

From occasional conversations with several of King Lunalilo's friends, Minister Peirce was assured that His Majesty entertained no thought of proposing the cession of the sovereignty of the kingdom to the United States or to any other power. Such a measure, in his opinion, would not "benefit himself or promote the happiness of the native people." Minister of Foreign Affairs C. R. Bishop favored preserving the country's independence as long as possible and was "strongly opposed to any change." Although annexation to the United States might eventually take place, it should not be considered until the few remaining chiefs of royal blood and the majority of the then living inhabitants had passed from the scene. Should the King ever entertain the matter favorably, Edwin O. Hall, minister of the interior, Elisha H. Allen, the chancellor and chief justice, and Attorney General Albert Francis Judd would be friendly to and support the measure. Robert Stirling, the minister of finance, was strongly opposed to the transfer under any condition whatever of any portion of the territory to the United States.

The twenty-five members of the privy council were about equally divided on the question. According to Peirce, a large majority of the American missionaries, planters, and merchants were anxious for the consummation of the measure, but more than three-fourths of the native inhabitants were opposed to a change of the sovereignty of

16. See *Pacific Commercial Advertiser*, June 7, 1873. Cf. my "Sandwich Islands Missionaries and Annexation," *Journal of Religious Thought*, 20 (1963–64), 137–45.

17. Davies to Granville, Aug. 26, 1873, No. 9, FO 58/136.

the country. In view of all the circumstances, he was of the opinion that the only proper course for the United States government to pursue was to await events. In the meantime, it seemed wise to accept the cession of Pearl Bay with reciprocity of commerce between the two countries: "This measure would bind these islands to the United States with hoops of steel." He was convinced that the Hawaiian nation was "destined to pass through the throes of a new national birth before it is prepared to adopt the proper measure to give security and prosperity to the people." The death of the King or a general bankruptcy of the people would perhaps "precipitate the desired event." [18]

In Washington there was no disposition to plan for the immediate annexation of Hawaii. Secretary of State Hamilton Fish, in answering the queries of a New York *Herald* correspondent, asserted that, although the State Department could not deny the possibility of annexation in the future, "for the present the government has no such arriere pensee." [19]

Only eight months after his accession, the melancholy fact could no longer be concealed that King Lunalilo, afflicted with pulmonary tuberculosis, would not long continue to reign. Apprehensive American residents requested Peirce to exert his influence to induce Commander J. S. Skerritt, of the U.S.S. *Portsmouth*, to remain in port until the 15th for any emergency that might arise. The September 7th mutiny of the Household Troops, about sixty in number and constituting the standing army of the nation,[20] accompanied by rumors of destruction of life and property, impelled the Minister to request Skerritt to tarry until the exigency of the occasion lapsed.[21] The unexpected arrival of Admiral Pennock's flagship, the U.S.S. *Saranac*, on October 19, dispatched from San Francisco in great haste on receipt of the news of the King's illness, and the preparations made for her protracted stay on something like a continual naval guard, reportedly caused the ailing King, Queen Emma, and the chiefs "great annoyance." [22]

18. Peirce to Fish, May 26, 1873, No. 206. Cf. my "Sandwich Islands Missionaries and Annexation," p. 143.

19. New York *Herald*, Jan. 8, 1873.

20. *Pacific Commercial Advertiser*, Sept. 13, 1873. Richard A. Greer, "Mutiny in the Royal Barracks," *Pacific Historical Review*, 21 (1962), 349–58.

21. Peirce to Fish, Sept. 2, 16, Oct. 13, 1873, Nos. 220, 223, 225, USDS, Dispatches, Hawaii, 15.

22. Davies to Granville, Nov. 7, 1873, No. 12, FO 58/136.

Lunalilo, like Kamehameha V, declined to name a successor, preferring that the selection devolve upon the people. The most eligible candidate by birth was David Kalakaua. This amiable prince of "polished manners and bearing" spoke English well, had supplemented his scholastic education at the Royal School with extensive reading and the assiduous study of international law in order to qualify himself for the duties of a sovereign, had engaged in various civic activities, held public office under Kamehameha V, and had been Lunalilo's only rival for the throne.[23] Peirce, nevertheless, considered Kalakaua flighty and vacillating, carrying "more sail than ballast." [24] A member of the Episcopal Church, he appeared thoroughly English in feeling and was unpopular with many, Americans, who believed him desperate and reckless enough to make an attempt to secure the crown for himself—by force if necessary. Davies appraised the Prince's character and capacity as follows: "He is a man of fair education, little intelligence, and I fear no principle. He is supremely Hawaiian in sympathies, bitterly opposed to American Missionaries and people and shows a great friendship and regard for Great Britain. This regard arises more from reliance on the honour and friendship of England, than actually attachment to English people or principles. It is probably a selfish motive, but it will always exert on his policy great influence." [25]

Kaleleonalani, or Queen Emma, known as the "good queen" and idolized by the lower classes for her charity, was Kalakaua's most formidable rival. She had pronounced British sympathies, was bitter toward American missionaries and their descendants, and particularly opposed their designs on Hawaiian territory.[26] Naturally, the English residents supported her for the succession.

One factor in the Prince's favor was the prospect that he presented of dynastic stability. The Dowager Queen Emma, who had decided not to remarry, could not found a dynasty or provide the kingdom with a guarantee of the future. David Kalakaua and his spouse, the Chiefess Kapiolani, were both young enough to have an heir, but

23. *Nuhou Hawaii*, Feb. 11, 1874.

24. Peirce to Fish, Dec. 18, 1872, No. 177, USDS, Dispatches, Hawaii, *15*. A year later Peirce reported that Kalakaua was "the natural son of an American mulatto and pugilist by the name of Blossom, who resided here about forty years since" (Peirce to Fish, Dec. 18, 1873, No. 231).

25. Davies to Granville, Nov. 7, 1873, No. 12, FO 58/136.

26. Ibid., July 24, 1873, No. 8. Wodehouse to FO, Dec. 26, 1867, FO 58/136. Queen Emma to Keliineewai, Aug. 20, 1873, AH, Queen Emma Collection (Nylen-Altman).

in default of this, his capable junior brother, William Pitt Leleiohoku Kalahoolewa (Shooting Star), could succeed him.

This eldest male representative of the princely Hawaiian family which stood next to the defunct Kamehameha line was willing to compromise and to adapt his policies to the welfare of the nation and the dictates of influential foreigners. He promised that his government would pursue the course of his predecessors: existing laws—specifically those prohibiting the sale of intoxicating liquors to native Hawaiians and requiring the "proper observance of the Sabbath"—would be preserved intact. Kalakaua announced to the world that "we have always welcomed foreigners to our shores. Let them come, and bring with them money and skill to develop the resources of the country. Here, as in the freest and strongest nation in the world, all men will be protected in their rights, under civilized law." [27] As time passed, a majority of Hawaiians inclined toward Kalakaua, and foreigners came to accept his election as inevitable.

King Lunalilo died on February 3, 1874, at the age of thirty-nine, after a reign of only a year and twenty-five days, during which the only amendment to the Constitution of 1864, which resident Americans hoped to see supplanted by a more liberal one, was the abolition of the property qualification for voting. An attempt to restore the division of the legislature into two houses sitting separately failed. The date for the election of a successor by the legislative assembly was set for February 12.[28] American residents in Honolulu were almost unanimous in favor of the election of David Kalakaua, convinced that if Emma came to the throne, British views and interests would predominate, that she would exert her influence toward making Bishop Staley a controlling power in the government, that the Anglican faith would be declared the state religion, and that there would be no hope of obtaining a reciprocity treaty with the United States.[29]

Opportunely, the U.S.S. *Tuscarora* had arrived in Honolulu Harbor from San Diego the day before, and the U.S.S. *Portsmouth*

27. See Kalakaua's letter to the *Pacific Commercial Advertiser*, Dec. 9, 1872, reprinted in the *Hawaiian Gazette*, Dec. 17, 1873. Peirce to Fish, Jan. 26, 1874, No. 235, USDS, Dispatches, Hawaii, 16. All of Peirce's dispatches for 1874 are in this volume.

28. *Hawaiian Gazette*, Feb. 4 (obituary notice), Feb. 11, 1874. *Pacific Commercial Advertiser*, Feb. 7, 1873. *Nuhou Hawaii*, Feb. 11, 1874. Peirce to Fish Feb. 5, 1874, No. 237.

29. Peirce to Fish, Feb. 7, 1874, No. 240. Cf. *For. Rels.* (1894), App. II, p. 574.

appeared from a surveying cruise on the very day of the King's demise. In view of the tension and feverish excitement, the United States Minister requested Commander George Belknap, of the *Tuscarora,* senior naval officer present, not to permit the crews of the vessels under his command shore liberty on the 12th. The commander of the H.B.M. *Tenedos* also agreed to the same restriction. Peirce verbally asked Belknap to be prepared to land an armed force in case one was required for the preservation of life and property. The necessary orders were given and the Minister was assured that the marines on the two United States warships would be prepared to act in concert with him in any emergency that might arise.[30] Unwilling to trammel himself with pledges, Peirce declined a proposal from James Wodehouse, Great Britain's commissioner, that in case the necessity arose to land forces from the warships in port, British and American officers should act in concert while occupying Honolulu.[31]

At the scheduled election the members of the Legislative Assembly cast thirty-nine votes for David Kalakaua and six for Queen Emma.[32] During the balloting a mob composed of the latter's adherents gathered outside the courthouse where the legislators were assembled. In spite of heroic efforts on the part of Sanford B. Dole and Charles C. Harris to warn back the rioters, they gained access to the building, proceeded to club members of the legislature who had dared to vote for Kalakaua, and sacked and vandalized the offices of the attorney general and Judge Hartwell. In the fracas several Hawaiian legislators were seriously injured when they fell some twenty feet from windows to the street below, and one died.[33] The rioters were careful not to attack the whites (except in one case), for the Hawaiians considered this election their own affair. Moreover, three men-of-war were in the harbor.

About forty policemen selected for duty during the day, when requested to arrest the rioters, removed their badges and disappeared among the crowd. The volunteer companies of militia were

30. Peirce to Belknap, Feb. 10, 1873, and Belknap to Peirce, Feb. 11, 1873, encls. Nos. 3 and 4, in Peirce to Fish, Feb. 7, 1874, No. 240.

31. Peirce to Fish, Feb. 7, 1874, No. 240.

32. *Pacific Commercial Advertiser,* Feb. 14, 1874.

33. Lorrin Andrews Thurston, *Memoirs of the Hawaiian Revolution* (Honolulu, 1936), pp. 17–18. Alexander Statement, *Morgan Report,* pp. 303, 351–52. Repetition and distance magnified the heroism of Dole and Harris, as illustrated in reports in the *Daily Alta California,* March 18, 1874, and the San Francisco *Chronicle,* March 19, 1874.

not called out to assist in maintaining order, for, being divided in their political persuasions, they could not be depended upon to act in an emergency. In this state of affairs the King elect, Charles R. Bishop, and Governor Dominis requested Minister Peirce to land an armed force. Within ten minutes 150 marines from the United States ships poured ashore, followed soon after by approximately seventy men from H.B.M. *Tenedos*. At their appearance the rioters reportedly ran from "the courthouse like rats out of a burning barn." Later, minor disturbances were quelled, and eight or ten leaders were arrested by the marines and turned over to the Hawaiian authorities. American forces set up quarters in the courthouse and armory, guarding those, as well as the treasury, prison, and station house. British forces, after dispersing the crowd that assembled on the grounds of Queen Emma's residence and making a few arrests of ringleaders, occupied the barracks and guarded Iolani Palace. Marines held the city for eight days.

Minister Peirce, Commissioner Wodehouse, and his French counterpart, one Ballieu, at 7:00 A.M. meeting on February 13 at the palace, recognized Kalakaua as sovereign of the Hawaiian kingdom. He was hastily sworn in at 11 o'clock that day in their presence, without taking an oath to support the Constitution. During the same morning Peirce called on Queen Emma and recommended that she accept the fact of the legality of Kalakaua's election as king and urge her people to do likewise and to commit no more acts of violence. That afternoon she publicly counseled her followers as had been suggested, and in a message to David Kalakaua recognized him as sovereign of the realm, promising that her adherents would do the same.[34] One of the first acts of the new ruler was the appointment, with the consent of the nobles, of his brother Leleiohoku, a well-educated and well-deported young prince of "correct morals," as successor to the throne.[35] Thus an issue that had agitated and excited the public mind for over half a decade was quietly settled. The new King seemed generally popular with the people, and soon "peace and good order" prevailed throughout the islands, the government was "respected and obeyed, and the Courts of law unobstructed in their operations." This tranquillity gave promise of continuing for a long time.[36]

34. Peirce to Fish, Feb. 17, 19, 20, 1874, Nos. 243–45, USDS, Dispatches.
35. Circular of Minister of Foreign Affairs to the legislature, Feb. 14, 1874, encl. 5 in Peirce's No. 243, ibid. *Pacific Commercial Advertiser*, Feb. 17, 1874. *Nuhou Hawaii*, Feb. 17, 1874.
36. Peirce to Fish, March 12, 19, April 1, 1874, Nos. 242, 255, 258.

Reciprocity Consummated

Immediately after the election, Minister Peirce commented upon the Hawaiian government's lamentable want of physical strength in protecting itself and foreign residents, and observed that the military and police force could not be relied upon to support the laws or to arrest their violators. He recommended that a national vessel should always be stationed at the islands under a system of relief, for a time might arrive when the United States government would "find it necessary for the interest of our nation, and its resident citizens here, to take possession of this country by military occupation." [1]

Peirce was not alone in stressing the need for the protection of American interests. As a result of the disorders attendant upon the election, eighty resident Americans, comprising all those in business, influential individuals, and ministers of the gospel at Honolulu, addressed to the United States legation a memorial expressing their congratulations for the security their flag afforded to the government of the kingdom and representing that the duty of protecting the persons and property of Americans there "in emergencies such as have arisen and may arise again, belongs naturally to our Government rather than to any other power." They maintained that "since the expansion of our own territory on the Pacific Coast has made us commercially and politically the near neighbor of the Hawaiian kingdom, it is on all accounts desirable that our interests here should be increasingly and abundantly protected." [2]

The State and Navy Departments in Washington cooperated with the United States Minister Resident in Honolulu in his request to have a national vessel in Hawaiian waters retained under a system of rotation. The U.S.S. *Portsmouth, Tuscarora, Benicia, Pensacola,* and *Lackawanna* appeared frequently in port, remained for periods of a few weeks up to months until relieved, transported King Kalakaua and his suite to and from San Francisco, and steamed to and fro on assignments to sound various ocean depths between the Hawaiian chain and Japan, Australia, and California. The officials of the kingdom, in their cordiality, even deference, to Americans, always extended a courteous welcome to the commanders of these vessels. Rear Admiral John J. Almy, commander of the North Pacific

1. Peirce to Fish, Feb. 17, March 3, 1874, Nos. 243, 250.
2. Memorial dated Feb. 26, 1874, encl. in Peirce's No. 250.

squadron, was persona grata with the King and other Hawaiian functionaries.[3] In fact, there is no indication in the press or in official documents of any resentment of the continual surveillance of American war vessels in the territorial waters of the kingdom. The real or imaginary danger from the partisans of Queen Emma, who at times created tension but were never large in number and always lacked efficient leadership, was sufficient justification for the presence of United States vessels in Hawaiian waters, which measure of precaution also benefited generally American interests in the archipelago.[4]

The constant vigil was intentionally broken on one occasion for the purpose of determining whether the disaffected portion of the native population would avail itself of the opportunity to create a disturbance and whether the Kalakaua regime was able to sustain itself and protect persons and property without the assistance of a foreign man-of-war. In early September 1874 the *Benicia* sailed on a fifteen-day training cruise, but the experiment proved nothing, for only twelve hours after the warship's departure, the H.B.M. *Scout* from South America appeared on the horizon with a party of scientists.[5]

King Kalakaua, accompanied by Henry A. Peirce, Governor Dominis, John M. Kapena, and several other Hawaiian dignitaries, on November 14, 1874, left Honolulu for the United States to further the reciprocity negotiations. This first sovereign of any state to visit the country spent December 12–23 as its guest in the national capital and paid a five-day visit to New York, financed by that City. His good-will tour, well publicized by the press, was helpful in promoting a friendly feeling toward Hawaii among the American people and government officials, and undoubtedly smoothed the way for reciprocity. A treaty was negotiated by Elisha H. Allen, H. A. P. Carter, and Hamilton Fish, providing that unrefined sugar, rice, arrowroot, castor oil, bananas, fruits, nuts, vegetables—dried and undried, preserved and unpreserved—hides and skins undressed,

3. Peirce to Fish, May 20, June 17, Sept. 14, 1875, Nos. 235, 238, 338. Cf. San Francisco *Morning Call*, March 24, 1875.

4. Peirce to Fish, July 24, 1874, No. 273. Cf. their letters of Jan. 26, Sept. 10, 1874, Nos. 236, 282.

5. Peirce to Fish, Sept. 10, 1874, No. 283. This premeditated test should be compared with similar action nineteen years later, when the U.S.S. *Boston*, with Minister John L. Stevens aboard, departed temporarily from Honolulu Harbor on the eve of the January 1893 *émeute*, but returned in the midst of it. See below, p. 130.

pulu[6] seeds, plants, shrubs or trees, and practically all other Hawaiian products would be admitted free of duty to the United States. On the other hand, American goods to be imported into Hawaii duty free would include virtually every product conceivable, with major emphasis on wool, iron, steel, and textiles. The treaty was to continue in force for a term of seven years; thereafter, it could be terminated by either party after twelve months' notice.

Minister Peirce, before leaving Honolulu, informed Secretary Fish of a reported offer by the Premier of New Zealand, Sir Julius Vogel, to negotiate a $3,000,000 loan for Hawaii, the security for which was to be a lien on the property and revenue of the kingdom, together with assurances that an effort would be made to admit Hawaiian sugar free of duty to New Zealand and Australia, and of the Premier's scheme to establish a great Polynesian company similar to the South Sea Company, a "Grand Dominion" of islands under British suzerainty near and south of the equator. The Minister warned that if the Senate did not ratify the reciprocity treaty, Hawaii would, of necessity, look for her future prosperity to Canada and the British colonies in the Pacific, with the prospect of the Hawaiian chain becoming eventually an appendage of the British Empire.[7] The State Department was apprised that Hawaii's entire sugar crop of 1876–77 would flow to British possessions. Peirce appeared before the Senate Committee on Foreign Relations and submitted this intelligence, which—along with warnings of other Americans (including the members of the Hawaiian Club of Boston and the Boston Board of Trade) interested in the fate of their Hawaiian investments and the destiny of the islands—caused some senators to realize that reciprocity was assuming a "graver importance"; as "political supremacy in the islands must inevitably follow commerce," a favorable atmosphere was created for an agreement." [8]

6. *Pulu* is a silky or woolly fiber which grows at the base of the fronds of the tree fern and is useful as a filling for mattresses and pillows.

7. Peirce to Fish, Oct. 20, 1874, No. 239. Cf. *Hawaiian Gazette*, Sept. 9, 1874.

8. *Morgan Report*, p. 469; *Sen. Docs.*, 56 Cong., 2 sess., No. 231, Pt. VI, p. 465. Actually, there is no official evidence available which indicates a threat of a Hawaiian swing toward Australasia in 1874–75 or in any other period, for that area was never able to offer what the United States afforded—a large and expanding market for sugar. See my "Canada's Interest in the Trade and the Sovereignty of Hawaii," *Canadian Historical Review*, 44 (1963), 21–26; "Australasian Interest in the Commerce and the Sovereignty of Hawaii," Australia and New Zealand, *Historical Studies*, 11 (1965), and "The Myth of Hawaii's Swing toward Australasia and Canada," *Pacific Historical Review*, 33 (1964), 276–81.

The United States Senate, after inserting an additional article, advised ratification of the convention on March 18, 1875, by a vote of 51 to 12, 8 more than the required two-thirds. The appended Article 4, without which the treaty probably would have been rejected, stipulated: "It is agreed, on the part of His Hawaiian Majesty, that as long as this treaty shall remain in force, he will not lease or otherwise dispose of or create any lien upon any port, harbor, or other territory in his dominions, or grant any special privilege or rights of use therein, to any other power, state, or government." [9]

According to the San Francisco *Morning Call*,[10] our government officials were probably motivated by the conviction that if we refused this offer for closer commercial relations, the islands would fall into the hands of England or France. Representative James Garfield of Ohio maintained that those two countries stood ready to make satisfactory arrangements with the Hawaiian government in case we should reject the convention. Some alliance would be sought by King Kalakaua, and we, after declining his overtures, could not consistently raise any objections to such a course. The Congressman favored the treaty as a satisfactory substitute for all probable schemes of annexation that might come up if this failed; it was the best solution of the question.[11]

King Kalakaua ratified the convention on April 18, and President Grant did the same on May 31, 1875. Congress, however, delayed over a year in passing the legislation necessary to implement the treaty. During this period it was received with varying degrees of enthusiasm in Hawaii and in the United States, depending upon the political or economic interests concerned. The principal objection voiced by Americans in the islands was that reciprocity would postpone annexation, while in this country the sugar and rice planters claimed that reciprocity would lead eventually to annexation. Another fraction of the opponents felt that the terms of the treaty had been dictated by California refiners, and by Claus Spreckels in particular, because high-grade sugars were not allowed free entry. In general, the Pacific coast favored closer economic and political ties with the Hawaiian Islands.

9. For a text of the treaty see *United States Statutes at Large*, 44 Cong. (1875–77), 19, 200, 666; *For. Rels.* (1894), App. II, p. 166. Cf. New York *Times*, March 19, 1875; San Francisco *Alta California*, March 19, 1875; *Pacific Commercial Advertiser*, April 10, 1875.

10. March 19, 1875.

11. *Cong. Record*, 44 Cong., 1 sess., pp. 2274–75. New York *Evening Post*, April 5, 1876.

The reciprocity treaty of 1875 was a perfect example of a commercial and economic negotiation dictated by political motives. It was designed primarily to extend American influence over the islands and only secondarily to secure economic benefits. The annexationist-minded Grant administration was aware of the prevailing anti-annexation feeling in the Congress. Hence, there was achieved through the execution of a commercial instrument the substance of a policy which would have been defeated if brought to an open fight on the floor of the Senate. This convention prevented any European power from gaining a political foothold in Hawaii, and at the same time—from the commercial point of view—rendered the archipelago a significant appendage of the United States.

To all outward appearances King Kalakaua was a popular monarch. His willingness to act upon the petition signed by the principal merchants and planters of the kingdom, advocating a commercial treaty with the United States,[12] and his journey to Washington to assist in securing it, indicated a deep concern for the welfare of his realm, extending even to cooperation with the influential resident foreign element to secure prosperity. For approximately six years following his accession there was no serious complaint from the American ministers resident on the policy of the Hawaiian government toward either the United States or its citizens in the islands. Nor was there anxiety over the succession. Leleiohoku, an intelligent, accomplished young prince, gave promise of becoming a wise and exemplary monarch. When the expectation of his future usefulness to the nation was suddenly terminated by his untimely death on April 10, 1877, the King immediately nominated his sister, the Princess Lydia Kamakaeha Liliuokalani (Lily of the Sky, Salt Air of Heaven, or Preservation of the Heavens), to succeed him if he died without issue.[13]

Hawaiian officials settled complications and complaints speedily and satisfactorily either through the regular diplomatic channels or through the enactment of preventive or palliative legislation. They did everything within their power to prevent the importation of sugar and rice from the Orient for fraudulent reshipment to the United States duty free under the reciprocity treaty. Legislation was enacted imposing a tariff of 2½ cents per pound upon such importa-

12. *Pacific Commercial Advertiser*, June 24, 1874.
13. *Hawaiian Gazette*, April 11, 1877.

tion of rice, an impost designed to be prohibitive and thus to relieve further apprehension on the matter in the United States.[14]

Trivial diplomatic differences were eventually settled.[15] Remaining unsolved and of grave concern to the United States Minister
and the State Department were the fundamental weaknesses in
Hawaiian society and polity: the persistent moral and physical decay of the nation, the increasing cosmopolitan nature of the ministries, the changing complexion of the Legislative Assembly, the
misjoinder of the producing with the expending power in the islands,
together with proposals to institute state socialism and to organize
and lead a Polynesian confederation.

Decadence

The impact of progressive Western civilization and beneficent
Christianity upon the hitherto insulated and isolated naïve Hawaiian
islanders had a doleful, even fatal, effect. The population of the
archipelago, estimated to be about 200,000 when discovered by
Captain James Cook in January 1778, declined in forty years to
about 125,000, or by 37 per cent. As time passed, the rate of decay
accelerated. According to the *Hawaiian Star*, the indigenes were
reduced to 57,135 in 1866, to 44,088 in 1878, and to 34,436 in 1890,
or by 72 per cent. In the twenty years preceding 1893, the loss was
nearly 40 per cent, and during the last twelve of those years 22 per
pent.[1]

Henry A. Peirce, a merchant of considerable residence in the
islands, predicted as early as 1837 the extinction of the Hawaiian
people, and declared that "foreigners and half breeds will take their

14. *Laws of His Majesty Kalakaua I, King of the Hawaiian Islands, Passed
by the Legislative Assembly at Its Session of 1880* (Honolulu, 1880), pp. 52–
53. Hereafter *Session Laws*. Cf. James M. Comly to Sec. of State William M.
Evarts, Aug. 31, Sept. 20, 1880, Nos. 122, 124, and encl. in the letter, USDS,
Dispatches, Hawaii, 19. All of Comly's dispatches of 1880 and 1881 are in
this volume.

15. For complications arising out of the Harriet W. Carlton case see Comly's
dispatches of Sept. 20, Oct. 28, Dec. 23, 1878, May 12, 1879, Nos. 49, 53, 67,
72, with encls. All in USDS, Dispatches, Hawaii, 18. For complaints against
"vexatious regulations" involved in a $2.00 hospital tax imposed on every for-
eigner entering the kingdom and in passport requirements, see dispatches of
Feb. 16, March 15, June 8, Sept. 22, Oct. 25, Nov. 18, 1880, Nos. 91, 95, 111,
126, 135, 138.

1. *Hawaiian Star*, May 9, 1893.

place." [2] Lunalilo and Kalakaua were deeply concerned over the precarious health and precipitant decline of their subjects, and early in their reigns both made recommendations and suggestions for checking the despondency, degeneration, and desolation.[3]

POPULATION OF THE HAWAIIAN ISLANDS IN 1878, 1884,[a] AND 1890[b]

Nationalities	1878	1884	Increase	1890
Hawaiian	44,088	40,014		34,436
Half-Hawaiian	3,402	4,218	798	6,186
Hawaiian-born of foreigners	947	2,040	1,093	7,495
Chinese	5,916	17,937	12,021	15,301
Portuguese	436	9,377	8,941	8,602
American	1,276	2,066	790	1,928
British	883	1,282	399	1,334
German	272	1,600	1,328	1,034
French	81	192	111	70
Other foreigners	664	1,850	1,186	419
Japanese		116		12,360
Polynesians				588
Norwegians				227
				89,990

Increase other than native	1878–1884	26,667	1884–1890	41,968
Native decrease	1878–1884	4,074	1884–1890	9,652
		22,593		

a. *For. Rel.* (1885), p. 472 (from the census of 1884 and 1878).
b. San Francisco *Morning Call*, Jan. 31, 1893.

Walter Murray Gibson, in an "Address to the Hawaiian People" in 1876, called attention to the "woeful condition" of their race, in which could be found "not more than 5,000 able bodied men." They, with their decaying and decreasing number of not more than 45,000, were helpless and already too few, with foreigners included, "to constitute an independent state qualified to hold diplomatic relations with other states," and would not be so recognized, "were it not for the courtesy and permission of great states whose ships of war patrol the great ocean." The vital question for the Hawaiian people to consider and act upon was not the succession, which was irrevocably settled, not reciprocity with the United States, for a

2. Peirce to James Hunnewell, Aug. 13, 1837, Hunnewell Papers, Harvard College Library.
3. *Pacific Commercial Advertiser*, Jan. 13, 1873; April 18, 1874.

treaty had been agreed upon and must be sustained in good faith, but repopulation.[4]

Ministers Peirce and Comly were convinced that the Hawaiian nation was dying by slow degrees and had to reach the end of its autonomy before many years elapsed.[5] The latter, without mentioning it by name, brought up the Yellow Peril and its implications for the mid-Pacific archipelago, where nearly one-fifth of the population was already Chinese, and, at the rate they were entering, they would have more than a majority before 1890. Coupled with the King's idea of a Polynesian confederacy was his "longing for a splendid alliance with the great oriental Empire of China." The Hawaiian Islands, Comly warned, comparatively insignificant politically, "in the hands of a small rabble of shiftless *Kanakas*,[6] would afford homes and subsistence for more than a million Chinamen, and would become an extremely important neighbor to our Pacific Coast." [7]

Secretary of State James G. Blaine reflected on positive steps to arrest the debilitation and thus preserve the islands for the Union. He instructed that the government of the United States would not tolerate "an arrangement which by diplomatic finesse or legal technicality" substituted for the native and legitimate constitutional government of Hawaii the controlling influence of a great foreign power. Neither could a Mongolian supremacy nor an Anglo-Indian coolie element supplant native control. The Hawaiian Islands could not be joined to the Asian system. If they drifted from their independent station, "it must be toward assimilation and identification with the American system, to which they belong by the operation of natural laws, and must belong by the operation of political necessity." [8]

The reciprocity treaty had made the archipelago a *Zollverein*, an outlying district of California. In view of the teachings of ethno-

4. W. M. Gibson, *Address to the Hawaiian People* (Honolulu, Jan. 31, 1876), pp. 4–6. Copy encl. in Peirce to Fish, Feb. 2, 1876, No. 332, USDS, Dispatches, Hawaii, *17*.

5. Peirce to Fish, March 3, 1874, No. 250. Comly to Frelinghuysen, April 10, 1882, No. 213, ibid., *20*, printed in *For. Rels.* (1882), pp. 334–37.

6. A Polynesian word meaning man, but now a despicable term. It was then used to connote a native of aboriginal blood.

7. Comly to Evarts, July 21, 1880, No. 121. Cf. Comly to Evarts, Oct. 25, 1880; Jan. 18, 1881; Nos. 136, 148.

8. Blaine to Comly, Nov. 19, Dec. 1, 1881, Nos. 111, 113, USDS, Instructions, Hawaii, *2*.

logical history, the decline of the native Hawaiian element, in the presence of newer and sturdier growths, had to be accepted as an inevitable fact. Since retrogression in the development of the islands could not be admitted without detriment to American interest in the North Pacific, the problem of replenishment of the vital forces of Hawaii had to be solved intelligently in an American, "not in an Asiatic or British sense."

Were the Hawaiian Islands, "by annexation or distinct protection, a part of the territory of the Union, their fertile resources for the growth of rice and sugar would not only be controlled by American capital, "but intelligent workers would be attracted thither from the United States. A purely American form of colonization in such a case would solve the problem. Even in the chosen alternative of maintaining Hawaiian independence, Blaine considered how the capital, the intelligence, and the necessary labor trained in the rice fields of the southern states could be induced to go to the islands, "not like coolies, practically enslaved, not as human machines, but as thinking intelligent working factors in the advancement of the material interests of the islands." He instructed James M. Comly to investigate this matter, and "in conversation with the leading man of Hawaii turn their thoughts discreetly in the direction of inviting American colonization there." The Secretary suggested that a Hawaiian homestead act for the benefit of actual American settlers, with remission of taxation during the time necessary to establish new plantations on a paying basis, might be in turn supplemented in the United States by voluntarily organized immigration schemes and cooperative aid to bone fide settlers.[9]

In a comprehensive reply addressed to Frederick T. Frelinghuysen, who succeeded Blaine at the State Department, Comly dealt at length with the decadence of the native race, which was not only in numbers "but in every component of strength known in the constituent elements of the state." Referring first to the appalling incidence of disease, he reported that out of a population of about 45,000 of aboriginal descent, there were over 700 condemned and isolated lepers at the Leper Settlement on Molokai, while physicians of the highest standing estimated that there were from 3,000 to 5,000 concealed lepers in the kingdom. Dr. George L. Fitch, the government physician at the Free Dispensary in Honolulu, declared

9. Blaine to Comly, Dec. 1, 1881, No. 114, ibid., which is separate from and more detailed than the general instructions of the same date intended for use with the Hawaiian minister of foreign affairs.

that the disease was everywhere; members of the police, soldiers, the band, pastors of churches, teachers, and students were all sufferers. He reported officially that out of 4055 new cases of diseases treated by him the first quarter of 1882, some 2748 were syphilis and 508 leprosy. There were 51 more cases of other venereal diseases.[10] One of the oldest and most reputable physicians in the islands stated his belief that four-fifths of the native population was afflicted with syphilis.

In addition to these maladies, then considered incurable, there were the "constantly increasing sterility and impotency, and in a large degree more and more foggy perceptions in sexual morals," all of which caused the physique to deteriorate frightfully. "The robust race of the ancient Kanaka" had shriveled and dwindled to a melancholy handful, too many of whom were crippled by disease. They were "crippled alike in person, in morals, and in fortune—in mind, body, and estate." Not one Hawaiian of pure blood in all the islands owned or exclusively operated a sugar plantation or a mercantile or manufacturing business. These were in the possession of Englishmen, Germans, and Americans, especially Hawaiian-born Americans. Rice cultivation was almost exclusively carried on by the Chinese; cattle ranches were largely operated by the Portuguese; while the little shops, bakeries, and restaurants belonged to the Chinese, Portuguese, and other foreigners. Already the Chinese constituted more than half the adult male population of the kingdom, and the Portuguese were also increasing rapidly. The American population, however, was not augmenting as quickly as American capital.

South Sea islanders, "savage and lawless, and without either the noble physique or the amiable character of the ancient Kanaka," had been brought at great expense to transfuse the blood of a so-called cognate race into the dying Hawaiian; the result had been failure. As fast as the newcomers' contracts expired, they preferred to return to their own islands. Even if successful, the experiment, in Comly's opinion, would have resulted in lowering the Polynesian type by the infusion of an inferior race. Large expenditures had also been incurred in bringing in Portuguese, Norwegians, and others as laborers and as permanent population; but this mostly resulted in the simple substitution of aliens for Hawaiians—a result which did "not greatly delay the ultimate absorption of the native

10. *Pacific Commercial Advertiser,* April 8, 1882.

race into a new fusion of different nationalities of more or less contradictory character and habitat originally." Leaving out of account "every consideration except the good of the Hawaiian Islands," Comly believed that "our own American colored race can supply a more desirable population, without drawing too heavily upon our resources, than any of these other races of people now in prospect." All the hungry hordes of foreigners brought with them "habits of industry and thrift, to which the poor Kanaka is nearly a stranger, and he is rapidly going to the wall, clutching wildly at every straw for national life."

Even more somber were the vital statistics for the chiefs. The House of Nobles, created by the sovereign, was not necessarily of chief blood. In 1882, nearly half of its members were whites or half whites. But the native Hawaiians were still of feudal temper, and their attachment to their allis was deep and abiding, incapable of transfer or substitution. The constitution required that the sovereign should be of the native alli, or high chief blood. Queen Kapiolani had borne no heir. Queen Dowager Emma was childless. The Princess Luka, Ruth Keelikolani, had produced no heir to her name on the long Kamehameha estate. Mrs. Bishop, daughter of the old Chief Paki, was also childless and had refused the nomination to the succession. The Minister might have added that the Princess Liliuo-kalani had mothered no children. Of all the royal family or collater-als there was but one frail little girl,[11] the half-white daughter of Princess Likelike, who represented the second generation. Unless the genealogical tables of the kingdom were reformed and enlarged, there was no other family left eligible to the throne. Only one deli-cate life constituted the reserve of high-chief power to draw from, and even that was not accepted wholeheartedly by the body of Hawaiians, who did not recognize the Kalakaua family as true high-chief blood. Minister Comly queried: "With the native race rapidly disappearing, and the high-chief blood nearly exhausted; with al-ready a majority of the adult males in the Kingdom of alien races; with a constitution resting upon a moribund constituency, and rely-ing for functional life upon nearly defunct agencies; what future is there for the native race and the existing dynasty of the Sandwich Islands?"[12]

11. Princess Victoria Kawekiu Kaiulani Luhalilo Kalaninuiahilaphlapa, then eight years old.

12. Comly to Frelinghuysen, April 10, 1882, No. 213, USDS, Dispatches, Hawaii, 20. For several suggestions to import colored Americans to labor on

The expectation of small independent farmers possessing and tilling their own lands in the islands was not bright. There were no homestead laws and, strictly speaking, no government lands in sufficient quantity "to make it practical to offer small holdings for immigrants." There were, however, opportunities offered by private parties to planters of sugar cane who wished to take up small quantities of land "on the shares"; but the acreage was for lease, not for sale.[13]

Cabinets and the Legislature

In spite of tranquillity in the islands and comity in international relations, Peirce was convinced that the increasing cosmopolitan character of the Hawaiian government and the national jealousies engendered thereby were pregnant with significance and dangerous to continued quiescence. The first cabinet appointed by King Kalakaua—composed of William L. Green, an Englishman, Alfred S. Hartwell, an American, Hermann A. Widemann, a German, and Governor P. Nahaolelua a Hawaiian noble—was of a more cosmopolitan nature than any preceding it, in spite of the fact that it was three-quarters foreign. Its members were all honest, experienced men of first-class ability who enjoyed the respect and confidence of the public. This ministry, which held office for nearly three years and carried through the treaty of reciprocity, resigned in December 1876.

The sovereign then named as minister of the interior and premier Dr. John Mott Smith, who had served the kingdom in several capacities; as minister of foreign affairs Henry A. P. Carter; as attorney general A. S. Hartwell, thus retaining his services; and as finance minister John M. Kapena, who had accompanied the King on his visit to the United States and who had acquired experience in the finance department. The second Kalakaua cabinet, formed when the country was entering a new economic era incident to reciprocity, was selected for its members' "talents, ability and integrity," as well as for their American proclivities.[1] Yet it was turned "out of bed and out of office" on the night of July 1–2, 1878, by a sudden de-

the Hawaiian sugar and rice plantations, see my "The Decadence of the Hawaiian Nation and Proposals to Import a Negro Labor Force," *Journal of Negro History*, 47 (1962), 256–63.

13. W. L. Green to Comly, March 28, 1882, No. 26, encl. No. 6, in Comly's No. 213 to Frelinghuysen, USDS, Dispatches, Hawaii, 20.

1. Peirce to Fish, Dec. 11, 1876, No. 381.

cision of the King, apparently under the pressure of demands from Claus Spreckels and W. H. Dimond for a lease of water rights on Maui and an extension and enlargement of the $48,000 government subsidy to the Pacific Mail Steamship Company,[2] and also because of the vigorous opposition of the native Hawaiian party in the legislature and the determination of Kalakaua to retain the support of that body for desired public and private appropriations. The cabinet was dismissed in spite of the fact that only a week before, a motion of want of confidence, brought before the legislative assembly by Walter M. Gibson, was defeated by a vote of 26 to 9. William De Witt Alexander considered this "Arbitrary and despotic act . . . without precedent in Hawaiian history."[3] No doubt, rumors which reached Spreckels to the effect that certain sugar planters on Maui would oppose this lease prompted the King to dismiss the cabinet peremptorily.[4] A more amenable, less conservative, and less American ministry succeeded, with Samuel G. Wilder at its head.

Premier Wilder was thoroughly American in his sympathies and deeply concerned over the investments of foreigners, for he possessed large shipping and other private interests in the islands. This energetic Yankee was unquestionably the most experienced and valuable member of a rather mediocre cabinet.[5] Kapena, who took charge of foreign affairs, was a man "of good ability, fairly friendly to the United States, but timid and somewhat vacillating." Simon K. Kaai, the new Minister of Finance, who reportedly had "left-handed blood of the Kamehamehas in him," was the ablest Hawaiian of pure unmixed blood in the kingdom, but he was "more than suspected of being corrupt." Preston, a capable attorney with considerable practice in Honolulu, including the legal transactions of Claus Spreckels, was an Englishman of unknown antecedents. He was represented to be "a hard drinker, fond of low company, and a bad subject generally in his private capacity."[6] Nevertheless, he

2. Comly to Evarts, July 8, 1878, No. 44, USDS, Dispatches, Hawaii, 18.

3. William D. Alexander, *History of the Later Years of the Hawaiian Monarchy and the Revolution of 1893* (Honolulu, 1896), p. 4.

4. Charles C. Harris to Elisha H. Allen, Oct. 4, 1878, Allen Papers, Library of Congress. Jacob Adler, "Claus Spreckels, Sugar King of Hawaii: Interaction of an Entrepreneur with an Island Economy" (dissertation, Columbia University, 1959), p. 60. For detailed story of the water rights see ibid., chap. 2.

5. George F. Nellist, ed., *The Story of Hawaii and Its Builders* (Honolulu, 1925), p. 186.

6. Comly to Evarts, July 8, 1878, No. 44, USDS, Dispatches, Hawaii, 18. Comly to Frelinghuysen, June 5, 1882, No. 221, ibid., 20.

proved to be a fairly able attorney general. This polygenetic cabinet offered a sharp contrast to the 100 per cent *haole*, British-American, sober, and somber missionary-dominated ministries of Kamehameha III, dignified by the preeminent statures of Wyllie, Judd, and Armstrong.

The concern of the United States residents and ministers was not confined to the composition of the cabinets; it extended also to the complexion of the legislature. In Peirce's opinion, native Hawaiians were incapable of legislating intelligently for the good of the country without receiving assistance from educated foreigners. In the elections of January 1874 for the legislative assembly, practically all Hawaiians were chosen. This the minister attributed to ill feeling toward foreigners planted in the minds of the people and cultivated by demagogues, under the pretense of being the true friends of Hawaii.[7] The outlook remained unchanged in the February 1876 biennial election for twenty-eight representatives to the legislative assembly. In the district of Honolulu, which was represented by four members, only one supporter of government policy was elected, the other three being members of the opposition, or Queen Emma party. As the legislature was about to assemble on April 29, some apprehension was felt that before its session closed there might be some dangerous exhibition of the disaffected members. For this reason Peirce recommended the retention of the U.S.S. *Lackawanna* in port for its "moral influence." [8]

One of the first acts of the Wilder cabinet was to grant the desired water-right on Maui to Claus Spreckels for thirty years at $500 per annum. Largely through the efforts of the efficient Premier, considered by William D. Alexander as probably the ablest administrator the Hawaiian kingdom ever had, the predominantly native legislature of 1878 was held in check and the opium and free liquor bills were killed. This experienced businessman infused new vigor into every department of government, promoted immigration—much to the satisfaction of the large sugar planters—carried out extensive public works, and at the close of the session was able to show cash in the treasury sufficient to pay off the existing national debt.[9]

In spite of this sanguine achievement, the election of February 4, 1880, was unsatisfactory to the business community. Only three

7. Peirce to Fish, March 3, 1874, No. 250.
8. Ibid., Feb. 3, April 23, 1876, Nos. 352, 359.
9. Alexander, *Hawaiian Monarchy*, p. 4.

white men were returned for the entire kingdom, and of these only W. M. Gibson had legislative experience. According to James Comly, the elect were "almost without exception ignorant natives, with little or no conception of the nature of their duties, and most of them with the wildest schemes for legislating good incomes for lazy people without work." The strong white candidates for Honolulu "were beaten by natives who promised to borrow ten million dollars and enrich the country, so that everybody can live without work." The King himself "entered the canvass with zeal" and authored the ten-million loan project, which was put forth in the name of Hoapili Baker. Some quite calm and dispassionate men predicted a revolution.[10]

The canvass of 1882 was far from reassuring. Again only three white men were elected on the islands. This was the first time the race issue superseded all other considerations with the native Hawaiian electorate, and white residents became increasingly alarmed over the mounting nationalism and the racial antagonism stirred up by Gibson's propaganda of "Hawaii for the Hawaiians."

"Wild" Proposals

The "inconsiderate and extravagant" measures of the legislature of 1880, particularly the so-called ten-million loan authorizing the minister of finance to issue bonds with coupons to bear interest not to exceed 6 per cent per annum—the proceeds from which were to be used for a system of public works and assistance to agriculture— aroused the bitterest opposition from the capitalist class. This act envisioned government aid in constructing railroads, roads, bridges, wharves, public buildings, schools, and hospitals, encouragement and assistance to planters and agriculturalists in opening new fields of cane, beets, sorghum, coffee, cocoa, rice, etc., and the establishment of defense installations. The most vulnerable spot in Section 4 of the bill, which dealt with loans and contained the list of twenty-one items for which stipulated sums were to be appropriated for specific purposes, was an unstated amount for "Subsidy for Foreign Steam Lines."[1]

Representing the propertied interests, the cabinet opposed this "utter bosh," this "crazy scheme" for public works and underwriting

10. Comly to Evarts, Feb. 16, 1880, No. 93, USDS, Dispatches, Hawaii, 19. Since all of Comly's dispatches of 1880 are in this volume, reference to it hereafter will be omitted.

1. A copy of the act encl. in Comly to Evarts, July 5, 1880, No. 113.

indigent Hawaiians at the expense of incurring a big debt. Minister Comly was convinced that "disastrous" proposals, involving the use of public funds and foreign loans for a program of internal improvements and assistance to destitute and debilitated Hawaiians threatened the security, the well-being, and, most important, the capital of the propertied class. Such "curiosity in legislation" indicated that it was "the duty of the government to go largely into debt, in order to provide money to assist its citizens in carrying on private enterprises—farms, plantations, and all ways of business calculated to make Kanakas rich without personal risk or effort." In addition, an army of soldiers would be kept at play, fortifications erected, railroads built, cables laid, hospitals erected on all the islands, "traveling physicians with medical stores and attendance provided free for the natives at their homes, and the like."[2] Thus Comly frowned upon efficacious projects to preserve the indigenous inhabitants. Yet Dr. Charles F. Guillou, lecturing under the auspices of the Honolulu Lyceum twenty-two years earlier, spoke forcibly of the need for hospitals, asserting that the only means of prolonging the existence of the Hawaiians was by bringing them within the protecting reach of medical aid.[3]

James Comly lent his moral support to the ministers, assured them "verbally and privately" of the approval of all sensible people of their determination to get out of debt, and let it be known without precisely saying so, "that the United States government could not allow American interests in these Islands to be jeopardized and crippled by the creation of an unnecessary and foolish indebtedness." [4]

Proponents of the loan, in defense of their project, prepared a pamphlet entitled *A Reply to the Ministerial Utterances*, justifying a loan for public purposes by comparing Hawaii's indebtedness with that of several other small states, like Mauritius, with only one-tenth of the area of the Hawaiian Islands and a debt thirteen times as large, but whose officials kept the country up to a position equal to the value of its indebtedness through public improvements, manufacturing, and educational, scientific, and charitable institutions, combined with armies and navies.[5] Final action on the ten-million loan was postponed on August 6 by a vote of 23 to 19, not on its

2. Comly to Evarts, April 10, 1880, No. 104.
3. *Pacific Commercial Advertiser*, April 29, 1858. *Polynesian*, May 1, 1858.
4. Comly to Evarts, April 10, 1880, No. 104.
5. Hoapili Baker, *A Reply to the Ministerial Utterances* (Honolulu, March 16, 1880), p. 4. Copy encl. in Comly to Evarts, April 10, 1880, No. 104.

merits but because it unconstitutionally embodied ten or twelve different objects in one bill.

The endeavors of the native legislators of 1880 were viewed by the United States representative as "grotesque efforts, which would be ludicrous if they were not pathetic." Since there was not a native Hawaiian in the islands who owned a sugar plantation or a substantial mercantile establishment, any debt obligation of the government would have had to be paid almost wholly by foreign invested capital. Comly feared that there was no limit to the amount of tax the legislators were disposed to levy. They might "practically confiscate half or even more of the American and other foreign capital in the Islands with their visionary attempts to better their own conditions at the expense of the Haole or foreigner." Americans having large interests at stake repeatedly called upon their representative to interpose personally with the King, and "demand that he protect them and their interests against profligate legislation in which they have no voice, but for which they must pay." Comly did everything he felt authorized to do toward meeting these demands, but he was not empowered to go so far as to make a personal demand upon Kalakaua.[6]

The Wilder cabinet wanted "no foreign loans," but favored government assistance for "the opening of Hawaii by railroads" and "a sectional dock or patent slip for the port." All the requirements of the railroads could be met, without borrowing. The Premier was definitely interested in, and was himself contemplating, the private and personal development of railways on the islands of Hawaii and Maui to facilitate the transportation of sugar. He also conceived the idea of a marine railway in Honolulu Harbor, which was completed in 1883, the first in the kingdom.[7] In spite of the inconsiderate legislation proposed and passed in the legislative assembly of 1880, Samuel Wilder succeeded in carrying several measures intended to strengthen the currency and commerce of the kingdom and to smooth Hawaiian-American relations.[8]

During the last week of the 1880 session, L. Aholo, a friend of the King, introduced a resolution to authorize the minister of finance

6. Comly to Evarts, July 31, 1880, No. 121. Cf. Comly to Evarts, Feb. 16, July 5, 1880, Nos. 93, 113, and Comly to Frelinghuysen, April 10, 1882, No. 213, USDS, Dispatches, Hawaii, 20.

7. Baker, p. 5. Nellist, Story of Hawaii, p. 186.

8. Session Laws (1880), pp. 51–53. Cf. Comly to Evarts, Aug. 31, 1880, No. 122.

to pay to the commissioners of crown lands $40,000 "for the purpose of cancelling certain notes of His Majesty now held by Capitalists, the money to be returned by said Commissioners into the Treasury with interest thereon at a rate not to exceed five per cent per annum, by payments from time to time, of one-fourth of the income of said lands." [9] Thus the loan made by Claus Spreckels in 1878, at the time the Maui water-rights were under consideration, reports of which had previously been held to be scandalous and were not openly discussed, became of record in the proceedings of the legislature and were paraded before the world, together with the opinion that it was not good for the King to have his independence destroyed by a personal pecuniary obligation to a foreign capitalist seeking valuable franchises in the kingdom. Aholo's proposal was referred to a special committee, and its report, together with a slightly modified resolution, was adopted by the legislature on August 12.[10] Although the repayment was to be made by King Kalakaua out of the income of the crown lands, the assumption of the debt by the kingdom was disturbing to those who advocated economy in government. The general opinion among the politically conscious public was one of "stern condemnation." [11]

After the legislature was prorogued at noon on Saturday, August 14, the cabinet relaxed; now that the intractable assembly had gone home, the ministers felt secure for another two years. Their satisfaction proved transitory, for, just an hour later, at about 1 P.M., the Wilder cabinet was summarily dismissed without a word of explanation. Doubtless the Premier's determination to administer the interior department in accordance with conservative business methods did not suit the sovereign. In a new and heterogeneous cabinet, King Kalakaua appointed Caesar Celso Moreno as premier and minister of foreign affairs.

The appearance on the Hawaiian scene of this clever Italian lobbyist—with several projects in which he interested King Kalakaua, the native legislators, and Chinese merchants—complicated still more the volatile political atmosphere. Moreno's proposal to secure $50,000 from the Hawaiian legislature to organize a company to lay a cable between the United States and China via Honolulu

9. AH, JL (1880), p. 264; *Pacific Commercial Advertiser*, Aug. 7, 1880; *Hawaiian Gazette*, Aug. 11, 1880. Cf. Comly to Evarts, Aug. 21, 1880, No. 122.
10. AH, JLA (1880), pp. 285–86; *Pacific Commercial Advertiser*, Aug. 14, 1880.
11. *Hawaiian Gazette*, Aug. 11, 18, 1880.

was defeated by adroitness on the part of Minister Wilder; but on July 28, 1880, the assembly took up and passed the formerly defeated appropriation of $24,000 for a subsidy to the China Merchants' Steam Navigation Company for a line of trans-Pacific steamers to run between China and San Francisco via Honolulu. Comly, however, was assured by Wilder that the contract would never be let to that company so long as he remained minister of the interior.[12]

Next, the legislature passed an opium bill, which through "pecuniary considerations in the matter of license," transferred "this large, lucrative and disgraceful trade from China" to Hawaii.[13] It provided for the sale of the license to a Chinese only, at a price of $60,000 per annum, whereas in China a similar license cost $400,-000 per annum. Through this favorable consideration, Moreno was able to secure enough contributions from the Chinese merchants of Honolulu to maintain himself in the capital. In the legislative assembly he tacked together his votes on the Chinese steamship subsidy and the opium bill and made an economical package deal by purchases of the members for the nominal payment of $50 to $100, except in the case of a highly principled representative, a former governor, whose vote allegedly cost $300.[14] Although the lobbyist confidentially expected to get a million for his projected Chinese cable, this bonus bill failed.

During the five-day crisis that followed the appointment of the Moreno cabinet, the United States minister played a decisive part— first, in declining an invitation of the British and French commissioners to intervene with a joint or collective diplomatic representative to the King, demanding the resignation or dismissal of the Italian adventurer, and, secondly, in urging and persuading Kalakaua of his own volition to dismiss the undesirable character. Eventually, New England town hall methods prevailed; a large mass meeting of native Hawaiians and a smaller one of foreigners protested against the King's arbitrary action. Three memorials were prepared and presented to Comly, one from resident American merchants, the second from Hawaiian citizens who were natives of the United States, and a third from the large and respectable element of German residents, most of them capitalists. Allegedly, the names on these memorials "represented more than half of all the capital in

12. Comly to Evarts, July 31, Aug. 21, 1880, Nos. 121, 122.
13. *Pacific Commercial Advertiser*, July 31, 1880.
14. Comly to Evarts, Aug. 21, 1880, No. 122.

the Kingdom and were still more weighty from the intelligence and respectability of the signers." [15]

After Comly's audience with King Kalakaua on August 18, the latter decided to remove the interloper. A message conveying this decision reached an assemblage of resident property owners meeting that day at 5 P.M. and voicing "an overwhelming public sentiment, equal to the work of changing the dynasty, if necessary." A committee of thirteen "solid men" was appointed to convey the thanks of the people to the sovereign, but coupled with these went new demands that the rest of the ministers go.[16] An all-haole cabinet, in the forming of which Claus Spreckels, who arrived in Honolulu in early September, took an active part, was headed by William L. Green, acting as minister of foreign affairs.

The legislative assembly of 1882 was no improvement over the "dangerous body of 1880." Comly reported that "the same wild schemes were brought forward in the canvass." A manifesto, similar to Hoapili Baker's, this one fathered by Lilikalani and subscribed by Walter Murray Gibson and others elected afterward, advocated "disastrous" proposals for the expenditure of public funds which men of substance considered "mischievous and dangerous," for they threatened practical confiscation of American and other foreign capital invested in the islands. Grave apprehension was felt among resident foreigners that a majority of the legislators would favor unrestricted loans and taxation, destructive of capital—the bulk of which was foreign, and four-fifths of that American. The opinion of foreign residents was that the assembly should be held in check by a careful and conservative executive, advised and guided by his constitutional ministers. The King, however, was the originator of the "wildest schemes for wasteful expenditures"; he did not consult his constitutional advisers on the projects, but hoped to carry them by personal solicitations of members, as he had done in 1880, acting directly against ministerial policy. The absurdity of the manifestoes of 1880 and 1882, Comly warned, should not mislead anybody as to the "mischievous and dangerous power over the native mind clothed with legislative functions." [17]

15. Comly to Evarts, Aug. 21, 1880, No. 122, with encls. Nos. 1–3.

16. Comly to Evarts, Aug. 21, 1880, No. 122. Cf. *Pacific Commercial Advertiser*, Aug. 21, 1880.

17. Comly to Frelinghuysen, Feb. 13, April 10, May 8, 1882, Nos. 208, 213, 217, USDS, Dispatches, Hawaii, 20. The last two are printed in *For. Rels.* (1882), pp. 332–37, 342–43.

Disaffection of the Propertied Class

Thus appeared in bold relief a socio-politico-economic phenomenon that had gained momentum for over a decade. The Hawaiian kingdom had presented an anomalous and unparalleled situation since the 1860's. With millions of dollars invested there, the majority of resident white people appeared content "under the domination of a primitive and inferior race," satisfied to share in the government and hoping to improve it, instead of overturning it altogether.[1] The enterprising capitalist class long had been apprehensive over the absence of representation of their capital in the legislative assembly and their inability to control appropriations. As early as April 1864, concern was voiced by the *Pacific Commercial Advertiser*, then an independent journal, over the danger of the legislature "being filled with men totally unfit to represent at least the foreign population and its capital, or to enact laws for the kingdom." The editor went so far as to advocate "a change in the organic law of the land," even if the constitution itself had to be revised.[2]

Deeply underlying the opposition to the policies of King Kalakaua was the mounting dissatisfaction of the propertied class—largely American, Hawaiian-American, and British—who had gradually acquired and developed the major resources of the kingdom, prudently conserved and invested their income, owned nearly all the estates, real and personal, and conducted almost all the substantial business. Thus this group, not the native Hawaiians, controlled the combination of labor and capital which organized the industry and commerce, and provided much of the revenue of the archipelago, yet had only an indirect, uncertain, and precarious control of policy. With the unprecedented prosperity and industrial expansion incident to reciprocity, the disparity between invested capital and political power became more pronounced, for American capital in Hawaii increased more rapidly than did the American population. During the first seven years of the operation of the treaty of reciprocity, property values advanced between two- and tenfold, and general extravagance in government was the natural result.[3] The

1. Capt. William Reynolds commented upon this condition as early as 1868, in Reynolds to Wells, Jan. 20, 1868, No. 3, U.S. Navy Dept., Captains' Letters, 1868.

2. April 23, 1864. Cf. ibid., May 7, 1864.

3. Daggett to Frelinghuysen, April 30, 1884, No. 144, USDS, Dispatches, Hawaii, 21.

propertied foreigners, numerically the smallest but economically the wealthiest element in the kingdom, paid the highest taxes to support a government which they were unable to manipulate and in which the native Hawaiian, owning practically no property, legislated the rate of taxation and the amount of expenditure. Even under the most favorable circumstances, this single misjoinder of the producing with the expending power would be looked upon with apprehension. But conditions in Hawaii were not favorable otherwise; they were "actively and menacingly unfavorable." [4]

4. Comly to Frelinghuysen, May 8, 1882, No. 217, ibid., Hawaii, 20. See Appendix II.

THE BLOODLESS REVOLUTION OF 1887

The legislature of 1882 was one of the weakest and most corrupt that ever sat in Honolulu.[1] At the opening of the session there was ample evidence that the Palace party, headed by the King and Walter Murray Gibson, leader of the native faction, controlled a majority of the members. The ministry was definitely at the mercy of the sovereign and his factotum, who would not be enticed or diverted from the attainment of his primary objective, the premiership. Consequently, the Green cabinet, without a vote of lack of confidence, resigned on May 19 and declined reappointment.

Unwillingness to alienate to Spreckels the crown land of Wailuku was not the sole reason for the resignation of this ministry. It was only the most apparent. Its members were resolutely opposed to the dangerous schemes of increased expenditures to be met by large foreign loans, and for some time they had not enjoyed the support of the predominantly native Hawaiian legislature and the confidence of the King, who depended more for advice upon Gibson than upon his constitutionally appointed cabinet. There was covert opposition to the ministry from the influential Planters' Association, whose members, anxious over the renewal of the reciprocity treaty, which was under severe attack in the United States, questioned whether the conservative Englishman's ministry would be willing

1. Alexander, *Hawaiian Monarchy*, p. 8. The characterization of the most corrupt is also applied to the legislature of 1892.

to make the necessary concessions (i.e. to cede Pearl Harbor) and cast about for a more tractable but still moderate body.

An active agent of the association called upon Gibson and strongly urged him to take a position in a new cabinet, under certain conditions, if it were offered to him. He declined to accept office under the proposed terms, shrewdly recognizing that "the game was in his own hands" and that when any change of ministry became necessary, Kalakaua would "call to his councils one who was the choice of both the native and foreign born populations." When offered the premiership, the appointee selected his colleagues to suit the King and himself, without consulting his would-be supporters in the Planters' Association, who retired crestfallen and cried out that the country was in danger. Then, as Green observed, "the red hot Reciprocity party subsided, and would have been glad to see even the old Ministry patched up, but it was too late, for a new set of performers had come upon the stage." [2]

The most significant and disturbing fact to the conservative business community and to foreigners exercised over the destiny of Hawaii was the emergence of Walter Murray Gibson as premier and foreign minister. This talented and versatile schemer, with a variegated and colorful career, was an unorthodox American, typical of neither the New England Presbyterio-Congregational Puritan school nor the Yankee trader-merchant class. Although Gibson appeared relatively late on the Hawaiian scene, he made a startling impression, wielded almost magical influence over the sovereign, was all but revered by Hawaiians of both royal and common blood, and became one of the most influential men in the kingdom in a period when the traditional American missionary party's influence was diminishing.

This Mormon apostate appealed to the nationalist feelings of the islanders by his popular slogan "Hawaii for Hawaiians." He became fluent in their language, especially identified his name with measures for their sanitary welfare—particularly for the control of smallpox—and with repopulation and immigration projects. As a member of

2. Green to the *Pacific Commercial Advertiser*, May 27, 1882. About the same time William Nevin Armstrong wrote a long letter to Senator George Boutwell of Massachusetts informing him of the influence in Hawaiian affairs of W. M. Gibson and of his policy to establish native rule, to discard foreign influence, and to break the treaty with the United States, with the idea that after the planters—chiefly foreigners—were ruined, the business of sugar growing could be resumed and made profitable with Chinese laborers. Boutwell to Elisha H. Allen, July 13, 1882, Allen Papers, Library of Congress.

the board of health and as an editor, he made the most of the smallpox epidemic of 1881 to excite the populace against the Green
ministry, just as the "Committee of Thirteen" had done in 1853 to
unseat Gerrit Judd. Gibson edited or controlled provocative newspapers, which became effective instruments for gross flattery of
the gullible King and for professions of undying devotion to the
decadent Hawaiian race. The first effort along this line was the
Nuhou Hawaii, which made its appearance on the last Tuesday in
February 1873, for the purpose of campaigning against the cession
of Pearl Harbor. The *Wednesday Press* or *Elele Poakolu*, a bilingual
paper, was published primarily for the native Hawaiian reader. In
both these journals the editor skillfully cultivated, and at the same
time denied, an antiforeign sentiment. His most ambitious journal-
istic effort was the purchase in 1880, allegedly at government expense, of the *Pacific Commercial Advertiser*, whose editorship he
resigned in 1882.

This man "of easy and agreeable address," "well informed on
world questions, unhampered by local business connections, ambitious of political leadership, devoid of any principles that would
prevent his scoring in any direction towards which his ambitions
pointed," [3] was by no means a novice in government when he was
elevated to the long-coveted premiership. On being appointed to the
privy council in 1880, he acquired considerable legislative experience, representing Lahaina, on Maui, during the long legislative
session of 1878, during which, among other activities, he supported
an appropriation bill for the erection of a new royal palace. At the
time he became premier he was the senior representative from
Honolulu and the recognized leader of the King's party in the
house.[4]

As for the other "performers," Simon K. Kaai, an inveterate inebriate, was transferred from the ministry of finance to the interior,
but was soon succeeded by J. M. Kapena. John E. Bush, a half-
white noted chiefly for his hatred of foreigners, became minister of
finance. Edward Preston was again named attorney general.[5] This
heterogeneous ministry represented what was called in the islands
the "Young Hawaiian" party, "embodying a Hawaiian 'Know Noth-

3. Thurston, *Memoirs*, pp. 74–76.
4. *Hawaiian Gazette*, May 24, 1882. Cf. Esther Lenora Sousa, "Walter
Murray Gibson's Rise to Power in Hawaii" (M.A. Thesis, University of Hawaii,
1942), pp. 104, 124–30, 149–92.
5. Alexander, *Hawaiian Monarchy*, pp. 8–9.

ing' sentiment of opposition to foreign influence in the government."
It suited the extreme native party, but was far from the liking of
the chagrined Planters' Association and was looked upon with apprehension by haoles who conducted the business and payed the
taxes of the kingdom. Americans were especially alarmed, for Hawaiians in the legislative assembly succeeded in defeating by the bare
majority of one a conservative American for president of that body,
and elected Godfrey Rhodes, an Englishman who had a pronounced
aversion to Americans and to the United States.[6]

Kalakaua and Gibson, at times dictated to and assisted by Spreckels, practically controlled the Hawaiian government for the following five years. During this period the Premier held each of the
ministerial posts, sometimes two or three of them simultaneously,
drawing a salary for each, as well as other positions to which he was
named by Kalakaua, who filled vacancy after vacancy with the name
of Walter Murray Gibson. The Premier was appointed commissioner
of crown lands in 1882, president of the Board of Education in 1883,
and secretary of War and the Navy in 1886. He pleased the King
and people by erecting a commemorative statue to Kamehameha
I, which still stands in Palace Square, by staging elaborate and ex-
pensive pageants that depicted and glorified their history and traditions, and by espousing a public works program, which was criticized
by his enemies for including "presumably Statues, Coronations, Ped-
igrees, Chinese Steamers, Steam Yachts." [7]

Although the members of this bizarre triumvirate had diverse
ambitions, their aims were complementary. The King was interested
in restoring the lost power of the crown and in reviving Hawaiian
nationalism. The Premier was an opportunist, an astute politician
apparently coveting power for the sake of power, used by Kalakaua
because he understood the ways of both Hawaiians and foreigners,
and spoke their languages. Thus he could furnish clever and intelligent leadership, while the entrepreneur provided lucre, the
element that strengthened and held the trio together while they
dominated the political scene. But Spreckels, as a daring capitalist
who had invested heavily in the kingdom, wanted political stability
and opposed the wilder schemes of the King and Premier.[8]

After six years on the throne, King Kalakaua had outgrown any

6. Comly to Frelinghuysen, June 5, 1882, No. 221, USDS, Dispatches,
Hawaii, 20.
7. *Hawaiian Gazette*, Feb. 1, 1882.
8. Adler, "Claus Spreckels," p. 26.

restraint that the opposition of the resident foreigners to his election had at first imposed upon him. His appetite for personal aggrandizement and his desire to be his own prime minister were fully developed.[9] Not satisfied with the appointment of the house of nobles, he interfered, after 1880, in the election of representatives by using his retainers, as well as liquor taken from the customhouse free—the most notable case being his active participation in the defeat for re-election of G. W. Pilipo, the "Lion of North Kona." [10] Kalakaua arbitrarily dismissed more than one cabinet, surrounded himself with advisers whom "righteous men" considered of disreputable character, and, like rulers in other lands, indulged in habits unbecoming a sovereign.[11] He was continuously in debt and resorted to unorthodox measures for raising money. Disgustingly, to pious Americans, he continued the "heathen" policies of Kamehameha V by permitting the *kahunas*[12] to organize themselves into a Hawaiian Board of Health.

Walter Gibson was adjuvant to this state of affairs. He played upon the vanity of the King and encouraged his grandiose and quietly nurtured dream of heading a Pacific empire of cognate peoples,[13] the first step toward its realization being an alliance with Malietoa of Samoa. The Chief Minister, like his esteemed predecessor, sanctioned the granting of favors, especially to Spreckels, who for a period made and unmade ministries and was disparagingly referred to as "His Majesty Spreckels." [14]

After an indefinite postponement motion was defeated, the legislature approved, on July 20, 1882, a bill "to authorize the Commissioners of Crown Lands to convey certain portions of such lands to Claus Spreckels in satisfaction of all claims he may have on such lands." [15] This measure engendered bitter debate, with Pilipo leading the opposition to the alienation of part of the Hawaiian heritage, claiming that the "taking of crown lands away from the crown and giving

9. Comly to Evarts, July 31, 1880, No. 121.

10. Alexander, p. 13. Thurston, p. 59.

11. Thurston, pp. 48, 50.

12. Soothsayers and sorcerers who saw only a supernatural agency in disease and remedy.

13. As early as July 1880 the King had confided this aspiration to Minister Comly; see Comly to Evarts, July 31, 1880, No. 221.

14. Honolulu *Bulletin*, Aug. 13, 1886.

15. *Session Laws* (1882), p. 11; *Pacific Commercial Advertiser*, July 21, 1882. The same day the land bill passed, Princess Ruth and her retinue were entertained at Spreckelsville; see *Hawaiian Gazette*, July 26, 1882.

them to another person is a step toward destroying the independence of the country." [16]

In addition to the obnoxious land bill, a "National Loan Act," which provided for a loan of $2,000,000 for specific purposes, the most important being encouragement of immigration and agriculture, as well as construction of roads, bridges, and government buildings, was passed. As the entire amount was allocated for these purposes and none of the proceeds were to be used for the current expenses of government, the bill had something of a claim upon public approval. There was no question, however, that the loan was authorized by a native legislature with the incentive and full knowledge that the burden of its payment would fall largely upon American and foreign property owners in the kingdom.[17]

Gibson, as premier, naturally came under the heaviest attack, but the opposition failed to dislodge him. Only loans from the friends of Charles R. Gulick, who was prevailed upon to accept the portfolio of the interior, tided the administration over until Spreckels decided to lend his support.[18] Paul Neumann, a Spreckels man, became attorney general.

The passage of the two million loan bill opened wide the doors of extravagance and peculation. Included in the expenditure were items for a belated coronation, for the education of Hawaiian youths abroad, for the relief of the board of genealogy, besides considerable sums for the military, the foreign embassy of the sovereign, and the new palace.[19] During the following two years the expenditures of the government—$3,216,406.05—exceeded the actual receipts by $793,220.63. The public debt, which on March 31, 1882, was $299,-200, reached $898,800 on April 1, 1884, and $1,048,800 on the 30th —$150,000 in bonds of the two million having been sold during the month.[20]

The first effective opposition to the policies of the triumvirate came in 1884, when a small but efficient group of Independents, organized for the purpose of checking extravagance and corruption

16. *Hawaiian Gazette*, July 26, 1882. Cf. AH, JLA, July 18, 1882.

17. *Session Laws* (1882), pp. 47–49. Cf. Daggett to Frelinghuysen, Sept. 20, 1882, No. 11, USDS, Dispatches, Hawaii, 20, printed in *For. Rels.* (1882), pp. 347–48.

18. Alexander, *Hawaiian Monarchy*, p. 10.

19. Ibid., p. 8.

20. Daggett to Frelinghuysen, April 30, 1884, No. 44, USDS, Dispatches, Hawaii, 21.

in government, were either elected or returned to the legislative assembly. A timely controversy between the Pacific Mail Steamship Company and Spreckels' Oceanic Steamship Company, favored by the Gibson regime, played into the hands of the opposition and was a significant factor in the canvass for this legislature.

Although the former company received a subsidy of $1,000 a month for carrying the Hawaiian mails, its primary interest was in the through traffic between Sydney and San Francisco, and it treated the tiny kingdom like a stepchild and Honolulu merely as a way station. Since the shipping requirements of the islands were not being met, the alert Claus Spreckels seized the opportunity to cater to the community's needs: under his son John's name and leadership, the Oceanic Steamship Company was incorporated in San Francisco in December 1881. This line offered a general freight and passenger service between San Francisco and the Hawaiian Islands, and proposed making special provision on its ships to adapt them to a tropical voyage, in the expectation of attracting more Californians to the islands as a pleasure resort.[21]

This steamship service was timely, for under the stimulus of reciprocity the economy of the islands was expanding more rapidly than the steamship service provided by the Pacific Mail. The lack of freighting accommodations, especially in the transport of sugar from Maui, was a serious drawback to commerce and a powerful argument in favor of encouraging another line of steamers.[22] Therefore, the ministry proposed to subsidize the Oceanic Steamship Company for carrying Hawaiian mail and to grant it the concession of transporting Chinese immigrants.

Independent candidates in the campaign for the 1884 legislature seized upon this example of discrimination to discredit Gibson's cabinet and Spreckel's influence. An Independent mass meeting in early December 1883 passed a resolution charging that the controversy was responsible for unfavorable sentiment in Washington, thus endangering the reciprocity treaty; for condemning action of the cabinet in withdrawing from the Pacific Mail the privilege of transporting Chinese immigrants; for expressing lack of confidence

21. *Pacific Commercial Advertiser*, March 26, 1880, May 21, 1881; Jan. 21, 1882. *Saturday Press*, June 11, 1881; Jan. 21, 1882. *Hawaiian Gazette*, Jan. 19, 1882.

22. *Pacific Commercial Advertiser*, May 6, 1882. Cf. *Hawaiian Gazette*, May 10, 1882.

in the ministry; and for calling for the election of Independent candidates to the legislature.[23]

There were repercussions over the inequitable monopoly in Washington, where both Henry Carter and Secretary of State Frelinghuysen received a communication from Edward Lauterback, representative in New York of the Pacific Mail, complaining that the transfer of the privilege of carrying Chinese immigrants violated "every principle of equity and justice," as well as the spirit of the commercial treaty.[24] Immediately, Minister Rollin M. Daggett in Honolulu was instructed to press upon the Hawaiian government the views of the State Department that the right to admit or to exclude from its dominions immigrants of any nationality or race was not for a moment questioned, "but the exclusive privilege of carrying immigrants who are admitted to Hawaii should be accorded to any one company owning a particular line of ships, whether American, Hawaiian or foreign to both countries, is believed to be itself unjust, and . . . inconsistent with the due maintenance of the treaty of 1849." The Pacific Mail had no right to demand an exclusive privilege in such carrying trade, but it might "with manifest propriety, under the terms of the treaty, insist that no discriminating measures against its vessels shall be maintained or permitted by the Hawaiian Government." [25]

Frelinghuysen let Carter know that the United States government felt bound to protest against "an inequitable monopoly being established on the ruins of a contract broken without cause." The Secretary of State frankly asserted "that no measure which does not freely open the Hawaiian foreign trade to any and all American citizens and American vessels without discrimination can be regarded as a just compliance with the spirit of the existing treaty." [26] Minister Carter was especially concerned over the effect of the controversy on the negotiations to renew the reciprocity treaty, for many people in the national capital regarded Spreckels' contracts

23. Honolulu *Bulletin*, Dec. 12, 1883.

24. Lauterback to Carter, Nov. 5, 1883, AH, folder "Minister and Special Commissioner to Washington, 1883."

25. Frelinghuysen to Daggett, Nov. 15, 1883, No. 38, USDS, Instructions, Hawaii, 2.

26. Frelinghuysen to Carter, Dec. 12, 1883, USDS, Hawaii, Notes to, in one vol. Cf. Henry A. P. Carter to Frelinghuysen, Dec. 6, 1883, ibid., Notes from, Vol. 2. Copy encl.

with the planters for the sale and freighting of Hawaii sugars "as an unfortunate and unsatisfactory outgrowth of the Treaty." [27]

Premier Gibson denied that the arrangement with the Oceanic Steamship Company violated Section 11 of the treaty of 1849 with the United States, and claimed that the Pacific Mail could not properly regulate immigration, but that Oceanic had offered to conduct that service in a manner satisfactory to Hawaiian authorities. The real grievance, the Premier discovered, "was that we had apparently engaged in too much business with one wealthy man." [28] A modified bill, providing a payment to Oceanic of $1500 a round trip from July 19, 1884, to March 31, 1886, instead of $2000 a trip, as originally proposed, eventually passed the legislature. [29]

After the election for the legislature of 1884, the Palace party retained control of metropolitan Honolulu as a stronghold, but the opposition at the opening of the session elected the speaker and controlled the organization of committees. During the session the most violent opposition to the Gibson ministry from the press and the foreign community was aroused by a bill drawn up in San Francisco. Its initiators were Spreckels and Frederick F. Low, and it provided for the chartering of a national bank for the islands enjoying certain tax exemptions and numerous privileges, including the right of deposit and exchange, the power to issue circulating notes, which were to be legal tender for all debts, public and private, except for custom duties and principal and interest on the public debt, and empowered to engage in a wide variety of nonbanking activities—namely, "to acquire by purchase, exchange, lease, hire or otherwise . . . ships, steamers, vessels, lands, buildings, plant, machinery, stock-in-trade, chattels or effect, either in the Hawaiian Kingdom or elsewhere." Low, president of the Anglo-California Bank of San Francisco, experienced in banking and familiar with the methods of lobbyists, brought the bill to Honolulu, expecting to steer it safely through the legislative assembly. [30] Several prominent businessmen of Honolulu were induced to join Spreckels and Low as the proposed incorporators.

In spite of the resistance of the Reform members and their friends

27. Carter to Gibson, Dec. 12, 1883, No. 51, AH, FO Ex., file "H. A. P. Carter, 1883."

28. Gibson to Carter, Dec. 14, 1883; Jan. 2, 1884; AH, Hawaiian Legation, Washington, D.C., Vol. 1.

29. *Session Laws* (1884), pp. 23–24.

30. Alexander, *Hawaiian Monarchy*, p. 11.

—as expressed in two mass meetings on June 7 and 23, the language of which hinted at revolution[31]—the objections of the powerful Honolulu Chamber of Commerce, buttressed by a constructive report on what was needed in a bank bill,[32] and the continuous assault of the opposition newspapers, Gibson was not overthrown. But the national bank bill was lost. By a vote of 25 to 2, on June 26, the bill was "indefinitely postponed," which meant it died an ignominious death.[33] Not even the four ministers dared, in the face of public opinion, to vote for it, as they voted for themselves on a resolution of want of confidence on June 28.[34] Its defeat marked the first dramatic check to Spreckels' domination of Hawaiian political life and portended his eclipse two years later on another financial measure, the London Loan. One constructive result of the acrimonious struggle was the eventual passage of a bank bill supported by the chamber of commerce after a cabinet bank bill failed.[35]

Despite the success of the Reform members and their friends in two areas of fiscal affairs—the other being the passage of an "Act to Regulate the Currency," the so-called Gold Law of 1884, which made gold coins of the United States the standard and legal tender for all debts, public and private[36]—the general appropriation bill of 1884 was, in the words of Minister Daggett, "an extraordinary exhibit of reckless legislation." It authorized the expenditure of double the expected ordinary revenues of the kingdom for the following biennial period and left to the ministry the discretion of determining which of the appropriations should be unprovided with funds. The outlook was improved somewhat when the members of the privy council struck out items in the bill to the aggregate amount of about $1,200,000 as impracticable, owing to a probable lack of funds.[37]

31. *Hawaiian Gazette,* June 9, 14, 1884. Honolulu *Bulletin,* June 24, 1884. Cf. Daggett to Frelinghuysen, June 14, 30, 1884, Nos. 159, 167, 168, USDS, Dispatches, Hawaii, *21.*

32. Honolulu *Bulletin,* June 5, 1884. *Hawaiian Gazette,* June 4, 1884.

33. Honolulu *Bulletin* and *Pacific Commercial Advertiser,* both June 30, 1884.

34. June 27, 1884.

35. Adler, "Claus Spreckels," pp. 302–11.

36. *Session Laws* (1884), pp. 20–23. Copy encl. in Daggett to Frelinghuysen, July 24, 1884, No. 179, USDS, Dispatches, Hawaii, 22. For details of the coinage controversy and Spreckels' role in the coinage, see Adler, chap. 7.

37. Daggett to Frelinghuysen, Aug. 31, Sept. 1, 1884, Nos. 189, 190, USDS, Dispatches, Hawaii, 22. Cf. Honolulu *Bulletin,* Aug 30, 1884.

In the canvass for the legislative assembly of 1886, Spreckels' influence in government was a significant issue and was scathingly attacked by the Independent candidates, especially attorneys William Kinney and Lorrin A. Thurston. The planters and merchants of the kingdom feared that the continued interference and unbounded influence of the California interloper in the Hawaiian government would threaten the renewal of the reciprocity treaty in Washington, where it had long been the opinion that the profits accruing to the United States were all made by one individual, where this same individual was held responsible for most of the evils emanating from the convention, and where the leading editors did not dare to support the treaty for fear of coming under the suspicion of being the hired agent of that person.[38]

In Honolulu the magnate was attacked as the power behind the throne, as "ex officio Emperor of the Hawaiian Islands," [39] as a maker and breaker of cabinets, and as being more powerful than the King himself. Much of the Californian's power and the antagonism to it stemmed from loans which he held and used as a weapon for furthering his own enterprises. In 1886 these encumberances

38. The continuance of that treaty was indeed doubtful, and it would not have been renewed except for a quid pro quo. In the executive session of the United States Senate on April 14, 1886, John T. Morgan, of Alabama, whose Committee on Foreign Relations had two years earlier justified the reciprocity treaty upon "higher considerations," presented another favorable report, but on this occasion proposed a significant insertion after Article 1, to the effect that the king of the Hawaiian Islands grants "to the Government of the United States the exclusive right to enter the Harbor of Pearl River, in the island of Oahu, and to establish and maintain there a coaling and repair station for the use of vessels of the United States, and to that end the United States may improve the entrance to said harbor and do all other things needful to the purpose aforesaid."

This second report called attention to the vexatious complications with European and Asian powers which might arise if the question of the control of the Hawaiian Islands should be reopened. The commodious harbor required only a little deepening at its entrance to admit the largest ships. It could be easily defended, and as there were forty miles of shore, including the indentations, all vessels would be out of reach of bombardment. In the unanimous opinion of the committee, this concession would be of great political advantage to the United States. *Journal of the Executive Proceedings of the Senate of the United States, 25* (1885–87), 419. Nowhere in the amendment is the word "cession" used in reference to Pearl River harbor. Cf. New York *Herald,* June 30, 1890.

39. Honolulu *Bulletin,* July 9, 1884.

mounted to more than half—$700,000—of the public debt of $1,300,-
000. Kalakaua, keenly humiliated by the position in which he was
placed and annoyed at frequent references to him as a second king,
decided to seek a loan in London to pay off his creditor and thus
free himself from this American's influence. Perhaps he also felt that
a creditor in distant London would be less likely to interfere in
affairs in Honolulu than one in nearby San Francisco.

Reaction in Washington

The details of the original loan bill—the second one amended by
"His Majesty Spreckels' Attorney General" John T. Dare in such a
way as to assure the capitalist the money owed him—and the revised bill which passed the assembly on October 13, 1886,[1] have
been thoroughly covered by Professor Jacob Adler.[2] Locally, the
most important consequence of the London loan was the end of
Spreckels' political influence in Hawaii. Although his economic interests continued paramount, they could no longer be extended by
preferential treatment from the government. After 1886, even these
gradually declined, until his death in 1908. Other results of the
struggle were the weakening of Walter Gibson, who never again
commanded the support he previously had been able to muster, and
the strengthening of the forces of the Independents, or the Reform
party, who in less than a year overthrew the Premier and forced
a new constitution on the sovereign.

Our primary interest is with the attitude in Washington toward
any loan made in Honolulu that might pledge the public revenues
of the Hawaiian kingdom as a collateral security, with possible impairment of sovereignty and loss of independence in case of default,
or, in this particular case, lead to the interference of Great Britain
in Hawaiian affairs. George W. Merrill apprised Secretary Thomas
F. Bayard of the $2,000,000 loan, the politics surrounding its negotia-
tion, and the Dare amendment in a general manner. The Minister

1. Honolulu *Bulletin*, Aug. 13, 1886. AH, JLA (1886), p. 380; *Session Laws*
(1886), pp. 19–20, 57–59. Cf. Merrill to Bayard, July 1, Sept. 2, Oct. 14,
1886, Nos. 69, 74, 84, USDS, Dispatches, Hawaii, 22.

2. Adler, "Claus Spreckels," chap. 8. Jacob Adler, "Claus Sprekels' Rise
and Fall in Hawaii, with Emphasis on London Loan of 1886," HHS Sixty-
Seventh *Report*, 1958 (Honolulu, 1959), pp. 7–21.

probably was not aware of the details of the final measure.[3] On the first page of the prospectus issued by the syndicate there were two indications that the principal and interest were "secured upon the consolidated revenue of the Hawaiian Kingdom." Although the final act, as amended by Representative L. Aholo, made only interest a charge on consolidated revenue, the proposed wording of a preliminary bond to be deposited in the Bank of England as security for the subscribers gave to the latter "a first mortgage on the Kingdom." [4]

Perhaps some hint of this from Honolulu, together with West Coast newspaper comments, prompted the Secretary of State to request Minister Carter to call at the Department. There Bayard explained that in consequence of some publications in the San Francisco papers and of information that "it was proposed to pledge the public revenues of the Hawaiian kingdom as a collateral security" for a loan negotiated in London, it appeared to him "that to give even a set of private creditors the necessary right of inspecting the exercise of the taxing power of a country, would virtually be creating a mortgage on that country, or, to use the language of the treaty between Hawaii and the United States, to create a lien in favor of third parties." To the Secretary of State "such a course was directly invasive of the rights and liberties of the Kingdom of Hawaii, and indirectly impairing the preferred rights of the United States under the agreement with Hawaii in the treaty of 1875." [5]

Carter concurred "in the unwisdom" of the pledge of the revenues of the kingdom. After communicating with his government, he called at the State Department with the information that the Secretary's suggestion had been successfully acted upon and that the pledge of the revenues of the Sandwich Islands for the payment of this loan had been withdrawn, so that the bond given in advance of the securities to be issued under the loan was simply the pledge of the minister of finance, and not a pledge of the taxing power of the government. As proof, he displayed a copy of the preliminary bond

3. Merrill to Bayard, July 27, Sept. 2, Oct. 14, 19, 1886, Nos. 74, 78, 84, 86, USDS, Dispatches, Hawaii, 22. A copy of the Dare amended act is in No. 78.

4. A copy of the prospectus is in AH, "Consul General at London, 1887." For the act which amended an act "To Authorize a National Loan and to Define the Uses to Which the Money Borrowed Shall Be Applied," see *Session Laws* (1886), pp. 57–59.

5. Memo. written by Bayard after a conversation with Carter, Nov. 30, 1886, Bayard Papers, Vol. 99.

to be deposited in London.[6] Thus he attempted to satisfy Bayard that the loan did not compromise Hawaiian sovereignty. He reported that Bayard was satisfied that the fears he had entertained were groundless, and that he had been actuated only by concern "that something might be done which would result in embarrassment at some future time." In answer to the Secretary's inquiry as to the purposes of the loan, Carter said, for improvement of Honolulu harbor and of the island itself. Yet, in the act was a provision of $150,000 for the encouragement of immigration.[7] The Minister further stated that the loan, although nominally two million dollars, would in reality not exceed one million, and that the result of the operation would be to increase the public debt of the kingdom about $700,000.[8]

In spite of the assurances given by Hawaii's representative, Secretary Bayard addressed a strong instruction to Minister Merrill in Honolulu on the subject of the two million dollar loan, whose reported terms "were practically the creation of a right of inspection and possible control, by foreign creditors, over the financial measures and administration of the Hawaiian Government, and as such were not in accordance with the spirit, if not of the letter, of the existing treaty between the Hawaiian Islands and the United States, which was intended to prevent any cession of territory or grant of a political nature by Hawaii to any other Government than that of the United States." The reasons for the Treaty of 1875 existed "in increased and still growing force." The political geography of the United States and the relation of the island groups of the Pacific Ocean to our Pacific coast and to the terminal points of its transcontinental railways had been importantly affected by the progress and natural operation of events since the ratification of that treaty. Bayard suggested that the Minister discretely intimate to King Kalakaua "the lively interest we feel in the autonomy and self-preserving force of his Government, and the satisfaction experienced by the President in learning that the late loan . . . did not involve a pledge of the revenues of his [Kalakaua's] Government, and the possible embarrassments to which he might otherwise have been internationally subjected." The letter concluded: "The safety and welfare of the Hawaiian group is obviously more interesting and important to the United States than to any other nation; and for

6. Memo. written after a conversation with Carter on Jan. 7, 1887, ibid., Vol. 101.
7. *Session Laws* (1886), p. 58.
8. Carter to Gibson, Jan. 7, 1887, AH, FO, Ex., "H. A. P. Carter."

that reason our ties of intercourse and amity should be cherished." [9]

Merrill called on the Hawaiian minister of finance in February 1887, requesting information on the true nature of the loan and the bond which had been executed as a pledge of the consolidated revenue of the kingdom for the payment of the principal and interest of all coupon bonds issued or to be issued, by virtue of the Loan Act. The latter frankly stated that a preliminary bond had been executed as a security for any advances, which might be made of a portion of the proposed two million loan, before the coupon bonds could be issued, and as a pledge that, as soon as they could be printed, the coupon bonds would be regularly issued and delivered as provided by the Loan Act, but that this preliminary bond had never been and would not be used. The next month the United States representative was informed that $500,000 of the loan had been placed by the London syndicate to the credit of the Hawaiian government in the Bank of California, in San Francisco, on condition that the money should be expended for one of the purposes named in the Loan Act and that vouchers be produced therefore, while the advancement of further sums would depend largely upon the judicious expenditure of this amount and the prompt payment of the interest thereon.[10]

Primacy in` Polynesia[1]

Anxiety in Washington was aroused also over Walter Murray Gibson's ambitious program to achieve primacy in Polynesia—initiated after he became premier—and especially by his August 23, 1883, protest over further annexations in the Pacific, addressed to twenty-six sovereign states.[2]

9. Bayard to Merrill, Jan. 8, 1887, No. 36, USDS, Instructions, Hawaii, 3, printed in U.S. Senate, *Hawaiian Islands: Report of the Committe on Foreign Relations*, 2 (Washington, D.C., 1873), and *House Ex. Docs.*, 53 Cong., 2 sess., No. 1, Pt. I, p. 1165, with variations in punctuation.

10. Merrill to Bayard, Feb. 14, March 14, 1887, Nos. 104, 109, USDS, Dispatches, Hawaii, 23.

1. Here used as the broad nineteenth-century geographical term, which comprehends a larger region than Polynesia applied in the anthropological and scientific sense, and actually includes Micronesia and some of the Melanesian islands, particularly those adjacent to northeast Australia.

2. For details of Gibson's proposals and their reception see my "Hawaii's Program of Primacy in Polynesia," *Oregon Historical Quarterly*, 61 (1960), 378–407. For historic precedents of his ambitious policy, see my "Hawaii's Early Interest in Polynesia," *Australiam Journal of Politics and History*, 7 (1961), 232–44.

At the time there was genuine danger of the division of South Pacific islands among the major powers. Queensland's precipitous action, on April 4, 1883, in annexing non-Dutch New Guinea in the name of Great Britain, allegedly to forestall Germany from acquiring the strategic area; the opposing ambitions of the French and Australasians in the New Hebrides; the designs of New Zealand statesmen on the "adjacent islands" extending to and including Fiji, Tonga, and the Cook and Samoan groups; and the expanding commercial enterprises of Germany in the Pacific—all caused deep concern in the kingdom of Hawaii.

In spite of this rivalry, the protest was not taken seriously by any of the powers. Only eight of the twenty-six recipients of the dispatch bothered to respond. The United States, alone of the major powers, considered Gibson's message, but refused to join Hawaii in diplomatic representations. Secretary of State Frelinghuysen discussed the proposal twice with Henry A. P. Carter, expressed regret that the Hawaiian action had taken the form of a protest rather than simply of an appeal to the powers,[3] and finally sent a guarded reply with the assurance that "the sympathies of this government and the people of this country are always in favor of good self-government by the independent communities of the world. While we could not therefore view with complacency any movement tending to the extinction of the national life of the intimately connected commonwealths of the Northern Pacific, the attitude of this Government towards the distant outlying groups of Polynesia is necessarily different."

The New Hebrides, the Solomon Islands, and those immediately adjacent to Australia were geographically allied to that continent rather than to Polynesia. Their material development, he concluded, had been largely due to their intercourse with the Australian system, and the United States government "would not feel called upon to view with concern any further strengthening of such an intercourse, when neither the sympathies of our people are touched, nor their direct political or commercial relations with those scattered communities threatened, by the proposed change."[4]

Neither Carter nor Gibson was satisfied with Frelinghuysen's reply, which indicated a lack of understanding of the true situation in the Pacific. Only the preceding day, December 5, 1883, the Sydney Inter-Colonial Conference adopted unanimously eight reso-

3. Carter to Gibson, Oct. 22, 1883, No. 36, AH, FO Ex.
4. Frelinghuysen to Carter, Dec. 6, 1883, USDS, Hawaii, Notes to.

lutions, which are often referred to as the Australasian Monroe Doctrine, the first of which declared "that further acquisition of dominion in the Pacific, south of the Equator, by any Foreign Power, would be highly detrimental to the safety and well-being of the British possessions in Australasia, and injurious to the interests of the Empire." [5] Nevertheless, Gibson instructed Carter that since the agitation for annexations in the Pacific appeared to have subsided, there was no need for him to press the issue further.[6] In reality, annexation pressures were still strong in Australasia, but the Hawaiian minister of foreign affairs was probably convinced that without support from the American Secretary of State, nothing positive was to be gained along the lines indicated in the protest.

Gibson's proposal of 1885 for confirming and strengthening the autonomy of the islands of central Polynesia was presented to Secretary of State Thomas F. Bayard, in a very broad and moderate approach, by Carter, who represented that Hawaii intended to supplement the efforts of American and Hawaiian missionaries in the islands, emphasized the extent of this evangelical activity, and urged that the United States join in suggesting to other powers that the past efforts of Hawaii on behalf of Pacific islanders should be acknowledged and that she "should be encouraged to take a leading part in aiding the people of these islands to group themselves into political communities and established forms of government in accordance with civilized usages.[7]

Bayard, after conferring with Sir Lionel Sackville-West, the British Minister, informed Carter that no general understanding existed as to the South Pacific regions, but that there was a partial understanding as to the Samoan kingdom, under which Great Britain, Germany, and the United States were jointly represented in a municipal government for the town of Apia and its surrounding district. He had had no information from either Great Britain or Germany of a desire to unite in declaring an extension of this principle to other islands, and he "would hesitate to propose it without some assurance that the proposition would be generally considered." The

5. New South Wales, Legislative Assembly, *Votes and Proceedings* (1883–84), *1*, 13–14. Victoria, Legislative Assembly, *Votes and Proceedings* (1884), *2*, Paper No. 25, pp. 14–15. Great Britain, House of Commons, *Sessional Papers* (1883), *54*, C. 3819, pp. 47–48. Cf. my "The Australasian Monroe Doctrine," *Political Science Quarterly*, 76 (1961), 264–84.

6. Gibson to Carter, Jan. 31, 1884, AH, Record of Hawaiian Legation, Washington, Bk. I.

7. Carter to Gibson, Nov. 10, 1885, AH, FO Ex., No. 9.

British disposition to control the traffic in liquor and firearms in certain of the groups, especially in the Ralik Islands, might be extended "so as to embrace a general recognition of the autonomy of the groups themselves, and so operate as a guarantee of their neutrality." He would be happy to see Hawaii, "the only established independent government in the Open Pacific, maintaining a recognized and honorable place in the family of nations . . . join in such an arrangement, if it be practicable." The proposal should be general and aim to secure autonomous neutrality. To limit it to a scheme for imposing restrictions would be a step in the opposite direction and one which the United States would not be disposed to favor.

Referring to the troubles in Samoa, the Secretary observed that the United States government

> could not be expected to view with favor the destruction of the autonomies of that group . . . We desire no domination in the Pacific ourselves nor can we be expected to sanction such a doctrine whereby any one among the Powers equally interested in trade and intercourse with those regions, might roam at will over the Pacific seas and absorb the jurisdiction of Islands, because unprotected or unadministered, thence to announce to other nations, whose rights are at least co-equal, the terms on which such islands may be visited or traded with.[8]

This encouraging reply came from an anti-imperialist statesman of a country not yet embarked upon an expansionist program in the Pacific. In Europe the situation was entirely different, as Carter learned from a mission to its capitals. An Anglo-German agreement had been reached the preceding April on partitioning New Guinea. The Vatican had successfully arbitrated the Caroline Islands dispute by assigning that archipelago to Spain, and Germany was compensated by being left free to acquire the Marshalls. The latter power had already given notice of a protectorate over that group, plus Brown and Providence Islands. She had also entered into arrangements with other powers interested in South Sea commerce to establish a demarcation of their mutual spheres of interest. Lord Salisbury made clear that Her Majesty's government would be unable to interfere in regard to islands recognized as wholly within the limits of German influence. Thus the area remaining in which to operate was small, and the islands insignificant and widely scattered. Since the Marshall Islands had been occupied by Germany, the task

8. Bayard to Carter, Nov. 11, 1885, USDS, Hawaii, Notes to.

of forming a government in the Gilberts would be more difficult and ran the risk of collision with a great power. The independence of central Polynesia could not be attained.[9]

The most significant aspect of Gibson's program to preserve the independence of the Pacific islands was his efforts to rescue Samoa from the clutches of the great powers, especially from German aggression, which endeavors led to the formation of the Hawaiian-Samoan Confederation. News reached Honolulu in January 1885 that a German agent the preceding November had forced the Samoan king and vice-king to sign an agreement that virtually made them puppets of the imperial German government. Although this arrangement was repudiated, the Hawaiian foreign minister was prompted to act. He secured cabinet council authorization to address to the Pacific powers dispatches regarding the archipelago, with pertinent documents revealing Samoa's 1875 request to Hawaii for recognition of its government and the latter's compliance.[10]

This diplomatic note, like the protest of August 1883, received no serious attention. Only Great Britain and the Netherlands were polite enough to acknowledge receipt of it. In Washington, Carter sought an interview with Thomas F. Bayard, who reportedly indicated that he regarded the Samoan matter as one solely concerning Great Britain and Germany, and felt that Hawaiian independence, because of the firm policy of the United States on that subject, was not jeopardized.[11] This was not a true representation of Bayard's attitude, for only the month before, shortly after taking up his duties in the State Department, he had instructed the American consul at Apia to oppose the annexation of Samoa.[12] In fact, throughout the 1880s the consular representatives of Germany, Great Britain, and the United States were highly suspicious of the annexationist designs of one another.

Despite his failure to receive diplomatic support or encouragement, Gibson did not remain indifferent to the fate of Samoa. Instead, he appointed his finance minister, John Edward Bush, to head a mission to Apia. The official instructions, which were not pub-

9. Carter to Gibson, Dec. 4, 20, 24, 1885, Nos. 12, 14, 15, AH, FO Ex.

10. AH, Cabinet Council Minute Book (1874–91), p. 320. Gibson to Bayard, March 26, 1885, AH, FO Ex.

11. Carter to Gibson, April 19, 1885, No. 106, AH, FO Ex.

12. Charles Gallen Tansill, *The Foreign Policy of Thomas Bayard, 1885–1897* (New York, 1940), p. 27. Cf. G. H. Ryden, *The Foreign Policy of the United States in Relation to Samoa* (New Haven, 1933), for a comprehensive treatment of our policy in Samoa.

lished, directed this agent to award to King Malietoa Laupepa the Grand Cross of the Royal Order of the Star of Oceania, newly established by the foreign minister, and to attempt to secure a confederation of Samoa with Hawaii which would "render them but one state in their relations to foreign powers." If he could only secure an exchange of courtesies with the King, Bush was to proceed to Tonga and negotiate a treaty of commerce and amity. If, however, he met with success in Samoa, he was to urge Tonga to join the confederation; then, if successful at the latter archipelago, he was to extend a similar invitation to the Cook islanders. Since Gibson considered the Gilbertese incapable of self-government, he recommended the annexation of their group by Hawaii. Thus he contemplated a Hawaiian-dominated Polynesian confederation, plus an extension of Hawaiian territory. But Bush was warned against committing Hawaii to any definite action in Samoa before attempting to end the strife between Malietoa and Vice-King Tamasese.[13]

The governments of the United States, Great Britain, and Germany were informed of the Hawaiian envoy's departure, but no intimation was given of the sweeping nature of his instructions. On the contrary, Gibson assured the powers that the mission was "no intermeddling of a petty State, but the earnest endeavor of a favored Polynesian ruler to assist and counsel for the best, one of the same race less fortunately situated." [14]

Unaware of the true nature of Bush's instructions, the Secretary of State expressed satisfaction at the mission.[15] Later, when H. von Alvensleben, the German minister in Washington, interviewed Bayard and in the course of the conversation inquired about the rumor "of the Sandwich Islands annexing Samoa," the reply was that "it was all nonsense"; the Hawaiian agent "was simply going there rather to evangelize those people than for anything else, and that his visit had no political significance." [16]

When Carter informed Bayard of the signing of the confederation agreement, the latter was both surprised and annoyed: surprised because he had regarded Bush's mission as purely advisory; annoyed because less than a month before he had assured Alvensleben that

13. Gibson to Bush, Dec. 24, 1886, AH, FO Ex.

14. Gibson to Carter, Jan. 18, 1887, No. 2, ibid. Gibson to Hoffnung, Jan. 18, 1887, No. 2, ibid.

15. Carter to Gibson, Feb. 4, 1887, No. 82, ibid.

16. Memo. written after conference with Alvensleben, Feb. 25, 1887, Bayard Papers, Vol. 107.

the rumor about Hawaii's annexing Samoa was "all nonsense."
Bayard regarded such a union as inadvisable. He felt that Hawaii
would risk her "political position in the family of nations" by being
drawn into the complications of Malietoa of Samoa.[17] At the time,
he was concentrating upon preparations for the three-power conference on Samoa, and desired to maintain the status quo and to
avoid giving Germany any pretext for precipitate action until the
conference convened. He hoped that no hasty steps would be taken,
but that Hawaii "would content itself with merely extending its
good offices in the way of good counsel and advice." The Secretary
of State was astonished at the plans made in Honolulu for arming
the *Kaimiloa* and for the purchase of a man-of-war in Great Britain,
and told Carter that he could see nothing in the arrangement "that
had a show of prudence or wisdom; that Samoa had not a breath
of power which Germany would care to respect; that the only reason
Malietoa had not been driven from the Island was the interest the
United States had taken in the matter, and the treaty made with
him." [18] From every point of view, it seemed to the Secretary of State
"ill advised" for Hawaii to take any ground while issues were pending in the origin of which she could have no concern and which
might bring her into conflict with other interests directly concerned.[19]

Interviews with Sackville-West and Alvensleben, who stated that
the German foreign office regarded the alliance between King
Kalakaua and Malietoa as "a travesty," and that this "political arrangement" would be entirely ignored in Berlin, convinced Bayard
that the representatives of the three major powers were in agreement on the inexpediency of the confederation treaty.[20] He then informed Carter that the British, German, and United States consuls
in Samoa were being instructed to maintain the status quo pending
a decision of the approaching Washington Conference.[21]

17. Carter to Gibson, March 16, 1887, with encl. Bayard to Carter, March
5, 1887, No. 87, AH, FO Ex.

18. Carter to Gibson, April 1, 1887, No. 94, ibid. Memo. written after conversation with Carter, April 1, 1887, Bayard Papers, Vol. 107. Cf. *Polynesian,*
Oct. 2, 1886, for the heated debate in the Legislative Assembly over this expenditure.

19. Bayard to Carter, April 12, 1887, USDS, Hawaii, Notes to.

20. Memo. written after conversations with Alvensleben, May 20 and June
20, and with Sackville-West, June 14, 1887, Bayard Papers, Vols. 108, 109.
Sackville-West to Salisbury, June 15, 1887, No. 156, copy encl. in Pauncefote to
Wodehouse, July 20, 1887, AH, British Commissioners Letter Book, No. 18.

21. Bayard to Carter, June 20, 1887, AH, FO Ex. USDS, Hawaii, Notes to.

By the summer of 1887 Gibson's position as leader of King Kalakaua's government had become untenable. The Premier realized that devoid of influential support at home and without the blessings or even the approval of the United States government for his Polynesian confederation, there was no hope of achieving his primacy program. Meanwhile, the conference in Washington, which convened on June 25 and held six sessions, adjourned after a month without reaching an agreement on Samoa. Carter informed Bayard, on August 15, of the recall of John Bush from Apia and of the termination of the Hawaiian mission in the South Pacific islands.[22] Six weeks before this note was written, a revolution in Honolulu had toppled Walter Gibson from power, and with his eclipse, Hawaii's dreams of primacy in Polynesia faded.

The Hawaiian League

The legislative session of 1886 was protracted for five and a half months by the determined opposition of the minority members to measures they regarded as inconsistent with the public welfare. This legislature proved as extravagant as its predecessors. After re-assembling in August, following a short vacation, instead of reducing expenses, as recommended by the King, and keeping expenditures to the limit of $2,633,169, as was proposed, the amount of the appropriation bill was increased to $4,552,477.17. After the resignation of the Spreckels' ministry, following the defeat of the Dare amendment to the Loan Bill, Gibson, notwithstanding that he was one of the ministers voting with the minority, was again called to form a new ministry, which this time included two native Hawaiians. To Merrill it appeared that Kalakaua's policy was to try the experiment of conducting the government exclusively by native Hawaiians, since not only in the cabinet but in nearly all departments Hawaiians were gradually displacing persons of foreign birth.[1]

As for the personal influence of the King in poiltics, it had increased by 1886 to an unprecedented degree, while the constitutional precedents of former reigns were disregarded. In the minds of some men, like the brilliant and versatile "mission boy," William

22. Carter to Bayard, Aug. 15, 1887, USDS, Hawaii, Notes from Vol. 3. Godfrey Brown to George W. Merrill, July 12, 1887, *For. Rels.* (1887), p. 581.

1. Merrill to Bayard, July 25, Oct. 14, 1886, Nos. 74, 84, USDS, Dispatches, Hawaii, 22.

DeWitt Alexander, "the government was in danger of becoming an Asiatic despotism like that of Johore." [2] In this state of affairs dissatisfaction grew. With no legal method of overriding the monarch, there seemed no hope of initiating desirable reforms by legislative methods, and sentiment became widespread among the propertied class in favor of a strong protest, backed by sufficient organized force to go further if necessary.

Apprehensive over the safety of their property and investments, exasperated opponents of the extravagant and corrupt policies of the irresponsible King banded together in a secret Hawaiian League. The idea of an organization, including all nationalities, that would force the King "to be decent, and reign, not rule, or take the consequences," was suggested to Lorrin A. Thurston on December 26, 1886, by Dr. S. G. Tucker, a homeopathic physician. The lawyer discussed the matter with William A. Kinney, an American attorney practicing in the island, who was enthusiastic[3] and broached it to others, all of whom favored the plan. After several preliminary meetings—the first being at the home of Sanford B. Dole[4]—a general one was held in the residence of Dr. Tucker where the constitution drafted by Thurston was adopted.

Deemed too dangerous to be retained, the preamble of this instrument was destroyed after the members had committed it to memory. It ran about as follows: "The Hawaiian League is a voluntary organization, organized to secure efficient, decent and honest government in Hawaii. To the securing and maintenance of government of this character, we do hereby pledge our lives, our property, and our sacred honor." [5] The initiates bound themselves to keep secret the existence and purposes of the league; not to "oppose or oppress the white citizens of this Kingdom"; to support their "military superiors in their necessary efforts to protect the white community against arbitrary or oppressive action of the Government, which may threaten the lives, liberty or property of the people"; and "at all hazards protect and defend the members of the league who may be jeopardized in its service." [6]

Information about the league was extended to chosen persons on other islands, and the response was hearty. Enrollment ceased on

2. Alexander Statement, *Morgan Report*, p. 322.
3. Thurston, *Memoirs*, p. 129.
4. Sanford B. Dole, *Memoirs of the Hawaiian Revolution* (Honolulu, 1936), p. 47.
5. Thurston, p. 131.
6. Ibid., p. 608.

June 30, 1887, with 405 members. Among the names were those of leading merchants, planters, business and professional men, and morticians. Meetings were generally held in the evening in different parts of Honolulu and rarely twice in succession in the same place. In spite of these precautions, the government became aware of the existence of the plotting organization, and some efforts were made by the police to secure information about the gatherings.

Activities of the league were not confined to secret meetings: the press, the public platform, and the petition procedure were all enlisted in its support. The charge was made that public funds which should have been expended on internal improvements had been diverted to the useless Samoan mission, to the support of extravagant and useless officials, and to unnecessary tours abroad.[7] Coupled with these complaints were vituperative charges of bribery, all of which caused political excitement to run very high. There were open mutterings against officials in the early part of June 1887, intimations that a change in the ministry and governmental policy might be forced, and expressions of lack of confidence in the King. Minister Merrill counseled moderation and the adoption of peaceful measures as the best method of bringing about a proper administration of affairs, and he especially urged them not to encourage or participate in any act whereby trade and commerce would be interrupted. Petitions stating their grievances addressed to their several representatives were circulated among American, British, and German residents, requesting their respective governments to act separately or unitedly "to secure a just, economical and faithful administration of public offices." To all questions as to how the United States would respond to such an entreaty, Merrill invariably replied that he was not authorized to make any promise, but that when such a petition was received, it would be forwarded promptly to the Department of State, where the decision would be made as to what action would be taken.[8] An eleven-page memorial presented to the Minister on June 6 by Peter C. Jones contained a ten-page recitation of evils, and concluded: "We are therefore of opinion that a due regard for our political and personal rights as American citizens

7. *Hawaiian Gazette*, March 24, 1887. Honolulu *Bulletin*, May 22, 1887. Honolulu *Daily Herald*, May 25, 1887.

8. Merrill to Bayard, June 6, July 30, 1887, Nos. 124, 135, USDS, Dispatches, Hawaii, 23. All of Merrill's dispatches for 1887 are in this volume. Extracts for his most important dispatches for the year are printed in *For. Rels.*, 1887. In the case of No. 135, p. 362, the most significant sections were deleted in printing.

domiciled abroad demand that we should thus *protest* against a continuance of the conditions which we have described as very prejudicial to our national and social welfare." [9]

Originally formed for the purpose of effecting a change in the ministry and reforms in the old constitution, as more members were admitted the league became permeated with more revolutionary ideas. Two factions developed within the organization: the radicals, who were in a minority, advocated the overthrow of the monarchy, establishment of a republic, annexation to the United States, and enjoyment of the fruits of victory—offices;[10] the strong conservative wing, convinced that less radical measures than the overthrow of the monarchy were required, exerted all its influence to check the radicals. Among the leaders of that wing were the "mission boys" —sons and grandsons of the early American missionaries—who wanted Hawaii to remain independent but felt that the king's powers should be limited by a new constitution. The radical policies advocated by V. V. Ashford led two of the staunchest conservatives, Sanford Ballard Dole and Peter Cushman Jones, to resign from the executive committee and the league.[11] Members of the secret society on other islands were generally in favor of a radical policy and of annexation to the United States.

One of the most important problems that arose as the organization developed in the first half of 1887 "was how to precipitate the issue with Kalakaua." [12] As the league believed that he would forcibly resist its proposals, the greatest energy was devoted to strengthening the body militarily. The first members were able to procure fire-arms and ammunition from Honolulu hardware stores. To fill the growing requirements, a supply of ammunition and Springfield rifles was ordered. Upon the arrival of the invoice, government authorities, suspicious of the destination of the items, refused to permit their delivery, whereupon the directors of the league—trained lawyers— instituted proceedings of replevin in the courts and obtained delivery.[13] The brother of the able and kindly disposed Clarence W. Ashford, Volney V. Ashford, was appointed by the executive committee to organize the military forces and was named "Colonel of the Honolulu Rifles," an old-time company of fifty or sixty men.

9. Merrill to Bayard, June 6, 1887, No. 124.
10. Ibid., July 30, 1887, No. 135.
11. Dole, *Memoirs*, p. 49.
12. Thurston, *Memoirs*, p. 137.
13. Dole, p. 48.

The expanded Rifles was soon brought to a high degree of efficiency and divided into three companies, composed largely of young Americans, officered by league members, and entirely independent of any authority of the Hawaiian government. Each member of the Hawaiian League was armed with a rifle and from five hundred to a thousand cartridges. Besides its own military, the league had the support of the *Drei Hundert,* commanded by Captain C. W. Ziegler and chiefly constituted of Germans who were reputed to have served in the Germany army. Although this organization numbered considerably less than three hundred, its support—both moral and military—was welcomed, and later, in the Revolution of 1893, proved vital.

Toward the end of June 1887 the executive committee of the Hawaiian League felt that the military force at its disposal was sufficient "and that the time was ripe to bring about a crisis." [14] The immediate occasion, but not the ulterior motive, was a bribery scandal connected with government licensing of the sale of opium under the law of 1886. [15] This, together with rumors that the King was fortifying the palace and organizing armed forces, and that orders had been issued to the collector general of customs not to permit any arms of ammunition which might arrive in port to be delivered to the consignees, resulted in a cabinet crisis which came to a head on June 28.

His Majesty sent for Merrill the night before to request his unofficial but friendly advice concerning the prevailing political situation, the causes for the excitement, and what could best be done to allay it. The caller informed his friend [16] of the general dissatisfaction, and expressed the opinion that the retention of the Gibson cabinet was daily intensifying the opposition and that it would be better for many reasons to heed the voice of "those who were paying the taxes, who had accumulated wealth in the country and were directly interested," and substitute men in whom the community had confidence. When the Minister left at 11 o'clock, he was told that there would be cabinet changes within twelve hours. The following morning he received information that Gibson and all

14. Thurston, pp. 141–42.

15. Dole, p. 48. Cf. *Hawaiian Gazette,* May 17, 1887, for opium disclosures, and Merrill to Bayard, May 31, 1887, with enclosures of copies of pertinent affidavits sworn to by William Castle. This dispatch, unnumbered, is bound out of order before No. 183, May 1, 1888, in USDS, Dispatches, Hawaii, 24.

16. King Kalakaua and Merrill had collaborated in writing a book entitled *Legends of Hawaii.*

the cabinet had resigned. The news spread rapidly throughout the city; speculation began as to who would be called to form a new ministry; but nothing definite was ascertained until the following day, when "it was generally known that Mr. W. L. Green had been called upon." [17]

Meanwhile, the arrival of the steamer *Australia* from San Francisco, on June 28, with a large quantity of arms and ammunition consigned to well-known firms in Honolulu, occasioned considerable excitement owing to the fact that rumors were circulated that the collector general would seize the arms and not permit their delivery to the several consignees, in which event it was understood that they would be taken by force; then the conflict would begin in earnest. No opposition, however, was made; the arms were delivered as consigned, and distributed soon thereafter to various individuals.[18] The executive committee of the league chose this propitious time to act.

The Bloodless Revolution

A great public meeting was convened on June 30 in the "Armory of the Rifles." On the motion of Sanford Dole, Peter Cushman Jones— president of C. Brewer and Co., Ltd., the largest American exporting house and sugar plantation agency in Hawaii—was elected chairman. This gathering, addressed by seventeen men, was dominated by Attorney Lorrin A. Thurston who, on the request of the chairman, introduced and read the resolutions "in a voice that reached the outer limits of the assemblage," a voice which five and a half years later in a similar public meeting in the same armory would serve its owner well. The citizens, residents, and taxpayers resolved, among other things, that the administration of the Hawaiian government had ceased, "through corruption and incompetence, to perform the functions and afford the protection to personal and property rights for which all governments exist." Some evils had to be remedied immediately, before a permanent reform movement could be inaugurated with any reasonable prospect of success. The King was requested to dismiss "at once and unconditionally" his cabinet and to invite one of four named persons to assist him in selecting a new cabinet, which should be committed to the policy of securing a new constitution. Walter Gibson was to be dismissed at once from

17. Merrill to Bayard, July 30, 1887, No. 135.
18. *Hawaiian Gazette*, July 5, 1887. Dole, *Memoirs*, pp. 51–52.

each and every office held by him under the government. Kalakaua was further requested to make immediate restitution of $71,000 involved in the opium scandal, and a five-point pledge was required that in the future he would not interfere either directly or indirectly with the election of representatives, or attempt to influence unduly legislation or legislators, or interfere with the constitutional administration of legislators or of his cabinet, or use his official position or patronage for private ends.[1]

Although it was generally known in Honolulu the day before the meeting that His Majesty had invited William Green to form a ministry, and during the course of the assemblage Charles Bishop presented a letter received that day from Kalakaua stating the same and promising that guarantees would at once be conceded to such administration, the English businessman, who had adopted somewhat the American point of view on economic questions and had served as premier in two of Kalakaua's cabinets, asserted that he knew no more than anyone present about the letter. He referred to the meeting of citizens in the Lyceum in June 1884 and the failure then of the sovereign to acknowledge receipt of the protest letter with the resolutions against the ministry numerously signed which had been sent him.[2] Sixteen others spoke briefly. Bishop observed that matters should be discussed peaceably. Several speakers raised the question whether the new instrument should be initiated by the legislature or by some shorter and more efficacious process. Paul Isenberg, Sr., and Henry P. Baldwin, both conservative wealthy sugar planters and businessmen, opposed the immediate promulgation of a new constitution and urged moderation. Being from the country, they did not share the extreme feeling of Honolulu. Thurston, however, wanted immediate action. "The only way was to change the constitution now." [3] He won his argument.

The resolutions of the meeting were unanimously adopted and a committee of thirteen, headed by Paul Isenberg, immediately called on the King, presented him with a certified copy of the resolutions, and informed him that he had twenty-four hours in which to answer. The latter maintained that the propositions contained therein had been substantially complied with on June 28, and refused to admit

1. Dole, p. 53.
2. This letter was acknowledged. See Daggett to Frelinghuysen, July 12, 1884, with encls., No. 172, USDS, Dispatches, Hawaii, 22.
3. Thurston, *Memoirs*, pp. 143, 158–61. Dole, p. 55. Kuykendall, *Constitutions of the Hawaiian Kingdom*, pp. 29–30.

the truth of the opium license charges, but he was willing to submit the whole subject to the new cabinet and to act according to their advice. He acceded to each of the specific pledges required and assured the committee of his readiness to cooperate with "our Councillors and advisers as well as with our intelligent and patriotic citizens in all matters touching the honor, welfare and prosperity of our Kingdom." [4]

The following morning, when the community was still in a state of suppressed excitement, Colonel Ashford proceeded to act substantially as if the country were under martial law. He arbitrarily dispatched soldiers to the home of Walter Gibson, arrested him and his son-in-law, marched them through the town, and confined them in a stone warehouse on the wharf at the foot of Nuuanu Street, with the intention of hanging the former. On the timely intervention of Thurston, the executive committee of the Hawaiian League repudiated Ashford's plans, and Gibson was afforded the opportunity of choosing either to stand trial "for high crimes and misdemeanors" or to depart for San Francisco.[5] The prisoner preferred the latter, and was sent from the country on July 12 on a sailing vessel. The following year he died of tuberculosis in California, not realizing his great ambition to have a funeral attended by many poor Hawaiians and to mingle his dust with the soil of Hawaii.[6]

Alarmed over the method of arresting Gibson, the presence of illegally armed men patrolling the streets, and not knowing what the next act would be, King Kalakaua, on July 1, sent for the American, British, French, Portuguese, and Japanese diplomatic representatives and expressed the desire to place the control of his kingdom's affairs in their hands. The gentlemen informed him that the offer could not be accepted, that they wanted him to remain in authority, and since he had agreed to the wishes of the people expressed at the mass meeting the previous day and would shortly so inform the committee in writing, they advised him at once to authorize Green to form a ministry; in their opinion the atmosphere would then become normal.[7]

Shortly before the revolution was consummated, Minister Merrill

4. *For. Rels.* (1887), pp. 583–84. *Sen. Reps.,* 53 Cong., 2 sess., *Report of the Committee on Foreign Relations, Hawaiian Islands,* p. 1611. This report is not in the congressional series. Cf. encl. in Merrill to Bayard, July 5, 1887, No. 126; *Hawaiian Gazette,* July 5, 1887; Thurston, pp. 149–50.

5. Thurston, pp. 150–52. Dole, pp. 54–56. *Hawaiian Gazette,* July 5, 1887.

6. *Hawaiian Gazette,* March 8, 1882.

7. Merrill to Bayard, July 30, 1887, No. 135.

was reportedly "indifferent if not hostile to the party of reform, but at the last moment changed in his expressions and did not interpose" on behalf of the monarch, as had been feared.[8] Both he and Commissioner Wodehouse took special interest in informing emotional people of the condition of affairs and in quieting the excitement in the street; their efforts met with success. During the crisis no violence occurred and no occasion arose for requesting assistance from the U.S.S. *Adams*, which had arrived opportunely from Acapulco on June 14. Merrill, however, obtained from the acting governor of Oahu authority to land armed forces in case of necessity, and the Minister kept in frequent communication with the commander of the ship.[9]

Meanwhile, in Washington, Secretary Bayard was importuned by H. A. P. Carter to take a definite position in regard to the use of force to support the reform element in Honolulu, and was assured that the revolution was being conducted by his (Carter's) friends and would be in the best interest of Hawaii. He pictured the state of affairs there as "very critical," and asserted that "corruption, perfidy, and weakness were the chief elements in the Government of Hawaii." He was anxious to know what action would be taken by the United States minister or the naval commander who might be there "in case the other foreign powers were to land forces for the purpose of protecting their citizens against what he called 'the mob.'" Bayard found it "simply impossible" to give "information upon a purely supposititious case," but he took it for granted that neither of our "officers would see American interests suffer." [10]

With the representation of Merrill and the importunities of Carter in mind, and with only the barest telegraphic knowledge of the June 30th disorders,[11] the Secretary of State directed his attention to the political upheaval in Honolulu. Already genuinely dis-

8. Charles L. Carter to Bayard, Feb. 3, 1894, Bayard Papers, Vol. 113. Young Carter wrote that this "seemed to corroborate what I learned from father."

9. Merrill to Bayard, July 5, 15, 30, 1887, Nos. 126, 132, 135. For newspaper coverage of the revolution see "A Sketch of Recent Events, Being a Short Account of Events Which Culminated on June 30, 1887, together with a Full Report of Great Reform Meeting and the Two Constitutions in Parallel Columns," from the *Hawaiian Gazette*, April 30–Oct. 16, 1887.

10. Memo. written by Bayard after a conversation with Carter, July 6, 1887, USDS, Hawaii, Notes from, Vol. 3. This memo. is not in the Bayard Papers.

11. Merrill to Bayard (telegram), July 1, 1887, No. 125.

turbed over the impairment and destruction of the South Sea islands' sovereignties and international rivalries in the Pacific, he regretted deeply the existence of domestic disorders in Hawaii at a time when he was attempting to deal with the Samoan situation. He observed in instructions to the Minister that it was the duty of the United States to see that the interests of American citizens were "not imperiled or injured, and to do all things necessary for their just protection." The treaty between the two countries, as was contemplated and intended by the parties thereto, "created and fostered commercial relations more intimate in their nature and of incomparably greater volume and value than Hawaii had or can have with any other government." The growth of this commerce and the consequent advancement of these islands in wealth and importance was "most satisfactory to the United States, and by reason of their geographical position and comparative propinquity to our own territory they possess an interest and importance to us far exceeding that with which they can be regarded by any other power."

In the absence of any detailed information on the changes which had taken place in the official corps of the Hawaiian government, Bayard could only give general instructions to Merrill which might be communicated in substance to the commanding officer of the United States government vessel or vessels in Hawaiian waters, with whom the Minister was to confer freely "in order that such prompt and efficient action may be taken as the circumstances may make necessary." The Secretary concluded: "Whilst we abstain from interference wtih the domestic affairs of Hawaii, in accordance with the policy and practice of the Government, yet obstruction to the channels of legitimate commerce under existing treaty must not be allowed, and American citizens in Hawaii must be protected in their persons and property by the representatives of their country's law and power, and no discord must be suffered to impair them." [12]

Before this instruction was prepared, the revolution of June 30, 1887, became a *fait accompli*. After July 5, the Minister was not apprehensive of further trouble, yet he believed that the presence of a United States vessel of war could not fail to exert a wholesome influence in favor of American interests in Hawaii, and he requested that one be permitted to remain in the vicinity for several months or at least until after the general elections under the new constitution.[13]

12. Bayard to Merrill, July 12, 1887, No. 52, USDS, Instructions, Hawaii, 3, printed in *For. Rels.* (1887), p. 580.
13. Merrill to Bayard, July 15, 1887, No. 132.

Not only did the *Adams* prolong her sojourn, but she was joined by the U.S.S. *Vandalia* on August 27, and both warships remained until after the elections on September 12. Although there were no indications of political disturbances, Merrill consulted frequently with the officers of these vessels in order to have "a full and complete understanding in the event of possible action being required." [14]

The Constitution of 1887

As soon as King Kalakaua agreed to cooperate with the reformers in improving his government, the ministry invited a number of capable men, including Chief Justice Albert Francis Judd, Justice Edward Preston, and Sanford Ballard Dole, to assist in the preparation of a new constitution. By remaining in almost continuous session day and night, the gentlemen completed the assignment in five days. After deliberation, they decided to retain as much of the text of the former constitution as was not clearly inconsistent with the reforms insisted upon by the Hawaiian League.[1] Nevertheless, the instrument, accepted by Kalakaua on July 6, 1887, and promulgated by official proclamation the following day, contained certain provisions far-reaching in the curtailment of the king's prerogatives. The object of the framers of this Bayonet Constitution was to end irresponsible personal government by making the ministry responsible only to the people through the legislature, and to widen the suffrage by extending it to male residents of Hawaiian, American, or European birth or descent, thus enfranchising white foreigners who had previously found naturalization difficult or undesirable.[2] Ameri-

14. Ibid., Aug. 30, 1887, No. 140.

1. *For. Rels.* (1894), App. II, pp. 602, 793–817. A copy of the Constitution of 1887 and the King's proclamation of July 7 are enclosed in Merrill to Bayard, July 11, 1887, No. 127. A printed copy is in *For. Rels.* (1887), pp. 574–79; Lorrin A. Thurston, *The Fundamental Law of Hawaii*, pp. 181–94; *Laws of Her Majesty Liliuokalani Queen of the Hawaiian Islands Passed by the Legislative Assembly at Its Session, 1892*, pp. 343–61. Hereafter *Session Laws, 1892*.

2. Under the Constitution of 1864 the law required five years' residence— and then the decision to sign the naturalization papers was left to the King's discretion. There were cases of rejection on political grounds. The Hawaiian government, however, issued letters patent to applicants which gave them the privileges of naturalized citizens without being thoroughly naturalized, for they did not abjure their own nationality. This was called denizenship, and men were required to be denizens before practicing certain professions—for example, law.

cans, Englishmen, Germans, Norwegians, Portuguese, and Frenchmen were thus able to retain their original citizenship and at the same time enjoy all the privileges and immunities of Hawaiians, but Chinese and Japanese, working alongside the Portuguese, were effectively excluded from the benefits of the same.

While the powers of the legislators were greatly enhanced, the king was divested of nearly all direct personal control in the government. The cabinet members were to be appointed and commissioned by the king, "removed by him only upon a vote of want of confidence passed by a majority of all the elective members of the Legislature, or upon conviction of felony," and subject to impeachment. The monarch remained "commander-in-chief of the army and navy, and of all other military forces of the Kingdom by sea and land." But he might not proclaim war nor organize a military or naval force without the consent of the legislature. The veto of a bill by the king could be overridden by a two-thirds vote of the legislature. Nobles were no longer to be appointed for life by the king, but were to be elected for a term of six years, and serve without pay, one third going out of office every two years.

Under this constitution the two houses of the legislature sat separately. The number of nobles was increased from twenty to twenty-four. To be eligible for election as a noble, besides the usual residence and citizenship requirement, a candidate was required to own taxable property worth $3,000, free of encumbrances, or receive an income of not less than $600 a year. The same financial qualifications were required of electors of nobles. To be eligible as a representative, one had to own real estate worth at least $500, free of encumbrances, or have an annual income of at least $250. The number of representatives was fixed at twenty-four and their compensation was increased to $250 for each biennial term. Although citizenship was one of the necessary qualifications of both nobles and representatives, it was not required of electors of either house. There was no property qualification of electors of representatives, but all voters had to be of Hawaiian, American, or European birth or descent, had to be able to read and write in Hawaiian, English, or "some European language," and had to take an oath to support the constitution and laws.[3]

A new and significant article (No. 78) was added, which provided: "Wherever by this constitution any act is to be done or performed by the King or the Sovereign, it shall, unless otherwise expressed,

3. *For. Rels.* (1887), p. 578. Kuykendall, *Constitutions*, p. 48.

mean that such act shall be done and performed by the Sovereign by and with the advice and consent of the cabinet."

Most of the changes incorporated in the constitution of 1887 were intended to strengthen the power of the propertied class. That they could have been brought about by regular amendments to the constitution of 1864 was universally admitted to have been impossible. Since the representatives of wealth were not strong enough in the legislature to command a two-thirds majority of both houses, they turned to other—and admittedly revolutionary—methods to secure their ends. Consequently, the allegation has been made that the 1887 instrument was not legally enacted. Lorrin Thurston asserts: "Unquestionably the constitution was not in accordance with law; neither was the Declaration of Independence from Great Britain. Both were revolutionary documents, which had to be forcibly effected and forcibly maintained." [4] William DeWitt Alexander also admitted that the methods used were revolutionary," and revolutions do not generally claim to be constitutional." [5] Chief Justice A. F. Judd was of the opinion that both the *coup d'état* of Kamehameha V and the Revolution of 1887, though accomplished without bloodshed, lessened the respect of Hawaiians for their constitution and encouraged the rebellious attempt of Robert Wilcox, in June 1889, to promulgate a constitution that would restore the lost royal prerogatives.[6] Theophilus H. Davies also wondered if this anomalous procedure "might not later become a source of confusion in the hands of disaffected foreigners, working with Hawaiians." [7]

In addition to the attack on the revolutionary manner in which the "Bayonet Constitution" was secured, a majority of Hawaiians objected to the subordinate position in which it placed them and their sovereign, their *alli*, who was reduced almost to the status of a ceremonial figurehead. In reality, the revisions did not deprive the native Hawaiians of any rights or privileges they had previously enjoyed (except the possibility, so far as a few of them were concerned, of appointment as nobles), but the privileges extended to haoles gave the latter a greatly increased power in the government and correspondingly reduced the Hawaiians to an inferior position in the political life of their nation.[8]

4. Thurston, *Memoirs*, p. 153.
5. Alexander Statement, *Morgan Report*, p. 320.
6. Kuykendall, *Constitutions*, p. 46.
7. Davies to Lord Salisbury, Sept. 9, 1887, FO 58/241.
8. Kuykendall, *Constitutions*, p. 50.

Status of American Residents

Immediately after the promulgation of the new constitution, numerous citizens of the United States residing in the kingdom inquired of Minister Merrill and Consul General J. H. Putnam whether by taking the oath prescribed by the constitution and exercising the right of suffrage thereunder, they would retain intact their citizenship at home. Many expressed deep anxiety over taking any obligation that would interfere with their rights of citizenship, either in Hawaii or in the United States. As only two months would intervene before the election for the next legislative assembly, in which these Americans were naturally desirous of participating, the Minister sought instructions from the State Department on this vital question.[1] In so doing, he referred to the earlier decision of that department in the case of Peter Cushman Jones.[2] The new obligation did not contain the word "allegiance," as the old denizen act did, but required only a declaration of fealty to the constitution and laws of the kingdom. Putnam inquired of the Assistant Secretary of State: "But does not the constitution and law practically constitute the Government; and is not an oath of fealty to them in reality fealty to the Kingdom?" The question was not as to the ability of Americans "to throw off their Hawaiian citizenship on returning to their homes," as that had been settled by former decisions, but as to "whether the changed wording of the oath *will permit them to exercise the privilege of Hawaiian citizenship here and at the same time be entitled to the protection accorded to American citizens. In short, can they be citizens of two countries at the same time?"* [3]

Secretary Bayard instructed "that citizens of the United States who take the oath of fealty prescribed by the new constitution of Hawaii remain citizens of the United States and are entitled to be regarded and treated as such by our Consular and Diplomatic officers." He indicated that this result was contemplated by the Hawaiian government, as appeared evident from the last sentence of the oath, which read: "Not hereby renouncing, but expressly reserving all allegiance and citizenship now owing or held by me."

The State Department was aware that this oath was indiscrimi-

1. Merrill to Bayard, July 25, 1887, No. 134.
2. Frelinghuysen to Comly, July 1, 1882, No. 122, USDS, Instructions, Hawaii, 2, printed in *For. Rels.* (1882), p. 346.
3. J. H. Putnam to Jas. D. Porter, Aug. 1, 1887, No. 125, *For. Rels.* (1895), Pt. II, p. 849.

nately required of citizens of other nations who were understood by their own governments to retain their nationality of origin. Inasmuch as the oath was a requisite condition for exercising any political privileges in the islands, to Bayard it was "evident that a refusal on the part of this government of the assent to taking it granted by other governments to their citizens would result in the destruction of any political power previously possessed by our citizens, and its transfer to citizens of other assenting nations." The United States Minister was directed "to relieve the minds of all *bona fide* American citizens who while honestly deserving to retain their American nationality are, in order to obtain the privileges necessary for a residence in the Islands, obliged under local law to take an oath to support the Constitution of the Hawaiian Kingdom." [4]

A new problem related to the same subject arose a few months later. The Reform cabinet decided that the Honolulu Rifles, which had hitherto been independent of any authority of the government, should be legalized. Since the Rifles was composed largely of young Americans, Putnam inquired of the State Department whether these men, who had "not verbally relinquished their allegiance to the United States," might be members of the body in question, subject to the military laws of Hawaii "and to the command of its officials, and still retain American citizenship." In other words, could Americans in foreign lands put themselves in a position to be required, should an emergency arise, to fight against countries with which the United States was at peace, or even against the United States itself? [5] The Consul General was apprised "that citizens of the United States do not lose their nationality by enlistment in foreign armies." [6]

The Insurrection of 1889

During the five and a half years that the constitution of 1887 remained in force, there were several proposals and a series of movements aimed at securing not only amendments to the constitution but a new instrument of government similar to that of 1864. These

4. Bayard to Merrill, Sept. 20, 1887, No. 61, USDS, Instructions, Hawaii, 3. Porter to J. H. Putnam, Aug. 18, 1887, No. 63, in *For. Rels.* (1895), Pt. II, p. 849.

5. Putnam to Asst. Sec. of State Adee, Dec. 5, 1887, No. 133, *For. Rels.* (1895), Pt. II, pp. 849–50.

6. Asst. Sec. of State Rives to Putnam, Jan. 5, 1888, No. 76 in ibid., p. 850.

efforts were defeated, and the final contest resulted in the *émeute* of January 1893. During the two and a half years following the revolutionary events of June 30–July 6, 1887, which witnessed a struggle for power between Kalakaua, with his supporters, and the cabinet forced upon him, we are concerned primarily with Hawaiian-American relations and with growing British influence in the islands.

The Reform, all-haole cabinet, composed of William L. Green, minister of finance, Lorrin A. Thurston, minister of interior, Godfrey Brown, minister of foreign affairs, and Clarence W. Ashford, attorney general, obviously represented the conservative businessman's outlook. The Reform party, which had successfully carried through the bloodless revolution of June 30, and among whom the descendants of American missionaries were prominent, gained a decisive majority in the election of September 12, 1887, which was quiet and orderly in Honolulu and in other parts of the kingdom. The race issue, which a few endeavored to inject into the campaign, did not meet with favor. There was no formidable opposition party, and the opposing candidates, poorly organized, promulgated no platform or declaration of principles. In general, all candidates publicly accepted the constitution, the only open criticism being the provision requiring property qualifications in voting for nobles. After the election, all nationalities living in the kingdom appeared "agreed upon sustaining a policy of administrative economy and internal improvements."

During the extra or special session of 1887 the contest for power centered round the veto—the question of whether under Article 78 of the new constitution the King could exercise a personal veto against the advice of his ministers. The struggle resulted in a division within the cabinet itself. Thus after the Reform ministry had been in power less than six months, there were indications that it did not "possess that cohesive power necessary to a long and harmonious existence."[1] The supreme court, notwithstanding Article 78 of the constitution, sustained the constitutional right of veto by the king under Article 48 of that instrument. Four justices concluded that "if the power of veto is vested in the Cabinet the practical result would be that no measure which they should oppose and veto against could become law unless two-thirds of the elective members favored it. This would give the Ministers a power unknown in any

1. Merrill to Bayard, Dec. 15, Dec. 24, 1887, Nos. 158, 162. *Hawaiian Gazette*, Dec. 10, 1887.

other country and completely obliterate the legislative power of the King." Associate Justice Dole dissented.[2] During the 1888 regular session a cabinet measure to organize the military force of the kingdom with Colonel V. V. Ashford as the commanding officer was passed over the sovereign's veto without considering his objections, and illustrated the continuing lack of harmony between him and his ministers.[3]

The publication intentionally of twelve affidavits touching the corruption of government officials in May 1888 aroused among foreign residents intense feeling against the King and expressions of opinion that a change must occur from the highest to the lowest official. Merrill heard remarks to the effect that no modification in government would be satisfactory unless it was one deposing the King, changing the constitution, and adopting a republican form of government. Repeatedly, he was asked when a United States vessel was expected in Honolulu, to which he could make no definite answer, yet he felt that the appearance of one in port would have a salutary effect on all parties.[4]

The Reform ministry gave Hawaii an efficient administration; the special session of the legislature eliminated many useless expenditures in the public service and also made considerable reductions in the civil list. This retrenchment continued in the regular session of 1888. Financially, the economy was in a better position at the beginning of that year than for several previous years, and the islands appeared on the road to prosperity, provided the reciprocity treaty with the United States remained in effect, for there had been a rise in the price of sugar and the forthcoming crop was expected to be a large one. The only "rock" ahead appeared to be Spreckels' project of raising sufficient sugar from the beet root in California for the consumption of the Pacific coast.[5]

In spite of efficiency in government and prosperity in the economy, the Reform ministry was not popular with all the electorate. For one thing, it included no Hawaiian or part-Hawaiian. Particularly was it opposed by the National Reform party, which drew its strength variously from native Hawaiians, friends of the King, and

2. Honolulu *Bulletin*, Feb. 7, 1888.

3. *Session Laws* (1888), pp. 55–60. Merrill to Bayard, July 2, 30, 1888, Nos. 192, 200, USDS, Dispatches, Hawaii, 24. All of Merrill's dispatches of 1888–89 are in this volume.

4. Merrill to Bayard, May 31, 1888.

5. Wodehouse to Salisbury, Jan. 17, 1888, No. 38, FO 58/241.

anti-American, antimissionary whites. This opposition soon expressed itself in the form of conspiracies and insurrections. Robert Wilcox and Robert Boyd, recalled from military schools in Italy toward the end of 1887 as a result of the economy program of the Reform ministry, disappointed in finding that cabinet in power and themselves without the high positions they had been led to expect from the Gibson regime, formed a secret league and held public meetings to propagandize native Hawaiians.

The first conspiracy occurred in early 1888, led by Wilcox, Charles B. Wilson, and Sam Nowlein, commander of the Household Guard. Its purpose was to force the abdication of King Kalakaua in favor of his sister, Princess Liliuokalani, at whose Palama residence the plans were made. It failed, for the King refused to abdicate voluntarily and the leaders feared that they were not strong enough to precipitate a fight. Some evidence was collected but never used against them.[6]

With political affairs critical and an outbreak imminent, the cabinet on July 29, 1889, forced the King to transfer to the minister of foreign affairs the control of certain Gatling guns and materiel stored in the barracks of the Royal Guards.[7] Before dawn of the following morning, about 150 insurrectionists, armed with guns and ammunition taken from the barracks and led by Robert Wilcox, occupied the palace yard and bungalow. No serious assault was made upon the palace, from which the King was absent. The cabinet held council with the diplomatic representatives of the United States, Great Britain, France, and Portugal and with Commander Edwin T. Woodward, of the U.S.S. *Adams,* then in port. It was decided to make a demand upon Wilcox, in the name of the government, to surrender.[8] Minister of Finance Samuel M. Damon, who carried the demand, was refused admission to the palace grounds.

The Honolulu Rifles, composed of some of the leading citizens of Honolulu, took up position and fired from the Opera House and the Royal Hotel grounds commanding the palace. They were assisted by strong armed youth, who threw giant powder cartridges from Palace Walk, between two and three hundred feet outside the high stone wall. Toward evening the insurgents were dislodged, seven of their followers having been killed, and twelve, including Robert

6. Thurston, *Memoirs,* pp. 182–83.
7. Ibid., p. 184. AH, Cabinet Council Minute Book (1874–91), p. 402.
8. Merrill to Blaine, Aug. 1, 1889, No. 255.

Boyd, wounded.[9] The serious casualties were confined to the insurgents.

Meanwhile, with the permission of Hawaiian authorities, Minister
Merrill arranged with Commander Woodward for the landing of
seventy marines from the *Adams* to assist in preserving peace during
the night. The bluejackets went ashore at about 5:00 P.M., marched
with fife and music to the United States legation, and with a
machine gun took a turn round the streets, finally quartering for the
night at the armory. In addition to the 10,000 rounds of ammunition
they loaned to the Honolulu Rifles, the presence of the marines on
land gave heart to the residents, who regarded with trepidation the
approaching darkness. The forces remained ashore that night, returning on board ship the following morning.[10]

Apparently King Kalakaua had conducted himself in such a
manner that whether the insurrection had been a success or a failure,
he would have been safe. If the insurgents had succeeded, he would
have gone up to the palace and proclaimed the old constitution; as
they failed, he denied that he was connected with the movement.
Princess Liliuokalani also disclaimed any knowledge of the conspiracy and collaboration with Wilcox,[11] who himself became a popular idol and, for a time, wielded considerable influence over the
native Hawaiians of Honolulu.

This insurrection convinced the cabinet that the massive masonry
wall around the palace grounds was a definite menace to public
peace, and should be removed. The sovereign strenuously opposed
the decision, but the ministers were adamant and prepared, in case
their demands were persistently refused, to move upon the palace
with an armed force and suppress all oppositions. Kalakaua capitulated and a crisis was averted.[12]

Soon after the July 30 disturbance a report gained credence that

9. Honolulu *Daily Bulletin*, July 31, 1889. Dole, *Memoirs*, pp. 60–65. Alexander Statement, *Morgan Report*, pp. 285–86. Merrill to Blaine, Aug. 1, 1889,
No. 255.

10. Austin to Merrill, Aug. 1, and telegram, Aug. 2, 1889. The U.S.S. *Adams*
was the only national vessel in port.

11. Honolulu *Bulletin*, July 31, 1889. Theo. H. Davies believed that Liliuokalani was implicated in the Wilcox insurrection, "a not unnatural counter-
plot against those who as she believed were betraying" the independence of
the islands "by sapping the King's power" (Memo. on Hawaiian Sovereigns,
encl. in Davies to Sir James Fergusson, Feb. 6, 1891, FO 58–259).

12. Dole, *Memoirs*, p. 65.

the object of the leaders of the insurrection was not so much the dethroning of the King as obtaining from him the promulgation of a new constitution and the dismissal of the Reform ministry. The conspirators were inbued with the belief that foreign residents and the cabinet were in league for the purpose of destroying the autonomy of the kingdom; in addition, native Hawaiians felt that they were not the recipients of a fair share of the official patronage under the all-haole cabinet, and that a change of ministry was desirable. Relying upon the result of the revolution of 1887, many malcontents believed that all that was necessary to effect the desired remedy was to make a show of force, surround the government building with armed guards, take possession of the palace and the King, demand the resignation of the cabinet and the appointment of another, and compel the promulgation of a new constitution.[13]

Some demagogues seized upon the insurrection to intensify race hatred and the cry of "Hawaii for the Hawaiians," and others, to agitate for annexation to the United States. According to Merrill, it was noticeable that among the American residents in Honolulu there were several "who, from personal motives, contemplate with satisfaction, periodical disquietude, in the Kingdom, hoping that frequent revolutionary epochs will force the United States Government to make this group a part of its territory." [14]

The Reform ministers became convinced in early August 1889 that the time had arrived when, in the interest of peace and good government, the powers and responsibilities of the ministers and the king should be clearly understood and defined, and so informed the diplomatic corps. After friendly advice from Merrill and Wode-house, King Kalakaua accepted an August 5th decision of the supreme court to the effect that he had no constitutional right to exercise his discretion and to withhold his approval of acts embraced in the demands presented by his ministers.[15] This concession resulted in a temporary easing of tension.

Serious dissension soon arose over the question of a free-trade convention with the United States, to be negotiated by Henry A. P. Carter and James G. Blaine, which would have provided for reciprocal free trade in the native products of each country, equality of treatment in respect to bounties, and a guarantee of the independ-

13. Merrill to Blaine, Aug. 6, Sept. 7, 1889, Nos. 257, 262.
14. Ibid., No. 262.
15. Ibid., No. 257. *Pacific Commercial Advertiser*, Aug. 5, 6, 1889.

ence of Hawaii by the United States.[16] The initial agreement of the King was obtained on September 24, 1889, but on December 20, in the absence in Canada of Clarence W. Ashford, His Majesty refused to sign the authorization for Minister Carter to negotiate, on the grounds that the absence of the Attorney General left the cabinet incomplete. Despite harsh words and a warning from Thurston that if His Majesty persisted in his course he might eventually lose his throne, the sovereign remained adamant.[17]

On Ashford's return from Canada, he advised Kalakaua not to sign the authorization and to resist advice on this subject from the other members of the cabinet, Thurston, Austin, and Damon. The Attorney General was particularly opposed to an article added to the proposed treaty by Secretary Blaine which pledged Hawaii to enter into no treaty engagements with other powers without the previous knowledge of the United States, for this was considered a surrender of independence and sovereignty, unworthy in itself, and also detrimental to some commercial arrangements with Canada.[18]

Fall of the Reform Ministry

The insurrection of July 30, 1889, and the acquittal of Wilcox indicated a tendency of opinion among native Hawaiians which expressed itself in the election of the legislature of 1890.[1] Although the insurrection failed to dislodge the Reform cabinet, political maneuvering was more successful. The humbled King rallied his forces, while native Hawaiians, wishing to restore the Constitution of 1864, formed the Political Economy Party. A copy of the Blaine-Carter Treaty, including an article canceled by the cabinet which

16. For a draft of the convention see Carter to Blaine, April 11, 1889, USDS, Hawaii.

17. Thurston, *Memoirs*, pp. 208–09. Cf. AH, Cabinet Council Minute Book. (1874–91), pp. 412–13.

18. John L. Stevens to Blaine May 28, 1890, No. 25, USDS, Dispatches, Hawaii, 24. All of Stevens' dispatches, as Minister Resident, Nos. 1–30, dated 1889 to Sept. 24, 1890, are in this volume. Nos. 1–96, as Envoy Extraordinary and Minister Plenipotentiary, are bound in Vol. 25. With the exception of No. 70, Oct. 8, 1892, and important parts of No. 20, Feb. 22, 1891, all of Stevens' dispatches that have significance in connection with Hawaiian-American relations are printed in *House Ex. Docs.*, 53 Cong., 2 sess., No. 48.

1. *Pacific Commercial Advertiser*, Oct. 14, 1889. Stevens to Blaine, Oct. 17, Nov. 14, 1889, Nos. 6, 10, 11.

authorized the landing of United States troops in certain contingencies, was shown to the British commissioner by the King,[2] and was allegedly furnished by him to a native Hawaiian newspaper for publication. The cry was raised that the ministry was "selling the country" to the United States.[3]

This effective propaganda, along with the refusal of Marshal John H. Soper to take further orders from the Attorney General, Thurston's brusque treatment of the King during the discussions of the Carter-Blaine Treaty—resented by many Hawaiians—and divisions within the Reform party itself resulted in a partial victory for the opposition, which was completed when the legislature convened. In the organization of that body the Reform party was in a minority. Two or three half- or native Hawaiian members, supported by the reformers, joined the opponents, who elected the speaker by a small majority and controlled the appointment of committees. As the session advanced, it was evident that the King and his party were again in control and that sooner or later the majority would force the resignation of the ministry. The situation was complicated by the fact that Attorney General Ashford deserted his colleagues, supported the King in his opposition to the Blaine-Carter treaty, and advocated a reciprocity treaty with Canada and an oceanic cable that would connect with the Canadian Pacific system, all of which led to the strong suspicion that he was under the pay of the company.[4] After a vote of want of confidence, with an amendment condemning the action of the Attorney General, failed to pass, the three other ministers offered their resignations on June 16, 1890, forcing the resignation of their colleague. Thus the Reform cabinet, which never possessed much cohesion or internal strength, was succeeded by one of the King's choice.[5]

Proposals for a New Constitution

Since the contending parties were nearly balanced, a compromise ministry, composed of conservative men, was appointed on June

2. Confidential Memo. respecting the Designs of the United States on the Hawaiian Islands, printed for the use of the FO, Nov. 29, 1889, encl. in Wodehouse to Salisbury, Sept. 26, 1889, No. 4, FO 58/241 and CO 537/136.

3. *Pacific Commercial Advertiser*, Sept. 30, 1889. Cf. ibid., Oct. 4, 1889. Stevens to Blaine, Oct. 7, 1889, No. 3.

4. Stevens to Blaine, Feb. 6, 10, May 28, 1890, Nos. 17, 18, 25.

5. Thurston, *Memoirs*, p. 213. Alexander Statement, *Morgan Report*, p. 287. Stevens to Blaine, May 28, 1890, No. 25.

17.[1] The Reform party was in a measure satisfied, for it survived the change better than it had at first expected. On the other hand, the King's party was dissatisfied, because it had only two of the four ministers, and those not of the most pronounced nationalist type. Although these men had less intellectual force than their predecessors and were "less decidedly American than the three best of the retiring cabinet," Minister John L. Stevens hoped that they would "favor strong friendly relations with the United States." [2]

The first months of the legislative session were somewhat stormy and engendered considerable public excitement, especially over the proposal of the King's party and supporters to secure a new Constitution. The movement, carefully organized and manipulated, had the endorsement of the King and the support of a large part of the native population. During the session numerous petitions were presented asking for the enactment of legislation to provide for a convention, the delegates to which were to be elected by universal suffrage, to frame a new instrument. Representative J. W. Kalua gave notice of his intention to introduce such a bill on June 30, only a fortnight after the resignation of the Reform cabinet.[3] Joseph Nawahi moved a resolution two days later that "whereas it is the universal wish of the people to have a Constitution giving equal rights to all, the ministers be requested to state if they intend to bring forward a new Constitution this session." This resolution was ruled out of order by the president of the assembly, who declared that the honorable members "might as well ask the Ministers if they intend to hold a revolution." [4]

Two mass meetings of native Hawaiians were held in Palace Square in support of a constitutional convention. A resolution signed by forty-three Hawaiian delegates from the various islands and formally presented to the sovereign declared that the petition of his subjects should be good cause for him to request the legislature to enact a law authorizing the calling of a constitutional convention. Kalakaua, without consulting or receiving the sanction of his

1. John A. Cummins, a successful half-Hawaiian large sugar planter, became minister of foreign affairs; Godfrey Brown returned as minister of finance; C. N. Spencer, a native of New York, became minister of the interior; and A. P. Peterson, a barrister from Massachusetts and regarded as the ablest member of the cabinet, served as attorney general.
2. Stevens to Blaine, June 26, 1890, No. 27.
3. AH, JL (1890), pp. 61–62, 64.
4. Ibid., July 2, 1890, p. 74, Kuykendall, *Constitutions*, p. 54.

cabinet, sent a special message to the legislature on August 15 commending the object of the petition.[5]

Since the Constitution of 1887 specifically provided that the legislature should initiate amendments that had to be submitted to and voted by another legislature two years hence, the businessmen and more responsible citizens of the islands were disturbed at the prospect of having the country convulsed by a constitutional convention. On the advice of the two ablest ministers and the most conservative members of the legislature, Commissioner Wodehouse and United States Minister John L. Stevens, in a confidential interview, counseled the King against the rash and dangerous step. His Majesty professed that he was neutral in the controversy and had only brought popular grievances to the attention of the legislature.[6]

The appropriate bill was introduced on August 15 by Representative Kalua and was defeated by a vote of 24 to 16. Amendments lowering the qualifications required of voters for nobles, however, were voted almost unanimously.[7] These amendments, passed through the first stage as required by the Constitution of 1887, did not restore to the sovereign any of the power taken from him by that instrument, and the functions of the legislature and of the ministry were not at all impaired.

In addition to fending off concerted efforts to call a constitutional convention, the legislative assembly of 1890 succeeded in enacting several laws that were satisfactory to the conservative business interests: a homestead act; one restricting the importation and sale of opium or derivatives thereof; one which aimed to prevent illicit traffic in spirituous liquors; and still another which stipulated that Chinese immigrants should "not engage in any other occupation than that of agricultural labor and defined all labor incident thereto." This legislature also authorized the government to contract for the construction and maintenance of a submarine electric cable "from and within the boundaries of the United States or elsewhere and some point upon one or more of the islands of this kingdom," and stipulated the rates to be charged messages on such a cable.[8] Finally, a resolution was passed, nearly unanimously, requesting the minister of foreign affairs to open negotiations with the government of the

5. Kuykendall, *Constitutions*, p. 55. Stevens to Blaine, Aug. 19, 1890, No. 30.
6. Ibid.
7. AH, JL (1890), pp. 281–82, 284, 347.
8. *Session Laws* (1890), pp. 51–53, 130–38, 145–49, 153–54.

United States for the purpose of enlarging the free list of the two countries under reciprocity.[9]

After a long and, at times, stormy session of 146 days, the legislative assembly of 1890 adjourned without undoing the reforms of 1887. The victory over Kalakaua, however, was not complete. In spite of the extension of the suffrage to white foreigners resident in Hawaii and the heavy property qualification written into the Constitution of 1887, the Reform party managed to elect majority to only one regular legislature in the four years following the bloodless revolution. Moreover, during the period of that party's incumbency, the cabinet was hopelessly divided on the question of controlling the king. In the haste of preparing a new instrument, the framers failed to specify that the sovereign must follow the advice of the cabinet.

Growing British Influence

While reporting to the State Department in September 1888 on the efforts of an agent of the Canadian Pacific Railway to secure the exclusive right to construct or land a submarine electric cable that would reach to or from a British possession to an island of the Hawaiian group, Minister Merrill wrote at length on the growing influence of the British in the archipelago and the importance of the United States or its citizens taking the initiative in constructing a telegraph cable between some point in the republic and the Hawaiian Islands. He apprehended that the principal danger to the permanent interests of the United States in the group was "a gradual, peaceful conquest of the political control of Hawaiian affairs and the diversion of trade and commerce to other channels and the sympathies of the people to other Governments than that of the United States, where it legitimately belongs." British capitalists were seeking investments in the different islands and were contemplating the purchase of large tracts of land suitable for agricultural purposes on the islands of Kauai and Hawaii, while an English company owned an exclusive right to build and operate a steel railway throughout Honolulu and suburbs for a term of years. These and similar projects directed trade and influence through British channels, encouraged British lines of commerce, and readily assisted any enterprise that tended to bind British interests to those of Hawaii. "With a steamship line and cable connection with the British possessions in

9. AH, RL (1890), pp. 394–95.

North America," Merrill observed, "the people of this island King-dom would naturally become imbued with the opinions of their commercial connections and imperceptibly absorb the sentiments and feelings of those controlling the source of their daily intelli-gence." He hoped that cable communication might "terminate on United States soil thus strengthening what ought to be an indissolu-ble commercial and political bond." The Minister emphasized the importance of a cable that would bring the Hawaiian people "in daily contact with the world, through United States sources," and thus "largely and imperceptibly aid in the natural gravitation of commerce and political influence to our country and would silently yet strongly tend to quiet the periodical unrest natural to a seg-regated ocean bound community." [1]

Rear Admiral Lewis A. Kimberly, commanding the Pacific sta-tion,[2] addressed a similar communication to Secretary of the Navy William C. Whitney. The Admiral was certain that the day was not far distant when the line of native Hawaiian kings and royalty would become extinct, "and if the Government here does not become Republican it will be because the U.S. has neglected her oppor-tunity." There was no doubt that a cable would be laid, and if the government of the United States desired "to impress its views, power, and intentions, in the future, on the Government of these islands, the effects of a cable in prompting such influences" were obvious.[3]

On the reported intention of King Kalakaua to place his kingdom under the protection of Great Britain, the subject of British influence arose again in 1889. The posture of the State Department on this prospect was similar to that taken on the London Loan. When Minister Carter suggested that the United States might deal with the situation by means of a treaty that would establish a protec-torate, taking control of the foreign affairs and revenues of the Hawaiian Islands, Secretary Bayard mentioned "that there was evidently in the United States a growing consciousness of the pos-session of large material resources—superabundant population, a great deal of money, and a disposition to extend themselves beyond

1. Merrill to Bayard, Sept. 29, 1888, No. 211.

2. From June 1866 to May 1878, the Pacific command was divided be-tween the North and South Pacific stations. In July 1878 these two were com-bined to form the Pacific station.

3. Kimberly to Whitney, Nov. 14, 1887, U.S. Navy Dept., R.G. Naval Records Collection of the Office of Naval Records and Library, Area 9 File, 1814–1910, Jan.–July 1887 folder.

their present boundaries." He referred to the interest in a Panama canal, the Nicaraguan treaty, and Senator Edmund's pet idea of acquiring political control of Central America, and thought all these things should be considered in respect to the conduct of affairs in the Sandwich Islands.[4]

Henry Carter was not only keenly interested in securing a combination free trade and protectorate treaty with the United States, but he was particularly concerned that Bayard's approach to the Samoan imbroglio would not establish a pattern or precedent for the treatment of Hawaii. In a later conversation with the Secretary of State, the Minister expressed the ardent hope that in the forthcoming conference in Berlin with reference to Samoa, "there would be no principle laid down that would embarrass Hawaii." He was especially anxious that the United States refuse any invitation to join the European maritime powers in a guarantee of Hawaii's independence—that Bayard make no promise never to annex the kingdom. Carter was assured that the State Department drew the line "sharply between our relations with Hawaii and our relations with the island groups of the South Pacific," and that the Secretary "had never for an instant confused the two or suggested any similarity between the cases of Hawaii and Samoa." [5]

Kalakaua's Last Visit

After years of intrigue, during which he was confronted with the "cession" of Pearl Harbor, a revolution, conspiracies, insurrections, and a losing struggle with his ministers, and "protected" by a disloyal guard in a wall-less palace, the ailing King, commander in chief of sixty to seventy men—a military simulacrum—and of a nonexistent navy, decided, in November 1890, to make an informal visit to California for health and recreation. The United States government graciously tendered the U.S.S. *Charleston*, flagship of Rear Admiral George Brown, commanding the Pacific squadron.

The government of Canada expressed anxiety to the Colonial

4. Memo. written after conversation with Carter, Jan. 5, 1889, Bayard Papers, Vol. 135.

5. Memo. written after a conversation with Carter, Feb. 15, 1889, ibid., Vol. 136. Carter's solicitude on this matter contrasted sharply with his attitude a dozen years earlier, when he proposed that the great powers jointly or severally declare the Hawaiian archipelago permanently neutralized. See Peirce to Fish, June 14, 1877, No. 396, USDS, Dispatches, Hawaii, *17*.

Office that influence might be brought to bear on Kalakaua during his sojourn on the mainland to induce him to consent to the annexation of his kingdom to the United States. On the suggestion of Lord Knutsford, Secretary of State for the colonies, Commissioner Wodehouse was instructed that in the event of such a project coming to his knowledge, he was immediately to take such steps as he might think judicious to protest against it on behalf of the British government.[1] The astute Englishman was apprehensive that the King might extend his visit to Washington and that an attempt would be made there to negotiate a cession or long lease of Pearl Harbor to the United States in exchange for a bounty on Hawaiian sugar; but relief came on receiving the intelligence that it was inadvisable for the indisposed King during the winter season to cross the continent. Instead, Carter was summoned to California.[2] Actually, the belief prevailed among the best informed in Honolulu that the fitting time to enter on new negotiations in Washington relative to reciprocity would not be before late winter or spring.[3]

In San Francisco, Carter had several conferences with King Kalakaua regarding Hawaiian-American relations. The Minister advised that it was unwise to sign a convention giving a long-term lease on Pearl Harbor for monetary compensation, as Hawaii would part with the strongest inducement she had to offer for reciprocal advantages which were worth more to her than any money consideration she was likely to get. He considered it out of the question then to ask Congress for the bounty; and although after April 1, 1891, the balance of advantages would be with the United States, he was of the opinion that after January 1, 1892, they would be in Hawaii's favor. There was also the chance that the duties on sugar might be restored for purposes of revenue; Carter therefore deemed it wise to wait to see what would happen. If the Hawaiian government extended the treaty and relinquished Pearl Harbor for a long term and

1. FO to Wodehouse, Jan. 8, 1891, No. 1, FO 58/259. Cf. FO to CO, Jan. 3, 1891, ibid. My "Great Britain and the Sovereignty of Hawaii," *Pacific Historical Review, 31* (1962), 336–37. My "Canada's Interest in the Commerce and the Sovereignty of Hawaii," *Canadian Historical Review, 44* (1963), 31.

2. Wodehouse to FO, Jan. 14, 1891, No. 2, FO 58/259. Two months later the British commissioner claimed that he was "well aware" that Kalakaua was prepared in San Francisco to carry out a "long lease of Pearl Harbor in exchange for some tariff advantages" (Wodehouse to FO, March 23, 1891, No. 12, ibid.).

3. Stevens to Blaine, Nov. 20, 1890, No. 8.

the duty was not restored on foreign sugar, "we should not have gained anything, and we should be bound by the terms of the Treaty preventing us from making arrangements with other powers, while the United States having the harbor would not be anxious to give us any other compensation." Apparently any negotiation at that time would have been advantageous to the United States. By waiting until January 1, 1892, "we can more accurately judge of the value of reciprocity to us, while their desire to secure the use of Pearl Harbor will probably be greater than it is now." [4]

On his arrival in San Francisco on December 4, the royal visitor was received with appropriate ceremony. The ocean voyage proved beneficial, and his health for a time appeared "materially improved." His Majesty was pleasantly entertained by friends and acquaintances not only in the Bay City but also in Los Angeles, San Diego, and Santa Barbara. Colonel E. C. Macfarlane, the royal chamberlain, remarked in an interview: "Never at any time were the relations so close and friendly as they are at the present time with the United States." [5] Although rumors circulated that the annexation of Hawaii formed no inconsiderable part of the sovereign's purpose in visiting the West Coast, these were ridiculed by his advisers, although they acknowledged that Kalakaua earnestly desired to see an extension of the reciprocity principle to all the products of the islands.[6]

The King was expected home on January 29, and elaborate preparations were made to receive him with a great ovation. In the meantime, his strength was overtaxed by entertainment, especially by a banquet in San Francisco on the 13th and festivities at the Mystic Shrine on the 14th. The symptoms of his malady, Bright's disease, aggravated by a cold, increased in severity, and he succumbed at 2:30 P.M. on January 20, 1891, in the Palace Hotel.[7]

No one in the islands had realized the critical state of King Kalakaua's health. In the absence of a trans-Pacific cable, news of his death did not reach Honolulu until the morning of January 29, when the U.S.S. *Charleston*, with her yards aslant and her flags at half-mast, appeared around Diamond Head bearing the royal remains. A city in holiday mood, gaily decorated with triumphal arches draped in colorful bunting, had hastily to change to somber

4. Ibid., Dec. 21, 1890.
5. San Francisco *Chronicle*, Dec. 5, 1890.
6. Ibid., Jan. 21, 1891.
7. Ibid.

funereal crepe. After the unparalleled shock to the populace, the question uppermost in many minds—especially in those of the Americans—was: Would the deceased King's strong-willed and capable sister, the Princess Liliuokalani, take the prescribed oath to support the constitution of 1887? Refusal to do so or even attempt to circumvent the requirement would be construed as a revolutionary step. Since the Princess was "a natural born politician" and, as regent, had gained some experience in statecraft, she was considered "a sovereign to be watched with a keen eye." [8]

8. Ibid.

LILIUOKALANI'S REIGN

The dramatic revelation of King Kalakaua's death, without warning or time to prepare for a crisis, caused grave apprehension among the resident Americans in Hawaii. Tension was partially relieved by the Queen's promptly, graciously, and solemnly swearing "in the presence of Almighty God to maintain the constitution of the Kingdom whole and inviolate, and to govern in conformity therewith."[1] Thus the sudden and unexpected change of sovereigns was made without commotion and with no extraordinary excitement.

Many in the country anticipated an improved state of affairs with Lydia Kapaakea Liliuokalani (pronounced Lil-lee-woke-a-lanny), "Lily of the Sky." The fifty-three-year-old sovereign, daughter of Kapaakea and Keohokalole, high chief and chiefess of the islands, was known to foreigners as Princess Lydia or Mrs. Dominis. She was comely, dignified, and talented; her bearing was noble, with "the ease and authoritative air of one accustomed to rule"; and she appeared well fitted to take a firm hold of the reins of government. Her political ideas were in some respects similar to those of her brother, but she possessed more tenacity and determination than did Kalakaua, and charged him with cowardice for signing the Constitution of 1887. The Queen had been educated at the Royal School in Honolulu, had accompanied Queen Kapiolani to

1. Art. 24, Constitution of 1887.

London in 1887 to attend the jubilee of Queen Victoria, and for
many years had been a social leader in the Hawaiian kingdom.
She had a perfect command of English and had had good literary
training. An accomplished musician, she composed more than a
hundred songs, the most famous being the nostalgic *Aloha Oe*,
written in the early years of her brother's reign,[2] and she could
perform well at the console.

Liliuokalani had served as regent during the three-months' absence of the ailing King and for a longer time when her brother
made a world tour in 1881; her management of the affairs of state
won her the highest admiration for tact and statecraft.[3] After her
accession, the Reverend Soreno E. Bishop, in a long article contributed to the *Review of Reviews*, praised Liliuokalani's moral
character, religious habits, and good works. For years she had been
an active member of the Woman's Board of Missions and a munif-
icent patroness of the Kawaiahea Seminary for training native
Hawaiian girls. As Queen, she gave evidence of having deeply at
heart the moral welfare of her people, and made a remarkable decision by excluding the "heathen" and "lascivious" hula-hula from
the palace during her brother's obsequies and by banishing the
"libidinous" dancing and chanting during the royal progress tour
of her dominions. Her influence secured the repeal of laws relating
to the supply of liquors to native Hawaiians, and she disapproved
of the *Kahunas,* those "sorcerers and medicine men, dealing in deadly
witchcraft and its antidotes of propitiation of demons by incantations
and sacrifices," who were licensed by Kamehameha V, and became
"ubiquitous and busy, to the ruin of life and health, and the subversion of moral influences." Thus there was an improved outlook for
the increase of the native race. The Queen's "large fund of good
sense" was "much needed to gain her people's confidence and to
guide a somewhat determined will." [4]

Bishop's complimentary appraisal of the new monarch was tem-
pered with certain reservations. He alluded to the distrust felt by
many whites, due mainly to her attitude after the Reform movement
of 1887 and during the Wilcox insurrection of July 30, 1889, when

2. See also her "He Mele Lahui Hawaii," published under the name of
Lilia K. Dominis, in the Hawaiian Club of Boston, *Hawaiian Club Papers*
(Boston, 1868), p. 116.

3. Comly to Evarts, Feb. 14, 1881, No. 152; printed in *For. Rels.* (1881),
pp. 619–20. Cf. San Francisco *Chronicle,* Jan. 21, 1891.

4. Sereno E. Bishop, "The Hawaiian Queen and Her Kingdom," *Review of
Reviews, 4* (New York, 1891), 147–48.

her Palama residence was reported to have been the headquarters for the conspirators. Many Americans doubted the sincerity of the Queen in the act of oath taking, he said, and expected her to seize an early "opportunity to reclaim the ancient powers of the crown." Commissioner Wodehouse (who believed that Liliuokalani had "something of the old determined spirit of the Kamehameha dynasty in her composition"[5]) and Theophilus Davies were convinced that Hawaiian interests were much safer under the new sovereign than they had been under either of the last two kings.[6] Yet Bishop indicated that the legislature of 1892 was expected to take affairs into its own hands, and that the Queen would thus "inevitably come, under a more or less severe pressure of events, to put herself into the hands of the most capable advisers obtainable."

After nearly a month of suspense and intrigue, the supreme court justices, at the request of the cabinet, rendered the opinion "that the death of His Late Majesty obliges you [the ministers] to tender your resignations to Her Majesty the Queen."[7] The members selected for the new cabinet were Samuel Parker, minister of foreign affairs, Charles N. Spencer, minister of the interior, Hermann A. Widemann, minister of finance, and William A. Whitney, attorney general, a newcomer to public office.

The Queen's first and chief condition for the incoming ministry was that Charles B. Wilson, superintendent of water works since 1881, should be designated marshal of the kingdom, with control of the police force of the islands. Righteous and respectable citizens resented this appointment, for they claimed that Wilson, a half-Tahitian, openly associated on intimate terms with Captain Whaley, "King of the opium ring," and drew around himself a gang of disreputable characters, "while opium joints, gambling dens, and other criminal resorts flourished and multiplied."[8] Some further asserted that the marshal was a palace favorite and exercised as much influence in the administration of public affairs as any member of the cabinet.

Another unpopular step of the new monarch was the repudiation

5. Wodehouse to FO, March 23, Oct. 22, 1891, Nos. 12, 30, FO 58/258.
6. Theo. H. Davies, Memo. on Hawaiian Sovereigns, encl. in Davies to Sir James Fergusson, Feb. 6, 1891, FO 58/259.
7. *Reports of Decisions Rendered by the Supreme Court of the Hawaiian Islands, Admiralty, Criminal, Divorce, Equity, Law and Probate* (Hereafter *Hawaiian Reports*), 8, 578–82. *Pacific Commercial Advertiser*, Feb. 25, 26, 1891.
8. Alexander Statement, *Morgan Report*, p. 290.

of the pledge given by her brother to allow the income from the crown lands at the rate of $20,000 a year to meet the $95,000 worth of bonds issued by the legislature of 1890 to pay his obligations.[9] The debt had to be borne by the State.

The Queen ascended the throne in the midst of a depression in her tropical kingdom caused by the McKinley tariff bill, approved on October 1, 1890. This legislation removed the duties on all raw suger—that is on sugar not above No. 16 Dutch standard—imported from foreign countries, and gave a bounty of two cents a pound to sugar planters in the United States.[10] Thus the differential advantage that Hawaiian sugar had previously enjoyed in the big American market over sugar produced in other foreign countries was swept aside, with disastrous results for the islands. The price of raw sugar dropped from $100 to $60 per ton, production fell off sharply, wages were cut, and unemployment increased. The United States minister in Honolulu calculated that Hawaiian property values depreciated not less than $14,000,000.[11] For the preceding fifteen years Hawaii's commercial prosperity had been due to the advantageous terms granted her by the United States. In the spring of 1891, however, owing to the heavy decline in the American market of the islands' principal product, matters looked very serious for the approaching summer and autumn. The opinion prevailed in Honolulu that a permanent reciprocity treaty would stimulate and encourage other industries in common with sugar, and would benefit all classes in the islands. Her Majesty's government in cabinet council agreed that further attempts should be made to modify or improve commercial relations with the United States.[12] But a treaty providing for complete free trade was not realized. The depression, coupled with mounting political uneasiness, created an atmosphere favorable for the fermentation of revolutionary ideas and for the growth of a movement among certain elements for annexation to the United States.

A secret league was organized by V. V. Ashford, R. W. Wilcox,

9. Statement of E. C. Jones, ibid., p. 564. Cf. "An Act for Relief of His Majesty the King," Session Laws (1890), pp. 74–75. For a general statement with statistics of the extravagance of King Kalakaua, see Thurston, Memoirs, pp. 23–25.

10. U.S. Statutes at Large, 26, 583–84.

11. Stevens to John W. Foster, Nov. 20, 1892, No. 74, USDS, Dispatches, Hawaii, 25. Stevens' dispatches hereafter cited are in this volume, unless otherwise indicated.

12. Samuel Parker to Carter, April 18, Aug. 10, 1891, AH, FO Ex., U.S. Minister to Washington file.

and J. E. Bush in the spring of 1892 for the alleged purpose of promoting justice and equal rights in the political government of Hawaii. The founders, opposed to white suffrage and white influence in the government, included in their objectives abolition of the monarchy, the establishment of a republic, and, ultimately, union with the United States. They were not annexationists in the usual sense, for their principal aim was control of the government. Over three hundred native Hawaiian and half-whites, mostly of the Radical Labor party, comprised the membership of the league. At first the Queen's party attempted to form an alliance with the "Equal Rights League," both parties being opposed, for different reasons, to the constitution of 1887. The overtures were finally rejected, whereupon Marshal Wilson arrested the principal members of the league under charges of conspiracy. All were finally discharged, but the weakness of the league was exposed and its leaders lost prestige.[13]

The Annexation Club

Smaller and more secretive, the Annexation Club was organized by "safe" conservative white businessmen in Honolulu after the Queen had had trouble with her cabinet and rumors were rife of her dissatisfaction with the Constitution of 1887 and her inclination to take action.[1]

Henry E. Cooper, an American lawyer who had formerly practiced in California and served as attorney for the Southern Pacific Railroad, suggested to Lorrin Thurston that the leaders of the Honolulu community should be organized to know exactly the men who thought alike and could be reached at a moment's notice, if action were necessary. In Cooper's opinion, the situation had gone so far that the only effective remedy was annexation to the United States. Thurston, who had long supported independence for Hawaii, had been forced reluctantly to the same conclusion, and he therefore considered Cooper's idea a good one. As a result of the conversation, about a dozen men of the same opinion gathered in Thurston's office upstairs over the old Bishop Bank on Merchant Street (where the Kaahumanu and Strangenwald Building was later erected) and

13. Alexander Statement, *Morgan Report*, pp. 289–90. Honolulu *Bulletin*, May 20, 1892.

1. The secret Annexation Club of 1892 should not be confused with the large Annexation Club of 1893, formed after the overthrow of the monarchy, and reactivated in 1897.

agreed to form the Annexation Club. Their "object was not to promote annexation" but, according to Thurston, "to be ready to act
quickly and intelligently, should Liliuokalani precipitate the necessity by some move against the constitution, tending to revert to
absolutism or anything of the nature." [2]

Unlike the large Hawaiian League, which instigated and carried
through the bloodless Revolution of 1887, the membership of this
new organization was small—never more than seventeen—but it
was cohesive, pertinacious, and thorough. Its members were conservative lawyers, merchants, planters, bankers, directors and part
owners of large corporations, stock brokers, realtors, and engineers
—men who had millions of dollars invested in their own names or
as trustees in property in Hawaii. Having an appreciation and sense
of wealth and property, they were not fanatical. Needless to say,
they were white, and the majority were American citizens or Hawaiian-born Americans. These men never overreached themselves by
talking before they were ready to act. No records were kept by the
club.

Thurston's Mission

The members of the Annexation Club felt that they should know in
advance the probable attitude of the United States government toward their objective. Accordingly, arrangements were made to send
the able and energetic Lorrin Andrews Thurston to Washington.
He sailed from Honolulu on March 29, 1892.

In San Francisco the agent discussed the situation thoroughly
with W. H. Dimond and Claus Spreckels, whom he knew well,
having acted as his attorney in Hawaii. In New York, Thurston
contacted Frederick Allen, the Hawaiian Consul, and visited Attorney William N. Armstrong.[1] In Washington, John Mott Smith,
Hawaiian minister, volunteered to introduce the emissary to Senator
Cushman K. Davis, Republican member of the Senate Foreign Relations Committee, and Representative James H. Blount, Democratic
chairman of the House Foreign Affairs Committee. The latter stated
that he was not well acquainted with the situation in Hawaii but
assured Thurston that if action became necessary in Honolulu and
the question arose of the attitude of the Democratic House of Representatives, the matter would "be treated here as a national one,

2. Thurston, *Memoirs*, p. 229.
1. Thurston, *Memoirs*, p. 230.

and not as a Democratic." [2] He advised his visitor to see the Secretary of State and report back what the latter said.

When Blaine was able to see Thurston, introduced by a letter from Minister John L. Stevens, the caller explained that the Annexation Club members had no intention of precipitating action in Honolulu, but conditions had gone so far that they felt the maintenance of peace to be impossible: they believed that Liliuokalani was likely at any time to attempt the promulgation of a new constitution. "If she tended toward absolutism," annexation to the United States would be sought, provided the proposal would be entertained by the State Department. A "nucleus had been formed in Honolulu to bring the plan to a focus, should occasion arise"; and the group had sent him to Washington "to ascertain the attitude of the authorities there." Since Blaine was "somewhat unwell," he suggested that Thurston call on Secretary of the Navy Benjamin F. Tracy, inform him of the situation, "and say to him that I think you should see the President. Do not see Mr. Blount again. I will attend to him. Come to me after you have seen President Harrison." [3]

Thurston immediately called on Secretary Tracy, and together they went to the White House. While the former waited in an outer room, the latter explained the mission to the President, who felt that he should not see Thurston, but authorized Tracy to say that "if conditions in Hawaii compel you people to act as you have indicated and you come to Washington with an annexation proposition, you will find an exceedingly sympathetic administration here." This was what Thurston wanted to hear, and he considered his mission successful. He called at the State Department again, but the Secretary was ill and absent from the office.[4] The eager emissary, who had to attend to business in Chicago and return to Honolulu for the session of the legislature, did not thereafter see Blaine or Blount; but on May 6, before sailing from San Francisco, he addressed to the Secretary of State a letter enclosing a six-page, typewritten memorandum on "The Annexation of Hawaii to the United States," which was a statement of the situation as the attorney understood it, with a suggested line of action.

According to Thurston, up to about 1890 few individuals in the

2. Ibid., p. 231
3. Ibid., pp. 231–32.
4. Subsequently Blaine was replaced by John W. Foster. Blaine died on Jan. 28, 1893, at the age of sixty-three, of a chronic kidney ailment and lung complications.

islands had wanted annexation. Now three classes of people "almost unanimously" favored it. These were: "1. Those who have
money invested there, and whose interest in the country is mainly
confined to a financial one; 2. Those foreigners and some natives
who, in addition to their financial interests, are permanent settlers
in the country, who have made, and propose to continue to make it
their home; 3. The leaders among the natives who are known as the
Liberal Party." The classes opposed to the proposition were "the
common natives," the "Queen and her immediate personal following," and an "English faction rallying around the British Commissioner, Mr. Wodehouse, and Mr. Cleghorn, a Scotchman, father of
the present heir to the throne."

Annexation was favored by foreign investors of capital "mainly
because of the changed conditions brought about by the McKinley
tariff bill." Prior to that legislation, the $33,000,000 of foreign capi-
tal invested in the sugar business in the islands, under the protection of the United States sugar tariff and the reciprocity treaty,
yielded a handsome profit. By the abolition of the duty on sugar,
the price of that product was reduced from approximately $100 to
approximately $60 a ton. Many planters were selling sugar at less
than the cost of production. Several plantations would probably
go out of existence after the next crop was harvested, and unless a
radical change occurred, more would collapse during the following year, with a loss of many million dollars. A continuance under
existing conditions was impossible. Any change promising even a
chance of preservation would be accepted as preferable to inevitable
destruction.

Annexation had hitherto been opposed by most planters, for the
reason that the Hawaiian system of labor contracts could no longer
be enforced; thus an entire revolution in labor conditions would
necessarily take place. This objection was still strong, but it was
offset by the fact that annexation to the United States would give
the planters the immediate benefit of the bounty paid for sugar,
which would help pay for the extra cost of labor. Island planters
were then paying practically the same wages as those paid by
Louisiana planters and more than double those in any other sugar-
producing country.

Annexation was favored by the Liberal leaders because they did
not possess the confidence of the Queen, who feared them and would
not appoint them to office. By reason of the high property qualifications for electors of the upper house, the Liberals had not been able

to gain control to the legislature, for their followers were mainly among the common natives, who did not possess the franchise so far as the upper chamber was concerned. They had therefore concluded "that under the continuance of the present regime, the loaves and fishes of office will be beyond their reach; while, they argue, that if the Islands should become a part of the United States, universal suffrage would prevail, thereby enabling them to become leaders of the native majority and control the official patronage."

Foreign residents believed that there was no prospect of securing any certainty of stable government, except by union in some form with the United States or England. "Every interest, political, commercial, financial and previous friendship points in the direction of the United States; but they feel that if they cannot secure the desired union with the United States, a union with England would be preferable to a continuance under existing circumstances."

Foreigners permanently settled in the kingdom favored annexation because the elements necessary to maintain a continuous strong government were not present. Four-fifths of the property of the country was owned by foreigners, while out of an electorate of 15,-000, only 4,000 voters were foreigners, thus placing the natives in an overwhelming majority. The situation in the Southern States was therefore duplicated in Hawaii, to wit an overwhelming electoral majority in one class, and the ownership of practically all the property in another class. The only way that the foreigners had been able to protect themselves against being taxed out of existence was by securing and maintaining control of the house of nobles by means of the property qualification for electors thereto, which, with the few representatives which they were able to secure, gave them control of the legislature. This fact was recognized by the native Hawaiians, and in conjunction with their natural jealousy of the foreigner, it had "tended to draw the line closely between parties on the color line, giving rise to much bitterness of feeling on the part of the natives against the foreigners."

This antagonism had increased, and was directed against the Queen, because some native Hawaiians felt that she worked more for foreign support than for that of her own people. In addition, the extreme diversity of nationality of the foreigners prevented any continuity of concerted action among them. So long as any common danger or matter of great public interest involving all classes existed, there was unity; as soon as the crisis passed, the community divided into factions, principally on national lines, the chief divi-

sions being American, English, German, and Portuguese. (Japanese
and Chinese were not allowed to participate in the franchise.) The
result of this situation was a dissatisfied native element and an irresponsible foreign element, who had everything to gain and nothing
to lose by a disturbance of the peace, and who were constantly,
more or less openly, threatening revolution and disturbance. The
government did not possess sufficient strength to protect itself against
a violent coup. It was extremely probably that but for the presence
of a United States man-of-war in the harbor of Honolulu, the existing government would have been overturned in a month.

Although there was no great probability of revolution or bloodshed, there was the constant possibility of it, which, coupled with
the knowledge that one element was ready to resort to violence,
prevented new capital from flowing into the country and drove
away what was already there. The effect of this was to arrest development of the islands.

The difficulties to be overcome at the islands were two: the disposition to be made of the Queen and the royal family, and the opposition of the common natives when the time arrived to act. Thurston
was of the opinion that by working through native leaders who were
then in favor of annexation, and securing the active assistance of
those who had not yet declared themselves, a majority of the common natives could be secured in favor of the annexation proposition.
The financial stringency in the islands affected the poorer class first,
and they were mostly natives. With the prospect of better times
as the result of annexation, a majority vote might before very long
be obtained in favor of the proposition. If not, it might "be necessary
to secure the formation of a provisional government by a coup
d'état as against the common natives as well as the Queen, but it is
not probable." Union with the United States might take the form of
a state, a territory, a colony along the lines of the British crown
colonies, or a government reservation under the direct control of
Congress on the same basis as the District of Columbia and government fortifications. The territorial form "would probably find a much
more general support among the natives than would the proposition to treat the Islands as a government reservation."

Finally, the Annexation Club's agent proposed the following line
of action: pending the presidential election in the United States, to
hold the public development of the subject in check; to reorganize
the cabinet and secure the appointment of ministers committed to
annexation; to proceed with the education of the island people in

favor of annexation, and to obtain the adherence of as many native leaders as possible; and to have the legislature adjourn when it finished business in August or September, instead of being prorogued as usual:

> If the sentiment in Washington is found to be favorable to the proposition next December when Congress meets, assemble the Legislature and, according as circumstances at the time seem to dictate, either submit a general proposition to the people, allowing them to vote upon the one question of annexation or not without going into detail, and thereupon appoint a commission with full powers to go to Washington and negotiate the terms of annexation; or in case this does not seem advisable, to take such action by the Legislature directly without submitting the question to the people.

This suggested line of action was subject to radical change if circumstances required it.[5] In his accompanying letter Thurston referred Blaine to W. N. Armstrong and W. H. Dimond, enthusiastic annexationists who were willing to do anything in their power to facilitate action.

Apparently the emissary's visit to Washington led to the discussion of the annexation of Hawaii in the House of Representatives Committee on Foreign Affairs. No definite proposal was made, but numerous informal discussions were held among committee members, and reportedly there was a general determination that the islands should not be permitted to fall into the possession of Great Britain.[6]

New Prospects of Annexation

In anticipation of the forthcoming biennial election, Minister Stevens informed the State Department that "as early as the first of December without fail . . . and for some time thereafter, there should be a United States vessel here to render things secure." The only legal force in Honolulu was the city police and the palace guard of sixty men, "both composed of natives and half-castes, a very frail and uncertain reliance in time of special need." The Rifle companies, comprised of whites, had been dissolved the year before by vote of

5. Memo. encl. in Thurston to Blaine, May 6, 1892, USDS, Misc. Letters, May 1892, Pt. II.
6. *Times,* May 9, 1892.

the legislature, mainly to propitiate native prejudices and to secure native votes. Stevens observed that the best and only permanent security "will be the moral pressure of the businessmen and of what are termed 'the missionary people,' and the presence in the harbor of Honolulu of an American man-of-war," which "not only operates strongly to secure good order among the many nationalities here, but it is a standing notice to foreign nations that the United States has a special care for these islands." [1]

To the planters, businessmen, and the more conservative citizens, the principal issue in the campaign was a free-trade treaty with the United States, which they believed had been negotiated by H. A. P. Carter and Secretary Blaine in Washington. The Liberals—composed of some responsible, and many irresponsible, white voters, some half-Hawaiians, and a large number of native Hawaiians—pushed their canvass on three lines: a new Constitution, opposition to the incumbent cabinet, and hostility to the proposed commercial treaty, whose articles granting to the United States exclusive and permanent control of Pearl Harbor and the right to land a military force would, they feared, alienate the sovereignty of the kingdom. As a result of the election of February 3, 1892, the members of the legislature were divided among the Reform party, the Liberals, and the National Reform party, with no one group commanding a majority.

Considering all that had been said abroad, since the beginning of the Queen's reign, designed to propagate the notion that the sovereign and Hawaiian people held national autonomy and independence so lightly that their surrender would be a matter of easy arrangement, a strong declaration made by Her Majesty at the opening of the legislative session on May 28 was significant. While fully recognizing that by the Constitution and laws of the kingdom her station was that of a constitutional monarch, Queen Liliuokalani declared that she would "firmly endeavor to preserve the autonomy and absolute independence of this Kingdom, and to assist in perpetuating the rights and privileges of all who are subject to our laws and in promoting their welfare and happiness." [2]

The memorable eight-month legislative session of 1892 was a bitter embattled one with ominous warnings of an approaching storm. A persistent struggle, resulting in five changes of ministries, was

1. Stevens to Blaine, Aug. 20, 1891, No. 30.
2. *Pacific Commercial Advertiser*, May 30, 1892.

waged between the contending factions. During the session the opposition parties and the Queen's supporters were both guilty of the most "shameless corruption and bribery ever known in a Hawaiian Legislature." Thurston, an expert on "subsidizing," asserted that in this session any vote could have been bought for $50.[3] The two fighting issues were a change of the Constitution and control of the cabinet. Two issues of lesser importance were the lottery and opium license bills. The members of the Reform party, led by the vigorous and vociferous Thurston, were determined to maintain legislative control of the government as distinguished from control by the crown, while the Queen was equally resolute in retaining her sovereign authority. Moreover, this was the session in which the Annexation Club planned to perfect its scheme for the dethronement of the Queen and annexation of the islands to the United States. Prospects of carrying through its proposed line of action seemed bright. The nobles, elected by the property holders and comparatively high-salaried voters, were nearly all conservatives and composed half the legislature. Through control of this upper house and some representatives in the lower chamber, the Reform party expected to exercise power.[4] In order to supplant the Queen's ministry with a cabinet favorable to annexation, the party made an unholy alliance with the Liberals. This action was in line with Thurston's avowed purpose of obtaining "the adhesion of as many native leaders as possible." Their cooperation was secured by promising them a share in the power to be gained. Throughout the first three to four months of the session this curious coalition checked the Palace party, accused of concerting with the opium and lottery rings.

During the early weeks of the assembly, numerous petitions, apparently inspired by the *Hui Kalaiaina* (Hawaiian Political Association), a patriotic organization, were directed to the legislature asking for a constitutional convention, a new constitution, or the abolition of the one of 1887. A bill, introduced by Representative William White of Lahaina on June 27, providing for a constitutional convention, after consideration by, and reports from a select committee and debate extending over a day and a half, came to the Liberals who under the complete domination of the Reform members, went

3. San Francisco *Morning Call*, Jan. 28, 1893.
4. Stevens to Blaine, Feb. 8, 1892, No. 46. "Conservative," as the term is here used, was not synonymous with Reform party. It apparently included some dissatisfied native Hawaiian liberals who favored annexation.

back on their campaign promise to propose a constitutional convention and helped defeat the measure.[5]

In the meantime, conspiracies, the arrest and trials for treason of the fomenters of the April conspiracy, and rumors of plots against Liliuokalani produced a reaction among the wavering, which resulted in a swinging of the pendulum against annexation and in favor of the Queen.[6] This also contributed to the difficulty of concentrating on overthrowing the old and naming a new cabinet, while at the same time the unholy allies could not agree on the choice of men to fill the different positions. Actually, the Reform members were unwilling to permit the Liberals to have a voice in the formation of the new ministry, and the determination of the former to take affairs into their own hands brought results when, on August 30, in conjunction with the Liberal party, they succeeded in voting the Parker cabinet out of office.

That accomplished, the Reform and Liberal coalition, led by the resourceful and indefatigable Thurston, attempted to initiate the principle—not to be found in the Hawaiin constitution or precedents —that the sovereign must appoint the cabinet on the dictation of whomsoever a majority of the legislature should nominate in caucus as a leader. Resolutions were prepared which maintained that in forming a new cabinet the will of the majority of the house was to be taken into consideration and to govern the selection of the members, and not the private preferences of the Queen, who had no right to obtrude her individual likes and dislikes into the transaction of public business; and that persons who held the delegated power of the people should be the advisers of the sovereign, "instead of the horde of irresponsible backstairs politicians."[7] These resolutions were presented on September 6, and the Queen replied on the following day, accepting the principle claimed by the legislature. She called Arthur P. Peterson, who attempted to form a cabinet without going into it himself.

His efforts proved unsuccessful, for several individuals were either deemed unavailable or, as in the case of Thurston, personally objectionable to Liliuokalani, who resolutely refused to accept as advisers men whose fidelity she had good reasons to suspect. Furthermore, it was learned that regardless of who was called as at-

5. AH, JL, June 27, Dec. 28, 1892, pp. 92, 504.
6. Thurston, *Memoirs*, p. 235. Honolulu *Bulletin*, May 20, 1892. *Pacific Commercial Advertiser*, June 8, 9, 18, 1893.
7. Ibid., Sept. 6, 9, 14, 1892.

torney general, the sovereign proposed to retain Charles B. Wilson as marshal of the kingdom.[8] The *Advertiser* of September 9 "earnestly" counseled the Queen, "in the interest of her own family and throne, to seek to govern as a constitutional monarch, with strict respect to the forms of law," asserting that the legislature would refuse to accept a cabinet not selected in the manner laid down by the majority. Resisting an innovation that she believed would overthrow the existing institutions of the country, Liliuokalani designated successively three ministries, each of which was voted out by the Reform-Liberal combination in pursuance of its stated object.

The E. C. Macfarlane ministry was forced out apparently because of the aversion of its recognized head to the United States minister.[9] Of Scotch-English parentage, Finance Minister Macfarlane, who had served as one of the agents in negotiating the London Loan of 1886 and had business interests considered hostile to the United States, allegedly intended to push another heavy loan in England, thus aiming to mortgage the islands to English bondholders.[10]

The Queen was then induced to form a cabinet with W. H. Cornwell as premier and minister of finance, a cabinet which two and a half hours after it presented itself to the legislature on November 1 was dismissed by a vote of 26 to 13 on a want of confidence resolution introduced by Thurston. Ejected in the shortest time on record, this ministry was jocularly dubbed a "Nancy Hanks" cabinet after a mare that had recently broken a trotting record.[11] The determined Assembly then adjourned until November 7, having refused to pass appropriation bills for the expenses of the government. Meanwhile, the overdue salaries of all officials remained unpaid. In such circumstances business was disturbed and at times came to a standstill, and treasury affairs daily became more serious, with no one but temporary incumbents to grapple with the confused situation. Later, Captain G. C. Wiltse was informed "that the Queen had been strongly advised to dissolve the legislature and order a new election, which would have been unconstitutional, and which

8. Resolutions moved by L. A. Thurston, W. C. Wilder, and S. K. Pau, expressing a want of confidence in Marshal Wilson, had been introduced in the legislature. Cf. AH, RLA (1892), No. 101.

9. See attacks on the U.S. Minister, the Consul General, and Capt. G. S. Wiltse in Honolulu *Bulletin*, Sept. 28, 29, 30, Oct. 1, 1892.

10. Stevens to Foster, Oct. 19, 1892, No. 71, printed in *For. Rels.* (1893), App. II, pp. 362–63.

11. AH, JL (1892), p. 326. AH, RLA (1892), No. 167. Thurston, *Memoirs*, pp. 227–28.

would probably have caused a revolution; but she was deterred by the presence of United States vessels of war." [12]

The Reform-Liberal coalition remained adamant in its demand that the sovereign comply with the desires of the majority of the legislature. As certain members of the opposition openly talked outside the house of the support which they claimed had been promised them, under certain circumstances, by the United States minister, the situation grew critical. After conferring with Major Wodehouse, who advised that no pretext be given for Stevens or Captain Wiltse to interfere,[13] Queen Liliuokalani, on November 4, either from sound judgment, sheer exhaustion, or shrewdly seeing an opportunity to split the coalition of Liberal and Reform parties, sent for George N. Wilcox, one of the three men recommended by the opposition, and requested him to form a ministry. He selected Peter Cushman Jones as minister of finance and Mark P. Robinson as minister of foreign affairs, both thoroughly American in feeling and purpose. Even Attorney General Cecil Brown, born in the islands of British subjects, was said "to be more American than English as to the future of Hawaii." After some vacillation, the Queen granted the men commissions on November 8. The crisis ended, and the Hawaiian government was again able to borrow money on the mainland at 5 per cent.

This conservative ministry enjoyed the confidence of the propertied class and was acceptable to the moderates of all parties. Its members were responsible men of high character, and none needed the salaries, as they were all comparatively wealthy, with their aggregate property estimated at nearly one million dollars. The appointment of this cabinet was regarded not only as a victory of the legislature over the Queen but also as a triumph of the "better citizens" of Hawaii over "the worse," and proof of American ascendency over British and other anti-American elements. This new body, more positively American than any since the fall of the Reform ministry in June 1890, was expected to exercise its power in a conservative manner until the 1894 elections. Stevens was happy to report that his "official and personal relations with the ministry" were "likely to be most friendly and cordial." [14] Wodehouse felt that if these ministers retained their positions until the end of the

12. Wiltse to Tracy, Nov. 9, 1892, in *For. Rels.* (1894), App. II, p. 188.
13. Wodehouse to Rosebery, Nov. 9, 1892, No. 20, FO 58/263.
14. Stevens to Foster, Nov. 8, 1892, No. 73, printed in *For. Rels.* (1894), App. II, p. 376. Cf. interview with J. O. Carter, ibid., p. 737.

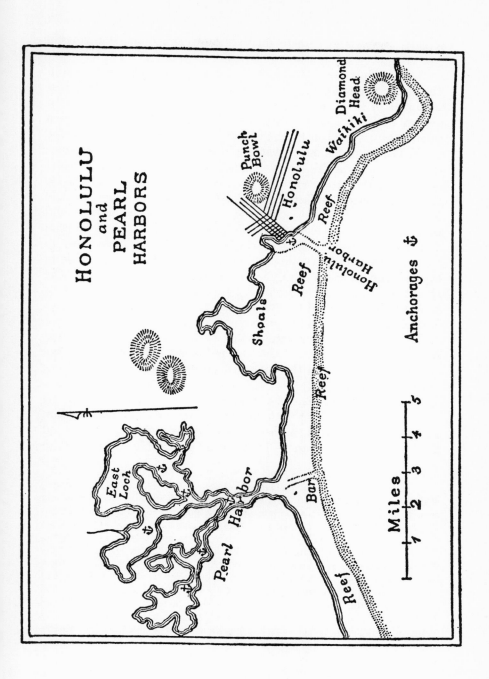

HONOLULU and PEARL HARBORS

Punch Bowl

Honolulu

Honolulu Harbor

Waikiki

Diamond Head

Reef

Reef

Reef

Reef

Reef

Bar

Shoals

East Loch

Pearl Harbor

Anchorages

Miles

1 2 3 4 5

127

session, they would be safe for two years, and hoped the trouble
was ended.[15]

Complicating the political atmosphere in November was a running correspondence in the *Hawaiian Gazette,* some of which was
reprinted in the *Pacific Commercial Advertiser,* pertaining to the
cession of Pearl Harbor. This epistolary battle[16] resulted from a
resolution proposed in the legislature on July 9 by Representative
R. W. Wilcox to the effect that the "disastrous financial depression"
stemmed from the McKinley bill, which deprived Hawaii's "chief
industry of the protection that was the principal consideration for
important concessions" made to the United States. Since she had
taken no action toward occupying or improving the lagoon, and
since the Hawaiian legislators believed "the geographical position
and natural advantages of Pearl Harbor" rendered it valuable to
any great nation as a coaling and naval station, it was reasonable to
expect concessions and privileges in exchange for the bay. The
House of Representatives resolved that a committee of five of its
members be appointed to visit Washington to ascertain the disposition of the United States government in regard to Pearl Harbor
and to report to the legislature what desirable arrangements could
be made for the cession of the harbor "for adequate compensation,
and in general to use their best efforts to obtain closer relations
with that country." [17]

Representative Williams O. Smith presented a report of the select
committee, which dealt with the Pearl Harbor resolution on January 5, 1893, proposed another similar to that of July 9, and named
L. A. Thurston to head a five-member committee to proceed to

15. Wodehouse to Rosebery, Dec. 7, 1892, No. 22, FO 58/263.

16. Engaged in by Alfred S. Hartwell, Theo. H. Davies, Lorrin A. Thurston,
William R. Castle, Charles L. Carter, John Emmeluth, William B. Oleson, and
Sereno E. Bishop. All these letters are available in a 29-page pamphlet en-
titled *Correspondence Reprinted from the Hawaiian Gazette for Mr. Theo. H.
Davies* (Honolulu, 1892), copies of which are in the University of Hawaii
Library and in FO 58/279. Castle's and Thurston's letters appeared in the
Pacific Commercial Advertiser, Nov. 19, 1892. Cf. ibid., Nov. 16, 17, 1892,
and Boston *Herald,* Jan. 13, 1893. Two months before, H. M. Waterhouse had
recommended the development of Pearl City as a site for seaside resorts, and
stated that if the United States did not wish to occupy and improve Pearl
Harbor, which was destined to become the center of a busy population, "let
some other nation or corporation, like the Vanderbilts or the Canadian Pacific,
step forward and do the work required to be done" (*Pacific Commercial
Advertiser,* Sept. 23, 1892).

17. AH, RLA (1892), No. 99.

Washington, at an expense of $5,000. A proposal of the Attorney General to limit the commission to three was amended on the following day by placing its appointment in the hands of the Queen.[18]

Thurston and William R. Castle, during the tense autumn of 1892 frequently visited Minister Stevens and Captain Wiltse, who could have well been considered members ex officio of the Annexation Club, and informally discussed the political situation, including the extent to which the annexationists might expect American assistance. The big problem in late 1892, as in early 1887, "was how to precipitate the issue," this time with Liliuokalani.

On the other hand, the November elections in the United States returned the Democrats to office, with Grover Cleveland in the White House for a second term. Would the "lame duck" session of Congress meeting in December look favorably upon annexation? Did the defeat of the Republican administration in the elections alter the outlook? The Reform party had not seized the reins early in the session, as Thurston had proposed in his line of action presented to Blaine. The legislature had not adjourned in August or September: it was still in session in November. Yet there was no avowed policy in Washington that would justify a decision either for a general plebiscite on annexation or direct action by the Hawaiian legislature.

A resolution of want of confidence was brought in on January 4, 1893, by John E. Bush, stating that the Wilcox-Jones cabinet had failed to fulfill the expectation of the country in its financial distress, had "shown a total want of capacity to lead the Legislature in matters of great moment or otherwise," and did "not represent the sentiment and wishes of the People at large." Only nineteen legislators supported the resolution, which consequently failed.[19]

The Queen Regains Control

Once the legislative work of the session had been nearly concluded and the principal appropriations voted, six white gentlemen—three nobles and two representatives—went to their homes. Minister Stevens, for the first time since his arrival in Honolulu on September 20, 1889, left Oahu on board the U.S.S. *Boston*, which sailed on January 4 for a ten-day cruise about the islands. Considerable un-

18. AH, JL (1892), Jan. 5, 6, 1893, pp. 531–32. Cf. AH, RLA (1892), Nos. 99, 113, 114, 196.

19. RLA (1892), No. 194. AH, JL (1892), p. 526.

easiness was felt in Honolulu when the ship steamed out to sea, for there were rumors in the street that the Wilcox-Jones ministry would be voted out of office. On the vessel's quarter deck Lieutenant Lucien Young mentioned these to Stevens, insisting that Sam Parker had already secured the votes of the Hawaiian members of the legislature, and that some of the whites would join them to form a majority to eject the ministry before the legislature adjourned. To these assertions the shrewd Stevens replied: "I do not see how they can do it; they have come in to stay during this Legislature and the next, and they will look out for American interests." [1] In spite of his apparent naïveté, Minister Stevens, as well as Captain Wiltse, was thoroughly acquainted with the explosive situation and knew exactly why the *Boston* left naval row that Wednesday.[2]

From the chain of events that followed the man-of-war's departure, it appears that the annexationists, aware that no proposal for union with the United States would ever receive the approval of the electorate, and cognizant of their inability to carry a project of annexation through the Hawaiian legislature, deliberately lured the Queen into a trap: they enticed her into committing a rash act which radically changed the political situation, and which, they hoped, would justify in Washington their own coup d'état and support for their plans from the Harrison administration before March 4, 1893.

By the cleverly premeditated actions of the Reform party itself, the Queen was allowed to regain control. The departure of six of the "best members" of the legislature before the close of the session permitted a belligerent majority to vote out the Wilcox-Jones ministry, which favored American interests and which, judging from the January 4 vote, appeared securely in power until the spring of 1894. Immediately, the supporters of the Queen and the opponents of the Reform ministry, now in a majority in the legislature, combined and marshaled their forces for the final battles of the session. The Liberals, not consulted in the formation of the cabinet and not represented in it, were so exasperated over the denial of the loaves and fishes that they joined hands with the National Reform or Palace party and proceeded to vote for measures which they had pre-

1. Statement of Lieut. Lucien Young, *Morgan Report*, p. 345.

2. The departure of the *Boston* certainly appears to me to have been arranged to test or to aggravate the political situation. A similar experiment was made under less critical circumstances in 1874. Cf. Peirce to Fish, Sept. 10, 1874, No. 283, USDS, Dispatches, Hawaii, 16; see above, p. 39.

viously denounced on the floor of the house: the pigeonholed lottery and opium license bills were called out of committee for passage.

In the summer of 1892, petitions had been circulated for the granting of a franchise to a lottery company. Signatures were obtained by a rapid canvass before publicity could be given to the proposal. Without reflection, some signed who afterward deeply regretted having done so. The bill was introduced in the legislature on August 30, but a powerful opposition developed, and resulted in the measure being referred to a committee where it was pigeonholed, as some supposed, forever.[3]

The "better" and "righteous" elements of the community, both white and native Hawaiians, were opposed to the lottery. The righteous, however, were not in the majority. According to W. H. Cornwell, "the measure was favored and supported by nearly all the Americans in Honolulu, the very men who revolted" and later claimed the lottery was the cause of the revolution. Even William DeWitt Alexander admitted that if the bill had been referred to the vote of the populace, it would have passed. In a special election held in October, a number of lottery men were elected as representatives from Honolulu. The lower class of native Hawaiians and half-Hawaiians either favored the bill or did not oppose it, contending that the white man had made money in the islands, that Hawaiians had not, and that it was not wrong to give them a chance. One or two speakers in the house emphasized that the lottery "would make money plentiful in Honolulu."[4]

The published prospectus, entitled *The Golden Era,* proclaimed: "It is bread and butter; it is dollars and cents. It is prosperity. It is the end of dull times. It is the dawn of a new order of things." These economic arguments, however specious, were convincing to the poor who, in terms of want, were suffering most from the depression in the sugar industry. The lottery would pay half a million a year in taxes; in addition, the officials and employees would spend at least $100,000 annually in Honolulu for household, office, and personal expenses. "Under the proposed arrangement there will be $20 in circulation where there is $1 now . . . With railroads, drives, avenues, parks, palatial hotels and thousands of tourists, the country would put on a different appearance"—would

3. For opposition to the lottery, see editorials in the *Pacific Commercial Advertiser,* Sept. 24, 27, 28, 1892; Jan. 11, 12, 13, 1893.

4. Cornwell to James H. Blount, April 24, 1893, *For. Rels.* (1894), App. II, p. 496. Alexander Statement, *Morgan Report,* p. 291.

"look like a park." Property "worth little or nothing would suddenly reach fancy figures. Talk about the Southern California boom! Why this country has a future such as boomers never dreamed of. Put a few millions of dollars into improvements and Hawaii would be the garden spot of the world!" [5]

Section 3 of the bill provided that the grantees and their successors and assignees should pay the Hawaiian government the sum of $500,000 annually for twenty-five years to be applied as follows: cable, $100,000; railroads on Oahu, $50,000; railroads on Hawaii, $50,000; Honolulu Harbor, $50,000; roads, bridges, wharves, etc., $175,000; encouragement of industry, $50,000; encouragement of tourist travel and immigration, $25,000.[6]

Queen Liliuokalani favored the lottery, for the anticipated revenue would render her independent of loans that would have to be approved by the legislature. Moreover, the members of the company seeking the franchise to operate the lottery were reported to represent a group that recently had been evicted from Louisiana, where they had dominated the government:[7] being outlawed in the United States, they could be relied upon to oppose any movement toward annexation.

Supporters of the lottery accused its righteous opponents, who had ample means, of not wanting to see any other influence in the islands that would interfere with their control and direction of men and affairs.[8] Noble Pau made this plea in the legislature: "The Government has been run on a moral and holy plan long enough. Let us try some of the schemes got up by the devil and see how they work . . . The Lottery bill will give us $14,000,000, and the missionaries will put them in their pockets fast enough and ask no questions . . . All this talk about the works of the devil will then wear out, and people will consider it very good money after all." [9]

Actually, the opposition of the conservatives, the propertied class, was not based entirely upon morality. They, too, were impressed by the economic arguments of the *Golden Era* and deeply concerned that the promised revenue from both the lottery and the proposed

5. *Golden Era* (Honolulu, Sept. 1, 1892). Printed in its entirety in Thurston, *Memoirs*, pp. 219–26.

6. *Session Laws* (1892), pp. 334–41. Thurston, *Memoirs*, p. 223.

7. Thurston, *Memoirs*, p. 219. Alexander Statement, *Morgan Report*, p. 293. For a study of American lotteries see John Samuel Ezell, *Fortune's Merry Wheel: The Lottery in America* (Cambridge, Mass., 1960).

8. Thurston, *Memoirs*, p. 223.

9. *Pacific Commercial Advertiser*, October 18, 1892.

opium license franchise would help render the sovereign independent of legislative control, while the relief from the financial distress precipitated by the McKinley tariff would diminish the urge for union with the United States. Annexationists were accused of forcing bankruptcy on the nation so that they could bring forward schemes for union with the United States, and of wanting to "ruin the country and then give away the wreck." [10]

Support for the lottery bill was secured during the last week of the session by "lavish and shameless bribery." For their vote some native members divulged that they were offered $300 a piece and a small annuity from the lottery company after its establishment. William White, who railroaded the lottery and opium bills through the house, boasted that he went down to the legislature with $2 in his pocket and returned with $800 and plenty of clothes.[11]

The lottery bill came up for final passage on the afternoon of January 11, and was carried by a vote of 23 to 20—a majority which would not have been possible if any three or four of the six absent Reform members had been present. At the last moment Lorrin A. Thurston and William O. Smith attached to the bill a rider requiring a deposit of $125,000 before the company could operate, thus hoping to hamper its implementation.[12]

The only white member of the legislature who favored the measure was A. P. Peterson. Two half-white leaders, Robert W. Wilcox and Bush, who earlier had opposed the legislation, now voted for it in order to compel the Reform cabinet to resign. By the same voters the opium license bill was passed. This act to provide for and regulate the import, sale, and use of opium, requiring four licenses costing a total of $45,000, was passed not alone as a revenue measure but for the purpose of checking the wholesale corruption which the smuggling of the drug entailed, and was a measure in favor of the morality of the country rather than one of debasement. The bill was supported by many planters, irrespective of political sentiments or party. Minister of Finance Cornwell favored it, since the Hawaiian government could not enforce prohibitive legislation owing to the facility for smuggling offered by the long extent of coast on the islands.[13] In the opinion of the supporters of these bills, the Wilcox

10. Thurston, *Memoirs*, p. 223.
11. Alexander Statement, *Morgan Report*, p. 291.
12. AH, JL (1892), p. 545. *Pacific Commercial Advertiser*, Jan. 12, 1893.
13. Cornwell to Blount, April 24, 1893, *For.. Rels.* (1894), App. II, p. 496. For a copy of the bill see *Session Laws* (1892), pp. 313–33.

ministry could not remain in office and execute obnoxious legislation which it had publicly and unequivocally opposed. But since the cabinet did not automatically resign, a vote of want of confidence was required.

Even with the cooperation of the members of the legislature subsidized by the lottery and opium rings, there was considerable difficulty in securing the requisite twenty-five votes. The Queen, however, brought her personal influence to bear with certain members, and the result of the ballot was 25 yeas and 16 noes.[14] Jones reported his "great relief," for "we felt all the time we were in office we were between the devil and the deep sea, the Queen and the Legislature." [15] Thus the conservative Wilcox-Jones ministry ended its sixty-six days in office. William Castle editorialized that it was removed "by a combination of opium smugglers, disappointed office seekers, intriguing office holders and haole haters, aided by the powerful influence of the Court and the Police Department, and the free use of bribery." [16]

Representative John W. Kapahu, in the course of a speech on the motion of want of confidence, indicated his reason for favoring it by inquiring: "How can we trust the cabinet to carry out the lottery bill? How do we know they will favor the change, the new constitution—carry out the wishes of the Queen in regard to the new constitution?" This was the first open declaration concerning the rumored new instrument.[17]

Attorney Thurston, Minister Stevens, and Captain Wiltse, however, for some time had warned Washington that the Queen was bent on securing certain constitutional changes. Thurston indicated this in his spring visit to that city, while the two American officials repeatedly stated that only the presence of a United States man-of-war in Honolulu harbor deterred the Queen from attempting a coup d'état.[18] Attorney Arthur P. Peterson had had a copy of Liliuokalani's proposed constitution in his possession during the month of November and had conferred with several lawyers on it.[19] The fact that anyone in gossipy Honolulu was consulted meant that the

14. AH, JL (1892), p. 551. AH, RLA (1892), No. 201.
15. Jones Statement, *Morgan Report*, p. 207.
16. *Pacific Commercial Advertiser*, Jan. 14, 1893.
17. Alexander Statement, *Morgan Report*, p. 292.
18. John L. Stevens to Foster, Oct. 19, 31, 1892, Nos. 71, 72; printed in *For. Rels.* (1894), App. II, 185–86, 362–63, 374. Wiltse to Tracy, Oct. 9, 1892, ibid., p. 188.
19. Liliuokalani, *Hawaii's Story by Hawaii's Queen* (Boston, 1898), p. 348.

annexationists were apprised of the existence of the document. Yet, in the face of these convictions and facts, on January 4, 1893, the U.S.S. *Boston*, with Minister John L. Stevens on board, sailed from Honolulu Harbor.

After the victory in removing the Reform Cabinet, the legislature recessed for two days while the Queen formed a new ministry, with Samuel Parker as minister of foreign affairs and premier. On the same day—January 13—the ministers recommended that the Queen sign the lottery and opium bills. She at first declined, wanting to please her "lady friends," [20] but her advisers felt there should be no hesitation on her part, as the house had passed these measures by a large majority and as they had been signed by the president and committee.[21] After placing her signature on these bills, Liliuokalani prepared to prorogue the legislature and promulgate the new constitution.

During the final days of the legislative session, energetic and determined American residents, other foreigners of substance, and Hawaiian-born Americans felt that they were living on a volcano. Temporizing did not satisfy them. William R. Castle was certain that a climax would soon be reached—that some radical change had to take place or the monarchy fall. The members of the Annexation Club and their closest friends and adherents had long been convinced that annexation to the United States was the solution to their problem. Now they speculated "as to when a change might come, how it would be forced and who would do it." During the last tense week of the session, the doubting Thomases and the lukewarm supporters of the Queen began to take a stand, and on Saturday, January 14, 1893, it was obvious to them that a change had to come.[22]

Preparing for Annexation

While annexationists in official positions and in private enterprises in Hawaii planned and labored for their goal, and their intermediator in Washington pursued his clandestine assignment to further their aims, the leading daily newspaper in the national capital,

20. Sworn statements of Rev. Oliver P. Emerson and of Alexander, *Morgan Report*, pp. 177, 292.
21. Liliuokalani, p. 383. Cf. AH, JL (1892), p. 552.
22. Emerson and Alexander statements, and Castle and G. N. Wilcox affidavits, *Morgan Report*, pp. 175, 301, 534–35, 583–84.

three on the West Coast, one in New York, an obscure one in Augusta, Maine, and the *Pacific Commercial Enterprise*, organ of the Reform party, then edited by William R. Castle, supported the cause. The *Ka Leo*, mouthpiece of the National party, which aimed to lead native Hawaiian opinion, alternated between expressions of devotion to the crown and hints of annexation. Editor John E. Bush expressed the opinion that Liliuokalani might be induced "to look favorably on a project of annexing the islands to the United States." [1] This was the first instance of the advocacy of annexation by native Hawaiians. The *Pacific Commercial Advertiser* editorialized on this "somewhat remarkable attitude of the Bush-Wilcox faction," observing that "there is no doubt that a strong undercurrent of sentiment in favor of annexation exists among the foreign element, and also that it meets with favor, to some extent among the natives." [2]

Far more serious were the mischievous reports about the Queen's health that were circulated in *Ka Leo* in the early autumn of 1891 and were reproduced on the mainland. The San Francisco *Examiner* published on October 6 an exaggerated and completely false article under the title "Liliuokalani Nearing Death," alleging that the Hawaiian Queen was in the throes of organic heart disease, for which her physician, Dr. Trousseau, could suggest no remedy, that Archibald Cleghorn, Commissioner Wodehouse, and other Englishmen were scheming to throw the islands into British hands, but that Americans were firm in their opposition. The impending struggle was bound to be fierce and bitter, for it was a foregone conclusion that American residents would take advantage of every opportunity to prevent the Princess Kaiulani from getting to the throne. The islanders were in sympathy with them and wanted either a republic or annexation to the United States, for "Hawaiians feel no loyalty towards a native ruler who has foreign blood in her veins." The situation was so critical, asserted the correspondent, "and there is so much certainty of riots and bloodshed, that the presence of two or three warships from the United States is an absolute necessity within the next few months" to "prevent any British element from taking the lead in affairs here." Not only was the Queen near death, but the Queen Dowager Kapiolani was also dangerously ill with paralysis and might die at any moment: "It is a settled fact that

1. "The Plan," *Ka Leo* (Honolulu), June 4, 1891.
2. Aug. 21, 1891. Cf. ibid., Aug. 18, 1891.

cannot be denied that the final end of Hawaiian royalty is near at hand."

There was absolutely no basis for this story. Dr. Trousseau publicly gave an emphatic denial to the statement concerning Liliuokalani's health. For months he had not been consulted by Her Majesty, he had never attended her but for trifling ailments, and had never expressed to her the opinion that she had organic disease of the heart. During October the Queen had been seen riding frequently, and when Wodehouse paid her a friendly visit at her private residence, he found her looking well and cheerful.[3]

The Washington *Post* referred most pointedly to the necessity of adopting an American policy with regard to the efforts Great Britain was making to neutralize the influence of the United States in the islands and to establish her own control there. Repeatedly during 1892, the *Post* editorialized on the condition of affairs in Samoa, rattled the saber over the Bering Sea controversy, and alleged that Britain was determined that the United States gain no foothold in the Hawaiian Islands, not even to the extent of acquiring Pearl River harbor as a naval station. "England is as mercenary and as grasping as ever and is attempting to create a feeling of revulsion against the United States for the benefit of her own tradesmen." The intelligent were not required to read between the lines to find indication that the condition of affairs in Hawaii could not continue in status quo.[4]

Hawaii was kept alive in the American press—no doubt intentionally by annexationists—in the spring of 1892, preceding and following Thurston's journey to Washington. The Boston *Herald* carried an article on March 25 with the caption: "She Wants to Come In," and maintained that the kingdom desired the closet possible trade relations with the United States. Five days later, the same journal reflected on "The Annexation of Hawaii," and stated that Minister Mott Smith had hinted at the possibility, free trade being the first desirable step. The New York *Mail and Express* published sensational news of "Fear of Rebels in Hawaii," on April 6, followed two days later by an article on "The Discontent in Hawaii." The

3. Wodehouse to FO, Oct. 22, 1891, No. 30, FO 58/258. Liliuokalani lived twenty-five more years, dying in 1917 at the age of seventy-nine.

4. Jan. 29, Feb. 14, March 14, 24, June 13, July 9, Aug. 7, 12, 13, 1892. Cf. my "British Opposition to the Cession of Pearl Harbor," *Pacific Historical Review*, 29 (1960), 381–94; and "Great Britain and the Sovereignty of Hawaii," ibid., 31 (1962), 327–48.

New York *Times* reported that the scare in Honolulu over the drill of the military guardians of the palace, who made breastworks of sand bags, appeared to have quickly subsided, but concluded that "we shall doubtless continue to hear from time to time of an alleged movement to overthrow the throne and to establish a republic." [5] The New York *World*, dealing with "Hawaii's Critical State," on the 14th, reported that the Queen was practically a prisoner and that bankruptcy was imminent. This article and the ones published in the *Mail and Express* were damaging and detrimental to the negotiations of the Carter-Blaine treaty. In an interview with Blaine, during which Mott Smith explained the causes which led to these disquieting rumors and stated his belief that no violence would be attempted, the Secretary interrupted with this significant remark: "but *I* expect to hear of a revolution there." [6]

Thurston's visit to the national capital served as an occasion for the newspaper press to enlarge and speculate upon the future of the Hawaiian Islands. The Boston *Evening Transcript* published a special dispatch from Washington on May 15 titled "Peaceful Conquest, Plan to Annex Cuba and Hawaii," which stated that the scheme to annex Hawaii had been discussed by members of the Senate Foreign Relations Committee and had caused some commotion in diplomatic circles. From information received from Hawaii, a strong sentiment prevailed among the American contingent of officials in favor of union. An intimation, therefore, from the United States government that the proposition would be received in a friendly spirit would ensure the success of the scheme. Reportedly, both President Harrison and Secretary of State Blaine had been approached on the subject, but neither seemed disposed to encourage the project at this time. A Dalziel agent of the *Times* reported that the matter had been discussed on May 6 in the Foreign Affairs Committee of the House of Representatives. [7]

Mott Smith considered these articles "mere newspaper talk." Dalziel had been misled as to facts. There had been no meeting of either the Foreign Affairs or Foreign Relations Committees of Congress on the subject of Hawaii. The haste of reporters to prophesy was incurable. The future of Hawaii was a favorite topic with political circles in Washington, "inseparable indeed from any treaty re-

5. April 9, 1892.
6. Mott Smith to Parker, April 14, 1892, AH, FO Ex., U.S. Minister, Washington.
7. *Times*, May 9, 1892.

lations discussion." The Minister, being unable to avoid interrogation, both officially and otherwise, always replied that his mission was to negotiate a treaty of reciprocity and that of other matters he had no official knowledge. He found that newspapers far outstripped public sentiment in the United States and certainly did not voice the ideas of Washington officials.[8]

Rear Admiral George Brown, commander of the Pacific squadron, visited and tarried in Honolulu on the cruiser *San Francisco* during the spring and summer of 1892, and frequently marched his battalions of bluejackets and marines through the city, reportedly as a manifestation of American strength "and an intention of American readiness to take a hand in whatever might be going on." [9] While in the kingdom Brown was interviewed by a visiting correspondent of the San Francisco *Examiner* who posed a question concerning the attitude of the flagship *San Francisco* to a possible disturbance on shore. The commander replied that in such a contingency his first duty would be to protect American citizens and property. Since he had the general authorization of the government to land troops at any time for "shore drill," he would avail himself "of this permission to send a guard, at once, to the American Ministry and Consulate, and to so dispose of my forces as to protect life and property." What he should do beyond that would be governed by his instructions, which, as a matter of course, he could not make public. "I am entirely prepared to take care of the lives and property of American residents," he asserted, "and as they are in the majority at Honolulu as regards the holding of property you can draw your inference as to what that may mean." [10]

It seemed to Major Wodehouse that the general permission granted to Admiral Brown was so unusual and the use he proposed to make of it might so jeopardize the independence of the kingdom that he felt impelled to indicate to the Queen the danger in the situation and to point out the usual course adopted by the commander of a national ship when he wished to land his men for shore

8. Mott Smith to Parker, May 20, 1892, AH, FO Ex., U.S. Minister, Washington. Five months before, on December 30 and 31, 1891, the Minister sent reassuring letters to Parker and the Queen, stating that in the event of an *émeute* involving dissident elements in Honolulu, the Hawaiian government could count upon the support of a U.S. national vessel (ibid.).

9. Wodehouse to Salisbury, March 29, April 7, 1892, Nos. 5, 52, FO 58/263.

10. "The Specter of Revolution—Admiral Brown Has Secret Orders," San Francisco *Examiner*, June 1, 1892.

drill. As the arrest of the ringleaders among the spring conspirators had momentarily allayed the danger, Her Majesty agreed with her visitor that it was better not to make any change in the permission granted to the Admiral, especially as he was due to leave for San Francisco on July 15. Nevertheless, the Queen believed that he intended to abuse the friendly permission given him to land his men for drill.[11]

At the time Brown sailed from Honolulu, he reported a strong sentiment among some native Hawaiians, Americans, and Germans "in favor of a change in the form of government looking toward the ultimate annexation of the islands to the United States," and disclosed that there existed in the capital an organization comprising the most prominent annexationists bent upon a change in government.[12]

In Honolulu the members of the Annexation Club were convinced in late August 1892 that prosperity could "be attained in Hawaii only by securing the establishment of a stable Government," that union with the United States would not only secure "stability of government, but would immediately cause an influx of capital and institute a period of prosperity and development of the resources of the country never before known," and that it would be "beneficial to every class and nationality" residing in the islands. Holding such belief, the members pledged themselves to unite their efforts "and use all lawful means to secure such political union with the United States." [13]

Considerable secrecy and mystery surrounded the proceedings in the United States Senate during the summer of 1892 over the civil appropriation bill, which provided for $250,000 to be expended toward the establishment of a naval station in Hawaii. This secrecy was necessary because the Senate had before it the confidential

11. Wodehouse to Rosebery, June 21, 1892, No. 11, FO 58/263. The procedure in regard to the landing of troops was quite different after the Queen was overthrown. Each time Admiral J. S. Skerritt wanted to land the crew of the *Boston* for battalion drill or to have the U.S.S. *Adams* engage in target practice within three marine leagues of Lahaina, a specific request to do so was made by the U.S. diplomatic representative. See Stevens to Dole, April 19, 1893; Blount to Dole, May 22, July 21, Aug. 5, 1893: AH, U.S. Ministers and Consuls, June–July 1893, July–Dec., 1893.

12. Brown to Tracy, Sept. 6, 1892, *For. Rels.* (1894), p. 183. Tracy sailed from Honolulu on Aug. 27, 1892.

13. Declaration of Aug. 23, 1892, Lorrin A. Thurston Papers, AH.

Schofield-Alexander report of the Pearl River lagoon made during the Cleveland administration,[14] and because the Foreign Relations Committee was considering Thurston's annexation proposal, which, like the Pearl River lagoon reports, was deemed impolitic at that moment to discuss in public session. The information provided in the generals' report and in the corroborative reports made by naval officers on the practicability and cost of removing the coral reef at the entrance of Pearl River harbor, plus, no doubt, Thurston's scheme, formed the basis of congressional action, which culminated in the adoption of Joseph N. Dolph's amendment to the Navy bill, appropriating $250,000 toward the establishment of a naval station at Pearl River, and a November offer made to the Annexation Club to pay Queen Liliuokalani a similar amount for the assignment of the sovereignty of the islands of the United States.

Annexation was frequently discussed in Hawaii by both its exponents and opponents during the latter part of 1892, and there was a general belief that any move for the overthrow of the Hawaiian government would receive the official recognition of Minister Stevens and the material support of Captain Wiltse. Very shortly after the Minister's arrival in the kingdom, he made clear that he considered annexation to the United States as the ultimate or "manifest" destiny of Hawaii, and the United States legation thus became the rendezvous of annexationist leaders.[15] Stevens showed his thinly veiled contempt for the monarchical system, the sovereign, and government to which he was accredited in his July 4, 1891, oration and his Memorial Day 1892 address. In the former he advocated positive action on the part of the United States.[16]

During the November ministerial crisis preceding the installation of the Jones-Wilcox cabinet, a friend of the Reform party warned the Queen that if she did not yield to the demands of the leaders of the opposition to name a ministry they would establish a provisional government and that Minister Stevens had agreed to order the troops from the *Boston* and the *Alliance* to support such a government against the royal power.[17] During the same month a private note was sent to Her Majesty informing her of the intentions of the

14. *Sen. Ex. Docs.*, 52 Cong., 2 sess., No. 76, pp. 150–54.
15. See Charles T. Gulick Statement, *For. Rels.* (1894), App. II, p. 818.
16. *Pacific Commercial Advertiser,* July 5, 1891. Cf. ibid., May 31, 1892.
17. *Examiner,* Nov. 21, 1892. This journal considered it absurd to believe that Stevens had made such a promise, but stated that he knew all that the opposition was doing.

American minister, with the aid of some residents, to perfect a scheme of annexation, and that the cabinet had knowledge of the fact. A similar note was received from the same informant on December 17. Her Majesty was advised to weigh this information "by the side of the bold open declarations and annexation campaign" made in the *Bulletin* by the Reverend Sereno Bishop, "the well-known mouthpiece of the annexation party"; she could then realize "that the enemy is in the household, and that the strictest watch ought to be kept on the members of the present cabinet." On receipt of this second note, the Queen sent for Major Wodehouse and asked him whether it would be wise for her to invite all the foreign representatives of the diplomatic and consular corps to discuss the matter. The Commissioner dissuaded Liliuokalani from her idea, as it was like acknowledging that there was actual peril.[18]

The San Francisco *Examiner* concluded that much of the November cabinet crisis in Honolulu was caused by Stevens' meddling in local politics: the Minister was a coadjutor of Secretary of State Blaine and was sent to Hawaii to promulgate his scheme in the Pacific islands. For misrepresenting everything and for making trouble Stevens had a "perfect genius." He had a willing reinforcement in the person of Captain Wiltse.[19]

Convinced that the matter was bound to come up in Washington during the winter, T. T. Williams, nationally-known editor of the *Examiner,* spent five weeks of the autumn in Honolulu, inquiring into the disposition of the people on the subject, and polling the members of the legislative assembly for their views. The results of his investigation were published in a three-page leader of his newspaper on November 21, 1892. Williams divided the annexationists into three classes: (1) those Americans who saw what a strategic advantage the possession of the islands would be to the United States and who were moved by patriotic feelings only—in other words, all the naval officers and diplomatic corps, except Minister Stevens, who was "less a patriot than a Blaine man, anxious to give the Maine statesman the credit of having carried out a brilliant

18. Liliuokalani, *Hawaii's Story,* pp. 382–83.

19. "Deplorable Meddling by United States Minister Stevens and the Captain of the Cruiser Boston," *Examiner,* Nov. 17, 1892. When the *Boston* arrived in Honolulu harbor, Stevens confidentially informed Foster that "Captain Wiltse will cooperate with me in exercising circumspection." Stevens to Foster, Sept. 14, 1892, No. 65, printed in *For. Rels.* (1894), p. 361.

stroke of policy in the Pacific Ocean"; (2) those Americans who owned land in the vicinity of or adjacent to Pearl Harbor, or had ocean-cable franchises which would be useful if Pearl Harbor became a grand United States rendezvous; and (3) those foreigners and native-born capitalists who feared for their investments "on account of the revolutionary tendency of Kanaka politicians," or who felt that "their financial plans could be operated to greater advantage if the islands were under the Stars and Stripes." In the latter class were the American sugar planters who wanted the United States bounty of $40 per ton; the sheep men who were anxious to sell their wool on the mainland at 20 cents a pound, instead of in England at 10 cents; those who would preserve fruit that was then subject to a duty in the United States; speculators who sought American loans; and many of the missionary element opposed to the rule of Queen Liliuokalani, who had not shown as much inclination to consult their wishes as some of the Kamehamehas in earlier years.

The opponents of annexation among the whites were "the patriotic British and those whose business interests would be injured by annexation." This opposition was "both selfish and patriotic, and sometimes intelligent."

Of the forty-two members of the legislature, ten regarded annexation as possible and desirable in case the Hawaiian government was disrupted. The thirty-one who were opposed were native Hawaiians who favored the autonomy of the kingdom, Americans who objected to a territorial form of government for the islands, and sugar planters who employed contract Japanese labor. One member declined to comment. Native Hawaiian representatives were in the overwhelming majority opposed to annexation and as a rule contented themselves with a direct negative. Typical of those who were vocal was Samuel K. Pua, who claimed that the people of Hawaii were satisfied with their relations with the United States, except as regards the McKinley act, which was not quite just. They wanted closer trade relations, but regarded annexation unfavorably.

The nobles' response to the question of annexation varied with their property interests. Some suggested only that the United States give consideration to treaty relations and "kill the sugar trust that keeps raw sugar low and refined sugar high." Those were convinced that a large majority of the Hawaiian people would oppose annexation to the United States, and asserted that annexation to Great Britain had never been seriously entertained. Others felt that the abolition of the contract labor system would "entail a greater loss on the sugar industry than any benefit which could possibly be derived through annexation."

The Reform group refrained from directly advocating annexation, but they asserted that all businessmen favored closer commercial relations with the United States, and admitted that the question had frequently been discussed and considered by many responsible citizens and residents during the preceding two years.

Several ministers or ex-ministers expressed their opposition, considering annexation contrary to the traditional policy the United States had pursued toward the little kingdom and desiring to see the nationality of Hawaii maintained, or emphasizing the native Hawaiians' love of their country and flag, and their preference for independence with closer commercial relations with the United States.

A week after the appearance of this comprehensive report in the San Francisco *Examiner,* the New York *Daily Tribune,* on the opposite side of the continent, attempted to create the impression that unrest in Hawaii would soon force the American people to consider the policy of forming a closer political tie with the island kingdom. Hawaiians understood perfectly that their future was "of necessity bound in ours; that . . . the United States are to them the source of life and safety. There is no other, and naturally the serious among them wish to bring about such conditions as will render our responsibility not merely one of interest, but of necessity." There would be unrest "so long as a system of government existed which was no longer in harmony with their aspirations, or so long as their claim upon our protection is based on anything less firm than a relation which enables them to fly the American flag. In some form, and sooner or later," the *Tribune* declared, "this must come about." [20]

Commissioner Wodehouse, undeceived by this newspaper propaganda, explained to Lord Rosebery that there had been a persistent misrepresentation for political purposes of the situation at Honolulu. Correspondents had predicted impending revolutions and disturbances, while everyone knew that "the political sky at least, as far as violence went," was as clear in Honolulu as in Washington. "The presence of two American Warships in the port of Honolulu," Wodehouse asserted, "is not, and has not been necessary as a 'preventive measure of security.' They have come here to bully and intimidate

20. Nov. 28, 1892, reprinted in *Kennebec Journal,* Dec. 2, 1892.

a little State struggling with many difficulties! A very unworthy position for a Great Power like the United States to assume toward little Hawaii." [21]

The annexation campaign continued in one form or another throughout December 1892 and into the new year. The Washington *Post,* on December 21, carried an article on "Our Hawaiian Interests," in which Pearl Harbor's value was stressed and the improvements required to make it available as indicated in the confidential reports of Generals Schofield and Alexander—information on which Congress based its appropriations of a quarter of a million. Nine days later the New York *Times* emphasized the "imperative necessity" that the United States take possession of the Pearl Harbor coaling station. The renewal of the exclusive right to enter that harbor and to establish and maintain there a naval station would amount to little if the Navy Department continued its policy of inactivity, if it favored Pago Pago and neglected Pearl Harbor, or if it allowed "any one of the three waiting European nations to take the only means of outside protection to our interests in the Pacific." [22]

Two Pacific coast dailies, the San Francisco *Morning Call* and the Portland *Oregonian,* remained alert to the Hawaiian situation. The former, in an article from its Washington correspondent entitled "An Eye on Hawaii, England Jealous of the United States, Trying to Divert Trade," reported that Great Britain was following her old policy of aiming to create ill feeling toward America, and reviewed the Washington *Post* agitation of the previous year.

The *Oregonian* reported real news of interest when, on January 3, it disclosed, without giving a source, a projected trip to Hawaii by a bipartisan group of forty-four representatives and senators who were either members of the present Congress or members-elect of the next one. It was not clear whether this meant the purchase of some island for a coaling station, or the making of arrangements for laying a cable, or the intention of entering into negotiations to acquire the entire group. The chief reason for the proposed journey was said to be the desire on the part of the United States government to counteract the influence Englishmen were exciting in the islands to limit American commerce. The reciprocity treaty with Hawaii would expire in fourteen months, and British interests were hard at

21. Wodehouse to Rosebery, Dec. 7, 1892, No. 22, FO 58/263.
22. "Pearl Harbor Coaling Station, Imperative Necessity that the United States Take Possession," *Times,* Jan. 9, 1893.

work trying to secure the same foothold in the islands which the
United States government had obtained. Since Congress had appropriated $250,000 for a coaling station, British interests feared that
the establishment of the station would ultimately mean American
control of the islands. England had been trying to convince the
islanders of this. The *Oregonian* concluded that United States interest in Hawaii might be very much benefited by the visit of
forty-four members of Congress. The New York *Morning Sun*
theorized on the purpose and results of the proposed junket, believing also that its main object was to counteract the influence of
Englishmen in the islands.[23] Dr. Mott Smith, however, considered
the jaunt only "a humorous lobby scheme" that had originated in the
brain of a subofficial of the House but that was not worthy of official
notice.[24]

An Overture from Washington

Within seven months of Lorrin A. Thurston's delicate exploratory
mission to Washington, the Harrison administration advanced a
proposal. The representative of the Annexation Club, acting on the
recommendation of Attorney William N. Armstrong, arranged a contact with Washington officials through Archibald Hopkins, a friend
of Armstrong and a clerk in the court of claims. This agent, in a communication to Thurston, stated in effect: "I am authorized to inform
you that the United States Government will pay to Queen Liliuokalani, and those connected with her, the sum of two hundred and
fifty thousand dollars, for the assignment to the United States of the
Sovereignty of Hawaii." [1]

Thurston submitted the letter to a meeting of the Annexation Club,
and its members had several consultations. Later, when the attorney
was en route to San Francisco on a brief "business trip," he wrote
Hopkins at length reporting that those members of the club who
were "more particularly favorable to the proposition" were unani-

23. Jan. 3, 1893; New York *Mail and Express*, Jan. 5, 1893.
24. Mott Smith to Mark P. Robinson, Jan. 10, 1893, AH, U.S. Minister,
Washington.
1. Hopkins to Thurston, Nov. 15, 1892, AH, Thurston Papers, printed in
Thurston, *Memoirs*, p. 233. Hopkins was promised a stipend of $75 per month
for his services with an expectation of further compensation proportionate to
the results. As late as Dec. 29, 1893, he had been paid nothing. (Thurston,
Memoirs, p. 243.)

mously of the opinion that there was "no probability of success in attempting to secure annexation within the time that you mentioned and upon the lines suggested." Minister Stevens, "with the fullest knowledge of the facts, and himself an enthusiastic advocate of annexation," concurred in this opinion.

Thurston set forth the problems involved in attempting to secure annexation along the lines suggested. To begin with, the diverse nationality and numerous conflicting interests of the population rendered "Hawaiian politics kaleidoscopic to the last degree, resulting in the most unexpected changes and combinations." He pointed to the abortive conspiracy of the radical native party the previous May, which had led to a swinging of the pendulum against annexation and in favor of the Queen. The opposition of native Hawaiians to annexation was based not so much upon personal support of Queen Liliuokalani or even royalty as it was "on a strong sentimental feeling in favor of independence intertwined with a strong race prejudice against foreigners, and the fear that with a loss of independence the control of the Government would be more likely to pass out of their hands, and that less offices would be filled by Hawaiians."

Secondly, the proposal to pay the Queen $250,000 was totally inadequate. She was already receiving about $80,000 a year in salary, prerequisites, and incidental expenses. So long as she was reasonably sure that governmental affairs would continue on their present basis, it would be a poor financial transaction for her to accept a sum the interest upon which would be only $15,000 per annum. She was in a more independent frame of mind than six months before and, unless under duress, would not accept so small a settlement. In addition to the financial objections, Thurston observed that the Queen was "of a stubborn headstrong disposition, jealous of royal prerogatives and desirous of extending rather than giving up any of the powers and privileges which she now possesses."

Thirdly, if Washington required the treaty of annexation to be approved by the legislature, two difficulties—the opposition of the native Hawaiian members and that of certain planters—would have to be surmounted. Out of a total of forty-eight members in the legislature, twenty-five were native or half-Hawaiian. Of these, if "subsidizing" was not resorted to, six would vote for annexation; of the remaining nineteen, probably fifteen could be controlled by subsidizing to the amount of $500 to $5,000 each. Some twelve to twenty native Hawaiian leaders outside the house would "have to be convinced" by a similar process on a similar scale.

Among the twenty-three foreigners in the legislature, thirteen would probably vote in favor of the treaty, four would be opposed irreconcilably, and six were impossible to predict, mainly because of the labor question. The uncertainty so raised would be due to the Hawaiian contract labor system whereby the planter advanced $75 for the Japanese and somewhat less for the Chinese to pay their expenses to the islands. If some method could be devised for enforcing repayment of the advance except by civil suit for damage, the objection of some of the wealthiest planters would be removed. In addition, some planters feared that the United States prohibition of Chinese immigration might be extended to the islands and perhaps ultimately made to include the Japanese, in which case the source of labor supply, "at living rates to the sugar planters," would be cut off, while the effect of annexation on other industries would increase the wages of labor in the country to such a point that the sugar and rice business could not operate profitably.

Thurston raised eight questions which required answers with "approximate definiteness" before action. Five of these concerned the signatures that might be required to the treaty. Two arose out of Hawaii's labor system and the possibility of the United States permitting Orientals to be brought to the islands to work there in the agricultural industries, yet not giving them the right thereby to enter the other portions of the Union if the laws of the United States prohibited it. The eighth query related to the spoils: Should appointment to Hawaiian offices "be made from among those who have resided a certain number of years, say 5, at the Islands?" This question was prompted by the fear of "carpet baggers" descending upon the country from the mainland. Finally, Thurston suggested postponing action. Delay would, to a certain extent, remove factious and personal, as well as political, feeling in the legislature, while precipitate action might stir up opposition for purely factious reasons.[2]

Stevens Presses Hard

In his letter to Archibald Hopkins, Thurston revealed that John L. Stevens had forwarded by the same mail an exhaustive dispatch to

2. Thurston to Hopkins, Dec. 14, 1892, AH, FO Ex., folder FO, Misc. Local, printed in Thurston, *Memoirs*, pp. 235–36. In San Francisco, Thurston again saw Claus Spreckels.

the State Department, which the Attorney had been permitted to read and in which he had "endorsed heartily every statement." This forty-four-page memorandum dealt with the political, financial, agricultural, social, and demographic conditions of the islands and suggested a line of action.[1] It was by no means the first of its kind, but it differed from previous ones in its comprehensiveness.

In reporting the results of the biennial election of February 1892, Stevens deemed it his official duty to provide Secretary Blaine with a statement of facts and reasons for the necessity of a "new departure" in United States relations with Hawaii. The political situation was feverish and the Minister could "see no prospect of its being permanently otherwise until these islands become a part of the American Union or a possession of Great Britain." The intelligent and responsible men in the kingdom, unaided by outside support, were too few in numbers to control political affairs and to secure good government. A protectorate was impracticable; annexation "must be the future remedy, or else Great Britain will be furnished with circumstances and opportunity to get a hold on these Islands which will cause future serious embarrassment to the United States." There was no immediate prospect of its being safe to have the harbor of Honolulu left without an American vessel of war.[2]

The following month Stevens considered the possibility that the Hawaiian monarchy might be overthrown "by an orderly and peaceful revolution," by first seizing the police station, then the palace, and finally the government building, and he wanted to know how far he and the naval commander "might deviate from established international rules and precedents" in such a contingency.[3]

In a private letter addressed to Secretary Blaine the Minister expressed the opinion that republican and annexation sentiment was "growing among the property owners and the white workingmen, tradesmen, and professional persons, and more or less among the Hawaiian natives." It was "very plain" that the present state of things could not continue—that the time was not distant "when the United States must say *yes* or *no* to the question of 'Annexation.'" With Britain in virtual control of the palace and with the young princess placed on the throne, $50,000 or less spent in a future election "could give England or the Canadian Dominion a legal

1. Stevens to Foster, Nov. 20, 1892, No. 74, printed in part in *For. Rels.* (1894), App. II, 377–84.
2. Stevens to Blaine, Feb. 8, 1892, No. 46, USDS, Dispatches, Hawaii, 25.
3. Ibid., March 8, 1892, No. 59.

ownership of the islands." Stevens bluntly asked Blaine: "Are you or are you not for annexation?" [4]

In his most comprehensive dispatch regarding the Hawaiian problem Stevens wrote: "Circumstances are pressing and no time should be lost in looking at the facts as they really exist." Several European powers were strongly inclined to gain possession of all the islands of the Pacific, except those expressly protected by the United States. The seizure of the Gilbert, Johnston, and other groups, and events in Samoa, emphatically indicated that England was not moderating her policy in that area. Undoubtedly the Canadian government was prompting this course, for the enormous cost of the Canadian Pacific Railway impelled its managers to make the most desperate efforts to secure freight and passengers—hence its aggressive plans to capture commerce and to gain political and commercial influence in the Hawaiian Islands. Powerful agencies were already working on the scheme of a British cable from Vancouver to Japan and China via Honolulu, and of establishing commercial and mail lines of steamers on the same route.[5] If the United States government did not promptly provide for laying a cable from San Francisco or San Diego to Honolulu or Hilo, it might be regarded as certain that a cable would "be laid by British capital and controlled by British managers." Therefore, to safeguard effectively American interests in the Pacific and in these islands, there was no time for hesitation and delay. Pearl Harbor for a coaling station and cable between California and Hawaii was of "immediate importance to American commercial and naval interests and to the maintenance of American influence on these islands."

The Minister asserted that the monarchy in Hawaii was an "absurd anachronism" with "nothing on which it logically or legitimately stands." It was "an impediment to good government— an obstruction to the prosperity and progress of the islands." The palace cost the little kingdom probably $150,000 a year, while a governor at $5,000 a year, acting in harmony with the responsible men of the legislature, would be far better for the islands. Under a territorial government, they could be as easily administered as any of the existing territories of the United States.

Hawaii had reached the parting of the ways which lead to Asia or to America. Two-fifths of the population were Chinese and

4. Ibid., March 25, 1892, bound incorrectly between Nos. 40–41.
5. See my "Canada's Interest," *Canadian Historical Review*, 44 (1963), 20–42.

Japanese. "If the present state of things is allowed to go on the Asiatics will soon largely predominate, for the native Hawaiians are now decreasing at the rate of nearly a thousand a year." To postpone American action would only add to the present unfavorable tendencies and make future possession more difficult. The diplomat observed that Queen Liliuokalani was not expected to live many years. The Princess Kaiulani, heir apparent, had always been and was likely to remain under British influence. She was in school in England, and her guardian there was Theo. H. Davies, a "Tory Englishman," who had lived in Honolulu for many years, still owned large properties there, and was a "resolute and persistent opponent of American predominance, bitterly denouncing even the American acquisition of Pearl Harbor." A sister of the Crown Princess was married to the eldest son of James H. Wodehouse. The death of the Queen "would virtually place an English princess on the Hawaiian throne, and put in the hands of the ultra-English the patronage and influence of the palace."

Turning to the business status of the islands, Minister Stevens reported that the McKinley tariff had resulted in a loss of not less than twelve million dollars to the owners of sugar plantations and mills, etc., and in the consequent depreciation of other property. A large portion of this loss had fallen on Americans residing in Hawaii and in California. Unless some positive measures of relief were granted, the depreciation of sugar property would continue.

One of two courses appeared absolutely necessary: "either bold and vigorous measures for annexation, or a 'customs union,' an ocean cable from the California coast to Honolulu, Pearl Harbor perpetually ceded to the United States with an implied but not necessarily stipulated American protectorate over the islands." Stevens considered the first course to be better, "more advantageous to the islands, and the cheapest and least embarrassing in the end for the United States." If it was wise thirty-eight years before, through Secretary Marcy, to offer to expend $100,000 to secure a treaty of annexation, it certainly could not be "chimerical or unwise to expend $100,000 to secure annexation in the near future." [6] The United States "has five times the wealth she possessed in 1854, and the reason now existing for annexation is much stronger than it was then." The Minister could not "refrain from expressing the opinion with emphasis that the golden hour is near at hand."

6. See my "Slavery and Racism as Deterrents to the Annexation of Hawaii, 1854–1855," *Journal of Negro History*, 47 (1962), 1–18.

To the argument that annexation would involve the obligation of paying to Hawaiian sugar producers the same rate of bounties paid to American producers, thus imposing a heavy burden on the United States Treasury, the Minister suggested that the terms of the agreement specifically provide that the United States government should "pay 6 mills per pound—$12 per ton—to the Hawaiian sugar raisers, and this only so long as the present sugar-bounty system of the United States shall be maintained." This limited and small bounty would tide the Hawaiian sugar planters over their alarming condition and save the islands from general business depletion and financial disaster.

Stevens did not recommend giving Hawaii a highly favorable treaty while she remained outside the American union, for the same advantages would necessarily be enjoyed by hostile foreigners who would continue to antagonize our commercial and political interests there, as well as those of American blood and sympathies. There was an apparent relationship between prosperity and the desire to be annexed. It was "a well authenticated fact" that American sentiment in Hawaii in 1890, the last year of the great prosperity under the sugar provisions of the reciprocity treaty, was much less manifest than before the treaty had gone into effect, and less pronounced than when Secretary Marcy authorized the negotiation of the annexation treaty in 1854. "It is equally true that the desire here at this time for annexation is much stronger than in 1889. Besides, so long as the islands retain their own independent government there remains the possibility that England or the Canadian Dominion might secure one of the Hawaiian harbors for a coaling station. Annexation excludes all dangers of this kind."

In a personal note attached to the memorandum, the Minister expressed the hope that it would be read by the President and by Secretary Tracy, and would also be "seen by Senators Morgan, Sherman, Frye, and such others" as Foster deemed "it expedient." Stevens was not certain that our statesmen were "yet ready to grapple boldly with the Hawaiian question." He was, however, "very confident that the sooner it is firmly taken hold of, the better it will be for the United States as well as for Hawaii." [7]

Secretary of State Foster sent for James H. Blount, chairman of the House Committee on Foreign Affairs, and voiced the hope that he would endeavor to bring the Democratic party to the support of

7. Stevens to Foster, dated Nov. 28, 1892, but encl. in No. 74, USDS, Dispatches, Hawaii, 25.

the annexation of the Hawaiian Islands. The latter was under the impression that a treaty had been negotiated; he expressed no opinion on the matter, as he had declared his intention to retire, but he did show copies of the letter to Congressmen R. R. Hitt and James B. McCreary.[8]

Stevens' lengthy confidential dispatches would, at best, only arrest the attention of a few government officials. The ardent and ebullient annexationist, desirous of publicizing more widely the necessity of acquiring the Hawaiian Islands, therefore turned to the medium of the Augusta, Maine, *Kennebec Journal*, of which he was still titular editor, to disseminate the view that the issue of annexation was imminent. In an unidentified editorial published on November 17, 1892, the journalist convincingly stated his views and asked: "Shall Americans sleep while others are awake to take from them their natural advantages? Time and tide wait neither for men nor nations." The article was reprinted on November 28 by the New York *Sun*, which assumed that its author was Minister Stevens, while the New York *Tribune* of November 30 asserted that "in some form, and sooner or later," annexation must be achieved.[9]

Thurston's letter to the Annexation Club's agent in Washington reached its destination on Christmas Day. Upon its receipt, Archibald Hopkins immediately made the contents known to Secretary of State John W. Foster, who had, no doubt, just received—if not read —Stevens' detailed memorandum. The Secretary was of the opinion that since the situation in Hawaii was as Thurston represented, it would be "useless to attempt to bring matters to a head during the short time which remains to this administration." Such being the case, he considered it not worthwhile to take up in detail the questions propounded, as his views might materially differ from those of his successor. He was disposed to think that the foreign policy of the incoming Cleveland administration would "tend to be, if not agressive, at least positive and active," and in the case that E. J. Phelps should be called to the State Department, he would "likely be favorable to the acquisition of Hawaii and to do all he could to push it." [10]

Hopkins requested Thurston to send him details on the Hawaiian

8. *Sen. Reps.*, 53 Cong., 2 sess., No. 227, pp. 403–05.
9. See *Kennebec Journal*, Nov. 30, Dec. 1, 2, 1892.
10. Hopkins to Thurston, Dec. 29, 1892, AH, FO Ex., Misc. Local Officials, printed in Thurston, *Memoirs*, pp. 242–43.

debt—the amount, how long it was to run, the rate of interest, etc.
—as this information would be important in any further negotiations.
He assured his correspondent that should "unexpected changes make
it seem best for you to act immediately, everything possible to second your plans will be done at this end of the line in the short
time that remains." [11] This assurance was all that Thurston and
Company required.

Before Washington considered further the annexation project, the
émeute of January 14–17, 1893, occurred. In the course of this crisis
the subversive and clandestine Annexation Club made its public
appearance in the guise of a committee of safety, which deposed
Queen Liliuokalani without the approval of either the legislature
or the electorate.

11. Ibid. This communication dated Dec. 29, 1892, canceled at Washington
at 4 P.M., Dec. 28, postmarked at San Francisco, Jan. 3, 1893, reached Honolulu on Jan. 11—the day before the collapse of the Reform cabinet and three
days before the attempted promulgation of a new constitution. Considering
the eagerness with which mainland mail was always anticipated and its arrival
heralded, Thurston was almost certain to have received and read this letter,
with the desired assurance, before the series of engrossing events of Jan. 14-17,
1893.

THE REVOLUTION OF 1893: FOUR DAYS

Saturday, January 14

On this particular Saturday morning the air of Honolulu was filled with rumors to the effect that Queen Liliuokalani was planning a radical move, perhaps the promulgation of a new constitution. In deciding to take this rash step, the Queen believed she was performing her duty as a monarch toward her people and her country. Constitutional revision was expected and longed for by many Hawaiians; during the election of February 1892 petitions requesting a constitutional convention had poured in from every part of the islands, supported and endorsed by the *Hui Kalaiaina* (Hawaiian Political Association), which had forwarded them to the sovereign. Out of a possible 9500 registered voters, an estimated 6500, or two-thirds, had signed them.[1] The Liberal party had been elected on a platform in which the main plank was the calling of a convention for the purpose of preparing a new constitution and submitting it to the people for ratification.

At the beginning of her reign Liliuokalani had been taunted by Hawaiians as being too much in favor and under the advice and influence of haoles, and against her own subjects and race. Smarting under such taunts, she had decided to demonstrate that a Hawaiian monarch's chief obligation was to redress the wrongs of the Ha-

1. Liliuokalani, *Hawaii's Story,* pp. 230–31, 384.

waiian people.[2] "To have ignored or disregarded so general a request," wrote the Queen, "I must have been deaf to the voice of
the people, which tradition tells us is the voice of God. No true
Hawaiian chief would have done other than to promise a consideration of their wishes." Although by law the legislature was the
designated body for formulating a new constitution and amendments, the Queen reasoned that when members were bribed and
the legislature corrupted, no one could depend on any good measure
being carried through the stipulated procedure. That method had
been tried and had failed. There was only one recourse: with the
signature of one of her ministers, she would promulgate a new instrument. There was no clause in the constitution of 1887 stating
that there should be no other but this. Many of the Queen's friends
advocated a new constitution, and Samuel Parker promised to sustain her when the proper time came.[3] Thus she took the fateful step.

The "new" and "revolutionary" constitution was practically a
restoration of the instrument under which the kingdom was governed during the reign of Kalakaua prior to the revolution of 1887.
Composed of clippings from the constitutions of 1864 and 1887, the
document had been prepared by Liliuokalani and two members of
the legislature before October 1892. She had given it to Attorney
General Peterson, asking him to correct it, and if he found any
defects to delete them and substitute such clauses as he thought
would be good for the people and the country. He had kept it a
month, during which time he consulted some lawyers and others in
regard to many points, and returned the draft without modification.
The Queen therefore concluded that it was satisfactory. A week before the closing of the legislature, she requested Peterson to prepare
a preamble. From him Colburn heard of the document. Samuel
Parker and W. H. Cornwell gave the sovereign assurance of their
support before their appointments on January 13.[4] Thus all the

2. Statement of C. B. Wilson, *For. Rels.* (1894), App. II, p. 1027. Cf. memo.
from the *Hui Kalaiaina* to J. H. Blount, showing why the people urged the
Queen to promulgate a new constitution, *House Ex. Docs.*, 53 Cong., 2 sess.,
No. 47, "Report of Commissioner to the Hawaiian Islands," pp. 17–18, here-
after *Blount Report; Sen. Ex. Docs.*, 52 Cong., 2 sess., No. 76, "Hawaiian
Islands," pp. 483–84; Statement of Liliuokalani Dominis, in *House Docs.*, 54
Cong., 1 sess., No. 1, Pt. II, *For. Rels.* (1895), p. 284.

3. Liliuokalani, pp. 23, 383, 391.

4. Ibid., pp. 384–85. Statement of A. F. Judd, Chief Justice of the Supreme
Court of the Hawaiian Islands, *Morgan Report*, p. 445; Affidavit of E. C. Jones,
ibid., p. 222.

cabinet members were aware of the existence of the constitution before Saturday, January 14, 1893.

The most significant proposed changes were these: Article 22 added Prince David Kawananakoa and Jonah Kuhio Kalanianaole as heirs to the throne. Article 42 provided that the cabinet "shall be appointed and commissioned by the Queen, and hold office during the Queen's pleasure, subject to impeachment, or upon a vote of want of confidence passed by a majority of all the members of the legislative assembly. No act of the Queen shall have any effect unless it be countersigned by a minister, who by that signature makes himself responsible." Article 57 empowered the sovereign to appoint the nobles, who should hold their appointment during life, but their number should not exceed twenty-four. Article 60 permitted the number of representatives to be increased from twenty-four to forty-eight. The practice under the constitution of 1864 of having the nobles and representatives sit together was restored. Article 62 extended the suffrage to male subjects who could read and write, and reduced the qualification so that those who possessed "real property to the value over and above all encumbrances of $150, or a leasehold property on which the rent was $25 per year, or of an income of not less than $75 per year, derived from any property or some lawful employment," might vote. Article 65 made the term of appointment of supreme court judges six years, instead of for life, as formerly, and omitted the existing provision that the pay of justices of the supreme court "shall not be diminished during their continuance in office." This provision "virtually destroyed the independence of the judiciary."[5] Finally, Article 78 of the constitution of 1887, which stipulated that whenever any act was to be done by the sovereign, "it shall, unless otherwise expressed, mean that such Act shall be done and performed by the Sovereign by and with the advice and consent of the Cabinet," was omitted.[6]

The most "revolutionary" articles, and those that particularly disturbed the substantial, responsible, and righteous elements of the community, were 57 and 62, which would have destroyed the gains of the revolution of 1887. Under the constitution of that year the

5. Judd Statement, ibid., p. 444.

6. For a purported copy and details of the constitution see *Blount Report*, pp. 581–90; Thurston, *Memoirs*, pp. 608–21; *For. Rels.* (1895), pp. 823 ff.; Doles, *Memoirs*, pp. 72–73. The opposition offered to pay $500 for the original copy of the Queen's constitution, but were not successful in their efforts; it was destroyed. Jones Statement, *Morgan Report*, p. 221.

white property-owning and high-salaried residents secured the
franchise without becoming citizens, without taking an oath of allegiance to the monarch; they simply had to swear to support the
constitution. The restriction on the franchise for electors of the upper
house gave three-fourths of the vote for the nobles to whites and
one-fourth to native Hawaiians.[7] By this restriction and by limiting
the number of representatives in the lower chamber to twenty-four,
the people of substance were enabled, so far at least as the legislature was concerned, to elect men who opposed measures destructive
of property interests and capital investments. Under Liliuokalani's
constitution, if the residents of the islands wished to enjoy the
suffrage, they had to become naturalized subjects, following the example that prevailed in other modern states. Dole estimated that
the proposed changes would have disfranchised over one-fourth of
the voters and the owners of nine-tenths of the private property of
the kingdom.[8] Moreover, Chief Justice A. F. Judd claimed that
Article 57 would have "virtually placed the whole legislative power
in the queen's hands," while Article 42 would have made her an
autocrat. He was certain that the "new constitution would have
made it impossible for white men to live here." With the legislators
bribed and changing their votes at the will of the sovereign, with
a hostile Queen and a subservient cabinet, "there was no safety for
us or our property. This justified the revolution."[9] Liliuokalani, however, maintained that these proposed changes did not deprive foreigners of any rights or privileges enjoyed by them under the constitution of 1887.[10]

Also ready, along with the new constitution, were a proclamation
of martial law and another calling upon all loyal citizens to gather
at the police station and government building to maintain law and
order.

At a 10 A.M. cabinet meeting, Liliuokalani informed the ministers
of her intention to promulgate a constitution. Since they had to meet
the legislature, the conference adjourned without securing their
approval of it. The Queen labored under the impression that she
must have the signatures of her ministers to make her proposed
action legal. No doubt she had in mind British practice, for the
third article of the Act of Union (1701) stipulated that the sover-

7. Blount Report, p. 112
8. Dole, Memoirs, p. 85.
9. Judd Statement, Morgan Report, p. 444.
10. Liliuokalani Dominis Statement, For. Rels. (1895), p. 824.

eign's ministers in the privy council should sign the measures they supported, and thus their responsibility could easily be proved by the evidence of their signatures. Moreover, Article 42 of her proposed constitution in part stated that "no act of the Queen shall have any effect unless it be countersigned by a minister, who, by that signature, makes himself responsible." On this point the legalistic-minded Thurston avers that the only necessity for the approval of the cabinet was the provision that she should have such approval; if "she had the power to abrogate any provision of the constitution, she had the power to abrogate every provision," provided that she had the requisite force behind her. The Queen's impression that any provision of the constitution was binding upon her and necessitated cabinet approval of a change was purely an assumption. "Fortunately for the community, her views prevented her taking the bull by the horns, abrogating the constitution, promulgating a new one, and putting her terms into effect by force." [11]

On leaving the palace, Minister of the Interior John F. Colburn went directly to the business section of the city to inform Alfred S. Hartwell, an old esteemed friend, of the Queen's intentions. Thurston and William O. Smith were invited to join them in the judge's office. The experienced Lorrin Thurston advised Colburn not to resign under any condition, but to resist the Queen's demands. The leader of the opposition promised to support the newly formed cabinet and stated his belief that Stevens would also if a firm stand were taken. [12]

At noon the legislature was prorogued with the usual formal ceremony. The sovereign, elegantly dressed, with a coronet of diamonds on her head, read, with great dignity, the address of prorogation, in which she expressed her "earnest endeavor to promote such Treaty relations with our Great and Friendly Neighbor,

11. Thurston, *Memoirs*, p. 274.

12. Colburn to Blount, April 15, 1893, *For. Rels.* (1894), App. II, p. 498. Hartwell to Richard Olney, Nov. 4, 1893, Richard Olney Papers, Vol. 11, Library of Congress. Statement of W. O. Smith of events prior to Jan. 17, 1893, *Blount Report*, p. 489. Judd Statement, *Morgan Report*, p. 443. Thurston's account in his *Memoirs*, p. 445, varies slightly from the above, for he reports that Colburn, an old school friend, burst into his (Thurston's) office exclaiming: "Lorrin, we're having a hell of a time up at the Palace and I have come to tell you about it." The conference actually occurred in Hartwell's office, at the corner of King and Merchant Streets. Thurston, however, was intimately associated with Hartwell, having started the study of law in the judge's office in 1876.

the United States of America, as may restore to Our Agricultural interests the measure of prosperity which we formerly enjoyed." She also noted, with gratification, that liberal encouragement had been extended to some infant industries.[13] According to Judge Sanford B. Dole, the ceremony was "an impressive function." [14]

Not more than two white legislators were in attendance, for the Reform members, wishing to express their disapproval of and opposition to the new cabinet, absented themselves from the hall. Actually, their leaders were consorting elsewhere. Local officials, supreme court judges, and members of the diplomatic corps were present, and after the ceremony they were invited by the chamberlain to a meeting to be held in the palace that afternoon.

Following the prorogation ceremonies in the legislative hall, the members of the diplomatic corps immediately requested an interview with the cabinet to ascertain whether a new constitution was to be promulgated that afternoon by the Queen. Parker replied that the ministers were not aware of it, but that they had heard rumors to that effect. To Major Wodehouse's inquiry as to what position the cabinet would take if the attempt were made, the ministers assured him that they would oppose it.[15]

Stevens remained silent during this conversation, but later inquired and learned that the Queen had signed the lottery bill and that the cabinet had acquiesced in the action. Instantly he raised his cane and stamped it on the floor, asserting that the passage and signing of that bill was "a direct attack on the United States," picked up his hat, and stalked out of the office, saying as he left that he wanted the cabinet to inform him at once if the sovereign attempted to promulgate a constitution.[16]

In the meantime Liliuokalani waited for her ministers in the blue room of the palace. After their delayed arrival at 1:30 P.M., she stated that at the request of some 8,000 Hawaiians, she had decided to promulgate a new constitution, in which the grievances of her petitioning subjects would be remedied, and she invited the gentlemen to proceed with her to the throne room, where the diplomatic

13. AH, JL (1892–93), pp. 552–53.

14. Dole, Memoirs, p. 70. Lieut. Lucien Young of the cruiser Boston, who brought the tourist point of view to the ceremony, described it as "about the funniest affair I ever saw in my life—a circus." In reporting on the palace reception, he claimed that the Queen was drunk (Morgan Report, pp. 328–29).

15. Colburn to Blount, April 15, 1893, For. Rels. (1894), App. II, p. 498.
16. Ibid.

corps, members of the supreme bench, and members of the legislature, besides a committee of the Hui Kalaiaina, were waiting.

The ministers demurred, saying that they thought it inadvisable to take such action, that there was danger of an uprising. In reply, the Queen explained that she would not have planned the promulgation if they had not encouraged her: "They had led me out to the edge of a precipice, and now were leaving me to take the step alone. It was humiliating." Then she entreated: "Why not give the people the constitution, and I will bear the brunt of all the blame afterwards." Peterson met this plea with the excuse: "We have not read the constitution." Liliuokalani reminded him that he had had it in his possession for a whole month.[17] At this, Colburn asked the Attorney General why this had not been revealed the previous night at a caucus of the party on the subject.

Ministers Colburn, Cornwell, and Peterson withdrew from the argument and left the more courageous Samuel Parker to try to dissuade the sovereign from her purpose. He remained at her side, fearing that if she were left alone she would proclaim the constitution from the palace balcony, and tell her anxious people to look out for her cabinet and judges, who would not approve it. Colburn and Peterson dropped in at W. O. Smith's office, which was crowded to capacity with a number of the leading businessmen of Honolulu, who were anxious to know if the Queen would promulgate the constitution. Colburn assured them that the cabinet would not allow her to do so as long as the residents of the islands were not agreed on the subject.[18]

When Cornwell, Colburn, and Peterson returned to the palace and the Queen asked them what they perceived injurious in the constitution, Attorney General Peterson replied that there were certain points that he thought were not exactly suitable. To this Liliuokalani rejoined that the legislature could make the necessary amendments. He entreated Her Majesty to wait for a fortnight; in the meantime the cabinet would be ready to present modifications to her. Chief Justice Judd also appealed to the Queen not to promulgate the constitution that afternoon. After more than two hours of argument and persuasion, she yielded, but at the same time called attention to the precedent which the Reform party had

17. Liliuokalani, *Hawaii's Story*, pp. 385, 392–93.
18. Colburn to Blount, April 15, 1893 *For. Rels.* (1894), App. II, p. 499.

created by the revolutionary constitution of 1887.[19] Justice Judd was
relieved that the trouble was over, and thought, "We may be able to
stop it yet."

In the interim the diplomatic corps, judges, and local officials
assembled in the throne room grew tired of waiting and left the
palace; only the people's delegates and representatives of the Hui
Kalaiaina remained. To these Liliuokalani announced that obstacles
had arisen which prevented her from promulgating the constitution
at that time, and that she had yielded to the advice of her ministers,
who had promised that on some future day she might proclaim a
new one. She then requested the guests to return home and await
in peace the time when a proper course could be adopted to carry
out the will of the people. Most of the delegates dispersed quietly;
but shortly thereafter, a crowd of interested Hawaiians gathered on
the palace grounds, and according to Minister Cornwell a few remarks were made by William White, the representative of Lahaina,
expressing regret at the Queen's inability to grant the wishes of
the people, but claiming that they would accept her assurance and
await the proper time, which, if they were successful in the next
election, would be at the meeting of the legislature in 1894.[20]

Meanwhile, Thurston and Smith went to the latter's office, where
dozens of men were excitedly discussing the situation. A declaration
was immediately drafted to this effect: "Since Liliuokalani had
announced her intention of subverting the constitution and arbitrarily promulgating a new one, the undersigned declared her to be
in attempted revolution against the constitution and government,
and pledged their support of the cabinet in resisting her." [21] Signatures were affixed and messengers were sent out to bring in other
men. Nearly a hundred leading businessmen signed this declaration
and pledge. The document lay on the table for several hours and
then disappeared, the general belief being that Paul Neumann had
sequestered it, for he later served as the Queen's attorney.[22]

Marshal Wilson, informed that Thurston and Smith were organizing and enlisting men to overthrow the monarchy, inquired at the

19. Liliuokalani, pp. 385–86; Cornwell to Blount, April 24, 1893, For. Rels.
(1894), App. II, p. 494.

20. Colburn to Blount, April 15, 1893, For. Rels. (1894), App. II, p. 499.
For a radically different report, see Statement of Lieut. L. Young, Morgan
Report, p. 332.

21. Thurston, Memoirs, p. 249.

22. Ibid.

latter's office, which was not more than eight hundred to a thousand yards from the police station. The attorneys explained that they were organizing simply to support the cabinet in opposing the Queen, in the event of her promulgating a new constitution in defiance of her ministers.[23]

Between three and four o'clock Thurston quietly remarked to Henry E. Cooper that the time had come for the Annexation Club to act. The latter agreed. The former proposed to the gathering that a committee of safety be appointed to devise ways and means of dealing with the political situation, and moved that Cooper be made chairman of a meeting to be held forthwith for the purpose of selecting such a committee. The motion carried. Cooper took the chair; then Thurston moved that the chairman be authorized to appoint a committee of safety, consisting of thirteen members, the chairman included. That motion carried unanimously; thereupon Cooper named his committeemen, all of whom were Annexation Club members except for George N. Wilcox. Immediately the room was cleared and the committee conferred.

Thurston again assumed the leadership and moved "that it is the sense of this meeting that the solution of the present situation is annexation to the United States." Cooper called for an expression of opinion. There was a general demand for annexation or any kind of stable government under the supervision of the United States. Even if the words that the Queen must be deposed or dethroned were not then spoken, the sentiment that it had to be done prevailed at, or even before, this January 14 meeting. All the members of the committee favored the motion except Wilcox, who, since he had no personal objects to accomplish and no friends whose interests he sought to further, resigned and returned to Kauai the following day. H. F. Glade, the German Consul, thought his name should not appear in the organization, but suggested the appointment of "Ed." Suhr, a clerk in the employ of H. Hackfeld and Company, Honolulu, a firm of which Glade was a senior member.[24]

What type of men were these who for nearly a year had secretly prepared for just such an occasion, had maneuvered to precipitate it, and whose clandestine organization was now transformed into a committee of public safety in which the prominent businessmen of Honolulu placed their trust?

The bold, earnest, and energetic ringleaders were Lorrin A.

23. Wilson Statement, *For. Rels.* (1894), App. II, p. 1028.
24. Thurston, *Memoirs*, pp. 250–51. Cf. *Morgan Report*, p. 453.

Thurston, William O. Smith, and William R. Castle, "old thunderbolts representing the white element." Thurston was born in the islands of the second generation. As organizer of the Hawaiian League, and, as a member of the legislature of 1886, he had taken a leading and vociferous part in the revolution of 1887, after which he was appointed minister of the interior, which office he filled for three years and was virtually premier. Thurston was considered the most influential and resolute member of the Reform party and the outstanding political leader and live wire of the islands. This man of marked ability and firm resolution, an indomitable dynamo of human energy and intrigue, was the Patrick Henry and the Samuel Adams of the Hawaiian Revolution. He was a shrewd, cold—if not Machiavellian—individual, with a tenacious purpose which made him utterly ruthless with those who did not support the cause. He, above all other annexationists, understood the value of propaganda and was capable of manipulating and directing it in channels suitable for his purpose. William O. Smith, born in Hawaii of American parents, had served and taken a leading part in the legislatures of 1878, 1884, 1887–88, and 1892, and had helped Thurston engineer the revolutionary movement of 1887, which resulted in the "Bayonet Constitution." [25] Closely associated with Thurston and Smith was another lawyer, William R. Castle, also of Hawaiian birth and American parentage, who had been a member of the legislature during five sessions. From carefully watching political affairs from 1876 to January 1893, he reached the conclusion that it would "never be possible to have a government of security to person and property in Hawaii under the old forms." [26]

Then there were Henry E. Cooper, in whose fecund brain the idea of an annexation club originated; William C. Wilder, a naturalized Hawaiian subject, president and manager of the Wilder Steamship Company, president of the Kahulii Railway Company, and a director of the Hawaiian Railroad Company;[27] C. Bolte, born in Bremen, Germany, a naturalized citizen of Hawaii, vice-president and managing partner of the wholesale importing house of M. G. Grinbaum and Company, and considered one of the most energetic and liberal businessmen of the community; Henry T. Waterhouse, of

25. Nellist, *Story of Hawaii*, pp. 773–74. San Francisco, *Morning Call*, Jan. 29, 1893.

26. *Morning Call*, Jan. 29, 1893. *Morgan Report*, p. 583.

27. *Morning Call*, Jan. 29, 1893. Affidavit of William C. Wilder, *Morgan Report*, p. 447.

English parentage and originally from Tasmania, a naturalized citizen of the kingdom, who served in the legislature in 1876 and 1887–88, played an active part in the revolution of 1887, and was one of the managing partners of the firm of John T. Waterhouse, general importers and wholesale and retail merchants; F. W. McChesney, an American citizen resident in Honolulu for ten years, and partner in and manager of the importing house of M. W. McChesney and Sons, wholesale dealers in groceries and provisions;[28] John A. McCandless, a United States citizen and an experienced engineer who had resided in the islands since 1880;[29] John Emmeluth, an American citizen, owner and director of the firm of J. Emmeluth and Company, the leading plumbing and house furnishings concern and hardware importers of the capital, as well as the principal owner and vice-president of the Hawaiian Fruit and Packing Company;[30] Andrew Brown, a Scotsman who had lived in Hawaii for fifteen years, and was foreman of the brass department of the Honolulu Iron Works and Foundry;[31] Theodore F. Lansing, a citizen of the United States owning and claiming allegiance thereto; and Ed. Suhr, a German subject and clerk in H. Hackfeld and Company.

On this dynamic and realistic committee of public safety there were no artists, no college professors, no dreamers, idealists, philosophers, or adventurers: there was no repetition of the Frankfort Assembly or of the French Constituent Assembly of 1848. All were experienced lawyers, legislators, merchants, managers of banking houses, trusts, or other corporations, directors of railways and steamship lines, engineers, or mechanics, who were considered "safe and conservative." They were not given to polemics or to debate of theoretical questions when matters of practical import were clamoring for solution. There was no particularism—no opposing factions with irreconcilable programs within the committee: all the members were bent upon the extirpation of the Hawaiian monarchy. Six of the thirteen had either legal training or experience in government or

28. *Morgan Report*, p. 453. *Morning Call*, Jan. 29, 1893.

29. *Morning Call*, Jan. 29, 1893. Cf. James Sutton McCandless, *A Brief History of the McCandless Brothers and Their Part in the Development of Artesian Well Water in the Hawaiian Islands, 1880–1936* (*Honolulu, 1936*), pp. 13, 20, 40.

30. Affidavit of John Emmeluth, *Morgan Report*, p. 455. *Morning Call*, Jan. 29, 1893.

31. *Morning Call*, Jan. 29, 1893.

both, and the men whom they entreated to join them in establishing a provisional government were of similar caliber.

The committee of safety instructed L. A. Thurston, W. C. Wilder, and H. F. Glade to inform Minister Stevens of the situation and to ascertain from him what if any "assistance could be afforded by the United States forces for the protection of life and property, the unanimous sentiment and feeling being that life and property were in danger." Wilder reported that Stevens replied to the effect that "if we obtained possession of the Government building, and became in fact the Government, he should of course recognize us." Henry Cooper visited Captain Wiltse on the U.S.S. *Boston* with a view of securing his cooperation, and later made an encouraging report to the committee.[32]

Marshal Wilson heard of this closed meeting in Smith's Office, and decided to send out special officers with instructions to report at once on the slightest signs of a disturbance. Other specials were assigned to shadow the principals, and instructions were given to the police to arrest all persons on the street found with arms and ammunition and to keep a strict watch on the premises of dealers in firearms. On the advice of the cabinet, the Marshal ordered the saloons closed at 9 P.M.—two and a half hours earlier than the regular time—in order to induce the usual Saturday night crowd to disperse. Peace and quiet prevailed throughout the city of Honolulu and nothing occurred that Saturday night to denote any sign of disturbance or change, except the decisions made in a gathering at the residence of Lorrin Thurston on Judd Street, which lasted late into the night.

The leader of the annexationists felt the need to call a small meeting to discuss further the explosive situation and the "means of bringing about the contemplated action," and particularly to ascertain the military force at their disposal.[33] Among the six men who attended, some difference of opinion arose as to the efficacy of forcibly setting aside the monarchy, and there were expressions of doubt as to whether the annexationists were strong enough to carry out such a program; but the feeling in favor of using force against Liliuokalani prevailed. Reportedly, Thurston stated that if the committee proclaimed a provisional government, Stevens would support them with troops from the U.S.S. *Boston*, and that their cause could

32. Wilder Affidavit, *Morgan Report*, p. 448. Cf. *House of Rep. Reps.*, 53 Cong., 2 sess., No. 243, p. 47.

33. Thurston, *Memoirs*, p. 251.

not succeed without those troops and the Minister's assistance. Re-
cruiting and arming had already started. Actually, the committee
could count on no more than seventy-five men and eighty stands of
arms: they needed more of both.[34]

Sunday, January 15

In spite of his serving as host to a late meeting the night before,
the vigorous Lorrin Thurston arose early on the Sabbath and at 6
o'clock went on horseback to the home of John C. Colburn, whom
he awakened to discuss the relation of the cabinet to the Queen.
The Minister of the Interior suggested that they go to the residence
of Attorney General Peterson. There Thurston informed the two that
the citizens were prepared to support the cabinet members against
Liliuokalani if they would declare her in revolution against the
government, proclaim the throne vacant and the monarchy abrogated, and seek annexation to the United States. He assured the
gentlemen that Stevens would land a force from the *Boston* to assist
in maintaining order and protecting property if they would consent
to sign the draft of a letter making such a request. If they would
lead, the committee of safety would back them; otherwise it would
act alone.[1] Both Colburn and Peterson declined to make an immediate decision on so grave a course. They recognized the anomalous position in which this offer placed them: they nominally would
remain as officers of the Queen, but actually would be seceding from
her and thus dividing the executive, so that while they would still
be in authority, they would actually be supporting the cause of
the rebels. The latter would thus accomplish their objective without risking their lives, while the ministers would become traitors
to the Queen and to her government. To this they could not agree,
and they asked for time to consider the proposition.[2] The first thing
that they did was to confer immediately with their colleagues.

Attorney General Peterson would not sanction the arrest of the
members of the committee of safety, as suggested by Marshal

34. Wilson Statement, *For. Rels.* (1894), App. II, p. 1029. Thurston,
Memoirs, p. 251. Cf. Dole, *Memoirs*, p. 74. Dole did "not remember that there
was then a conclusion in favor of changing the form of government."
   1. Thurston, *Memoirs*, pp. 25–52.
   2. Colburn to Blount, April 15, 1893, *For. Rels.* (1894), App. II, 499–500.
Cornwell to Blount, April 24, 1893, ibid., p. 494. Wilson Statement, ibid., pp.
1029–30.

Wilson, for he feared that such action would precipitate a conflict with American troops; he was most anxious to avoid any possible reasons for the landing of forces. If they were to land for any purpose other than to protect the United States consulate and legation, Wilson wanted the Hawaiian government to resist: then the United States would have to fight. He doubted if Stevens had authority to declare war against a friendly nation. Since not more than 175 troops could be landed, Wilson thought that the government, with 500 men, 10 Gatling guns, and a battery of artillery of about 12 pieces (rifled Austrian breechloaders), was in a position to resist.[3]

The ministers themselves were reluctant to adopt Wilson's proposals. Instead, they decided to inquire from Stevens how far he intended to support the plotters with United States marines, to seek advice from at least six responsible and conservative businessmen who were friendly to the Queen's government, and to confer with the consuls and diplomatic corps. Accordingly, the cabinet summoned the businessmen for a 1:30 P.M. meeting, and sought their views on Thurston's proposals. When they were told that the Queen had abandoned altogether the idea of promulgating a new constitution, they recommended that she and the cabinet issue a proclamation assuring the community that the matter was ended.

After the businessmen dictated the proclamation, on the suggestion of the ministers, one and all decided that the cabinet should inform the committee of safety that their proposition for landing troops would not be considered, and should request the members to accept the assurances given in the proclamation. The businessmen also raised the question of the government's ability to suppress any uprising, and were informed that it was ready and able to cope with any emergency that might arise. Whereupon Samuel M. Damon declared that the troops of the *Boston* were going to be landed.[4]

The cabinet members, joined by Wilson, dined at the Hawaiian Hotel and discussed the results of the afternoon meeting. At 7 P.M., Parker and Peterson called at the United States legation to secure some definite information as to Stevens' intentions in the event of an uprising. He reportedly informed his visitors that he was ready to support a provisional government with troops from the *Boston*.

3. Wilson Statement, p. 1030. Colburn to Blount, April 15, 1893, ibid., p. 500. Liliuokalani, *Hawaii's Story*, p. 387.

4. Liliuokalani, p. 387. Wilson Statement, *For. Rels.* (1894), App. II, p. 1031.

In an 8:30 meeting at the Attorney General's home, the cabinet members discussed the legality of the landing of troops, the violation of international law involved, the ways and means of overcoming the action of the conspirators in case of an uprising, the force, arms, and ammunition at the disposal of the government, the Queen's proclamation, and the propriety of holding a mass meeting. The Marshal proposed that the ringleaders be arrested at once, that all arms and ammunition in Honolulu be seized, and that the islands be placed under martial law until the arrests were affected. Peterson and Neumann both objected on the grounds that such action would precipitate a conflict, as Minister Stevens had already declared himself; at all hazards, a clash with United States troops had to be avoided. A committee was appointed to issue a call for a mass meeting and to draw up a resolution in support of the cabinet's action. Finally, the ministers decided to make the police station their headquarters.[5]

That same day, the committee of public safety had assembled at 10 A.M. at the residence of William Castle and had approved the action taken at the subcommittee meeting the evening before, as well as Thurston's proposal to Colburn and Peterson. The members had decided to call a mass meeting at the Rifles Armory for Monday at 2 P.M. to report to the citizenry on the state of affairs, to ask it to confirm the appointment of the committee of safety, and to authorize the members to take whatever measures they considered necessary to protect the public interest. Arrangements were made for the printing and posting of the announcement and to take care of other details of the proposed mass meeting. Colonel John H. Soper, an American citizen who had served for a time in Kalakaua's reign as marshal of the kingdom, was selected to command the military forces, and W. W. Hall, son of Edwin O. Hall, a printer and assistant secular agent of the Sandwich Islands Mission from 1835 to 1850, appointed to organize the commissary.

After adjournment, Thurston and Smith called on Stevens to inform him of the action taken. Since there was a feeling of great unrest in the community, they were uneasy. Among other things they discussed what should be done in case of their arrest or of extreme or violent measures being taken against them. The Minister indicated that he could not recognize any revolutionary government

5. Ibid.

until it was actually established, and that the United States forces, if landed, would not take sides with either party, but would protect Americans.[6]

Earlier, the committee had sent a request to the commander of the *Boston* to land troops for the preservation of public peace. They were cognizant of the fact that, according to all law and precedent, this landing could be done legally only on the request of the existing government; but having failed to utilize the Queen's cabinet for that purpose, the insurgents took matters into their own hands. No response was made to their plea, which later in the day was withdrawn. Yet, despite the withdrawal, Captain Wiltse, reportedly acting upon his sense of duty to Americans in Honolulu, concluded that troops should be landed, and made preparation for that purpose by lowering the boats, filling the cartridge belts of his men, and supplying them with the proper accouterment for a stay on shore. For the first time in the history of the tiny kingdom, preparations were made for the landing of American forces without the consent of, or even notice to, the existing government—in fact, over its vehement opposition.

On this Sabbath there was constant coming and going at the homes of Ministers Stevens, William R. Castle, Henry Waterhouse, W. W. Hall, and F. W. Wundenberg. Throughout the day, several committee members and others friendly to the cause of annexation were riding on horseback or in hacks round the city working up support. A survey of available arms and ammunition was made, and a roster of those who could rally at any moment was prepared. The *Drei Hundert,* captained by Charles W. Ziegler, offered to support the movement. The Honolulu Rifles, officially disbanded in 1890, reappeared. Actually, its members had continued to wear uniforms and carry arms in the streets of the capital under the guise of membership in the Knights of Pythias, and they had kept their arms and ammunition in readiness. Now as a crisis threatened, the Rifles was revived with some changes in personnel and with several sons and grandsons of missionaries enrolled in it. There was no dearth of either young or experienced volunteers, while arms and ammunition were in the hands of private individuals who had retained them since the revolution of 1887. Men armed themselves for mutual protection in the event of an emergency. The Reverend Oliver P.

6. Thurston, *Memoirs,* p. 252. Dole, *Memoirs,* p. 75.

Emerson was of the opinion that hundreds would have risen had there been a necessity.[7] On a day set apart for worship and solemnly observed at the islands, many business and professional gentleman and able-bodied young riflemen, despite the fact they might be mission boys, were not in their pews at church services. The proverbial ox was truly in the pit. Appropriately and characteristically, Hawaiian pastors conducted a prayer meeting at Iolani Palace for the distressed Liliuokalani. By evening the members of the committee of safety and their supporters had irrevocably determined on the dethronement of the Queen. They generally understood that in the event of their occupying the government building and proclaiming a provisional government, Minister Stevens would recognize it as the de facto government.[8]

Monday, January 16

At 9 o'clock Monday morning the committee of safety met in the office of Lorrin Thurston, upstairs over the Bishop Bank, on Kaahumanu and Merchant streets, "right under the nose of the police station," to organize and carry forward the preparations for the afternoon mass meeting. Meanwhile, the Marshal again requested authority from the cabinet to arrest the committeemen, but the inexperienced ministers were still fearful that such action would precipitate trouble and cause Stevens to land a naval force. On their suggestion, Wilson went over personally to persuade the committee to desist. When he told the group that they had gone too far, since the matter of the promulgation of the constitution was now settled and a proclamation would be issued by the Queen to that effect, Thurston responded: "I am sorry for the country, but what guaranty have we that this will not happen again? It is living on a volcano; there is no telling when it will explode." The Marshal argued that if the foreign representatives were satisfied with the proclamation, the committee of safety should be. But the adamant attorney had decided to take no further chances and "to wind affairs up now." After warning the men that they were wrong and to desist, Wilson departed, feeling that the condition of affairs would have been totally changed if he had been permitted to make the desired arrests.

7. See Hartwell to Olney, Dec. 5, 1893, Olney Papers, Vol. 12; and Emerson and Judd Statements, *Morgan Report*, pp. 183, 185, 446.

8. *House of Rep. Reps.*, 53 Cong., 2 sess., No. 234, pp. 48–49.

In his opinion, he could have completely knocked out the committee and its project to overthrow the monarchy.[1]

Shortly after Wilson's departure, Governor Archibald Cleghorn appeared. Speaking to Thurston alone in the hall, the Governor entreated him to consider the claim of Princess Kaiulani, pleading: "You can appoint a board of regents to act during her minority, and I assure you that the community will have a very different state of affairs to deal with from that which Kalakaua and Liliuokalani have presented." To this plea Thurston replied that he thought very highly of Kaiulani and that if conditions were different he would be glad to promote the suggestion, but that matters had progressed too far for Cleghorn's plan to be an adequate answer to the situation: "We are going to abrogate the Monarchy entirely, and nothing can be done to stop us, so far as I can see!" The disappointed Scotsman looked as though he were about to weep as he bowed his head and retreated down the stairway.[2]

Having heard on Sunday evening that the conspiring committee of public safety had decided to establish a provisional government, the cabinet members invited the diplomatic corps to a meeting on Monday morning to consult on the situation and to inform them of the government's intentions. Representatives of England, France, Japan, and Portugal attended. Minister Stevens declined, but this was no surprise, for it was known that his sympathies were with the revolutionists.

The Queen's ministers had decided to follow the advice of the six businessmen with whom they had conferred on Sunday. Since the stated reason for the plans to establish a provisional government was the attempt of the sovereign to violate the constitution, they would advise Her Majesty to issue the prepared proclamation, giving assurance that any changes desired in the fundamental law of the land would be sought by the methods provided in the constitution. The diplomatic corps considered this a wise procedure, which would no doubt prove satisfactory.[3] Between 11:30 A.M. and 12:30 P.M., the proclamation was printed and distributed, and assurances were sent to the foreign representatives.

1. Wilson Statement, *For. Rels.* (1894), App. II, p. 1023. Thurston, *Memoirs,* pp. 253–54.

2. Thurston, *Memoirs,* p. 255. Cleghorn, in his Diary (MS in AH) mentions going into the city in the morning, but does not give the details of what transpired on this "bad day for Hawaii."

3. Cornwell to Blount, April 24, 1893, *For. Rels.* (1894), App. II, p. 495.

The "By Authority" proclamation expressed the ministers' appreciation for the quiet and order which had prevailed since the events of Saturday, and stated "that the position taken by Her Majesty in regard to the promulgation of a new Constitution was under the stress of her native subjects." Assurance was given "that any changes desired in the fundamental law of the land will be sought only by methods provided in the Constitution itself." All citizens were requested "to accept the assurance of Her Majesty in the same spirit in which it is given." This proclamation, signed by the Queen and her four ministers, was published in an extra issue of the Hawaiian language paper *La Le o Ka Lahui,* along with a call for a public meeting of Liliuokalani's supporters for 2 P.M. in Palace Square, at which time the purposes of the Queen would be explained. It was stated in the extra that representatives of the foreign countries, except for the United States, had met and decided to support the cabinet. The annexationists were seeking some pretext to injure the Queen and to "order the American naval force on shore to protect their property without knowing what they are afraid of." The banks of Bishop and Spreckels were ready to help the government with money, and some merchants were also offering their support. Only certain missionaries were "secretly meeting and seeking a riot as a reason for landing the men of war when there is no reason." [4]

At the open-air meeting, several hundred Hawaiians and half-Hawaiians were cautioned by their leaders against any action of violence or turbulence, and urged to support the course of Her Majesty's cabinet. The Queen's proclamation was read and endorsed, and a resolution was unanimously passed, accepting as satisfactory the assurances contained in the notice and pledging the "cordial support" of the citizens to the administration. Thus, in an apparently contradictory manner, the nationalist leaders who had previously advocated and petitioned for a new constitution, now, in a moment of grave danger to the kingdom, voted an expression of thanks to their Queen for renouncing her attempt to promulgate one. [5]

In the former Rifles Armory, then serving as a skating rink, there assembled on Monday afternoon the largest meeting ever held in

---

4. Blount to Gresham, July 17, 1893, printed in *For. Rels.* (1894) in App. II, p. 582. Alexander, *Hawaiian Monarchy,* pp. 41–42. Thurston, *Memoirs,* p. 256.

5. Alexander, *Hawaiian Monarchy,* pp. 50–51.

Honolulu up to that date, with a crowd variously estimated at from twelve to fifteen hundred. A report of the committee of safety was read, narrating events since Saturday noon and containing a set of six resolutions. These condemned the action of Her Majesty Liliuo-kalani in "attempting to abrogate the existing Constitution and proclaim a new one in subversion of the rights of the people," endorsed the action taken by the committee of safety, and empowered the committee to consider "the situation and further devise such ways and means as may be necessary to secure the permanent maintenance of law and order and the protection of life, liberty and property in Hawaii."

In the course of the meeting a messenger arrived with a statement from the Queen promising that "changes in the fundamental law of the land would be sought only by methods provided in the Constitution itself." After the declaration had been made light of by Thurston, who questioned the value of Liliuokalani's word and asserted that it was "not her fault that the streets have not run red with blood," the resolutions were adopted without a dissenting vote.[6] The phrases "dethronement of Liliuokalani" and "abrogation of the Monarchy" were not publicly used at the meeting, but according to Thurston, there was a unanimous understanding that dethronement and abrogation were intended.[7]

The "unanimous understanding," however, was confined to the members of the committee of safety and their supporters; it certainly did not exist in the minds of the hundreds who were present at the mass meeting. Perhaps not fifty others understood or desired that any further steps should be taken. Many prominent citizens attended simply for the purpose of participating in a public expression of disapproval of the step which the Queen had desired to take, and believed that the matter would end there,[8] while many ordinary men went along merely for the excitement. By 4 P.M. that excitement appeared to have ended, for the people had dispersed to their homes or places of business, and normal order prevailed on the streets.[9]

Immediately following the Armory meeting, the members of the

6. Thurston, *Memoirs*, pp. 261–67. *Hawaiian Gazette, Two Weeks of Hawaiian History January 14–28*, 1893 (1st ed. Honolulu, 1893), pp. 17–26. Cf. Emerson Statement, Jones Affidavit, Alexander Statement, *Morgan Report*, pp. 185, 232, 302.

7. Thurston, *Memoirs*, p. 267. Cf. Jones Affidavit, *Morgan Report*, p. 232. This was understood the preceding Saturday.

8. Cornwell to Blount, April 24, 1893, *For. Rels.* (1894), App. II, p. 494.

9. Wilson Statement, ibid., p. 1034.

committee of safety gathered in the office of William O. Smith to consider their precarious position. Their plans were inchoate: they had no program of action to meet the Queen's government, should it move first. They lacked organized troops and even particulars as to the number of volunteers at their command. They did not know whether Minister Stevens proposed to land armed forces from the *Boston* before further action, what the government intended, and what it would do if the troops were brought ashore. According to Judge Dole and William R. Castle, the committee of safety, realizing that the community was in a state of unrest, and responding to the demands of numerous citizens who feared the burning of their property, requested the United States Minister to land troops. Castle recollects that the committee arrived at the decision on Monday forenoon.[10] He claims that the written request represented that the public safety was menaced, that lives and property were in peril, and that the "Queen with the aid of armed force, and accompanied by threats of violence and bloodshed from those with whom she was acting, attempted to proclaim a new constitution; and while prevented for the time from accomplishing her object declared publicly that she would only defer her action." Such circumstances "created general alarm and terror." The committee averred: "We are unable to protect ourselves without aid and therefore pray for the protection of the United States forces." Signed by all the members of the committee of safety, the appeal was delivered to Minister Stevens by Castle and Thurston after the mass meeting.[11]

Quite a different and conflicting report is given by Lorrin Thurston, who states that, after the action taken at the mass meeting, time for thought and planning was "overwhelmingly essential." Since a landing of troops might have precipitated action by the government before the committee of safety had evolved a plan, he and Smith waited upon the United States Minister immediately to urge him to delay the landing of troops, if he had this in view. They called at his residence and were informed that he had gone aboard the *Boston*. After he returned and was told of the visitors' mission, Mr. Stevens replied:

> I do not know what your plans are, gentlemen, and I cannot afford to take chances to find out what the plans of the govern-

10. Dole, *Memoirs*, pp. 75–76. Castle Affidavit, *Morgan Report*, p. 586.
11. Citizens Committee of Safety to Stevens, Jan. 16, 1893, *For. Rels.* (1894), App. II, p. 501.

ment may be. The conditions are so serious, and the possibilities of trouble so great, that it is my duty to protect the lives and property of American citizens with every available means within my power; and I am going to land American troops immediately for that purpose. I have already given orders to that effect, and it will not be long before the troops are ashore. That's all I have to say.[12]

The note which the Minister addressed to Captain Wiltse reads as follows: "In view of the existing critical circumstances in Honolulu, including an inadequate legal force, I request you to land marines and sailors from the ship under your command for the protection of the United States legation and United States consulate, and to secure the safety of American life and property." [13]

Lieutenant Young, of the *Boston*, gave yet another version of the decision and order to land forces. According to him, Captain Wiltse on Sunday came to the conclusion that troops should be landed, and acting on his own authority, made preliminary preparation for such. At about 10:30 A.M. on Monday, convinced that the Queen's government could not under any circumstances protect life and property, he decided he would have to order his men ashore. He informed Lieutenant Young that he was acting under instructions from the Navy Department and from Admiral Brown of San Francisco, then commanding the Pacific squadron. The gist of those instructions was that "you will use every means and endeavor to act in concert with the minister to preserve and protect our treaty rights with the Sandwich Islands, even if necessary to use force." When, at three o'clock, Minister Stevens came aboard the *Boston* to consult with Wiltse, the Captain remarked that he had already decided to land troops, that they were all ready, and that they would go ashore at four o'clock. When asked by one of his officers what should be done in case the troops should be attacked by one of the contending parties, the Commander replied: "The situation is such that it will require a great deal of judgment on the part of you officers who are going ashore; you have been here a number of months, and know all the Americans and their property; that is what I want you to protect, and I want you to be careful and remain as neutral as you can." Stevens then made the comment: "I am very glad you are

12. Thurston, *Memoirs*, pp. 268–69.
13. Stevens to Wiltse, Jan. 16, 1893, encl. in Stevens to Foster, Jan. 18, 1893, No. 79, printed in *For. Rels.* (1894), App. II, p. 208.

177

going to land them, because I think it is absolutely necessary." [14]

Regardless of who made the ultimate decision to land troops, three companies of bluejackets, one of artillery, and one of marines, making a total of 154, along with ten officers, proceeded ashore. Two Gatling guns and two .37 revolving cannons, as well as a hospital unit, accompanied them. The men were armed and equipped for heavy marching order, with knapsacks and double belts of cartridges holding from sixty to eighty rounds. Lieutenant Young had the caisson filled, taking in all about 14,000 rounds of caliber .45 for the rifle and Gatling, 1200 rounds of caliber .38 for the revolvers, and 174 common explosive shells for the revolving cannon.

Once landed, the force formed in a body immediately, with the artillery in the rear. Lieutenant Commander Swinburne was in command. From Brewer and Company's and Charlton's wharf, the troops marched up to the corner of Fort and Merchant streets, where a marine company was left to protect the American legation and consulate. The rest of the battalions turned and marched down King Street. As they passed Iolani Palace, where Queen Liliuokalani was standing on the balcony, they gave her the royal salute, with a drooping of the colors and four ruffles on the drums. They marched beyond the palace 250 yards, and there halted in front of Hopper's residence, on the south corner of the palace enclosure, in full view of the Queen, until they could find some place to bivouac. An effort was made first to get the old armory near the wharf, so as to be close to their base of supplies, but this building had been engaged for the volunteer riflemen. Swinburne then tried to secure the Opera House. These were the only two empty buildings near the center of the town, and failing to get either one the men marched about six hundred yards further out King Street to the property of Joseph B. Atherton, president of the firm of Castle and Cooke, where they were served lemonade and bananas, and bivouacked under the trees in the rain until about 9:30 P.M.[15] Then they obtained Arion Hall, a low wooden building in the rear of the Opera House but not more than two hundred yards in front of Iolani Palace, and separated from the government building by a strip of land about twenty feet wide. This became Camp Boston. Later Cornwell commented: "If the troops were landed solely for the protection of American property, the placing of them so far away from the center of the

14. *Morgan Report*, pp. 333–34, 336, 368.
15. Ibid., pp. 335–36.

property of Americans and so very close to the property of the Hawaiian Government was remarkable and very suggestive." In a similar vein Admiral J. S. Skerrett observed: "The American troops were well located if designed to promote the movement for the Provisional Government and very improperly located if only intended to protect American citizens in person and property." [16] On the other hand, Chief Justice Alfred F. Judd contended that Arion Hall did not command the palace, the government building, or the barracks. It was the only place convenient for men to sleep in that was then available. In his mind the location was not "significant of any intention on the part of the United States troops to defend any uprising against the Queen's Government." [17]

As these forces marched through the streets of Honolulu, they encountered not a single policeman or guard; the former, numbering eighty, in the command of Marshal Wilson, were safe in the station house; the latter, numbering about sixty, remained inactive in their barracks, hesitating to come out for fear of precipitating bloodshed. No one was in the streets to protect life or property.

Immediately after the force began to land, Parker, Colburn, and Cleghorn drove in haste to Stevens' residence, where the first-named gentleman informed the United States Minister that the Hawaiian government was in a position to offer protection to everyone and to suppress any rebellion. Stevens rejoined that he could not help the matter of landing, and that since the troops were ashore, they would remain ashore. Colburn asked Stevens if he intended to annex the country, to which the latter replied No, and further stated that the troops were ashore "to preserve the Queen on her throne, you gentlemen in your offices, and to offer protection to the community at large." The ministers again emphasized that they did not want the troops ashore, and that they themselves could preserve law and order. Stevens concluded the conference by saying: "Make your protest in writing and if you make it in a friendly spirit I will answer in the same tone." [18]

The protest was immediately forthcoming. Minister Stevens ac-

16. *For. Rels.* (1894), App. II, pp. 495, 585. Cf. Liliuokalani, *Hawaii's Story*, p. 386.

17. *Morgan Report*, p. 445. The marines remained in Arion Hall for two days and then moved 300 yards to the old Bishop Building on King St.

18. *For. Rels.* (1894), App. II, pp. 495, 500. See above, p. 89, for the customary procedure for the landing of forces from a national vessel. Cleghorn, in his Diary, Jan. 16, 1893, mentions his presence with the ministers; he also called on the British and French commissioners.

knowledged it the following day and at the same time gave assurance that "in whatever the United States diplomatic representatives have done or may do at this critical hour of Hawaiian affairs, we shall be guided by the kindest feelings and views for all the parties concerned, and by the warmest sentiments from the Hawaiian people and the persons of all nationalities." [19]

Governor Cleghorn also solemnly protested, in writing, the landing of an armed force without permission, and reminded Stevens that when he had desired to land naval forces for drill, permission by the local authorities had been readily accorded. On this occasion the circumstances were different: "ostensibly the present landing is for the discharge of functions which are distinctly responsible duties of the Hawaiian Government." Such being the case, the Governor felt compelled to impress upon the Minister "the international question involved in the matter and the grave responsibility thereby assumed." In his reply to this protest, Stevens assured Cleghorn "that in whatever responsibility the American diplomatic and naval representatives have assumed or may assume, we shall do our utmost to regard the welfare of all present and interests concerned." [20]

In a desperate effort to inform the world of her plight, Queen Liliuokalani and her ministers prepared an account of the situation in Honolulu and, through the British consul, sent it on the S.S. *Alameda* leaving for Auckland and Sydney in the evening, to be cabled to the foreign office on the steamer's arrival in New Zealand.

That same Monday evening the committee of safety offered John H. Soper, a former marshal of the kingdom, the command of the forces supporting the movement, which reportedly he accepted only after assurances from committee members and Stevens that troops from the *Boston* could be counted upon to bolster the provisional government after its installation in the government building.[21]

Early in the evening Bolte called at Dole's home and apprised him of the committee's wish to have him lead the scheme to suppress the monarchy and organize a new government. The judge declined and suggested that Thurston was the logical man for the

19. Stevens to Parker, Jan. 17, 1893, AH, U.S. Minister and Consuls.

20. Cleghorn to Stevens, Jan. 16, 1893, and Stevens to Cleghorn, Jan. 17, 1893, *For. Rels.* (1894), App. II, p. 1038.

21. For these conflicting assertions see A Report from Wundenburg to Blount, encl. No. 4 in Blount to Gresham, April 26, 1893, *For. Rels.* (1894), App. II, p. 493, No. 2; ibid., p. 584; Committee of Safety, 1893, Jan. 16, 1893, Thurston Papers; Affidavit of J. H. Soper, *Morgan Report,* pp. 450–51.

position, to which Bolte replied that Thurston was "sick abed." Weakened by a previous bout of grippe and continuous pressure, he had gone home and collapsed. On Bolte's suggestion, Dole attended the meeting to hear what the committee had to say, and discovered that the gathering was unanimously in favor of setting aside the monarchy, with the view of eventual annexation to the United States. When the Hawaiian-born justice suggested, instead of their proposal, that Liliuokalani be deposed, that they hold the power of the throne in a trust, and that a regency be established to govern until the Princess Kaiulani reached her majority, the committee of safety informed him very positively that they were unanimous in the opinion that no more trial should be accorded the Kalakaua family and that as his suggestion was wholly impractical, it would receive no support. They were definitely bent upon the extirpation of the monarch and determined to carry through a genuine revolution, for they understood clearly that Washington would not consent to annexation so long as the existing monarchy was opposed to union. After some further discussion, Judge Dole informed the gathering that he would consider the proposition overnight and deliver his decision to the executive council.[22]

The night of January 16–17, 1893, was a tense one in Honolulu. The Queen's Household Guards stood to arms at their barracks and in the palace grounds, the police barricaded their station and set up two Gatling guns; and the revolutionary volunteers mustered at three rendezvous, with their sentries alert. Since rumors floated that the royalists were plotting to burn the houses of the insurgent leaders and set fire to the business quarter, fire patrols marched through the street all night. Women and children were taken to Waikiki for safety. After the American troops went into Camp Boston, they sent out a grand guard—a company in one direction and then in another—for the purpose of seeing that American property was not molested, and also to prevent any incendiarism. Swinburne, however, dispatched no separate patrol and posted no sentinels over the city or the buildings. Although two fires occurred, the night passed without fighting. The training in discipline and forbearance, for which the missionary teachers were chiefly responsible, paid handsome dividends in the orderliness displayed by native Hawaiians at this most unhappy period in their history.

22. Dole to his brother George H. Dole, Jan. 19, 1893, Letters of Sanford Ballard Dole to George H. Dole, 1859–1912, Robert E. Van Dyke Foundation, Honolulu. Dole, *Memoirs*, p. 77.

Tuesday, January 17

During the night Judge Dole reflected on the proposal to head the revolutionary government, and after calling on several friends early the next morning, all of whom favored the proposition, he returned home to breakfast, disposed to accept the assignment of the committee of safety and anticipating the establishment of a new government and annexation to the United States within a few months.

Sanford Ballard Dole's adhesion added tremendously to the prestige of the committee. He had never before favored annexation; now, with the deepest regret and in the firm conviction that there was no other method of securing peace and safety to life and property in the islands, combined with a sense of duty, he accepted the position of president of the provisional government.[1] Dole had gained valuable experience as a member of the legislatures of 1884 and 1886, where he was one of the most vocal leaders of the opposition to Walter Murray Gibson's extravagance and corruption. After the revolution of 1887, he had been appointed an associate justice of the supreme court, which position he held with great credit until his resignation on the morning of January 17, 1893. Although not a director or part owner of a corporation or as affluent as most of his associates—in 1892 he paid taxes amounting to $6.00—S. B. Dole was a polished gentleman of commanding mien and was recognized as one of the leaders of thought and progress in Hawaii.

Also of inestimable value was the cooperation of wealthy Peter C. Jones, but it was not easily secured. Early that Tuesday morning the financier was alerted by Charles L. Carter that he and Bolte would call after breakfast to extend an invitation to join the executive council of the provisional government to be established that afternoon. Jones informed Carter that he was not fitted for such a position; that his experience in government had made him "heartily sick of politics"; that joining the council might look as though he was going in for revenge for the fall of the Wilcox cabinet; and that he could see no reason why he should accept the position.[2] The fifty-four-year-old man also feared that "there was great danger to his life," and this anxiety grew upon him during the day. Since he had

1. Dole, pp. 77–78. Theo. H. Davies, in a letter to the *Times*, published on Jan. 30, 1893, referred to Dole's "unimpeachable character" and stated that his appointment "is a guarantee of the integrity with which the crisis would be met."

2. Jones Statement, *Morgan Report*, p. 202.

retired from active business two years before, he wished to live the remainder of his life in peaceful enjoyment of his possessions. But the pressure from business associates, friends, and his wife, who argued that he owed a duty to the country in which he had accumulated his wealth, finally led him to take the position of minister of finance in the provisional government, provided Dole accepted the presidency.[3]

Meanwhile, Justice Dole and Captain J. A. King, of the Rifles, assembled in Smith's office with the members of the committee of safety—except for the incapacitated Castle[4] and Thurston—and listened to the reading of the proclamation abrogating the monarchy and establishing a provisional government, which document had been drafted and dictated that morning by the bedridden Thurston from copies of a declaration found in a book describing the French Revolution.[5] Jones was informed of Dole's decision and invited to join the party in the afternoon. This enlarged group, now consisting of an executive council of four members and an advisory council of fourteen, arranged to reassemble at 1 P.M. in Smith's office preparatory to taking over *Aliiolani Hale*, the seat of the government, at three o'clock. Captain King hastened off to alert the volunteer riflemen and to brief them on their afternoon assignment.

Another valuable addition to the advisory council was the able financier Samuel M. Damon, who had previously served as Kalakaua's and Liliuokalani's minister of finance. At nine o'clock that Tuesday morning he called at the palace and informed the Queen that he had been invited to join a revolutionary council, but that he had declined. He asked Her Majesty what he should do, whether he should join the advisory or the executive council, suggesting that perhaps he might be of service to her; she advised him to be-

3. *Morning Call*, Jan. 29, 1893. Nellist, *Story of Hawaii*, pp. 129–30. The similarity to Robert Morris, financier of the American Revolution, is notable. See Frank Gaylord Cook, "Robert Morris," *Atlantic Monthly*, 66 (1890), 607–10, 617–18. Jones was the older man, being fifty-four in 1893, while Morris was only forty-two at the beginning of the American Revolution.

4. The exhausted Castle was stricken with an asthmatic attack. The reader should bear in mind that both Thurston and Castle, born in the kingdom, were Hawaiians subject to arrest for treason. Consequently, to remain housebound was good for their health. On Thurston's fears for his safety see his *Memoirs*, pp. 252–54, and *Morgan Report*, p. 369. Without the aid of antibiotics, both men somehow recovered speedily and were able to set out on the long wintry journey to Washington on January 19.

5. Thurston, *Memoirs*, p. 129.

come a member of the former group, having no idea that they intended to establish a new government.[6]

As arranged, the members of the executive and advisory councils reassembled as Smith's office after lunch, completed the organization of the provisional government, reread and signed the proclamation, and were generally nervous and fidgety awaiting the appointed hour to divide into groups and take different routes for the hazardous walk from Fort Street to the government offices in Aliiolani Hale. A supporter was sent over to the building to ascertain who was there, and returned with the information that no government forces were on the grounds. In the meantime, the collection of arms and the registration of volunteers proceeded. Marshal Wilson, aware of these developments, made plans to guard the government building, and posted police across the street from the Opera House to arrest Dole and the council members when they should emerge from Smith's office.

At about one o'clock Parker and Peterson called on Minister Stevens and were informed that in the event the Queen's troops assailed the insurrectionary forces he would intervene.[7] During that Tuesday afternoon there were rumors frequently repeated on the streets that a move for deposing the Queen would be made during the day, and that "it was all right, as Stevens had promised to support the movement."[8] Cleghorn reports that Joseph Marsden, an influential Englishman, suggested that the Queen abdicate in favor of Kaiulani.[9]

Just before 2:30 P.M., a wagon left E. O. Hall and Son Hardware Store with munitions for the insurgents, and the deputy marshal sent a squad of Hawaiian policemen to stop it. Captain John Good, chief of ordnance for the provisional government, who was convoying the wagon, drew his revolver and shot the foremost officer, one Leleialoha, in the shoulder, whereupon the driver lashed his horse and the vehicle dashed away. The resulting commotion attracted the police who had been guarding Smith's office and also served as a magnet drawing into King Street toward Fort a crowd of about one hundred Hawaiians who had gathered on the steps of the Opera House. In the midst of this fortuitous confusion the committeemen started their precarious journey before the appointed hour. They

6. Liliuokalani, *Hawaii's Story*, pp. 386–87.
7. *For. Rels.* (1894), App. II, p. 585.
8. Statement of Charles T. Gulick, ibid., p. 819.
9. Cleghorn Diary, Jan. 17, 1893.

proceeded from Fort Street to Merchant Street toward the government building. Some took a different route up Queen Street. Preceding them, Charles L. Carter rode hastily on horseback to Arion Hall and delivered a letter to Captain Wiltse, who was himself in charge of the American troops on this crucial day. The latter read the communication, nodding his satisfaction to the bearer, who then withdrew.[10]

On arriving at the government building some twenty minutes ahead of schedule, the council members found only one of their volunteer riflemen in the corridor, along with Charles J. McCarthy, a man of military experience and a former clerk of the legislature, who had spent Monday night in the building waiting in vain for a government force of fifty to one hundred. The ministers were at the police station, and only eight clerks, too startled to offer any resistance, were in the offices. When the council demanded possession of the building from the chief clerk of the interior office, he gave it up politely. From the steps of the building, Attorney Henry E. Cooper, designated vice-president of the provisional government, read the proclamation in the presence of the members of the councils, the clerks, and one Hawaiian member of the legislature.[11]

This proclamation of the "citizens and residents of the Hawaiian Islands, organized and acting for the public safety and the common good," declared that "representative and responsible government, able to protect itself from revolutionary uprisings and royal aggression, is no longer possible in Hawaii under the existing system of Government." Five uprisings or conspiracies had occurred in five years and seven months; the culminating revolutionary attempt of the preceding Saturday would, unless radical measures were taken, "wreck our already damaged credit abroad and precipitate to final ruin our already overstrained financial condition, and the guarantees of protection to life, liberty, and property will steadily decrease and the political situation rapidly grow worse." In the firm belief that the action taken would be "for the best personal, political and property interests of every citizen of the land," the Hawaiian monarchy was abrogated and a provisional government established "to exist until terms of union with the United States of America have been negotiated and agreed upon."

The provisional government was to consist of an executive council of four members, who were declared to be Sanford B. Dole, James

10. *For. Rels.* (1894), App. II, p. 495. Liliuokalani, pp. 386–89.
11. Dole, *Memoirs,* pp. 77, 81. Judd Statement, *Morgan Report,* p. 446.

A. King, Peter C. Jones, and William O. Smith, and who should administer the executive departments of the government, "the first named acting as president and chairman of such council and administering the department of foreign affairs, and the others severally administering the departments of interior, finance, and attorney general respectively," and also of an advisory council, which was to consist of fourteen members. Ten of the officers of the provisional government were drawn from the committee of safety, which in turn was composed of the members of the Annexation Club. The advisory council was to have general legislative authority. The executive and advisory councils, acting jointly, were empowered to remove any member of either council and to fill such or any other vacancy.

With the exception of Queen Liliuokalani, the members of her cabinet, and Charles B. Wilson, all officers under the previous government were requested to continue the exercise of their functions and to perform the duties of their respective offices. All Hawaiian laws and constitutional principles not inconsistent with the proclamation were to continue in force until further order of the executive and advisory councils.[12]

During the reading of the proclamation, which ceremony was completed at 2:45, one rifleman was standing in the corridor, a group of spectators gathered, and soon thereafter volunteers arrived, some straggling in and some in formation. The first body of riflemen to march up double-quick was Company A, the *Drei Hundert*, numbering forty to sixty men, under Captain Zeigler. Company B, composed of Americans and Englishmen, soon reached the enclosure, cleared the grounds of spectators, and set guards at the gates. In less than half an hour one hundred riflemen were drawn up in front of the building, awaiting orders. An hour later, an estimated two hundred were present, nearly all of whom had assisted in breaking up the 1889 conspiracy.[13] Thus the provisional government was duly and securely installed in the official headquarters.

The phenomenal success of this nearly bloodless coup was prob-

12. *For. Rels.* (1894), App. II, pp. 388–90. Dole, *Memoirs*, pp. 83–87.

13. Alexander and Emmeluth Statements, *Morgan Report*, pp. 298, 455. After the *coup d'état*, there were conflicting reports of the order of the companies' arrival at the scene, as Americans wanted to claim credit for being there first. Most documentary evidence supports the above statements. There is also some testimony to the effect that no forces reached the government building until nearly a half hour after the appearance of the officials of the provisional government.

ably due to one revolver shot and a twenty minute to a half-hour difference in timing. Had the shot not been fired down at Hall's Hardware, the police would have been on hand to seize the committee members as they emerged from Smith's office.[14] Had the revolutionists waited until 3 o'clock, the Queen's guards might have been at the office building, although on this latter supposition there is some doubt. The over-all controlling factor in the situation was the presence of United States marines, drawn up under arms and with artillery in readiness only seventy-six yards from the government building.[15] Yet, these forces were not actually used to assist in the overthrow of the Queen or in the establishment of the provisional government.[16]

The seizure of this key structure was significant and necessarily the first step in the revolution; it was required for Stevens' recognition of the provisional government as de facto. Aliiolani Hale had always been considered as the visible seat of government. Together with the two smaller attached buildings, it contained all the offices of the departments of government, the chambers of the supreme court and the court of records, the land office, the registry of conveyances, the government archives, and the treasury. The Queen's cause was weakened initially by the action of her cabinet in abandoning their offices and seeking refuge in the police station.

W. H. Cornwell explained that the ministers had decided not to place guards in the government building, "as the immediate vicinity of the United States troops would endanger the lives of the men from the *Boston* in case of a conflict with the rebels, and the Government desired, at all hazards, to avoid giving Minister Stevens any excuse or pretense for his hostile actions." [17]

14. Later $200 was contributed by the grateful citizens of Honolulu and the purse was sent through S. B. Dole, not to Leleialoha, the victim of the incident, but to Capt. John Good, who fired the decisive shot (San Francisco *Morning Call*, Jan. 29, 1893). Good was officially exonerated for his act and named captain in the new provisional government army (AH, Proceedings of the Executive and Advisory Councils of the Provisional Government, pp. 36–37).

15. Cleveland's Special Message, Dec. 18, 1893, in James D. Richardson, ed., *A Compilation of the Messages and Papers of the President* (10 vols. Washington, 1896–99), 9, 467. Cf. *For. Rels.* (1894), App. II, p. 585.

16. The annexationists persistently emphasized this fact. See Committee of Safety, 1893, Jan. 16, 1893, Thurston Papers. *Morgan Report*, pp. 276, 444, 455. The annexationist press always maintained that U.S. troops were used only to protect the interests of American citizens.

17. *For. Rels.* (1894), App. II, p. 495.

Marshal Wilson wanted to fight to dislodge the intruders. He proposed to bombard the rebels from the palace roof opposite the government building and enfilade with Gatling guns the streets approaching Palace Square. But Queen Liliuokalani was confused, her ministers were in disagreement and in panic, and the royalist volunteers who thronged into the police station were unarmed, frightened, and disorganized.

After securing possession of Aliiolani Hale, the executive council assembled, officially appointed Colonel John Soper as commander of the provisional government forces, and attended to other matters that required prompt attention, such as notifying the diplomatic corps of the existence of the new regime. This duty was facilitated by the presence in the building of a few experienced secretaries, and especially of Frank P. Hastings, first assistant in the Foreign Office, and Prince David Kawananakoa, who were immediately employed by the new government.[18] The writ of habeas corpus was suspended and martial law proclaimed until further notice. All saloons were closed, and all citizens were expected to be off the streets after 9:30 P.M.

A short time after the reading of the proclamation, Lieutenant Young was sent over to the government building with a message from Captain Wiltse, extending his compliments to President Dole and inquiring if he had absolute control of the government, police force, and guard; if he did not, Captain Wiltse could not recognize him. Dole responded: "We have not control of the military forces and police, but we have a sufficient force to maintain us," to which Young replied: "If you have not charge of the Government, I am requested to inform you that we can have nothing to do with You." [19]

President Dole immediately directed to Minister Stevens a note announcing the action taken and suggesting the cooperation of United States troops with the citizen volunteers in maintaining order during the night, which request was refused. The President also sent a message to Swinburne, who commanded the troops near the Opera House, asking him to come over to the government building. Instead, Captain Wiltse called and refused Dole's oral request for assistance from American forces. Moreover, he asserted that the provisional government could not be recognized as a de facto gov-

18. Dole, *Memoirs*, pp. 82–83. "The Passing of 'Hawaii's Grand Old Man,'" *Paradise of the Pacific* (Honolulu), 39 (1926), 12.

19. *Morgan Report*, p. 345.

ernment until it had possession of the police station and the army barracks.[20]

Fifteen minutes after the reading of the proclamation, James S. Walker, president of the legislative assembly, called at the palace with the painful duty of apprising the Queen that the opposition party had requested that she abdicate. Liliuokalani informed him that she had no idea of doing so and that she would like to see Paul Neumann.[21] As soon as her ministers received information that a provisional government had been established, they dispatched a letter from the station house to Minister Stevens inquiring whether he had recognized the new government and requesting the assistance of the United States government in maintaining the peace of the country. After asking for an immediate reply and waiting an hour for it, a letter was handed to Noble Charles L. Hopkins, who served as courier, stating that Stevens had "recognized the Provisional Government because they were in possession of the Government building and he intended to support them." The letter reached the ministers at five minutes to four.[22] Thus the United States minister recognized the provisional government before the chief defense points of the Queen—the station house and the barracks—had surrendered. They would not have capitulated but for that recognition.[23]

Thereafter, Samuel M. Damon and C. Bolte, members of the advisory council, went to the police station and officially informed the Queen's ministers of the proclamation and asked for the delivery of the station house, Damon emphasizing that, since the provisional government had been recognized by the United States minister, any struggle would cause useless bloodshed.

After considerable conferring between the two factions in Dole's office at the government building, and a long discussion between the Queen and her friends, it was agreed that the monarch should surrender under protest pending a settlement in Washington, during which period, Damon said, it was understood that she would remain at the palace and continue to fly the royal standard. On this condition she agreed to concede her authority.[24]

20. Dole, *Memoirs*, pp. 83–84. *Morgan Report*, pp. 261, 229, 345.

21. Liliuokalani, *Hawaii's Story*, p. 387.

22. *For. Rels.* (1894), App. II, pp. 495, 500–01; Parker's and Stevens' letters are printed ibid., p. 589. For an annexationist's view of the nature of de facto recognition, see Statement of John L. Stevens, *Morgan Report*, pp. 478–79.

23. Blount to Gresham, May 4, 1893, *For. Rels.* (1894), App. II, pp. 502–03, No. 4. Cf. ibid., p. 590.

24. Ibid., pp. 495, 501, 739, 769. Liliuokalani, pp. 387–88.

Thus Liliuokalani resorted to the "life-of-the-land" policy of her predecessors in earlier periods of stress during which the sovereignty of the kingdom was in jeopardy, and yielded "to the superior force of the United States," who minister had caused "troops to be landed at Honolulu, and declared that he would support said Provisional Government." The suddenness of the landing and Stevens' speedy recognition of the new government suggested that the President of the United States had no knowledge of these occurrences, and must know of and approve or disapprove of what had transpired. The royal protest concluded: "Now, to avoid any collision of armed forces and perhaps the loss of life, I do, under this protest, and impelled by said forces, yield my authority until such time as the Government of the United States shall, upon the facts being presented to it, undo the action of its representatives and reinstate me in the authority which I claim as the constitutional sovereign of the Hawaiian Islands." [25]

Samuel Damon and the defunct cabinet returned to Aliiolani Hale and presented the Queen's protest to President Dole, who endorsed the same. This was about 7 P.M., or approximately three hours after Minister Stevens had acknowledged that he recognized the provisional government. Marshal Wilson, however, was not prepared to surrender without an order from the Queen. This official order, signed by Liliuokalani and her ministers, directing the Marshal to surrender the police station, the barracks, Oahu Prison, and all government property in his possession or under his control, was forthcoming at about 8 P.M.[26] Meanwhile, Colonel Soper sent squads of the volunteer corps into the suburbs to patrol the residential areas. American troops remained at their posts or in Camp Boston. In this somber setting an historic day drew to a close. To the credit of native Hawaiians, the night of January 17–18, 1893, passed without any disturbance in Honolulu. Exhausted men, who during the afternoon had borne heavy responsibilities, made historic decisions, and risked their lives, went home at about ten and slept safely, if not soundly. There was profound thankfulness that the blow had not cost a single life. There was no feeling of bitterness toward Hawaiians, and none would have regretted the shedding of native blood more sincerely than those mission boys and Hawaiian-Americans who had played and grown up with the islanders.[27] The members

25. Ibid., *Blount Report,* p. 120. *For. Rels.* (1894), App. II, p. 586.
26. Wilson Statement, *For. Rels.* (1894), App. II, p. 1039.
27. *Morgan Report,* p. 259. *Pacific Commercial Advertiser,* Jan. 19, 1893.

of the provisional government were surprised to see how quickly and quietly the opposition yielded, and considered this as "an evidence of the rottenness of the monarchy which fell as soon as any resistance was made." [28]

The Aftermath

The morning after the revolution, all was quiet in the Hawaiian capital. At 10 A.M., Queen Liliuokalani voluntarily retired to Washington Place, her private residence. Thus the palace, government building, police station, army barracks, all public buildings, and the entire city with all the government stores and ammunition were in the hands of the provisional government, which was completely master of the situation. Official recognition of that government had been received from representatives of the United States, the Netherlands, Sweden, Germany, Austria, Hungary, Belgium, Russia, and China. Of the leading powers, only Great Britain and Japan had not responded. Hastily prepared petitions were circulated by the annexationists among the Hawaiians directed to President Harrison, asking the United States to annex the islands and thus end the people's troubles, or *pilikias*, as they called them. Women and children returned home from Waikiki and some ladies drove about the streets of Honolulu in their carriages.

Editorially, the *Pacific Commercial Advertiser* maintained that there was only one government—the provisional government, which did not and could not acknowledge the claim of any aspirant to a throne which no longer existed: "All sovereigns abdicate under protest; and there is no ground for interfering with their enjoyment of so empty a luxury." The existing government did not derive its title from any abdication, whether made with a protest or without. Legally speaking, its authority came from the fact that it was *de jure* because is was the only *de facto* government.[1]

Wodehouse, sent for by the Queen, agreed to transmit a letter to Her Majesty Queen Victoria. Liliuokalani expressed the wish that the reply be directed to Sir Julian Pauncefote in Washington, so

28. Thurston, *Memoirs*, pp. 270, 276. *Morgan Report*, pp. 203, 333, 343.
1. *Pacific Commercial Advertiser*, Jan. 20, 1893.
2. Wodehouse to Rosebery (telegram), Jan. 18, 1893, FO 58/279. Liliuokalani's letter, ibid. This communication was returned by Queen Victoria to the foreign office without comment; thus it became a problem for that office to handle diplomatically. See my "Great Britain and the Sovereignty of Hawaii," *Pacific Historical Review*, 31 (1962), 342.

that her confidential agent, Paul Neumann, who was leaving for that city, might become acquainted with its contents there.

A special committee of five members—composed of four Americans (Lorrin A. Thurston, William R. Castle, William C. Wilder, and Charles L. Carter) and of Joseph Marsden, considered one of the most representative and influential Englishmen in the islands—was designated to journey to Washington to negotiate a treaty of annexation. This procedure was almost identical with that described by Thurston in his annexation memorandum seven months before as one of the several possible alternatives in case such a project should prove desirable.

On Thursday, January 19, Major Wodehouse informed the executive council that he recognized the provisional government as the existing de facto government pending instructions from London.[3] That morning the commissioners embarked for San Francisco on the *Claudine*, of the Wilder Steamship Company, expecting to reach that port in eight days—before, it was hoped, the *Alameda* arrived in Auckland. They refused to allow a representative of Liliuokalani to travel to San Francisco with them, later justifying their action by stating that there were at least two other inter-island steamers quite as capable of making the trip to the mainland and that there was no reason why the Queen should not have chartered a steamer for her own envoy. As they allowed her mail to be sent by the chartered steamer, they saw no reason for financially assisting her in dispatching to Washington an agent hostile to the provisional government and its objects.[4]

The deposed Queen, in letters forwarded on the *Claudine*, appealed to both President Benjamin Harrison and President-elect Grover Cleveland, requesting the former to reach no conclusions and to take no step "until my cause can be heard by you," and informing him of her intention to dispatch an envoy and in due time a statement of facts relating to the revolution. She explained that her submission to force was prompted by three reasons: "the futility of a conflict with the United States, the desire to avoid violence and

3. On Feb. 10 Lord Rosebery telegraphed approval of this recognition and stated that it was not "desirable to send a man of war unless there is real risk to British life and property, which at present I cannot see" (FO draft telegram to Wodehouse, Feb. 10, 1893, FO 58/279).

4. The Commissioners of the Hawaiian Provisional Government to Foster, Feb. 11, 1893, *For. Rels.* (1894), App. II, pp. 236–38. *Morning Call*, Jan. 29, 1893.

bloodshed and the destruction of life and property, and the certainty which I feel that your government will right whatever wrongs may have been inflicted upon us in the premises." Lilioukalani felt comforted to have the boon of Cleveland's "personal friendship and good will," and begged him to give his "friendly assistance in granting redress for a wrong which we claim has been done to us, under color of the assistance of the naval forces, of the United States, in a friendly port." She left her grievances in his hands, confident of his sympathy and aid.[5]

On the day before the departure of the *Claudine*, the provisional government adopted an order to disband the Household Guards and paid the members until February 1. Liliuokalani, who was provided with an honorary guard of sixteen men, hoisted her royal standard the following morning, but as she was notified to pull it down, she did so herself, weeping bitterly. Sanford Dole regretted the whole affair and the path that the nation had taken. If his views had prevailed, he would have employed far more tactful ways than the treatment rendered. But he trusted "that history will bear with us and not be critical for we have done what we know to be right and we are but men and I but one, and just an opinion, against the destiny of a nation." [6]

5. Liliuokalani, *Hawaii's Story*, pp. 388–90. *For. Rels.* (1894), App. II, pp. 219–20, 1278. Cleveland Papers, 2d ser. Vol. 250. Library of Congress. On Jan. 31 Paul Neumann, with Prince David Kawananakoa and E. C. Macfarlane, left for Washington to negotiate for the restoration of the Queen and, failing that, to get the best financial consideration for her and Kaiulani (Liliuokalani, p. 390).

6. Dole to George H. Dole, Jan. 19, 1893, Letters of S. B. Dole to G. H. Dole, 1859–1912.

AMERICAN REACTION

In the absence of cable connections between Hawaii and California, the utmost haste was required if the provisional government's commissioners were to reach San Francisco and break the news of the momentous events in Honolulu in a form advantageous to the revolutionists in advance of the *Alameda's* arrival in New Zealand.

The *Claudine*, one of the staunchest vessels of the Wilder Steamship Company built for and used in the inter-island trade,[1] was chartered for the journey at $300 per day until return. She beat the record by short distance from Honolulu to San Francisco, making the total run of 2,002 miles in eight days and sixteen hours steaming time, averaging 202 to 253 miles daily[2] Between games of cribbage, the commissioners worked on the draft of a treaty of annexation, news releases for the mainland press, and letters to prominent friends and acquaintances in the States. Arriving off the Golden Gate on Friday night, January 27, the *Claudine* took on a surprised pilot at 10:15 P.M. and anchored off the Presidio at 2 o'clock. Thurston, vio-

1. The *Claudine* was built by Napier, Shanks, and Belt at Glasgow, in 1890; she was 785 tons reg., her length 184 ft., beam 32, depth of hold 15.9 (San Francisco *Morning Call*, Jan. 30, 1893).

2. W. R. Castle, Diary (Jan. 19, 1893), pp. 1, 40, transcript copy University of Hawaii Library. The letter of J. R. Macaulay, the *Claudine's* chief officer, to Castle, Sept. 10, 1917, differs somewhat in facts from the article in the *Call*. The *Claudine* steamed homeward on Feb. 2, 1893.

lating the regulations of the port, went ashore with a customs officer at 3 A.M. and proceeded at once to the *Examiner,* while a messenger took dispatches to the *Morning Call* and the *Chronicle.* Advance telephone calls stopped the presses, with the result that these three newspapers, off the press just a little late, were able to break the sensational news of the Hawaiian revolution on the morning of Saturday, January 28, 1893.[3]

In an effort to inform and gain the support of all California newspapers and leading business interests, the commissioners spent Saturday and Sunday in press conferences, in offices of editors and business executives, in meetings with interested and concerned groups, and in otherwise disseminating information on the causes of and justification for the revolution and the legality of the existing provisional government. Of assistance in this task were W. H. Dimond, who was with the commissioners "heart and soul," Claus Spreckels, the "Sugar King," proprietor of the *Morning Call* and the *Examiner,* and his sons, Gus S. and John D. The latter arranged for Thurston to see M.D. De Young, editor of the *Chronicle,* who was opposed in principle to annexing Hawaii or any territory. As a result, the first day ashore the commissioners were able to convert to their point of view the leading newspapermen of San Francisco. The three evening journals, the *Bulletin, Record,* and *Post,* on January 28 came out with strong editorials in favor of annexing Hawaii. On the 29th the *Morning Call* and the *Examiner* did likewise, while, less enthusiastically, the *Chronicle* fell into line.[4] Thurston reported that the only dissenting voice that appeared in the area was that of E. L. C. Steele, editor of the San Francisco *Newsletter,* who denounced the whole revolution as "a fraud and a humbug."

After meeting with a group of businessmen keenly interested in Hawaii, who organized themselves into a bureau of assistance,[5] and after Thurston's assurance to the editors of the *Chronicle* and the *Call* that it was not intended that Hawaii come into the Union as a state,[6] the delegation, still besieged by reporters, left San Francisco for Washington on January 29, via the Northwestern Railway on the Overland Express. They made the best of interviews

3. Castle Diary, Jan. 28, 1893, pp. 2–4. Thurston to Dole, Jan. 29, 1893, AH, Hawaiian Officials Abroad, U.S. Minister and Commissioners, Washington. All the correspondence between the Hawaiian minister and commissioners and the officers of the provisional government are so filed in the Archives of Hawaii.
4. Thurston to Dole, Jan. 29, 1893.
5. Ibid., Castle Diary (Jan. 28, 29, 1893), pp. 3–5.
6. *Chronicle,* Feb. 2, 1893. *Morning Call,* Feb. 2, 1893.

at every major stop, including the bus trip from the Northwestern terminal to the Pennsylvania station in Chicago, during which reporters sat on the commissioners' laps or took notes the best they could standing. Arriving in Washington on February 3, the gentlemen took up headquarters at the Wormley Hotel, an old and decayed hostelry living on its ancient reputation.

Information regarding their presence on American soil and of their mission had reached the State Department and the Hawaiian legation on January 28. The Secretary of State had already published Minister Stevens' telegram of January 18, announcing that the provisional government was in full possession of the islands and had been promptly recognized by all the diplomatic representatives accredited to Honolulu, as well as Foster's reply approving of the Minister's action in recognizing the de facto government and instructing him to cooperate with the United States naval commander for the protection of American interests and property and for the preservation of good order.[7]

Official Reaction

In the national capital there was considerable diversity of opinion on the Hawaiian question. Reportedly, several members of the Cabinet expressed themselves in favor of annexation. President Harrison also approved, and although the course pursued by Minister Stevens in ordering the *Boston's* marines on shore was without explicit instructions from Washington, his action was fully sanctioned by the President. John W. Foster, James G. Blaine's successor as Secretary of State, regarded the question of annexation of the Hawaiian Islands as vital to our country and one "which could not be decided permanently in the negative without grave peril to our interests in the Pacific Ocean." It seemed apparent to him that if the islands did not become American territory, they would inevitably pass under the control of Great Britain or Japan, and he looked upon either of these contingencies as contrary to the interests of the United States.[1]

Interviews on Capitol Hill indicated that the sentiment generally in the upper chamber, especially among Democrats, was favorable

7. Foster to Stevens (telegram), Jan. 28, 1893, USDS, Instructions, Hawaii, 3, printed in *For. Rels.* (1894), App. II, p. 299. Cf. New York *Times*, Feb. 6, 1893.

1. John W. Foster, *Diplomatic Memoirs* (2 vols. Boston and New York, 1909), 167.

to annexation. Among them the opinion prevailed that the United States had quite enough to do looking after affairs within her present borders without extending her possessions.[2] Annexation was opposed for several reasons, including Hawaii's distance from the United States, the poor quality of the island's citizens, the expense of protecting outlying territory, the danger of inaugurating a new foreign policy that might involve the United States in serious difficulties,[3] and the violation of the fundamental principles of the constitution.[4] A majority of the Committee on Foreign Relations, however, favored the establishment of United States dominion over the islands. Senator John T. Morgan of Alabama, who was to become chairman of that committee in the reorganized Senate, was strongly in favor of annexation, considering the matter as one of the most important that had come under his notice since his incumbency in a senatorial seat.[5] The chairman of the committee on territories, Senator Orville Platt, Republican from Connecticut, urged action. He was convinced that the Hawaiian Islands and the Nicaragua Canal were two things the United States should control.[6]

William E. Chandler of New York offered a resolution requesting the President to enter into negotiations with the provisional government of Hawaii "for the admission of the islands as a territory into the United States, and to lay any convention which he may make before Congress for ratification by legislation." The purpose of that language was to permit the House of Representatives to share in the responsibility for the disposition of the subject, and not to have action taken behind closed doors. As the resolution was objected to by Senator Stephen M. White of California, it lay over for a time, but was referred to the Committee on Foreign Relations on February 2.[7] In the interim there was considerable discussion of the Hawaiian question in executive session and in committee and cloakrooms; Senator Joseph N. Dolph of Oregon offered the only extended remarks that were published, and these were in connection with an appropriation bill. He emphasized the importance of the islands to the United States in securing her share of Pacific trade,

2. Washington *Post* and San Francisco *Morning Call*, Feb. 1 and 2, 1893.
3. San Francisco *Examiner*, Jan. 29, 1893.
4. R. F. Pettigrew, *The Course of Empire: An Official Record* (New York, 1920), p. 75.
5. Washington *Post*, Jan. 29, 1893. San Francisco *Morning Call*, Jan. 31, 1893.
6. San Francisco *Examiner*, Jan. 29, 1893.
7. *Cong. Record*, 52 Cong., 2 sess., pp. 939, 1093.

and considered annexation the natural result of a long period of close relations between the two countries, as attested by numerous assertions of presidents and secretaries of state.[8]

On the request of the Senate, the President had Secretary of State Foster, on February 6, submit the unratified treaty of 1854, with all correspondence that had passed between Commissioner David L. Gregg and Secretary of State Marcy.[9] In the early part of the month petitions or memorials arrived from the legislatures of Oregon, California, Colorado, Pennsylvania, Illinois, and New York, and from the Portland, Oregon, and San Francisco Chambers of Commerce, and the latter's city Board of Trade, urging Congress to annex Hawaii.[10]

In the House of Representatives the majority was either clearly averse to annexation or noncommittal. The Monroe Doctrine was mentioned as a cardinal principle in our foreign policy and as demanding the exclusion of European domination over territory so near our shores. The most vociferous opponents were the anti-imperialists, who were convinced that annexation of overseas territory was unwise and that the acquisition of the islands through the machinations of Minister Stevens and the annexationists in Hawaii should be out of the question.[11] Eventually, four resolutions favoring annexation were introduced.[12]

After some deliberation and a weekend of reflection following the first flush of enthusiasm and exultation over the dramatic events in Honolulu, many members of Congress modified their views as expressed upon receipt of the first news. Considering all the circumstances attending the revolution, which doubtless was encouraged by the presence of the *Boston* and her marines, most senators were certain that England, Germany, and the other powers would regard our act as utterly inconsistent with our previously expressed foreign policy and might unite in demanding "hands off." The situa-

8. Ibid., pp. 999–1002.

9. Ibid., pp. 1174, 1246. *Sen. Ex. Docs.*, 52 Cong., 2 sess., No. 45. Cf. my "Slavery and Racism," *Journal of Negro History, 47* (1962), 1–15.

10. *Cong. Record*, 52 Cong., 2 sess., pp. 1027, 1091, 1170, 1563, 1605, 2086. *Morning Call*, Jan. 29, 20, Feb. 1, 7, 1893. New York *Times*, Jan. 30, 1893. Washington *Evening News*, Feb. 2, 1893. New York *World*, Feb. 9, 1893. A Boston member of Massachusetts House of Representatives, on Feb. 8, was refused leave to introduce a similar memorial (New York *World*, Feb. 9, 1893).

11. *Washington Post*, Jan. 29, 1893.

12. *Cong. Record*, 52 Cong., 2 sess., pp. 1037, 1406, 2032, 2086.

tion was considered serious.[13] So many obstacles loomed and so many objections were raised, the Washington *Evening News* reported on January 31, "that could a vote be taken on the question of annexation now, with the limited information at hand, a good two-thirds majority would be recorded against it." Only a minority boldly favored immediate action, with Senators Chandler and Dolph and Representative J. Logan Chipman from Michigan being the most outspoken.

The Treaty

On the first day of the negotiations Secretary of State Foster drew attention to the protest addressed to President Harrison by ex-Queen Liliuokalani, to which the commissioners promised to reply. On receiving their propositions formulating the basis on which, in their opinion, the union of the Hawaiian Islands with the United States might be effected,[1] the Secretary remarked that whether Hawaii should be annexed as a state or a territory was secondary; there would be opposition to annexation in any form. He suggested that the treaty cover annexation alone, leaving the status of Hawaii for future consideration[2]—a recommendation which the commissioners accepted.

Foster, knowing what was judicious from the point of view of international law and what stipulations and details in the draft would be likely to cause partisan strife, placed before the commissioners comments on their propositions and what, in a general way, constituted his ideas. He considered as unnecessary the incorporation in the treaty of an agreement to lay a cable to Honolulu, for it was contrary to the policy of the United States government to engage in such activities, and one of the first and necessary results of annexation would be the establishment of cable connections with the islands. Regarding the proposition that the United States should,

---

13. *Morning Call*, Jan. 31, 1893. Other journals, voicing the opinion that Great Britain would interfere, felt that her protest would not be serious, or should not be heeded. See my "Great Britain and the Sovereignty of Hawaii," *Pacific Historical Review, 31* (1962), 337–44.

1. These proposals are in USDS, Hawaii, Notes from, under date of Feb. 4, 1893, printed in Thurston, *Memoirs*, pp. 284–85.

2. For a scholarly treatment of this subject see Charles H. Hunter, "Statehood and the Hawaiian Annexation Treaty of 1893," HHS, Fifty-Ninth *Report*, 1950 (Honolulu, 1951).

within a given period, open and improve Pearl River Harbor and establish there a naval station, he thought that American officials should not be confined in their discretion to improving any one harbor when another might suit them better for the purposes of a naval station. Moreover, he felt that United States exclusion laws applying to Chinese would have to operate at the islands; that the bounty on sugar, if incorporated in the treaty, would be one of the most serious obstacles to its passage; and that the President might desire a plebiscite in Hawaii.[3]

A tentative draft of a treaty was provided the commissioners on February 9, at which time Foster stated that, after further consideration and consultation with the President, other members of the Cabinet, and members of the Senate Committee on Foreign Relations, he had concluded that it would be utterly impossible to get the Senate to consent to any bounty;[4] that since the end of the session was so near, it would be difficult to gain the consideration of the treaty under any circumstances; and that the only hope of getting it through would be the omission of all objectionable details which might be employed for defeating the treaty as a whole. By dropping the bounty and the tariff the greatest cause for opposition would be eliminated. The commissioners should have no fears, for once the islands were incorporated as part of American territory, there would be no disposition to discriminate against that portion of the Union. He so modified the wording of the proposed treaty that the existing labor system in Hawaii would continue until changed by positive legislation at Washington.[5]

As the terms set forth in the Secretary of State's draft treaty differed so materially from their original instructions and the new or amended ones of January 31, brought by Charles M. Cooke, the commissioners were reluctant to accept the convention. They were anxious to ascertain that these were the best terms that could be obtained and that the object of their mission would be accomplished.[6] They desired some discussion of the following points:

3. Protocol of the Second Conference between Secretary of State and Hawaiian Commissioners, Feb. 7, 1893. Castle Diary, Feb. 7, 8, 9, 1893, pp. 9–10.

4. Foster, *Memoirs*, 2, 168. Cf. Blount's testimony, *Morgan Report*, p. 404.

5. Protocol of the Third Conference between Secretary of State and Thurston, Feb. 9, 1893.

6. Protocol of the Fourth Conference between Secretary of State and Thurston, Feb. 10, 1893. Dole instructed the commissioners that if they found "it absolutely necessary" for the success of their mission to negotiate a

1) a time limit in reference to final and complete commercial union with the United States; 2) retention of the Hawaiian flag as the local emblem; 3) in the interim period, until Congress legislated on a permanent form of government, permission for the provisional government to remove officials; 4) provision for the registry of Hawaiian ships; 5) the right of Chinese lawfully domiciled, but absent from the islands, to return, and the prohibition as to immigration not in terms perpetual; 6) a clause permitting cancellation of the treaty should Congress not eliminate duties on imports from Hawaii within a definite period. Secretary Foster felt that the last proposition would not meet with favor in the Senate, and suggested, in lieu thereof, that there should be inserted a clause guaranteeing that such legislation would take place within one year after the ratification of the treaty. Provision for registry of vessels might be safely left to Congress, and the Chinese already domiciled might return. These statements were accepted by the commissioners as satisfactory. The Secretary promised to take into consideration the other three points.[7]

On the question of compensation for the Queen and Princess, Foster suggested $200,000 for the former and $100,000 for the latter. A discussion ensued as to whether this should be in money or in the form of government securities. Dr. Mott Smith favored securities and thought that $300,000 to the Queen and $200,000 to the Princess would be reasonable. Thurston felt that the larger the sum the less likelihood there would be of Congress agreeing to it; that the United States ought not to pay more than was requisite; and that Liliuokalani had "no legal, moral or any other claim on them for a cent." In reference to the citizenship provision, Foster inquired as to who were considered "citizens of Hawaii." Thurston promised to provide the Secretary the following morning with a full report on that subject, as well as a statement as to the public lands, and the allowances to and revenue of the royal family.[8]

---

preliminary treaty of political union which should "go into operation immediately without ratification by the Hawaiian government, leaving all questions of details of such union to be settled through subsequent legislation." He also authorized them, should circumstances render such a course advisable, to ask that the United States government establish a protectorate over the Hawaiian Islands covering the time required for the negotiations. (Dole to Hawaiian Commissioners, Jan. 31, 1893.)

7. Protocol of the Fifth Conference between Secretary of State and Hawaiian Commissioners, Feb. 10, 1893.

8. Stenographic Notes of the Fifth Conference, Feb. 10, 1893, pp. 6–7.

After examining the facts furnished by Thurston, Foster decided that it would be best to eliminate all references to citizenship and thus leave Congress free to deal with it. He also felt that no provision should be included in the treaty touching on the Hawaiian flag, for the people might use it locally if it were not made equal or paramount to the national flag; and that if the commissioners desired, he would write them a letter to that effect.[9] He modified Article 4 on the right of the provisional government to remove officers in the sense suggested by the commissioners in the conference the preceding day. To the Chinese exclusion article he added to the first sentence the words: "until Congress shall otherwise provide," which made it clear that the prohibition should not necessarily be perpetual. Article 6, providing for the royal family, was modified so as to stipulate for an annuity of $20,000 for the Queen, and a gross sum of $150,000 for the Princess. To these modifications and conclusions of February 14 the commissioners signified their assent, and the treaty as thus amended was prepared for signatures.[10]

The envoys' reply to Liliuokalani's protest contradicted all claims of illegality in the establishment of a provisional government. In denying that American forces had aided the revolution, they offered as proof the following so-called "facts": (1) At the beginning of the disturbance, the American minister and the *Boston* were both absent from Honolulu and had been for ten days previous thereto. (2) The first exhibition of force was made by the Queen on January 14 "by the public parading of the entire military force, armed with repeating rifles and carrying a full supply of ball cartridges." In addition, there was located at the palace, barracks, and police station 540 armed men. (3) The first call to arms in opposition to the Queen was issued by the cabinet on the afternoon of January 14. (4) Although from January 14 to 16, the most intense feelings of hostility were publicly manifested, American troops did not arrive on the scene until 5 P.M. on January 16. (5) A guard was placed at the United States legation and consulate, while the rest of the marines were stationed at a public hall: "No demonstration was made by the troops in any manner whatever. The uniform of the United States was not seen upon the streets, except upon the persons of the individual officers passing between the points at which troops were located in the execution of their business." (6) "At the time the Provisional Government took possession of the Government build-

9. See Foster to Thurston, Feb. 23, 1893, USDS, Hawaii, Notes to, 2.
10. Carter to Foster, Feb. 11, 1893, USDS, Hawaii, Notes from, Vol. 4.

ings, no American troops or officers were present or took part in such proceedings in any manner whatever. No public recognition was accorded the Provisional Government by the American Minister, until they were in possession of the Government buildings, the Archives and the Treasury, supported by several hundred armed men, after the abdication of the queen and the surrender to the Provisional Government of her forces.

The commissioners concluded that the submission of this statement of facts amply met "the charge by the queen that American troops coerced her action in abdicating." They also refuted the second contention of Liliuokalani: that they engaged the only vessel available to sail to San Francisco, claiming that the fleet of twenty inter-island steamers, two others were as fully capable of making the trip as was the *Claudine*.[11]

With a few "slight literal corrections," the treaty was ready for signature on February 14, exactly thirty-one days after the initiation of the scheme for a provisional government, fifteen of which were spent by the commissioners in their journey to Washington.[12] They requested that the document be withheld from the Senate until the following day, when the S.S. *Australia was* due to sail from San Francisco; thus the text would not go to Honolulu until some one of them could carry it to explain and defend its provisions.[13]

The commissioners' version of the revolution, with the sixth point of their statement of facts incorporated, formed the basis of Secretary of State Foster's letter that accompanied the treaty when it was submitted to President Harrison, who likewise accepted the "facts" as presented to him, and passed them on to the Senate. In his letter Foster took pains to point out that the State Department

11. Commissioners to Foster, Feb. 11, 1893, ibid; printed in *Sen. Ex. Docs.*, 52 Cong., 2 sess., No. 76, pp. 40–42. This statement was released to the press and circulated by the commissioners in circles where it promised to be most effective.

12. Protocol of the Seventh Conference between Secretary of State and Hawaiian Commissioners, Feb. 14, 1893. Four drafts of the treaty, are preserved in USDS, Hawaii, Notes from, 4. The treaty, as signed Feb. 14, 1893, is printed in *Sen. Ex. Docs.*, 52 Cong., 2 sess., No. 76, "Annexation Treaty with the Hawaiian Islands," pp. 28–40; in *Sen. Reps.*, 55 Cong. 2 sess., No. 681, pp. 94–96; and also in *Report of the Minister of Foreign Affairs to the President and Members of the Executive and Advisory Councils (March 21), 1894* (Honolulu, 1894), pp. 29–34. Cf. New York *Tribune*, Feb. 16, 1893.

13. Castle Diary (Feb. 14, 1893), p. 12. For a documentary history of the negotiations see Ralph S. Kuykendall, "Negotiation of the Hawaiian Annexation Treaty of 1893," HHS, 51st *Report*, 1942 (Honolulu, 1943), pp. 6–64.

had had no hand in the proceedings at Honolulu; that no officers or troops of the United States had been present at the time the provisional government took possession of the government; and that the annexation proposal was a voluntary offering brought to Washington by the special commission. In reviewing the United States' past relations with the kingdom, he asserted that annexation was the natural culmination of the government's Hawaiian policy and entirely consistent with its declared attitude toward the islands. Annexation had been "on more than one occasion avowed as a policy and attempted as a fact." [14]

In transmitting this treaty, with a view to ratification, the President deemed it unnecessary "to discuss at length" the conditions which had resulted in this decisive action. The policy of his administration had been "not only to respect but to encourage the continuance of an independent government in the Hawaiian Islands so long as it afforded suitable guaranties for the protection of life and property and maintained a stability and strength that gave adequate security against the domination of any other power." The United States' moral support had "continually manifested itself in the most friendly diplomatic relations and in many acts of courtesy to the Hawaiian rulers." The "overthrow of the monarch was not in any way promoted by this Government, but had its origin in what seems to have been a reactionary and revolutionary policy on the part of Queen Liliuokalani, which put in serious peril not only the large and preponderant interests of the United States in the islands, but all foreign interests, and, indeed, the decent administration of civil affairs and the peace of the islands." The monarchy had become effete and the government "so weak and inadequate as to be the prey of designing and unscrupulous persons." The restoration of Queen Liliuokalani to her thrown was "undesirable, if not impossible, and unless actively supported by the United States would be accompanied by serious disaster and the disorganization of all business interests. The influence and interests of the United States in the islands must be increased and not diminished."

Only two courses were open: "one the establishment of a protectorate by the United States, and the other annexation full and complete." The latter course would be highly promotive of the best interests of the Hawaiian people, and was the only one that would adequately secure the interests of the United States. It was essential that one of the great powers should secure the islands. Prompt

14. *Sen. Ex. Docs.*, 52 Cong., 2 sess., No. 76, pp. 5, 198.

action upon the treaty was very desirable. If it met the approval of the Senate, peace and good order would be secured in the islands under existing laws until such time as Congress could provide by legislation a permanent form of government for the islands.[15]

In the light of past policy and these apparently unassailable arguments in favor of annexation, together with a generally favorable press reaction and predictions of congressional approbation, prompt senatorial approval of the Hawaiian treaty appeared a foregone conclusion.

Early Reaction

The press of the United States was divided on the Hawaiian issue, with some of the leading metropolitan journals and those of the national capital taking opposite points of view, while a few remained cautious and skeptical. Among those favoring and campaigning for annexation were, first and foremost, the Washington *Post*, New York *Tribune*, New York *Sun*, New York *Independent*, Chicago *Tribune*, and, naturally, the *Kennebec Journal* of Augusta, Maine. Also supporting the acquisition of the mid-Pacific group were the *Commercial Advertiser, Morning Advertiser, Mail and Express, Observer*, and *Christian at Work*, all of New York, the Brooklyn *Standard Union*, Philadelphia *Inquirer*, Boston *Evening Transcript*, Albany *Times Union*, Rochester *Chronicle*, Detroit *Tribune*, San Francisco *Morning Call*, San Francisco *Bulletin*, and St. Louis *Republican*. The views of these pro-annexationist newspapers encouraged and, at times, tended to make the Hawaiian commissioners overoptimistic.

On the other hand, some journals, such as the Chicago *Herald* and the New York *Herald*, took a pronounced stand against annexation. The former maintained: "We already have Negroes, Chinamen, Greasers, Indians, Jerry Simpson and Mrs. Lease, and we don't want any more in the combination."[1] Others, such as the New York *Times*, New York *Evening Post*, and Washington *Evening News*, were cautious or skeptical. In this same category, varying in their intensity of opposition to union, with some favoring a protectorate instead of annexation, were the New York *World*, Brooklyn *Citizen*, Washington *Evening Star*, Boston *Advertiser*, Boston *Herald*, Troy,

15. Richardson, *Messages and Papers of the Presidents*, 9, 348–49. *Sen. Ex. Docs.*, 52 Cong., 2 sess., No. 76, pp. 1–2.
1. Jan. 30, 1893.

New York, *Times, Cincinnati Journal and Messenger,* San Francisco *Chronicle,* San Francisco *Newsletter,* and *Harper's Weekly.*

From the beginning, the Democratic New York *World,* owned by Joseph Pulitzer, hinted at the part played by Minister Stevens and the *Boston* in the revolution. An article entitled "Cruiser and Queen," published on January 29, carried the descriptive caption "The Warship Boston Cuts a Big Figure in Hawaii's Revolution." The "Queen's Side of the Story" was aired on February 9 in a letter written by her former minister of the interior, John F. Colburn, to J. H. Gantz of St. Louis. The day after the treaty was submitted to the Senate, the *World* raised the question: "Was Hawaii Stolen?" and reported that Minister Stevens was said to have "given the backbone to the revolution" and made possible the "steal" by preventing the former Queen's government from protecting itself.

In reporting that Liliuokalani yielded not to the revolutionists but to the superior force of the United States, the independent Washington *Evening News* cautioned its readers to bear in mind that the source of the information provided to the press was a commission of revolutionists who had chartered a special steamer to have their statements and views presented to the American people before the Queen's side had had a similar opportunity. "That there is another side goes without saying, or such haste would not have been made in putting their case." The revolution was engineered by parties desirous of improving their financial condition by inducing the United States to restore to them the advantages they received under the reciprocity treaty previous to the passage of the McKinley Bill. Under this treaty the planters made from 75 to 100 per cent on their plantation investments, or about $6,000,000 a year. After the McKinley tariff, not more than 10 per cent could be realized on sugar cultivation; consequently, they were anxious to secure the 2 cents a pound bonus.[2]

Provincial newspapers were also divided, with those of the South, Mid-west, and West generally opposed to annexation, but there was no clear-cut geographical cleavage on the question; rather, the division tended toward party lines.

The American press in February generally anticipated that the necessary two-thirds vote of the Senate would materialize. The New York *Tribune,* as early as February 11, suspected that the Democratic senators were trying to scuttle the pact; yet that same journal, a fortnight later, reported: "there is a constitutional majority in the

2. Jan. 30, Feb. 1, 1893.

Senate as it stands today in favor of ratification." The *Kennebec Journal* expressed a similar opinion on February 20, while a poll of the New York *Herald* disclosed that only three out of thirty-eight senators opposed annexation.

The greatest obstacle that the commissioners encountered was the popular belief or suspicion often voiced in the press that the sugar planters and the sugar trust controlled by Claus Spreckels were behind the annexation scheme. In the words of William R. Castle: "Our bitterest enemies are those who charge a job against us—that sugar has done this thing—or Spreckels, or someone else. It is not admitted that we can be honest or patriotic." [3] The New York *Herald,* no doubt borrowing the phraseology from the Albany *Times-Union,* which earlier had observed that the Hawaiian sugar interest "is the nigger in the fence, the cat in the meal tub, the milk in the coconut," queried six times on its editorial page of February 7 and 10: "Is Spreckels & Co. the nigger in the fence of the sugar islands?" Later the same journal commented that "there is more sugar than statesmanship and more jingoism than patriotism in the hasty movement." [4] The New York *Post,* on February 22, characterized the overthrow of Queen Liliuokalani as a "revolution of sugar for sugar," which was echoed the following week by the *Nation,* decrying the revolution "of sugar by sugar and for sugar" carried through by "a plutocracy of merchants and planters." [5] Similarly, the St. Louis *Republican* asserted that the revolution was "for the benefit of Claus Spreckels to help him make a dollar." [6]

Several Republican, some independent, and a few Democratic journals expressed concern over the serious situation presented by the strategic location of the Hawaiian Islands in the Pacific, and drew a comparison with the three British fortifications at Halifax, Bermuda, and Saint Lucia. Each of these bases permitted a hostile fleet to replenish its bunkers and reach our coast in about a two days' sail. Furthermore, Esquimalt had greatly increased our need for coast defense afloat and ashore. [7]

3. Castle Diary (Feb. 24, 1893), p. 18.
4. Feb. 24, 1893.
5. March 2, 1893.
6. Quoted by the New York *Herald,* Feb. 15, 1893.
7. This important North Pacific Harbor and naval station is situated on the southwest coast of Vancouver Island, on the Juan de Fuca Strait, about three miles from Victoria, the capital of British Columbia. After the opening of the Canadian Pacific Railway, the importance of Esquimalt became evident, and in 1893 it was fortified with strong armaments and all the accouterment of a

An anonymous contributor to the New York *Tribune* dealt with the archipelago's relation to isthmian trade and defense in an article entitled "Hawaii in Our System." By means of a geopolitical map, attention was directed to the British system of naval bases at Halifax, Bermuda, Esquimalt, and elsewhere; the author warned of the threat to the coasts and communications of the United States and of the danger that England might add Hawaii to this system, thereby controlling the routes from the West Coast and the isthmus of Panama to the Orient, and declared that a government aware of these facts could not do otherwise than accept the proffered union.[8]

The New York *Press* warned that the Hawaiian archipelago left to Great Britain would finish a "cordon of menacing strongholds," and asserted that "we must plant the stars and stripes in Honolulu." Likewise, the Atlanta *Constitution* observed that England was "drawing a cordon of bayonets around us—Canada, the Bermudas, Jamaica, British Guiana, British Honduras . . . strongholds, depots of supplies, rallying points bristling with guns."[9] The Philadelphia *Press* contended that "our failure to control the Hawaiian Islands would triple our future expenditure for defense in peace and render war possible."[10]

On the other hand, the Boston *Herald* was opposed to the added defense burden we would assume, for Hawaii would be our one weak point, liable to assault by the enemy in a foreign war, requiring a much larger naval force than was previously needed.[11] The Democratic Minneapolis *Times*, convinced that England would protest our annexation of Hawaii, considered the islands not worth a war. Security in the use of their harbors on equal terms with other nations trading in the Pacific Ocean was all that we required or could in justice demand.[12]

Interested individuals and the press were also divided on the efficacy of establishing a protectorate over the Hawaiian Islands, instead of annexing them. Since many opponents of union harbored

---

first-class naval arsenal. See "England in the Pacific, A New Move, Fortifying Esquimault Harbour," *Auckland* (New Zealand) *Star*, March 2, 1893.

8. Feb. 6, 1893. This sounded very much like Captain Alfred Thayer Mahan, who expounded practically the same arguments in the March 1893 issue of the *Forum*, 15, 1–13.

9. Both March 7, 1893.

10. March 14, 1893. Similar views were expressed by the San Francisco *Examiner* and the Denver *Republican*, Feb. 1 and 4, 1893, respectively.

11. Editorial, Jan. 30, 1893.

12. Feb. 2, 1893.

the opinion that the archipelago should not be allowed to drift into the hands of a foreign power, some proposed as a way out of the dilemma that we assume a protectorate. George W. Merrill, of Los Angeles, United States minister resident in Hawaii from 1885 to 1889, considered this the best solution. In his opinion a harbor and a coaling station on one of the islands of the group and a cable extending from some point in the United States to Honolulu would accomplish for us every advantage we might hope to derive through annexation.[13]

Edwin L. Godkin, editor of the *Nation*, was also of the conviction that whatever privileges we might desire in the way of a coaling station or naval stores in those islands, we either had at our disposal or could have for the asking. He felt that we should have a predominating influence there if things went on as they were, or if we assumed a simple protectorate: "If, by the latter method, we can get all the advantages, with few or none of the tremendous drawbacks of annexation, why rush headlong into so grave an experiment?" [14] Similarly, the New York *World*, persistent in its advocacy of a protectorate, contended that the alien population and the formidable distance from our shores militated against any closer union.[15]

Yet there was little enthusiasm in either the United States or Hawaii for a protectorate. As early as the first week in April 1893, Thurston thought such a settlement could be headed off, as he had not yet found an advocate of the proposition who, as soon as the details were studied, had not abandoned it as impracticable from the standpoint of the United States, who would assume all the responsibility without any of the advantages of outright possession.[16] Annexationists generally maintained that a protectorate would "give us the Maximum of responsibility, with a Minimum of power and influence." [17]

A Protectorate

In Honolulu there was an interim of uncertainty. Although troops from the cruiser *Boston* remained ashore, moving to a new camp in

13. New York *Post*, Feb. 11, 1893.
14. *Nation*, 56 (1893), 154. *Review of Reviews*, 7 (New York, 1893), 263.
15. Feb. 2, 1893.
16. Thurston to Dole, April 7, 1893.
17. M. Woodhull to Sen. W. E. Chandler, Feb. 2, 1893, Chandler Papers, Vol. 88, Library of Congress.

an unoccupied hotel in King Street, the officials of the provisional government were uneasy. The revolution was a *fait accompli*, but its leaders were uncertain of the future. On two occasions James H. Wodehouse interviewed President Dole on the continued presence on shore of the naval force from the *Boston*, and was given to understand that it would shortly return to that vessel. By the end of January it had not. Since the provisional government had "a force more than sufficient to maintain 'Law and Order,' and to afford an adequate protection to life and property," Her Britannic Majesty's representative again inquired why the foreign troops had not been recalled to their ships.[1] The British corvette *Garnet* was also expected, and the provisional ministers feared a new coup by either Japan or Great Britain.

Furthermore, there was unrest among the 20,000 Japanese contract laborers in Hawaii, for the royalists were reported to have promised them full citizenship if the monarchy were restored. At one point some four hundred Japanese laborers from a sugar plantation about twenty miles from Honolulu marched on the city, armed with cane knives. Fortunately, their consular representative intercepted them and sent them back to the plantation.

This event prompted the provisional government to request Stevens to raise the flag of the United States and extend temporary protection to the islands. There was conferred upon the government of the United States freedom of occupation of the public buildings and of the soil of the country, so far as might be necessary for the exercise of such protection.[2] On February 1 the American forces marched from their quarters in King Street to the government building, and a force was also dispatched to the Charles R. Bishop's residence and grounds. The enthusiastic Minister proclaimed Hawaii a protectorate of the United States, ordered the Stars and Stripes raised, and advised the Secretary of State: "The Hawaiian pear is now fully ripe, and this is the golden hour for the United States to pluck it. If annexation does not take place promptly, if all is held in doubt and suspense for six or ten months, there certainly will be here a revulsion to despair, and these people, by their necessities, might be forced towards becoming a British colony." Stevens main-

1. Wodehouse to Dole, Jan. 30, 1893, encl. in Wodehouse to Rosebery, Feb. 9, 1893, No. 1, FO 58/279. Cf. Stevens to Gresham, March 7, 1893, No. 91, printed in *For. Rels.* (1894), App. II, pp. 414–15.

2. Provisional Government to Stevens, Jan. 21, 1893, encl. No. 2 in Stevens to Foster, Feb. 1, 1893, No. 84.

tained that only his prompt action in taking this decisive step had prevented the British and Japanese from intervening, and he requested the dispatch to Honolulu of the "most powerful American ship available" to support his position.[3] Nine days later the U.S.S. *Mohican* arrived in port, and Rear Admiral J. S. Skerrett, commander-in-chief of United States forces in the Pacific, took charge of the protectorate. Under this regime the atmosphere became calm: the volunteer soldiers were allowed to return to their regular occupations, and on February 5 the order for martial law was rescinded and the writ of habeas corpus restored.[4] This salutary order represented a return to stability and safety.

The provisional government would assign no reason for an American protectorate other than that it was necessary "for the preservation of law and order, and for the protection of life and property." Wodehouse reported that there was no more truth in this statement than in the one that he, aided by the presence of a British man-of-war, might press unduly the provisional government. Sanford Dole admitted to a friend of the Englishman that the United States flag was hoisted for a purely political purpose,[5] and to his brother he confided that he was not fully in sympathy with the move, that he was doubtful about the need as well as the policy of it, but that since "it was strongly urged by the Council and supported by nearly the unanimous vote," he acted on it. The establishment of a protectorate did "not change the status politically or in relation to the negotiation, in any way." [6]

Secretary Foster disavowed this unauthorized act of the United States representative, but did not rebuke him. Written and telegraphed instructions commended the Minister for protecting American lives and property from apprehended disorders. But so far as his action might "appear to overstep that limit, by setting the authority and power of the United States above that of the Government of the Hawaiian Islands, in the capacity of Protector, or to impair in any way the independent sovereignty of the Hawaiian Government by substituting the flag and power of the United States,

---

3. Stevens to Foster, Feb. 1, 1893, No. 84, printed in *For. Rels.* (1894), App. II, pp. 244, 402. Cf. ibid., p. 245.

4. Dole, *Memoirs*, p. 92. Cf. *Pacific Commercial Advertiser*, Feb. 6, 1893, editorial.

5. Wodehouse to Rosebery, March 9, 1893, No. 4, FO 58/279.

6. Dole to George H. Dole, Feb. 1, 1893, Letters of S. B. Dole to G. H. Dole.

as the symbol and manifestation of paramount authority," it was disavowed. Careful distinction was to be drawn "between those functions of voluntary or accorded protection and the assumption of a Protectorate" over a government which the United States had recognized as sovereign and which we treated on terms of Sovereign equality.[7]

News of Stevens' audacious and unauthorized action in Honolulu caused a mixed reaction in the United States. The *Kennebec Journal* immediately approved and applauded the Minister's course as "eminently wise and proper." The Washington *Post*, New York *Sun*, and New York *Tribune* sustained the diplomatic representative, who had "acted with tact and good judgment . . . precisely the right thing."[8] To the New York *World*, Stevens' article in the November 24, 1892, *Kennebec Journal*, foreshadowing the revolution in Hawaii and the succession of events that "followed hard upon," did not "entirely exclude the idea of *malice prepense.*"

As for the reception of the news in the two houses of Congress, the Washington *Post* reported that the senators generally were glad, and that there was "a subdued hum of gratulation among them"; whereas James H. Blount of Georgia, chairman of the House Committee on Foreign Affairs, thought that the assumption of a protectorate "looked a little lively," and that Stevens' letter to Secretary Foster "manifested some passing beyond the proprieties for an American representative in a foreign country."[9]

Outside of Congress, Carl Schurz went further and condemned the protectorate as illegal. The executive power of this country had "no right to assume responsibilities of this character except in great emergencies, and for the purpose of protecting the lives and property of American citizens." There was no evidence of any such occasion for the exercise of sovereignty in Honolulu by this government, for there was no sign of an outbreak in the capital or anywhere else in the islands. The plain people of the United States wondered "why the republic departs from its ancient traditions of fairness and justice in order to take away not only the power of an unoffending royal family but the territory of a friendly people."

7. Foster to Stevens, Feb. 11, 1893, and telegram of Feb. 14, 1893, USDS, Instructions, Hawaii, 3, printed in *For. Rels.* (1894), App. II, pp. 240–42, 406–07.

8. Feb. 10, 11, 1893. For further press reaction to the protectorate see the *Literary Digest*, 6 (1893), 444.

9. *Morgan Report*, p. 404.

Ratification Delayed

In spite of early optimistic predictions that Hawaii would be annexed to the United States forthwith, events proved otherwise. Since
little more than a fortnight remained for Harrison's administration
when the treaty reached the upper chamber, the problem was one
of time. An attempt to hasten ratification would have created the
impression that the task had to be completed before Liliuokalani's
side was heard.[1] The New York *Times,* which did not have enough
information to take a real stand on the question, felt that there was
too much haste. It not only raised the question of the Queen's side,
but could not accept Foster's assertion that there had been no col-
lusion between Stevens and the revolutionists.[2] The New York *Post,*
as early as February 6, recommended a second sober thought, not
annexation by a rush or "hoop-la." Ten days later, it intimated that
President Harrison was attempting to push the treaty through the
Senate in order to give "a sort of sunset glory to a dying Administration" which was leaving numerous perplexing problems. The New
York *World* censured this "Snap-shot diplomacy," and considered
the whole matter "an administrative plot," "a set-up job," one that
Harrison and his officials had been in on from the beginning.[3] Also
opposed to snap action by the outgoing Harrison administration was
Carl Schurz, who, through the medium of *Harper's Weekly*—then
a force in American life—asserted that "if the Republican party takes
advantage of the last days of its power to effect the annexation of
the Hawaiian Islands to the United States, it will commit an act
utterly inconsistent with the true spirit of democratic government."[4]

Grover Cleveland conferred at Lakewood, New Jersey, on February 22, with Walter Quintin Gresham and three other chosen cabinet
members, at which conference Queen Liliuokalani's letter to the
president-elect, as well as the one addressed to President Harrison,
requesting delay until her side might be heard, were considered.
John G. Carlisle, a former senator and the prospective secretary of
the treasury, journeyed to Washington reportedly bearing a message
from Cleveland which influenced the ex-senator's party associates to
have annexation postponed for the consideration of the new ad-

1. "The Hawaiian Situation," *Harper's Weekly,* 37 (1893), 299.
2. Feb. 10, 17, 1893.
3. Feb. 16–18, 22, 1893.
4. "The Hawaiian Business," *Harper's Weekly,* 37 (1893), 170.

ministration.[5] Foster was of the opinion that this action was prompted by incoming Secretary of State Gresham's hostility to Harrison.[6] Whether this was true or not, the senators were not inclined to act speedily, and by the first of March it was clear that there would be no snap annexation of the Hawaiian Islands, for not more than a third of the Senate favored it.

Perhaps the most significant reason for the delay in ratifying the treaty was the arrival of the Queen's delegation, headed by Paul Neumann. Liliuokalani's surrender under protest had already created considerable sympathy for her and much doubt as to the legality of Stevens' activity during the revolution. Since the treaty was negotiated, signed, and transmitted to the Senate before the arrival of the royal agents, a feeling prevailed that it was not only right and proper but "indispensable that both sides of the question should be candidly heard." [7]

From San Francisco, where he arrived on February 9, Neumann sent Secretary Foster a telegram, received on the 10th—five days before the treaty was transmitted to the Senate—in which the hope was expressed that "no action will be taken by the president in relation to the affairs of the Hawaiian Islands, until my arrival." [8] The Secretary of State finally received Neumann on February 21, but not in the character of a diplomat. The envoy explained that many who were in favor of annexation disliked the provisional government, and that the Queen demanded a popular referendum on the question of whether the Hawaiian people wished her restoration or the continuance of the existing government. He asserted that there were not more than eighty or a hundred respectable men behind the provisional government, and insisted: "we do not want annexation that would leave the present Government there." The Secretary of State pressed his caller to the unwilling admission that his greatest objection was to the provisional government, and that he was duty bound to represent and defend Liliuokalani's case. Neumann then handed Foster a thirteen-page statement of facts in relation to recent events in the Hawaiian kingdom, with the request that it be presented to the Senate. The Secretary accepted the same,

5. Matilda Gresham, *Life of Walter Quintin Gresham 1832–1875* (2 vols. Chicago, 1919) 2, 168.

6. Foster, *Memoirs*, 2, 168.

7. Editorial, Washington *Post*, and "Envoys of the Queen Bring Different Story," New York *Herald*, both Feb. 10, 1893.

8. USDS, Hawaii, Notes from, 4.

but could not promise that it would be sent to the upper chamber without the President's instructions.

An expansion of the Queen's protest, this statement blamed the capitulation on the forces from the *Boston* who were landed "against the remonstrance of the Constitutional Government." John L. Stevens had given advance assurance that he would "espouse the cause of the usurpers . . . The usurpation of authority would not have lasted an hour without such armed support and encouragement by the United States Minister." Finally, the protectorate, which Stevens proclaimed on February 1, demonstrated that the provisional government had "no strength of its own, either to preserve the peace or enforce obedience to its edicts." It had "neither the moral nor the physical support of the masses of the Hawaiian people, who protest, with their Queen against the continuance of its usurpation, and pray for a restoration of their Constitutional Government and sovereignty." Proof of this was in the fact that 3,411 qualified electors had signed a petition against the provisional government.[9] Neumann also sent Senator Stephen White of California a letter setting forth the Queen's claims and protesting against the confirmation of the treaty, which the Senator certainly shared with his colleagues.[10]

In reporting Neumann's mission and the Queen's protest, the New York *World* posed two questions: "Why did not Secretary of State Foster give this out? Was it because of the light thrown on Minister Stevens' acts?" The haste with which the administration agreed to the treaty of annexation was not excused by any possible plea of necessity: "It was unjust and indecent. The care taken to suppress the Queen's side of the story in order that the treaty might be made irrevocable before public opinion could judge the facts is more than suspicious. If the statements of Mr. Neumann are true the treaty ought not to be confirmed at all, and Minister Stevens should be dismissed in disgrace from the diplomatic service. Let us have all the facts before we act upon them." [11]

Following hard upon the royal agents' visit, Princess Kaiulani, accompanied by her distinguished guardian Theo. H. Davies, arrived in New York and immediately issued a poignant appeal to the American people, reminding them that "seventy years ago Christian America sent us Christian men and women, who have given us religion, civilization, and the Gospel. We, in return, gave

9. Neumann to Foster, Feb. 21, 1893, ibid.
10. San Francisco *Morning Call*, March 10, 1893.
11. Feb. 24 (editorial, Feb. 25, 1893).

them welcome. This made the nation learn to love and trust America. To-day three sons of those missionaries are at your capital, asking you to undo the work of your fathers . . . asking this great nation to take away my little vineyard . . . They leave me without a home, a name, or a nation." [12] Davies felt certain that neither the government nor the people of the United States had any idea of the actual circumstances in which they were to be involved. He knew that sooner or later the fact would have to be disclosed that out of 14,000 electors, at least 10,000 would be utterly averse to annexation, and believed that the American people would reject with scorn the proposal that they should thus violate their own pledge of friendship, especially to a weak nation. Furthermore, hopeless as the effort seemed at the time, Kaiulani was concerned that if she did not go to Washington, Hawaiians would say to her thereafter: "You might have saved us, and you did not try." [13] So the two crossed "the wintry sea."

In the national capital, where they arrived on March 8, the President received them and Mrs. Cleveland entertained for the winsome Princess, who made a favorable impression on all who met her. Yet the visit was, in Thurston's opinion, of no consequence at all.[14] After a few weeks the first effect of the appearance of the charming royal visitor almost entirely disappeared.

Another apparent reason for delay in ratification of the treaty was that, with the failure of the British government to give a single sign of opposition to the proposed annexation, ardor in the United States was cooling off. This indifference was most annoying to annexationists, who had counted on the "threatening hand of Great Britain" to bring the desired action in Washington. Newspaper com-

12. New York *Times*, March 2, 1893. the *Times* (London), March 3, 1893. Thurston was the grandson of a missionary. Cf. New York *Times* and other papers, Feb. 21, 1893, for Kaiulani's earlier appeal "To the American People."

13. Theophilus Harris Davies, "The Hawaiian Situation," *North American Review*, 156 (1893), 608–09. Davies again visited Washington September 28–30, 1893, and gave his views freely to the press, but could not report the slightest evidence in favor of restoration of the monarchy. The Cleveland administration was still preserving the greatest silence on that question (Hastings to Dole, Sept. 30, 1893).

14. Thurston to Dole, March 16, 1893. Thurston was also of the opinion that Neumann's presence had no radical effect upon the final result (ibid.). Mott Smith gleaned that the State Department considered that Neumann's visit was related solely to an increase of the allowance made for the Queen in the treaty (Mott Smith to Dole, Feb. 25, 1893).

ment indicated that a protest would be forthcoming.[15] But an official denial of such action was made in London on January 31, and information to that effect appeared in the New York *Times,* along with a statement that officials at the Admiralty denied that British warships had been ordered to proceed to Hawaii from Australia.

Anglo-American diplomatic relations remained cordial, with Sir Julian Pauncefote stating that his government did not desire the Hawaiian group, was only interested in seeing stable government maintained there, and indicating that Wodehouse, "a man of very little ability" and of "not much consequence," would be very promptly relieved of his post in Honolulu if Secretary Gresham should say "that in his judgment he deemed it necessary for the maintenance of harmony and good feeling." [16] As the New York *Evening Post* commented: "The irrational conduct of Sir Julian Pauncefote in not sending a protest to the State Department against the annexation of Hawaii, or against the overthrow of the Queen, or against the landing of '300 blue jackets' from the 'Boston,' or against something, is most exasperating." It was "characteristic of British policy to do the very opposite of what the newspaper men predict." The *Post* guessed that John Bull was "holding back his protest in the belief that Uncle Sam's appetite for Hawaii will cool if he finds that nobody has any objection to his taking it. This would be just like the crafty, sinister, double-dealing British policy." [17] Since England had shown, in the words of the *Nation,* "a most provoking indifference to the whole affair, and as the glory was mostly to be won from vexing and triumphing over her, her calm unconcern has robbed the enterprise of all its glamour." [18]

Yet the absence of a protest did not eliminate the British bugbear.

15. See most American newspapers, including the New York *Tribune,* New York *Herald,* New York *Globe,* Boston *Herald,* San Francisco *Morning Call,* San Francisco *Chronicle,* Atlanta *Constitution,* Washington *Evening Star,* and Washington *Post,* Jan. 30, 31, Feb. 1, 1893, as well as the Montreal *Gazette* and the *Pall Mall Gazette,* Jan. 31, 1893.

16. Memos. of Conversations with the Secretary of State 1893–98, Conversation with Sir Julian Pauncefote, March 16, 1893, USDS, Misc. Archives. Cf. my "Great Britain and the Sovereignty of Hawaii," *Pacific Historical Review,* 31, 337–43.

17. Feb. 1, 1893. It was alleged later that Pauncefote did not protest because he was posted as to the action Cleveland intended to take; consequently, there was no need for Lord Salisbury to say a word (F. M. Hatch to H. E. Cooper, minister of foreign affairs, June 9, 1897, AH, Hawaiian Officials Abroad, U.S. Minister, Washington).

18. Vol. 56, March 2, 1893.

Commissioner Marsden, in a February 26 interview in Chicago while en route to Honolulu, was reported as saying that unless the Democrats speedily annexed the islands, the United States would not be afforded another chance. England was prepared to act at a moment's notice in the event of a failure of the negotiations, and British warships were already on their way to the islands to be on hand to intervene.[19]

The treaty, duly approved by the Foreign Relations Committee, was reported back to the Senate and placed on the calendar. The wave of apparent sanction which had greeted the advent of the commissioners was succeeded by a perceptible reaction: as time passed, so many dissident elements became apparent—particularly among the Democrats, who indicated their unwillingness to vote for the treaty, which they considered a purely Republican measure, and also among senators from states producing both cane and beet sugars, who opposed the entry of Hawaiian coolie labor into competition with their products in the American sugar market[20]—that friends of union believed it inexpedient to force a test vote. A number of Democratic senators intimated to a New York *Times* correspondent before adjournment that, while there was no opposition on their part to the acquisition of Hawaii, they did not approve of the method adopted by the Harrison administration, and if Hawaii came under the United States flag, the arrangements would have to be far different from those proposed.[21] Senator Orville H. Platt told Minister Mott Smith on February 24 that were all the senators present, the two-thirds vote would be easy, but that with a daily attendance of only fifty out of eighty-eight, the margin was so close that it would be unsafe to force a vote. Finally, Foster resigned and left for Paris to assume his duties there as one of the United States members of the Behring Sea Commission, leaving behind an expression of his desire to see the ratification accomplished in the Harrison administration. His departure was considered most unfortunate by the Hawaiian deputation.[22]

Individual Influence

Lorrin A. Thurston and William R. Castle made a specialty of meeting the editors of the most influential journals, particularly those

19. *Times,* Feb. 28, 1893.
20. Ibid., Feb. 24, 1893.
21. New York *Times,* March 10, 1893.
22. Mott Smith to Dole, Feb. 25, 1893. Castle Diary (Feb. 24, 1893), p. 18.

opposed to annexation, such as the New York *Post,* the *Nation,* the New York *World,* the Chicago *Herald,* and the Chicago *Post.* All made their strongest fight on the grounds that the proposed treaty was, as the *Nation* put it, "a job by, of and for sugar." After hearing Thurston's convincing explanation of the sugar situation, most editors expressed their satisfaction and somewhat modified their attack. E. L. Godkin, editor of both the New York *Post* and the *Nation,* explained that although he did not believe in annexation and would continue to oppose it, he would thereafter eliminate the sugar job from his argument. Thurston considered this a significant victory, for with this elimination the opponents of the treaty had simply the stock argument that annexation was contrary to American policy —an argument which found very slight response among the people.[1]

Thurston and Carter, as well as Castle before his departure for Honolulu, grasped every opportunity to educate the American public in the direction of annexation, "bringing the question home to the intelligent portion of the community, who have influence with members of Congress." In churches, by presenting simply the religious and social side of the case, "which tells with Christian people," Castle was able to convince his audiences that the annexation movement was not a job, and to convert their members to union. Charles L. Carter attempted to win over a large and attentive assemblage of the National Georgraphic Society.[2] Thurston lectured to groups in Montclair and Trenton, New Jersey, to the Norwalk Club, the Cornell University student body, and the Union League of Chicago, one of the strongest political organizations in the West. He revised a paper on "American Interest in Hawaii," which the preceding autumn he had read at the Social Science Club in Honolulu, and had it published in the March 1893 issue of the *North American Review* under the new title "The Advantages of Annexation." After reviewing Hawaiian-American diplomatic and economic relations, with supporting statistical data, and analyzing the benefits to American trade and commerce of the reciprocity treaties, Thurston expressed the belief that the United States would not "allow these islands to be forced, by untoward circumstances, to seek the commercial alliance and political friendship of other nations—America's rivals," thus losing "the accrued benefits of sixty years of statesmanship."[3] This was for public consumption. The

1. Thurston to Dole, Feb. 9, April 7, 1893, in Thurston, *Memoirs,* pp. 291–95.
2. Castle Diary (Feb. 24, March 10, 1893), pp. 18–19, 31.
3. Vol. 156, 80–81; cf. pp. 265–81.

shrewd agent knew and expressed to President Dole the simple fact that "we have no market for anything except the United States . . . I can see nothing in sight for us, in the direction of England, and other countries are out of the question." [4] It was simply annexation to the United States or nothing, and the commissioner bent his utmost efforts—noble and ignoble—toward that end.

Another of the delegation's means was that of securing Americans who had resided in, or had been associated in some way with, Hawaii to speak out for union. Charles R. Bishop, in an interview in San Francisco, asserted that it was "absolutely essential that some strong foreign power should assume a protectorate over the islands as we are tired of native rule." A republic was out of the question; if it should come to that, he would not be long in getting rid of his interests there.[5] Benjamin F. Dillingham, who was in New York seeking a loan for his Hawaiian railroad enterprises, declared that Claus Spreckels was innocent of any political intriguing to foment the revolution; the Queen alone was responsible for the trouble.[6] Rear Admiral George Brown, only a week back from command of the Pacific squadron, described Liliuokalani as "an obstinate, stubborn, woman, self-willed and unpopular." It was absolutely necessary that she be deposed.[7] Jack W. Girvin, Hawaiian consul at San Diego, and W. H. Dimond kept annexation to the front on the West Coast —the former by getting columns in the newspapers squelching unfavorable dispatches, the latter by securing the unanimous endorsement of the San Francisco Chamber of Commerce to the proposal.

General Samuel C. Armstrong, principal of Hampton Institute, in a long letter published in the February 2, 1893, edition of the New York *Post* and reproduced in the *Pacific Commercial Advertiser*,[8] made an urgent plea for annexation based upon religious, moral, and commercial grounds. He argued that since "the late Queen is unscrupulous to the last degree, of no moral standing whatever, and not entitled to the least confidence or respect," her restoration to

4. Thurston to Dole, June 13, 1893, printed in Thurston, *Memoirs*, pp. 296–301. See my "Myth of Hawaii's Swing," *Pacific Historical Review, 33* (1964), p. 290.

5. San Francisco *Morning Call*, Feb. 2, 1893.

6. Ibid., Jan. 31, 1893.

7. Boston *Evening Transcript*, Jan. 30, 1893. When Castle visited Brown in the Navy Department on February 14, the Admiral was friendly, but discreetly "kept his mouth shut on annexation matters." Castle Diary (Feb. 14, 1893), p. 34.

8. Feb. 23, 1893.

power "would mean destruction of the progressive element in Hawaiian life and the collapse of all hope for that people." The United States now had an opportunity to establish her influence in the Pacific Ocean, and it was not wise bluntly and stubbornly "to object to taking territory which lies in a position so vital to American commerce in the future." Since the General and former head of the Freedmen's Bureau was well known and respected, his letter carried considerable weight. Henry N. Castle, brother of William R. Castle, and Professor William B. Oleson helped the cause through articles published in the New York *Independent*, a Congregational weekly, "paying little attention to congregationalism, but much to national policies," [9] and having close ties with the missionary element in the Hawaiian Islands. Oleson also performed a beneficial service among the newspaper editors of the eastern cities and with the American Board of Commissioners for Foreign Missions in Boston.

That Board, at a meeting in Worcester, Massachusetts, October 10–13, 1893, adopted a memorial which called attention "to the obligation resting on the United States to assume some adequate responsibility for civil order and tranquillity in Hawaii." Whether that responsibility should take the form of annexation or of a protectorate was not in the province of the Board to say, but it respectfully urged such action as would "secure stability in the government of Hawaii, and promote peace among her people." [10]

Gorham D. Gilman, of Boston, espoused with alacrity the cause of the revolutionists, repeating and vouching for the political slander directed against the deposed Liliuokalani.[11] Although an ardent Republican himself, he was on intimate and friendly terms with all the newspapermen of his home city, and went out of his way to introduce Castle and Thurston to the editors of the Boston journals. This enthusiastic advocate of annexation reportedly spent as much time booming Hawaii—writing articles to newspapers, lecturing upon the subject, and furthering the ends of the commissioners—as

9. Frank Luther Mott, *American Journalism—A History of Newspapers in the United States through 260 Years: 1690 to 1950* (New York, 1950), p. 378. See the May 18 and Dec. 14, 1893, issues of the *Independent* (New York), Vol. 45.

10. *Eighty-Third Annual Report of the American Board of Commissioners for Foreign Missions Presented at the Meeting Held at Worcester, Massachusetts, October 10–13, 1893* (Boston, 1893), p. xiv. Cf. *Pacific Commercial Advertiser,* Aug. 13, 1898.

11. Liliuokalani, *Hawaii's Story,* pp. 332–33. Cf. Albert N. Marquis, ed., *Who's Who in New England* (1st ed. Chicago, 1909).

he did upon his own business of wholesale drugs. Thurston succeeded in having him rewarded for his assistance by securing his appointment as Hawaiian consul at Boston, replacing Lawrence Bond, who did not take enthusiastically to the new order. Although the Minister recognized that it was a disagreeable thing to turn a man out of office for no specific act, Hawaiian officials needed to pull all the strings they could; and Gilman, "with his live active ways and the authority which he as Hawaiian representative" would wield, was naturally considered more valuable to the cause in the Boston vicinity than Bond.[12]

One of the most effective weapons wielded by the annexationists was the defamation of Queen Liliuokalani. After pressure was removed from Claus Spreckels and the sugar planters as fomenters of the revolution, foul accusations were flung at the dethroned monarch, charging her as being a "battered harpy"—idolatrous, wicked, heathen, and immoral. These charges were made by men who, according to Theo. H. Davies, never refused, for themselves or their daughters, "invitations to sit at the Queen's table . . . to the very eve of the revolution." [13] Even the Reverend Sereno E. Bishop who had written an article about the Queen[14] bearing testimony to her excellent character and her zeal in Christian work, resorted— after failing to have Hawaii annexed by praising the islands, their people, and their Queen—to vile falsehoods to accomplish the objective, employing the columns of the New York *Independent* to carry on a tirade against a "debauched" Queen and "heathenish monarchy," on whose side were "the kahuana sorcerers and idolators, all the white corruptionists, and those who wish to make Honolulu a center for the manufacture and distribution of opium, together with the lewd and drunken majority of the native race, who live largely by

12. Thurston to Dole, Aug. 11, 1893. Cf. G. D. Gilman, Sept. 13, 1893, Consul's Commissions, Aug. 1879–July 1898, p. 182; *Pacific Commercial Advertiser*, Nov. 30, 1898; July 11, 1902.

13. Theo. H. Davies' letter of July 15, 1893, Honolulu *Daily Bulletin*, Aug. 9, 1893. Cf. Theo. H. Davies, *Letters upon the Political Crisis in Hawaii*, January 1893 to January 1894 (Honolulu, 1894), p. 19.

14. *Review of Reviews*, 4 (New York, 1891), 147–63. The same article, entitled "Her Majesty 'Lily-of-the-Sky' Queen of the Sandwich Islands," appeared in the London edition of the *Review of Reviews*, 4 (1891), 227–34. Entire sections of Bishop's paper were published in the San Francisco *Examiner* of January 29, 1893, with the parts complimentary to Queen Liliuokalani omitted.

the lucrative prostitution of their females to the wifeless Chinese and Japanese." [15]

John L. Stevens, homeward bound, issued a statement to the American press in May 1893 in which he attempted to show "how utterly vicious and demoralizing" the monarchy had become under the "semi-barbaric" King Kalakaua and his sister Liliuokalani. He accused her of having appointed "to the chief executive office of the islands the Tahitian half-white, who had sustained scandalous relations to her," and whom she had installed in her palace, though he had a lawfully married wife.[16] Instead of appointing ministers possessing the confidence of the legislative majority and the business-men of the islands, she selected those of her own type of character, those whom she knew would retain her illicit palace-favorite in power. The *Review of Reviews* for June 1893 carried a passage from "a forthcoming history of Hawaii" by one of its "most eminent citizens," which read: "The Church has never gone to her in vain for pecuniary aid, yet she is known to have danced the hula herself and to have maintained the institution at Iolani Palace. It may be the fashion, here and there, to say that the queen has been badly treated, but the blunt truth about her is that she stood for in-decency, paganism and commercial distress, and that she deserved the fate that came to her." [17] Such statements, published after the revolution and intended to place the former Queen in an awkward or utterly false position, were also calculated to deceive the Ameri-can people on the important topic of annexation—and they did. Senator George Frisbie Hoar of Massachusetts, in drafting the Re-publican party platform of 1894, included a plank which read: "No barbarous Queen beheading men in Hawaii." Later he learned that Liliuokalani was a true Christian woman, and on several occa-

15. "Freedom in Hawaii at Bay," *Independent*, 45 (1894), 5.

16. The marshal of the kingdom lived with his wife in a bungalow situated on a corner of the palace grounds and in a cottage at Washington Place. Mrs. Wilson, daughter of an American, John S. Townsend, who deserted his Hawaiian wife and children, was reared by Liliuokalani before she came to the throne.

17. *Review of Reviews*, 7 (New York 1893), 595. Cf. Liliuokalani, pp. 248, 327–28; Julius W. Pratt, *Expansionists of 1898: The Acquisition of Hawaii and the Spanish Islands* (Baltimore, 1936), pp. 160 ff.; *Harper's Weekly* (Dec. 2, 1893), p. 1146; S. C. Armstrong's letter published in the New York *Post*, Feb. 3, 1893; James Schouler, "A Review of the Hawaiian Controversy," *Forum*, 16 (1894), 677; Stevens' statement, *Hawaiian Star*, June 14, 1893; editorial, ibid., June 15, 1893.

sions publicly retracted his statement deriding her,[18] but the damage was irreparable.

The Strategists' Point of View

Immediately after news of the Hawaiian revolution reached the United States, Alfred Thayer Mahan, president of the Naval War College, Newport, Rhode Island, and author of *The Influence of Sea Power on History, 1660–1783* invited attention, in a letter to the editor of the New York *Times,* to one aspect of the situation which had not been mentioned but which to him appeared significant, namely "the relation of the islands not merely to our own and to European countries, but to China." How vitally important the group might become in the future was evident from the great number of Chinese, relative to the whole population, already settled in the archipelago. The question for the whole civilized world to consider was "whether the Sandwich Islands, with their geographical and military importance unrivaled by that of any other position in the North Pacific, shall in the future be an outpost of European civilization or of comparative barbarism of China." [1]

This letter attracted the attention of Walter Hines Page, editor of the *Forum,* who requested an article developing the argument. The result was an essay entitled "Hawaii and Our Future Sea Power," which urged annexation of the Hawaiian Islands by the United States. This would be "a first fruit and a token that the nation in evolution has aroused itself to the necessity of carrying its life . . . beyond the borders which have heretofore sufficed for its activities." Mahan referred to two chains of British possessions— one being Gibraltar, Malta, Cyprus, Egypt, Aden, and India, and the other, Halifax, Bermuda, Saint Lucia, and Jamaica—which strengthened the British hold upon the Atlantic, the Caribbean, and the Isthmus of Panama. In the Pacific, where her position was much less satisfactory, Great Britain was again found holding the two extremities of a line—British Columbia in the northeast and Australia and New Zealand in the southwest—between which she must inevitably desire the intermediate links; there was no "good reason why she should not have them, except the superior, more urgent,

18. George Frisbie Hoar, *Autobiography of Seventy Years* (2 vols., New York, 1903), 2, 262–65.

1. Letter to the editor of the New York *Times,* Feb. 1, 1893.

more vital necessities of another people—our own." Of these links, the Hawaiian group possessed "unique importance—not from its intrinsic commercial value but from its favorable position for maritime and military control."

Mahan indicated that the strategic importance of the Hawaiian Islands depended upon such factors as situation, strength, and resources. Geographical situation was of the most consequence, because it resulted from the nature of things and was not within the power of man to change. The other two factors, when deficient, could be artificially supplied in whole or in part. Fortifications remedy the weakness of position, while foresight accumulates beforehand the resources that nature does not yield. In viewing a map of the Pacific, two circumstances were immediately apparent. The Hawaiian Islands stand by themselves in a state of comparative isolation. They, however, also form the center of a large circle whose radius is approximately the distance from Honolulu to San Francisco. The circumference of this circle on the west and south passes through the outer fringe of the system of South Pacific archipelagoes. Within the circle a few scattered islets, barren and unimportant, seem to emphasize the failure of nature to bridge the interval separating Hawaii from her peers in the Southern Pacific. The proximity of that country and the relationship of its people to the United States, the most powerful community bordering on the Pacific, naturally makes the islands more important to her than to any other state.[2]

Rear Admiral George E. Belknap, an unyielding annexationist, was also convinced that the Hawaiian group was of momentous and vital concern to Americans. In a letter to the Boston *Herald* he applied the doctrine of propinquity to Hawaiian-United States relations. It appeared that nature had established the Hawaiian Islands to be ultimately occupied as an outpost of the great Western republic on its western border. The time had now arrived for the fulfillment of that design. Commercial and political benefits to both peoples would be assured by the consummation of annexation. "Not to take the fruit within our grasp and annex the group now begging us to take it would be folly, indeed a mistake of the gravest nature, both for the statesmen of the day and for the men among us of high commercial views and great enterprises." He warned that if the

2. *Forum*, 15 (1893), 1–13. Cf. "The Bermuda of the Pacific," *Hawaiian Star* (April 25, 1893), editorial.

British lion "got her paws on that group," Honolulu would become one of her most important strongholds of power. At the same time he opposed joint control with Great Britain: "We want no entangling alliances, we have had enough of that business at Samoa. We want no joint protectorate; no occupation there by any European power; no Pacific Egypt. We need the group as part and parcel of the United States and should take what is offered us, even at the hazard of war." Our statesmen should act in this matter in the spirit and resolve that obtained for us the vast Louisiana purchase, the annexation of Texas, and the acquisition of California. The administration that secured to the United States this "coign of vantage" would "score a great measure of beneficent achievement to the credit side of its account." [3]

Although not a naval strategist, Dr. J. C. McGrew, an American resident of Honolulu, founder and leading member of the Annexation Club, established after the revolution, and editor of the *Hawaiian Star*, voiced similar concern and recommendations. He was certain that Great Britain, if engaged in conflict with the United States, would promptly occupy the Hawaiian Islands, excusing herself to their government by the plea of "imperious necessity." Rather than run the risk of the islands falling to England in time of war, or to wait for such an emergency before seizing them as a matter of defense, the United States ought to go ahead and take them at a time when they would come easily. McGrew indicated the parallel of the Hawaiian group as an outwork to Heligoland which, after much diplomatic bartering, Kaiser Wilhelm II obtained in 1890. His astute military mind perceived that this strategic island in the North Sea adjacent to Hamburg would be a dangerous part of the offensive military equipment of a power with which Germany might be at war. But the latter country, using Heligoland as a base of maritime operations, could attack any squadron from the rear which might undertake to annoy her frontiers, or could at least divert from the neighborhood of those frontiers a large part of the hostile demonstration.[4] Heligoland was therefore vital to Germany's defensive system.

Strategists generally argued that a definitive American control of Hawaii would materially lessen the naval force that our growing commercial interests in the Pacific would require if there were

3. Boston *Herald*, Jan. 31, 1893. San Francisco *Examiner*, Feb. 1, 1893. *Sen. Reps.*, 55 Cong., 2 sess., No. 681, pp. 106–07. Belknap retired on Jan. 22, 1894.

4. *Hawaiian Star* (May 11, 12, 1893), editorials.

doubts about the control of that archipelago, or if rival powers shared our rights and privileges there. Our possession of the "key" to the North Pacific would make for permanent peace in that quarter and, at the same time, for comparatively small armaments.

CLEVELAND'S POLICY

Whatever may have been the cause of delay in ratifying the annexation treaty, the Hawaiian issue was not disposed of before March 4, 1893, when the Democratic, anti-imperialist Grover Cleveland returned to the presidency. A friend of both Queen Liliuokalani and Sanford Dole, he was chagrined by the rapidity with which the provisional government had been recognized and the equally hasty conclusion of the treaty. Cleveland was by no means unfamiliar with Hawaiian affairs. When he had entered the White House in 1885, the reciprocity convention, with the amendment leasing Pearl Harbor to the United States for its exclusive use as a naval base, was pending. It was later ratified by the Senate, and proclaimed by him. In his second annual message he had expressed the conviction that the intimacy of our relations with Hawaii should be encouraged. From inferences in his annual messages of 1886 and 1888, the conclusion was drawn that he favored appropriations by the United States government for building a cable to Hawaii. In his first administration he reportedly had favored the annexation not only of Hawaii but also of Cuba.[1]

Five days after his second inauguration, just as the Senate was

1. Sen. John T. Morgan claimed that he could name at least one confidential friend of Cleveland who could support this belief (New York *Times*, Jan. 25, 1898).

to consider further the treaty, Cleveland, upon the advice of Walter Quintin Gresham, his Secretary of State, sent a terse one-sentence message to the chamber in which he took the unusual though not unprecedented step of withdrawing the treaty for re-examination.[2] He appointed as special commissioner to Hawaii James H. Blount, an avowed anti-imperialist, who had represented Georgia in the house continually from 1872 to 1893, when he declined further service. During his last term he had chaired the Committee on Foreign Affairs. The letter of credence of this "special commissioner" declared that "in all matters pertaining to the existing government of the Islands, the authority of Mr. Blount is paramount." [3]

While some Republican senators were indignant at this procedure, declaring that Cleveland's action was presumptuous and showed want of good taste, if not disrespect, for ex-President Harrison, a number of their Democratic counterparts complimented Cleveland on his "iron nerve." Mott Smith felt that the step might mean modification of the terms and conditions of annexation, mainly proposed to give the negotiations and treaty a Democratic flavor, or to show an indisposition to consummate the negotiation until, through a plebiscite or a visit of a senatorial commission to the islands, information could be obtained proving that native Hawaiians were agreeable to annexation. Thurston's private opinion, drawn from secret agents and informants, was that Harrison's course in moving so quickly had piqued Cleveland; that he had withdrawn the treaty to show that he was in control of the situation; and that if resubmitted, it would contain some revisions as a justification for his action. The only amendments suggested were the addition of a clause specifically renouncing all claim to a bounty on Hawaiian sugar, and one reducing the amount to be paid to the Queen and to Princess Kaiulani. The commissioners did not intend to make any fight on either of these points, for after the most cursory examination of the situation in Washington, they were convinced of the utter impossibility of getting one cent of bounty out of the United States Treasury on their sugar, and Thurston considered that they were

2. Richardson, ed., *Messages and Papers of the Presidents*, 9, 393. Cleveland withdrew from the Senate, in 1885, a treaty which his immediate predecessor had negotiated with Nicaragua for the construction by the United States of a canal through Nicaraguan territory. He also withdrew pending reciprocity treaties with Spain and the Dominican Republic.

3. Gresham to Blount, March 11, 1893; encl. Cleveland to Dole and Gresham to Stevens, both March 11, 1893—all printed in *For. Rels.* (1894), App. II, pp. 467–69.

under no obligation to procure for the Queen "a high salary for having gotten things into a mess." [4] Charles L. Carter, through some of Cleveland's friends in New York, discovered that the treaty had aroused the President's suspicions against the Republican administration, and that he would send a commission to Honolulu to investigate the revolution. Once a report favorable to union was submitted, they expected that another treaty with some modifications would be negotiated and promptly ratified at a special session of Congress.[5]

Although Secretary of State Gresham remained noncommittal, there was considerable press opinion that annexation, being inevitable, was only delayed. The numerical strength and power of the expansionist Democrats in the Senate, the fact that several leading Democratic newspapers were pro-annexation, Cleveland's and Bayard's policy in furthering reciprocity with Hawaii in 1885, and the former's insight into the importance of that kingdom—all lent support to the idea that his policy would not be unfriendly to the closer unity of the two countries. Some editors thought that the President intended to restore the Queen and then negotiate with her for annexation of her kingdom to the United States. The New York *Times* believed that he favored a protectorate rather than annexation. Editorially, that newspaper pointed out that withdrawal of the treaty was in no sense a prejudgment of the case; it was, on the contrary, a definite step to prevent the case from being prejudged. The treaty had not been approved by public opinion: "The simple fact is that there was no public opinion, and no means of forming any." Cleveland might be trusted to deal with the situation "in a sensible and broad way." [6]

On the other hand, certain Republican organs and those elements in the country "personally interested in the proposed steal" either disapproved or condemned as a political blunder the President's action, claiming that in interfering in the Hawaiian matter, he violated one of the most necessary traditions of our government: that an act of one executive is binding on another and should not be re-

4. Mott Smith to Dole, and Thurston to Dole, both March 10, 1893, AH, Hawaiian Officials Abroad, U.S. Minister, Washington. The communications hereafter of Hawaiian Officials with each other, unless otherwise indicated, are contained in this file.

5. Carter to Dole, March 22, 29, 1893.

6. New York *Times*, New York *Herald*, Boston *Evening Transcript*, Philadelphia *Inquirer*, March 10, 1893. New York *Sun*, March 10, 11, 1893. Charleston *News and Courier*, March 20, 1893. *North American Review*, 7 (1893), 399.

versed. Of this opinion were the New York *Tribune,* New York *Press,* and Chicago *Inter-Ocean.*

Carl Schurz, apparently considering the procedure tantamount to a rejection of annexation, jubilantly declared:

> President Cleveland deserves the thanks of the country for the prompt withdrawal of the Hawaiian treaty from the Senate . . . What he has really done is to protect the republic against the injection into its system of a dangerous element of weakness . . . The possession of the Hawaiian Islands as part of our national domain, or of any similar distant possession, with all the responsibilities this involves, would, therefore, in our present condition, not be an element of strength, but an element of weakness.

In Schurz's opinion it wuold be an evil day when the American people embarked upon an expansionist program that would entail the burden of immense armaments.[7] The distinguished publicist sent a copy of this *Harper's Weekly* article to President Cleveland, who read it with "great satisfaction," and observed: "I do not now say that I should hold annexation in all circumstances unwise, but I am sure we ought to stop and look and think. That's exactly what we are doing now." [8]

The Initial Approach

During their first audience with the new Secretary of State on March 9, the Hawaiian commissioners found themselves confronted with an austere and frowning gentleman, determined to impress his stern disapproval of the policy of the preceding administration. William Castle sensed trouble, even ruin, ahead if "this dark and vengeful man" dictated the policy of the Cleveland administration. Efforts on the part of Thurston and Castle the following day to ascertain the intentions of the new administration from Gresham resulted only in the statement that the subject of the treaty had been "precipitated upon the administration upon such short notice," that, because of insufficient knowledge of the facts and details, "we desire

7. "The Annexation Policy," *Harper's Weekly,* 37 (1893), 246. Schurz enlarged upon this same theme in a nine-page article entitled "Manifest Destiny," which appeared in *Harper's Magazine,* 87 (1897), 737–46.

8. Frederic Bancroft, ed., *Speeches, Correspondence and Political Papers of Carl Schurz* (6 vols. New York, 1913), 5, 131, 133–34.

time for consideration of the subject," and that the treaty had been withdrawn for that purpose. A second call at the State Department, where they were coldly received by the Secretary, convinced the two commissioners that the probability of any favorable action on Hawaiian annexation was "not only faint, but almost nugatory." They then realized "their error in risking and staking all on Foster's success," and "that they ought to have got the ear of Cleveland." [1]

The course that the President intended to pursue was indicated by Secretary Gresham in a conversation with the Russian minister, Prince Cantacuzene, on March 16, when the former succinctly stated that he thought so far as the Hawaiian Islands were concerned, the administration was inclined to be conservative and would adhere to and be consistent with the traditional policy of the United States. He implied that it would not favor principles and a course looking to the acquisition of foreign territory.[2] This proved to be the case. Nevertheless, in the interval between Blount's appointment and the submission of his report, the President and his Secretary of State maintained a sphinxlike silence, refusing to commit themselves on the disposition of the Hawaiian question.

Blount arrived in Honolulu on March 29, 1893, under circumstances far from auspicious for assembling an objective report, for both royalists and revolutionists schemed to influence him. Having been informed by President Dole that the provisional government could preserve order without United States assistance, and convinced that a fair and impartial investigation could not be made until the protectorate was abolished, the commissioner, acting under instructions that he might use his own discretion but that no blood was to be shed,[3] on March 31 ordered Admiral Skerrett to haul

1. Castle Diary (March 9, 10, 14, 1893), pp. 30–31, 35. Thurston to Dole, March 10, 1893, USDS, Miscellaneous Archives, Memoranda of Conversations with Secretary of State, 1893–98. Cf. "Hawaii Must Wait a While," New York Times, March 11, 1893.

2. Ibid.

3. Blount to Gresham, April 6, 1893, Blount Report, pp. 4–5. Commissioner and Minister Blount's dispatches, with lengthy enclosures, are printed in this volume. The early ones, as commissioner, are not in USDS, Dispatches, Hawaii, 25. His entries in the latter begin with No. 1, May 24, 1893. Stevens was recalled and left Honolulu on that date. Consequently, Blount's dispatches, as minister, commence where Stevens' end, No. 96, May 18, 1893. Blount's Nos. 1–5, May 24–June 23, 1893, are printed in For. Rels. (1894), App. II, pp. 421–30, and in House Ex. Docs., 53 Cong., 2 sess., No. 48, "Hawaiian Correspondence," pp. 155–64.

down the United States flag from the government building and
re-embark the troops on the cruiser *Boston*. The Admiral, under protest, complied with these orders from a civilian, his critical attitude
being in line with naval opinion. There was no public manifestation
of excitement, but later Rear Admiral George Belknap asserted that
Blount's commission empowering him to pull down the flag was in
direct violation of naval regulations.[4]

Like other dramatic events associated with Hawaii, the hauling
down of the American emblem brought a mixed reaction in the
United States. In the national capital the withdrawal of the protectorate was received "with signs of popular regret." The New York
Times, Boston *Herald,* Boston *Evening Transcript,* and *Review of
Reviews* took a calm and reasoned view of Cleveland's action, stating that it did not necessarily mean that the United States had
abandoned annexation. Thurston reported that the Republican
papers in the Midwest "had fairly torn their shirts off," while the
Democratic ones had "been as mild as sucking does." [5] In the words
of Carl Schurz, "no end of senseless rant was indulged in about the
'hauling down of the American flag' from the Hawaiian state-house
—as if any man of self-respect would deny that wherever the flag
floats in dishonor, honor commands it to be hauled down." [6] The
keynote of opposition to tampering with the United States emblem
was perhaps struck in an April 14 editorial of the vexed, anti-
Democratic *Commercial Advertiser* of New York, which fulminated:
"In ordering 'Old Glory' pulled down at Honolulu President Cleveland turned back the hands on the dial of civilization. Native rule,
ignorant, naked, heathen, is re-established; and the dream of an
American republic at the cross-roads of the Pacific—a dream which
Seward and Marcy and Blaine indulged, and the fulfillment of which
the more enlightened of our 65,000,000 people awaited with glad
anticipation, has been shattered by Grover Cleveland, the Buffalo
Lilliputian!"

Theodore Roosevelt felt very strong about the matter. In a private
letter to an acquaintance he wrote: "I am a bit of believer in the
manifest destiny doctrine; I believe in more ships; I believe in
ultimately driving every European power off this continent, and I

4. *Morgan Report,* pp. 388, 395–97, 401, 714–16.
5. Thurston to Dole, April 23, 1893.
6. "Grover Cleveland's Second Administration," *McClure's Magazine,* 9
(1897), 364.

don't want to see our flag hauled down where it has been hauled up."[7]

President Dole, however, was not at all disturbed, for he felt that Hawaii's case had not been prejudiced and understood Cleveland's feeling that the existence of a protectorate confused the situation and was "an obstacle to the clear understanding of the strength and character of the Provisional Government."[8] As for William R. Castle, he was of the opinion that "taking down the flag and compelling us to stand on our own feet is going to be a good thing for us."[9]

The Blount Investigation

Although Blount's visit was regarded by the Queen's supporters as entirely in their favor, they were soon somewhat disabused of that idea when they found that the commissioner was taciturn and that he listened to everything, but made no reply. Three moot points which disturbed the annexationists in Hawaii were settled by the publication in the Honolulu press, on May 15 and 16, 1893, of the text of Blount's instructions. They made known that: (1) the commissioner brought with him no authority to restore the ex-Queen, nor to interfere in any way with the domestic policy of the provisional government; (2) the power of the United States would be exercised against foreign aggrandizement upon these islands; and (3) the settlement of annexation did not fall within the scope of the commissioner's duty, but was especially reserved to the President and Congress.

While Blount's appointment was harshly criticized by annexationists at home and in Honolulu, he conducted an independent and judicious investigation, and refused to have anything to do with the scheme of three mainland journalists to arrange Liliuokalani's abdication on a pension.[1] After three and a half months of careful in-

7. Roosevelt to James C. Clarkson, April 22, 1893, in Elting E. Morison, ed., *Letters of Theodore Roosevelt* (8 vols., Cambridge, Mass., 1951), *1*, 313, No. 400.

8. Dole to Thurston, April 6, 1893.

9. Castle to Thurston, April 8, 1893.

1. Blount to Gresham, April 26, May 24, 1893, *Blount Report*, Nos. 3, 7. All of Blount's dispatches as minister referred to hereafter are in this volume. Most are printed in *For. Rels.* (1894), App. II. For details of the machination and the outcome see *Morgan Report*, pp. 393, 666–74, 691–92; *Blount Report*, pp. 13–15, 22.

quiry, which included taking testimony from both royalists and revolutionists, although some of the latter declined to testify, he submitted a final report, dated July 11, 1893, which indicated that on moral and legal grounds the treaty of annexation was unjustified. In both his report and his dispatches to the Secretary of State, Blount condemned Stevens' action before, during, and after the revolution, particularly the use of marines and his unwarranted proclamation of a protectorate. The leaders of the revolutionary movement would not have undertaken it but for the Minister's promise to protect them; had it not been for this, no request to land troops would have been made; had the troops not been landed, no measures for the organization of a new government would have been taken. Most significant of all, Blount furnished evidence that the revolution did not rest upon the will of the majority. "If the votes of persons claiming allegiance to foreign countries were excluded," he reported, "it [annexation] would be defeated by more than five to one." Native Hawaiians who signed petitions for it did so under pressure from the sugar planters; furthermore, there was not an annexationist who would dare to submit the question to popular vote. Economic motives, revolving around sugar and large shipping interests, were the strongest elements in the movement for annexation.[2]

Under difficult and trying circumstances, two thousand miles from home and with nobody to talk to but Admiral Skerrett and a stenographer,[3] the Minister discharged his duties to the best of his abilities. He described his method of procedure in these words:

> I was impressed when I came to the investigation with the conviction that I had very much at stake. I had confidence in the integrity and high purposes of the President, and felt that I could give him no higher offense than to misinform him. I felt that any other than a truthful, an exhaustive, and impartial ex-

2. *Blount Report*, which was not released until a leak in the State Department caused its publication late in Nov. 1893. Cf. *For. Rels.* (1894), App. II, pp. 421 ff.

3. Sworn Statement of James H. Blount, *Morgan Report*, p. 415. Blount, according to James Wodehouse, frequently discussed with him the Hawaiian situation and encouraged an expression of views (Wodehouse to Rosebery, July 18, 1893, No. 10, FO 58/279). Judge Alfred S. Hartwell claimed that Blount avoided taking statements from many prominent persons who were known to be averse to the monarchy, while some of those whose statements he received in its favor were not generally regarded in Honolulu "as unprejudiced, and in some instances as persons of veracity" (Hartwell to Olney, Dec. 5, 1893, Olney Papers, Vol. 12).

amination would bring about the contempt of the American people. I was, therefore, timid—over cautious, perhaps, in all my conduct in reference to it. I kept from their social life. I did not intimate any opinion to these people one way or the other. When I left those islands nobody had any idea, so far as I could gather, what my report was. Each side claimed in the newspaper that I was in favor of it. I studiously avoided communicating anything to anybody, and I turned the facts over and over again in my mind. I felt that I was alone, without anybody on earth to consult with, counsel with, and I often felt the need of somebody to advise with. But there was no impartial person to whom I could talk at all, and so the responsibility I felt the greater, and went on in that groove to the end.[4]

In a final personal letter to Secretary Gresham, informing him that private affairs made it necessary for him to return home, Blount stated that anxiety over the action of the United States would continue until the proposition to annex was accepted or rejected. In the latter contingency no sudden movement would occur. The provisional government "only rests on the use of military force, possessed of most of the arms in the islands, with a small white population to draw from to strengthen it. Ultimately it will fall. It may preserve its existence for a year or two, but not longer."[5] Rear Admiral J. S. Skerrett, writing a month earlier of unjustified arrests and the holding of persons in custody without bail, observed that "it would appear that the iron heel of military law is really what serves to keep the Provisional Government in authority."[6]

The Cleveland administration moved slowly after receiving Blount's report, studying it thoroughly, but neither releasing it immediately nor formulating a definite policy on Hawaii for more than two months, too late for the Congress to take action, as was generally expected during the extra session held from August 7 to November 3, 1893. While maintaining silence, this administration insisted upon complete impartiality. Rear Admiral Skerrett and those serving under his command were enjoined to strict neutrality,[7] and

4. *Morgan Report*, p. 389.
5. Blount to Gresham, July 31, 1893, *For. Rels.* (1894), App. II, p. 630.
6. Skerrett to Secretary of the Navy, June 28, 1893, copy in USDS, Misc. Letters, June 1893, Pt. II.
7. H. A. Herbert to Skerrett, Oct. 3, 1893, U.S. Navy Dept., R.G. 24, Bureau of Navigation, Division of Officers and Fleet, Official Confidential Correspondence.

the new commander of the Pacific station, Rear Admiral John Irwin, issued a general order in November calling the attention of all under his command to the manifest impropriety in taking sides with either political party in Hawaii. The expression of political opinion or the wearing of badges was strictly forbidden.[8]

Gresham's Position

The documentary evidence in Blount's dispatches and in his final report, received in early August 1893, indicated that the provisional government "was recognized when it had little other than a paper existence, and when the legitimate government was in full possession and control of the palace and barracks and the police station." Stevens' well-known hostility and the threatening presence of the force landed from the *Boston* "excited serious apprehension in the minds of the queen, her officers and loyal supporters." Troops were landed, "not to protect American life and property, but to aid in overthrowing the existing government." The provisional government was established with the support and sympathy of the Minister, and its continued existence was "due to the belief of the Hawaiians that if they made an effort to overthrow it they would encounter the armed forces of the United States." Stevens and the marines had overstepped their duties, and the treaty should not be resubmitted to the Senate. In a letter to the President, embracing this decision, Secretary of State Gresham asked:

> Should not the great wrong done to a feeble but independent State, by an abuse of the authority of the United States, be undone by restoring the legitimate Government? Anything short of that will not . . . satisfy the demands of justice. Can the United States consistently insist that other nations shall respect the independence of Hawaii while not respecting it themselves? Our Government was the first to recognize the independence of the Islands and it should be the last to acquire sovereignty over them by force and fraud.[1]

8. John Irwin, General Order No. 2, Nov. 29, 1893, encl. in Irwin to Secretary of the Navy, Jan. 1, 1894, ibid., copy in Cleveland Papers, Vol. 285.

1. Gresham to Cleveland, Oct. 18, 1893, *For. Rels.* (1894), App. II, pp. 459–63. New York *Times*, Washington *Post*, and other newspapers, Nov. 11, 1893, with variations in punctuation and capitalization. Over a month earlier the Secretary of State had confided practically the same to Carl Schurz. See Gresham to Schurz, Sept. 14, 1893, Schurz Papers, Vol. 109, Library of Congress; Gresham Papers, Schurz to Gresham, Sept. 24, 1893, Vol. 41, ibid.

This forthright letter, released on November 10 and published the following day, shocked many in official circles who had expected quite a different outcome from the investigation. It also brought forth a typical reaction from the American press, with several influential journals, including the New York *Times,* New York *Evening Post,* Chicago *Herald,* and Louisville *Courier Journal* supporting Gresham and Cleveland. Considerable adverse comment was generated, however, even in some Democratic and independent journals. Leading Washington papers condemned Gresham's letter. The New York *World* was mildly critical and advocated noninterference, while the New York *Sun* expressed more specifically the opposition point of view in an editorial of November 12, entitled "The Policy of Infamy," asserting: "It is not the American policy. It it not the policy of the United States Government, or of the people of this republic. It is not yet, thank God! the policy of the Democratic party. It is neither more or less than the personal determination of an executive officer, charged with temporary power, to use that power to enforce a personal conclusion, and to commit this country to his personal conclusion, regardless of consequences in infamy or blood." Cleveland's purpose was "to employ the armed power as well as the moral influence of the United States to thrust back upon a civilized people, American in their instincts and habits and aspirations, a barbarous monarchy, in the person of a vile and ridiculous person whom they have driven from the throne."

The New York *Herald,* while remaining silent editorially, published a telegram from Stevens to the effect that Gresham's position was "so extraordinary, so void of real foundation of truth, so calumnious of the living and dead," that no extended reply would be made by the former Minister at that time. Rather, he preferred "to let time and events and history decide as to the issue the Secretary has raised against the provisional government and the aspersions he sees fit to cast upon the deceased Captain of the Boston, the officers under his command and myself." [2]

The high moral position of the Cleveland administration was applauded by some of the finest spirits in American life, as attested by letters addressed to the President and his Secretary of State, excerpts from two of which will suffice. Former Secretary of State Thomas F. Bayard, ambassador at the Court of St. James, expressed his great

2. Nov. 11, 1893. Friends of Capt. G. C. Wiltse felt that his fatal illness was in part due to mortification over his removal and the qualified disapproval of his action by the Harrison administration (ibid.).

satisfaction with "the dignity and justice" of Gresham's "treatment of the Sandwich Islands matter—Our country is too great and aspires to too high a place in civilization to stoop to the small arts of trickery and bullying." [3] Charles Francis Adams, Jr., acknowledged "that it requires courage in a public man to do what he is persuaded is right, when so doing is tantamount to a defiance of 'jingoism.'" He remembered "no stand taken by a government so morally sound and dignified as that now taken by Sect. Gresham and your administration . . . It is not easy to see how the United States can protest against the policy of force pursued by England and France in their dealings with semi-civilized natives and races if we ourselves are quite unable to resist the temptation to have an occasional hack at them on our own account." [4]

In spite of the contention of some that Gresham was actuated by a grudge against President Harrison in particular and the Republican party in general, the majority opinion appeared to be that the Secretary of State was prompted by principles of morality and justice. The most apparent fact in his life, as statesman and jurist, observed the New York *Times,* was "his strict impartiality, his unswerving integrity, his courage in doing what he believes to be right. . . With Secretary Gresham, and with Judge Gresham, Justice rules over all." [5]

In a cabinet meeting of October 18, 1893, the moral view of the Secretary of State was criticized as impracticable by Attorney General Richard Olney and Secretary of the Treasury John G. Carlisle. Nine days earlier the former had sent a comprehensive seven-page private letter on the subject to Gresham, which the President had seen. The memorandum expressed the view "that a great wrong was done under the auspices" of Minister Stevens and that this should be rectified by restoring as far as possible the status quo at the time of the perpetration of the wrong. Since the Queen's government was overthrown by an exhibition of force, if it could be reinstated by a like exhibition of force without actual resort to it, there would not be any general ground for hesitation, hardly any criticism, and probably universal commendation of "an act of substantial justice." It

3. Bayard to Gresham, Nov. 25, 1893, Gresham Papers, Vol. 41. Cf. Robert Duval to Gresham, Nov. 15, 1893, and Oliver T. Morton to Gresham, Nov. 17, 1893, ibid.

4. Adams to Cleveland, Nov. 18, 1893, Cleveland Papers, Vol. 283. Cf. Allan Nevins, ed., *Letters of Grover Cleveland, 1850–1908* (Boston and New York, 1933), p. 339.

5. Dec. 17, 1893.

would be the short way out of the complication if the Stevens' government were a thing of a few hours or even of a few days existence.

The situation, however, was not so simple. The provisional government had been recognized by foreign powers and had been in authority with our acquiescence for many months. While all parties had awaited the action of the United States, that government had had complete possession of the country and its resources:

> Its acts, unless shown to be *mala fide,* ought to be recognized as legal to all intents and purposes . . . It must ever be remembered that the Stevens' government is our government; that it was set up by our Minister by the aid of our naval and military forces and was accorded the protection of our flag; and that whatever be the views of this administration, its predecessor practically sanctioned everything Minister Stevens took upon himself to do. Under such circumstances, to permit the men who were Stevens' instruments . . . to be hung or banished, or despoiled of their estates, or otherwise punished for the connection with the Stevens' government, or to leave them exposed to the risks of such consequences,

would be grossly unfair and would deservedly bring the government of the United States into great disrepute both at home and abroad.

Application of superior military force would be clearly an act of war, however righteous the cause, and would be beyond the President's constitutional power. "To hand over to the Queen's government a country more or less devastated, a people more or less diminished in number and alienated in feeling by a contest of arms, would produce a result that would be a poor substitute for that peaceful control over an uninjured territory and undecimated population which the Queen's government enjoyed at the time of U. States Minister Stevens' lawless intervention in its affairs." Since the provisional government had secured a strong backing "in the intelligent public sentiment both of Hawaii and of this country . . . the administration in undertaking to reinstate the Queen's government by force of arms would be open to the reproach of sacrificing the interests of the country and its people to the interests of the Queen's government and of her dynasty." They were not the only and first consideration. "The paramount objects of our care should be the people of Hawaii and their interests"; we had "no right to redeem the original wrong by the commission of another still greater wrong, to wit, the imposition upon Hawaii of a government not wanted by its people."

In conclusion, the Attorney General stated that in addition to providing for the security of the Queen's person pending efforts to reinstate her government, there should be required of her "full power and authority to negotiate and bring about the restoration of her government on such reasonable terms and conditions" as the United States might approve and find to be practicable. It being understood that Washington would insist upon fair dealing for all concerned, the doubts being dispelled and all apprehension of severe or vindicative measures toward the adherents of the Stevens' government being removed, Olney anticipated that they would readily follow the course recommended by the United States.[6]

Instructions were drafted to Albert S. Willis of Louisville, Kentucky, the newly confirmed minister to Hawaii, on the basis of Gresham's suggestions. The envoy, who had served in Congress from 1876 to 1886, had, in frequent conversations with the President and Secretary of State during a period of three weeks, become thoroughly familiar with their views and acquainted with the material of the Blount report. He was furnished with a letter of credence to the provisional government and with confidential instructions to inform the Queen of Cleveland's determination that the movement against her, "if not instigated, was encouraged and supported by the representative of this Government in Honolulu . . . ," and to express his "sincere regret that the reprehensible conduct of the American minister and the unauthorized presence on land of a military force of the United States obliged her to surrender her sovereignty . . . and to rely on the justice of this Government to undo the flagrant wrong." When reinstated, the President expected that she would pursue a magnanimous course by granting full amnesty to all who had participated in the movement against her. Also, all obligations created by the provisional government in due course of administration should be assumed. Having secured Liliuokalani's agreement "to pursue this wise and humane policy," the Minister was to advise the executive and ministers of the provisional government of the President's determination of the question, and to state that they were expected promptly to "relinquish to her her constitutional authority." Should the Queen decline to pursue the liberal course suggested, or should the provisional government refuse to abide by

6. Olney to Gresham, Oct. 9, 1893, Olney Papers, Vol. 11; Gresham Papers, Vol. 41.

the President's decision, the envoy was to report the facts and await further instructions. In dealing with this "delicate situation," he was to be guided largely by his own good judgment.[7]

Willis' Mission

The envoy secured a private interview with the deposed sovereign on November 13, at which time he offered her protection on either a United States warship or at the legation, and conveyed the President's assurances and regrets, along with the expectation that when she was reinstated she would show "forgiveness and magnanimity," that she would "wish to be Queen of all the people," and that she would "make haste to secure their love and loyalty and to establish peace, friendship, and good government." When asked if she would grant complete amnesty to all persons connected with the provisional government, Liliuokalani reported the reply that it was beyond her powers "as a constitutional sovereign," that this "was a matter for the privy council and for the cabinet," and that "our laws read that those who were guilty of treason should suffer the penalty of death." [1] According to Willis, she answered as follows: "There are certain laws of my Government by which I shall abide. My decision would be, as the law directs, that such persons should be beheaded and their property confiscated." When the Minister asked if Liliuokalani would carry out that law, she, according to her memory, responded that they "would be more inclined personally to punish them by banishment, and confiscation of their property to the government." The official report states: "These people were the cause of the revolution and constitution of 1887. There will never be any peace while they are here. They must be sent out of the country or punished, and their property confiscated." [2] The

7. Gresham to Willis, Oct. 18, 1893, No. 4, USDS, Instructions, Hawaii, 3, printed in *For. Rels.* (1894), App. II, pp. 463–64, and New York *Times*, Dec. 19, 1893.

1. The Penal Code, Chap. 4, Sec. 9, reads: "Whoever shall commit the crime of treason shall suffer the punishment of death and all his property shall be confiscated to the Government."

2. Willis to Gresham, Nov. 16, 1893, No. 3, USDS, Dispatches, Hawaii, 26. Willis' dispatches dated Sept. 19, 1893, to June 30, 1894, are contained in this volume, and printed in *For. Rels.* (1894), App. II, pp. 434, 1241–43. Cf. J. H. Soper, Interview of U.S. Minister Willis with Pres. Dole, re the Queen's Statement to Willis "Banish or Behead," AH, S. B. Dole file.

Queen, who regarded the interview as an informal conversation as to the future of her country, repeated to Willis her wish to consult her ministers before deciding on any definite action.[3]

These extreme views prompted Willis to request the Secretary of State to withhold Blount's report "for the present," and to send further instructions. Gresham telegraphed on November 24: "You will insist upon amnesty and recognition of obligations of the provisional government as essential conditions of restoration." Instructions followed to the effect that should the Queen refuse assent to the written conditions, she was to be informed that the President would cease interposition in her behalf and that further efforts in that direction would depend upon her "unqualified agreement that all obligations created by the Provisional Government in a proper course of administration shall be assumed." If the provisional government inquired whether the United States would hold the Queen to the fulfillment of stipulated conditions, Willis was to say that "acting under dictates of honor and duty, as he had done in endeavoring to effect restoration," the President would "do all in his constitutional power to cause the observance of the conditions imposed."[4] He, however, could not use force to restore the monarch without the consent of Congress.

Meanwhile, the publication in Honolulu, on November 24, of Gresham's letter to the President created a sensation: crowds gathered on the streets, and all friends of the provisional government were called to a public meeting, to be held the following night and addressed by the leading annexationists.[5] President Dole and Attorney General W. O. Smith called upon Willis to ask what the United States intended to do. Dole rescinded the privilege of Admiral Skerrett to land his troops for drilling purposes, and on the 29th addressed a second communication to the Minister inquiring as

3. For Liliuokalani's version of her interviews with Willis, see her *Hawaii's Story*, pp. 246–49. Unfortunately for posterity, all the Queen's private papers, including her diary in which she recorded the gist of these interviews, were taken from her private residence, without a search warrant, by A. F. Judd on Jan. 17, 1895, the day after she was arrested and imprisoned in a room in the palace. Only her deed was returned (ibid., pp. 270–71).

4. Gresham to Willis (telegrams), Nov. 24, Dec. 3, 1893, USDS, Instructions, Hawaii, 3, printed in *For. Rels.* (1894), App. II, pp. 437, 464–65.

5. *Hawaiian Gazette*, Nov. 25, 27, 1893. *Hawaiian Star*, Nov. 27, 1893. Numerous clippings are printed in *House Ex. Docs.*, 53 Cong., 2 sess., No. 70, pp. 7–16.

to the authenticity of the Secretary of State's letter and the intentions of the President of the United States.[6]

These intentions were concisely stated by Cleveland in his annual message to Congress of December 4, 1893, in which he briefly reviewed events in Hawaii and announced that Blount's report showed "beyond all question that the constitutional Government of Hawaii had been subverted with the active aid of our representative to that Government and through the intimidation caused by the presence of an armed naval force of the United States which was landed for that purpose at the instance of our minister." The chief executive felt that "the only honorable course" for the United States to pursue "was to undo the wrong that had been done by those representing us and to restore as far as practicable the status existing at the time of our forcible intervention. With a view of accomplishing this result within the constitutional limits of executive power, and recognizing all our obligations and responsibilities growing out of any changed conditions brought about by our unjustifiable interference, our present minister at Honolulu had received appropriate instructions." Cleveland promised to send additional information, whenever it should arrive, to Congress, accompanied by a special executive message fully detailing all the "facts necessary to a complete understanding of the case." [7]

Willis had a second interview with Liliuokalani on December 16, at which he read to the ex-Queen what he said were notes of their first interview and asked if they were correct. She replied in the affirmative. Had she been permitted to read and examine the paper, she would have noticed that there was a clause which declared that she would have her opponents beheaded. That was a form of punishment which had never been used in the Hawaiian Islands, either before or since the coming of foreigners, and it was most unfortunate that she should have been so misrepresented or that she "should have been so overburdened by the many aspects of the painful situation" as to have been "ignorant or unconscious of the importance of the precise words" read in her presence. When Willis asked if her views were the same as when they met the first time, she answered Yes. Joseph O. Carter, who was present, inquired if she rescinded so much of Mr. Willis' report as related to the execution of the death penalty upon those in revolt. Her reply was: "I do in that

6. Willis to Gresham, Dec. 5, 1893, No. 8, *For. Rels.* (1894), App. II, p. 1246.

7. Richardson, *Messages and Papers*, 9, 441–42.

respect." Two days later she clung to this idea, admitting of some clemency to the extent that the offenders, both parents and children, should be permanently removed from the country, instead of being punished, according to the laws, by death. Soon after the interview, however, she sent to Minister Willis her written acceptance of Cleveland's conditions and a pledge that if restored she would grant amnesty, sustain the constitution of 1887, and assume the obligations entered into by the provisional government.[8]

The United States representative, in an interview with President Dole and his ministers on December 19, communicated President Cleveland's determination of the question, along with the written assurance of Liliuokalani, and stated: "you are expected to promptly relinquish to her constitutional authority." Earnestly hoping that their answer would "be inspired by that high patriotism which forgets all self-interest," he submitted the question: "Are you willing to abide by the decision of the President?"[9]

Sanford Dole delivered in person, at midnight on December 23, the eighteen-page, typewritten answer of the provisional government, expounding the reasons for refusing to surrender its authority to the ex-Queen, and declared that its members did not recognize the right of President Cleveland to interfere in their domestic affairs. Such right could be conferred upon him by the act of the government alone or could be acquired by conquest. Briefly, Dole's position was this:

> If the American forces illegally assisted the revolutionists in the establishment of the Provisional Government, that Government is not responsible for their wrong doing. It was purely a private matter for discipline between the United States Government and its own officers. There is . . . no precedent in international law for the theory that such action of the American troops has conferred upon the United States authority over the internal affairs of this Government. Should it be true . . . that the American Government made itself responsible to the Queen, who it is alleged lost her throne through such action, that is not a matter for me to discuss, except to submit that, if such be the case, it is a matter for the American Government and her to settle.

8. Encl. in Willis to Gresham, Dec. 18–20, 1893, Nos. 14–16, *For. Rels.* (1894), App. II, pp. 1236–70.

9. Encl. No. 2 in Willis to Gresham, Dec. 20, 1893, No. 17, ibid., pp. 1274–75.

While accepting the decision not to annex the islands as the final
conclusion of the Cleveland administration, President Dole wrote:
"We do not feel inclined to regard it as the last word of the American Government upon the subject . . . We shall therefore continue
the project of political union with the United States as a conspicuous
feature of our foreign policy, confidentially hoping that sooner or
later it will be crowned with success, to the lasting benefit of both
countries." [10]

The provisional government prepared to defend itself by placing
sandbags about its buildings and by an issuance of arms to its supporters. So far as the revolutionists were concerned, the Queen's fall
was final and irrevocable; she could be restored only by an American army. Sereno E. Bishop reported that "no deeper insult could
have been given to this intelligent and cultivated American colony
than to order it remanded by force under the heel of a vile, heathenish monarchy, which had thrown off the restraints that had hitherto
made a native monarch endurable by civilized whites. This order will
not be executed so long as the Provisional Government and its 1,200
armed supporters are able to resist by the sacrifice of their lives the
forces which the United States may bring against them." [11]

Mass meetings of protest were held in Hawaii, while in the United
States the press clamor increased against the administration's policy
and the secrecy in which it was invested. The receipt of Willis'
detailed report of his first conference with Liliuokalani pointed up
the predicament for the United States.

Cleveland's Message to Congress

In the meantime, the state of affairs in Hawaii was causing President Cleveland much anxiety. In a cabinet meeting of December 7,
1893, the decision had been made to lay the whole matter before
Congress. As a special message on the subject, prepared by Gresham
on Cleveland's request, was not completely satisfactory, Attorney
General Olney was asked by the President to see what he "could do
with it." Accordingly, he went over Blount's report and other papers
on Hawaii, and submitted a draft which was accepted by the chief
executive and which "forms by far the larger part of the message"

10. Dole to Willis, Dec. 23, 1893, encl. in Willis to Gresham, Dec. 23,
1893, No. 18, ibid., pp. 1276–82. Dole Papers, 1890–1900, AH.

11. *Independent*, 46 (1894), 5.

actually sent to Congress on December 18.[1] The scholarly and capable Massachusetts judge went loyally and willingly along on the legal-moral issue, but he helped to persuade the administration to regard a wider range of facts, equities, and problems than were at first considered, and he certainly exerted considerable influence in the President's arriving at the final decision to take no drastic action in Hawaii.

Cleveland's six-thousand-word message on the Hawaiian revolution reviewed in a logical, forcible, and impressive manner the formidable and irrefutable evidence of his major conclusion that the provisional government owed its existence to the machinations of the United States minister and the presence on shore of United States forces. He drew the attention of the Senate to "the extraordinary haste, not to say precipitancy characterizing all the transactions connected with the treaty," and referred to President Harrison's declaration when submitting the treaty to the Senate that "the overthrow of the monarchy was not in any way promoted by this Government," stating that both the President and the Senate had been misled.

After quoting Secretary Foster's letter to Harrison, which averred that "at the time the Provisional Government took possession of the government building no troops or officers of the United States were present," and that no public recognition was accorded that government by Minister Stevens "until after the Queen's abdication and when they were in effective possession of . . . all the potential machinery of the Government," Cleveland observed that the Queen's protest "explicitly stated that she yielded to the superior force of the United States, whose minister had caused United States troops to be landed at Honolulu and declared that he would support such Provisional Government." The truth or falsity of this protest, which was surely of the first importance, was not investigated before the submission of the treaty.

Cleveland then quoted from three dispatches and letters of Minister Stevens to show a "disposition and condition of mind" of this avowed annexationist:[2] "To a minister of this temper, full of zeal for annexation, there seemed to arise in January, 1893, the precise opportunity for which he was watchfully waiting—an opportunity

1. Autobiographical Memo., p. 11, Olney Papers in box. Cf. Henry James, *Richard Olney and His Public Service* (New York, 1923), p. 92. New York *Times*, Dec. 8, 1893.
2. March 8, Nov. 12, 1892; Feb. 1, 1893.

which by timely 'deviation from established international rules and precedents' might be improved to successfully accomplish the great object in view."

The President asserted that the landing of troops from the *Boston* "upon the soil of Honolulu was of itself an act of war, unless made either with the consent of the Government of Hawaii or for the bona fide purpose of protecting the imperiled lives and property of citizens of the United States." There was no pretense of any such consent on the part of the Queen's government, "which at that time was undisputed and was both the *de facto* and the *de jure* Government. In point of fact, the existing Government, instead of requesting the presence of an armed force, protested against it." There was little basis for the pretense that such forces were landed for the security of American life and property. "If so, they would have been stationed in the vicinity of such property and so as to protect it, instead of at a distance and so as to command the Hawaiian Government building and palace."

As Cleveland apprehended the situation, the United States was confronted with the following conditions:

> The lawful Government of Hawaii was overthrown without the drawing of a sword or the firing of a shot by a process every step of which, it may be safely asserted, is directly traceable to and dependent for its success upon the agency of the United States acting through its diplomatic and naval representatives.
>
> But for the notorious predilections of the United States minister for annexation the committee of safety, which should be called the committee of annexation, would never have existed.
>
> But for the landing of United States forces upon false pretexts respecting the danger to life and property the committee would never have exposed themselves to the pains and penalties of treason by undertaking the subversion of the Queen's Government.
>
> But for the presence of the United States forces in the immediate vicinity and in position to afford all needed protection and support the committee would not have proclaimed the Provisional Government from the steps of the Government building.
>
> And finally, but for the lawless occupation of Honolulu under false pretexts by the United States forces, and but for Minister Stevens' recognition of the Provisional Government when the United States forces were its sole support and constituted its

only military strength, the Queen and her Government would never have yielded to the Provisional Government, even for a time and for the sole purpose of submitting her case to the enlightened justice of the United States. . .

She surrendered, not to the Provisional Government, but to the United States. She surrendered, not absolutely and permanently, but temporarily and conditionally until such time as the facts could be considered by the United States. Furthermore, the Provisional Government acquiesced in her surrender in that manner and on those terms, not only by tacit consent, but through the positive acts of some members of that Government, who urged her peaceable submission, not merely to avoid bloodshed, but because she could place implicit reliance upon the justice of the United States and that the whole subject would be finally considered at Washington.

The chief executive, believing that the United States could not, under the circumstances, annex the Hawaiian Islands "without justly incurring the imputation of acquiring them by unjustifiable methods," informed the Congress that he would not again submit the treaty of annexation to the Senate for its consideration. Our duty did not end with refusing to consummate this questionable transaction. "The United States could not refuse to allow itself to redress an injury inflicted through an abuse of power by officers clothed with its authority and wearing its uniform." He had hoped that the restoration of the monarchy could be effected upon terms providing for a general amnesty to those involved in establishing the provisional government, a recognition of all its bona fide acts and obligations, and justice to all parties concerned. These conditions did not prove acceptable. Thus his plans encountered a check, "while unfortunate public misrepresentation of the situation and exaggerated statements of the sentiments of our people" injured the prospects of successful executive moderation.

In recommending the subject to "the extended powers and wide discretion of the Congress," Cleveland added the assurance that he would cooperate in any legislative plan which might be devised for the solution of the problem which was "consistent with American honor, integrity, and morality." [3] In so doing, he invited the legislative department to "give a lead" to the executive in its conduct of

3. Richardson, *Messages and Papers*, 9, 460–72. *For. Rels.* (1894). App. II, 445–58. *Blount Report*, iii–xvi. New York *Times*, Dec. 19, 1893.

foreign affairs—a rather surprising invitation from a President who was jealous of his prerogatives.

William Adam Russ, Jr., in his scholarly study of the Hawaiian revolution, expresses the opinion that "a more practical alternative and a wiser move for the President would have been to withdraw the treaty of annexation, let time take its course, and permit history to deal with Harrison and Stevens." When Cleveland "threw the question into the turmoil of Congress he was asking for what he got: interparty and intraparty strife." While the historian condemns Harrison and Foster "for a too hasty attempt to get their treaty accepted before the facts were known," he criticizes Cleveland and Gresham for "quixoticism" in foreign policy, "for their impractical endeavor to undo what could not be undone without involvement in questionable international proceedings and complications." [4]

Allan Nevins, also, is of the opinion that Cleveland and Gresham will incur a certain amount of censure from history for their failure to think their problem through at the outset and to foresee all its implications; nevertheless, this able historian concedes that the President's "final policy deserves not blame but praise . . . In an era of international land-grabbing Cleveland, despite angry sneers, had insisted that the United States should meet the loftiest obligations of honesty and unselfishness; in an era when the rights of small nations were almost universally trampled on, he had displayed a sensitive consideration for one of the weakest of them all." [5]

Carl Schurz, in assessing Cleveland's services to the country and in evaluating his second administration, wrote: "In declining to profit from an illegitimate use of the power of the United States, and in endeavoring, as far as possible, to redress a wrong done through it, Mr. Cleveland's Administration gave to the world a proof of our fairness, justice and good faith in dealing with weaker nations which could not fail greatly to raise the character of this Republic in the esteem and confidence of mankind." [6]

Grover Cleveland, in a statement released to the Associated Press early in 1898, declared that his opposition to Hawaiian annexation was not based merely upon dissatisfaction with the treaty pending before the Senate in March 1893; he objected "to annexation as

4. William Adam Russ, Jr. *The Hawaiian Revolution* (1893–94) (Sellingsgrove, Pa., 1959), pp. 350–51.

5. Allan Nevins, *Grover Cleveland: A Study in Courage* (New York, 1934), p. 561.

6. *McClure's Magazine*, 9 (1897), 641; cf. pp. 633–44.

such," and regarded the proposed acquisition of these islands "as not only opposed to our National Policy, but as a perversion of our National mission. The mission of our Nation is to build up and make a greater community out of what we have, instead of annexing islands."[7]

Congressional Action

The President's message and the accompanying documents requested by Representative Robert R. Hitt of Illinois precipitated a prolonged, acrimonious, and sometimes disorderly debate in the lower chamber, in which the Republican minority nettled the Democratic majority with resolutions favoring the annexation of the Hawaiian Islands and inquiring by what authority the naval forces had been placed under Mr. Blount.[1]

James B. McCreary of Kentucky, a Democrat, who had already proposed a resolution upholding Cleveland and Blount, brought it back on December 21, 1893, slightly modified in wording, as the majority report of the committee on foreign affairs.[2] Five days of partisan debate ensued, before the Populists, anxious to clear the way for Bland's silver coinage bill, voted to make a quorum, and the resolution finally passed on February 7, 1894, by a vote of 177 yeas, 78 nays, and 96 abstentions, the antisilverites abstaining.[3] This vote represented only a partial victory for Cleveland, as the resolution did not expressly support intervention against the provisional government. Furthermore, it could hardly be called an unqualified vindication when only 177 out of 215 Democrats were willing to uphold the executive.

The Senate commenced the new year with William P. Frye of Maine proposing, on January 3, noninterference in Hawaiian affairs during the investigation of the Senate Committee on Foreign Relations. George F. Hoar, of Massachusetts, moved that the Secretary of the Treasury be directed to inform the Senate what sums had

7. New York Times, Jan. 24, 1898. Cleveland Papers, Vol. 353. Cf. Nevins, Letters of Grover Cleveland, pp. 491–92. This statement was released in reply to an assertion of Senator Morgan that Cleveland was not opposed to Hawaiian annexation per se.

1. Cong. Record, 53 Cong., 2 sess., pp. 398–401, 446, 468–69, 478. House Misc. Docs., 53 Cong., 2 sess., No. 43, one page only.

2. Misc. Docs., 53 Cong., 2 sess., No. 44. Cong. Record, 53 Cong., 2 sess., pp. 471, 478, 2001.

3. Ibid., pp. 2000–07.

been paid to Blount, while William E. Chandler, of New Hampshire, questioned the President's policy of dispatching diplomatic agents without the consent of the Senate. Senator David Turpie, of Indiana, five days later introduced a resolution which declared: "it is unwise, inexpedient, and not in accordance with the character and dignity of the United States to consider further at this time either the treaty or project of annexation of the Hawaiian territory to this country; that the Provisional Government there in having been duly recognized, the highest international interests require that it shall pursue its own line of polity. Foreign intervention in the political affairs of these islands will be regarded as an act unfriendly to the Government of the United States." [4] For nearly five months thereafter, the senators engaged in heated polemics over the philosophies of imperialism and anti-imperialism, with some questioning the legality of Blount's appointment and condemning it.[5]

On February 24, 1894, the Senate Foreign Relations Committee presented its report, a bulky volume of 809 pages of testimony and accompanying findings, commonly called the *Morgan Report*, for John T. Morgan, chairman of the committee. This collection of statements, often repetitious and sometimes contradictory, described by the New York *Times* as a "rather picturesque bit of patchwork," and by the Philadelphia *Record* as "a mere incoherent yawp of jingoism," was generally representative of annexationist opinion, since great weight and space were devoted to the testimony or sworn statements of members of the committee of safety, as well as of Finance Minister Peter C. Jones, Colonel Z. S. Spalding, Lieutenant Commander W. T. Swinburne, Lientenant Lucien Young, John L. Stevens, and especially to that scholarly mission boy, William DeWitt Alexander, whose biased *History of Later Years of the Hawaiian Monarchy and the Revolution of 1893* was referred to frequently and whose "Sketch of the constitutional history of the Hawaiian Islands" and "Personal Recollections of the Revolution of 1893" were incorporated in the report. In taking oral testimony, Chairman Morgan asked many provocative leading questions, phrased appropriately to bring out the facts or impressions he wished to emphasize, and frequently interrupted the testimony and answers abruptly, or shrewdly directed them to other channels when

4. Ibid., pp. 483, 490, 519, 523, 621. Cf. *Sen. Misc. Docs.*, 53 Cong., 2 sess., Nos. 23, 24, 28, 29, 46.

5. *Cong. Record*, 53 Cong., 2 sess., pp. 621–28, 694–707, 1233, 1309, 1311, 1447, 1574–79.

they threatened to become derogatory. The Republican annexationist members of the committee interjected numerous queries intended to place the President, his Secretary of State, and his special "paramount" commissioner either in error or in bad light.[6]

As a result of the investigation, not even a majority of the committee members could agree upon a general conclusion and recommendations. They split in a ratio of 4:4:1, thus revealing the prevailing difference of opinion among the members toward the revolution and Cleveland's policy. What is sometimes referred to as the report proper or the "majority report" was presented by Senator Morgan, the only committee member who signed it. His two objectives, apparently, were to controvert the findings of the Blount report and to exonerate every American official involved, thus giving the United States government a clean slate. In contrast, he berated Queen Liliuokalani, claiming that "at the moment when she made public her decision to absolve herself from her oath to support the constitution of 1887 her abdication was complete." He also felt that her ministers had to bear some of the responsibility for the revolution, for they had misled the sovereign by working with her in drafting the new constitution, but had deserted her at the last moment.

The report cleared Cleveland's record. He, believing that the information in his possession "was not sufficient to justify summary annexation, could not have done justice to himself, to his country, to the people of Hawaii, to the Provisional Government, to Liliuokalani, without having made an effort to employ his good offices for the purpose of ascertaining whether it was practicable that the Queen should be restored to her authority."

The objection that Blount had been dispatched illegally was disposed of by stating that many precedents could be cited to show that such power had been exercised by a president on various occasions without dissent on the part of the Congress or the people of the United States. There was no irregularity in entrusting to Blount authority to remove the American flag from the government building in Honolulu, to disclaim openly and practically the protectorate which had been announced by Stevens, and to return the troops to the *Boston*. Even the commissioner's action was approved. He had in an impartial manner presented an instructive report; but popular feeling made it next to impossible to secure unprejudiced facts.

The committee discovered nothing to criticize in the speedy nego-

6. *Sen. Reps.*, 53 Cong., 2 sess., No. 227, pp. 309–312, 387, 406–08, 567–69, 586–87, 590–91.

tiation of the treaty of annexation, which action was desirable for obvious reasons, among which were "the injurious disturbance of commerce and danger to the public peace growing out of a protracted agitation of so grave a matter."

In conclusion, the report stated that in his dealings with the Hawaiian government, Minister Stevens' "conduct was characterized by becoming dignity and reserve and was not in any way harsh or offensive." Based upon the evidence which accompanied the report, Senator Morgan was of the opinion that the "only substantial irregularity that existed in the conduct of any officer of the United States" was that of Stevens in declaring a protectorate of the United States over Hawaii. This had been done illegally, without authority and the approval of Washington. No actual harm resulted from this act, but as a precedent it was "not to be considered as being justified." It was disavowed by Secretary Foster and rebuked by Secretary Gresham, and the order to abandon the protectorate and haul down the flag "was in accordance with the duty and honor of the United States." [7]

In entire accord with the essential findings of the report submitted by the chairman were the four Republican and annexationist members of the committee. They were, nevertheless, prompted to state their opinion on five points: (1) The appointment on March 11, 1893, without the advice and consent of the Senate, of James H. Blount as "special commissioner" to the Hawaiian government was an unconstitutional act. (2) The orders of the executive department placing the naval force of the United States in the harbor of Honolulu under the command of Blount or Willis "were without authority or warrant of law." (3) The commissioner's order to Admiral Skerrett to lower the United States ensign from the government building in Honolulu and to embark the troops on their ships was unlawful. (4) After the right of the provisional government to exist had been conclusively settled, the President of the United States had no authority to attempt to reopen such a determined question, "and to endeavor by any means whatever to overthrow the Provisional Government or to restore the monarchy which it had displaced." (5) The policy of Cleveland which indicated that it was the duty of this government to reinstate the Queen upon her throne by all constitutional methods was open to criticism.[8]

7. *Morgan Report*, pp. 4–6, 19–20, 24–25, 27–28, 44–45, 365–66, 387–90, 394–95.

8. Ibid., pp. 33–34, 395–96. The report was signed by John Sherman, William P. Frye, Joseph N. Dolph, and Cushman K. Davis.

Additional views were submitted by the four Democratic or administrative senators on the committee, who presented a brief minority report. They agreed with the conclusions submitted by the chairman that no irregularities were committed either in the appointment of Commissioner Blount or in the instructions given him by the President; but they especially dissented from that portion of Morgan's report which declared that the only substantial irregularity in Stevens' conduct was his declaration of a protectorate. They maintained that "there is nothing in international law, in sound public policy, or in our past history and traditions which justifies a representative of this Government in interfering officiously or improperly in the domestic or political affairs of a foreign country, whatever may be the character of its rulers, its form of government, or its political condition." In short, they were convinced that Stevens' "inopportune zeal" in the project of annexation "caused him to exceed the proper limits of his official duty"; his conduct was "seriously reprehensible and deserving of public censure." [9]

After the presentation of this report, Senator Turpie attempted, on March 20, to secure an agreement from the Republicans to vote on his resolution, but Senator Dolph objected. Senator James Z. George seized the opportunity to present a lengthy defense of Blount and his appointment, citing precedents, while Hoar retaliated, with the result that nothing was accomplished, except the addition of more repetitious arguments to the record. [10]

The Hawaiian government exerted all its power to get action on the Turpie resolution. Thurston, who had returned to Honolulu, [11] appealed to several senators urging its acceptance, arguing that so long as the United States left the question unsettled, native Hawaiians

9. Ibid., pp. 34–36, 397–98. The report bore the signatures of Matthew C. Butler, David Turpie, John W. Daniel, and George Gray.

10. Cong. Record. 53 Cong., 2 sess., pp. 3127–39.

11. Thurston overstepped his position as diplomat in early 1895 by writing one paragraph of an article and permitting other parts to be copied from records at the Hawaiian legation, as extracts from letters written by a "prominent lawyer in Honolulu," which were sent out by the United Press on Feb. 12, 1895, and published in the afternoon newspapers of that day and the morning papers of the 13th. After admitting this in an interview with Gresham on Feb. 21, the latter requested the Minister's recall. The chief overt act of discourtesy charged against him was the publication of official correspondence before it had been submitted to the Secretary of State. After considerable delay, Thurston was removed and Francis March Hatch sent to Washington. (Gresham to Willis, Feb. 21 and April 17, 18, 1895, Nos. 65, 79, and telegram, USDS, Instructions, Hawaii, 5). Cf. For. Rels. (1895), pp. 877, 880; New York Times, March 21, 1895.

would be restive and the provisional government unable to solidify
its position. A simple resolution to the effect that no intervention
would be permitted was all that was required.[12] In spite of the propaganda and pressure efforts of Frank Hastings at the Hawaiian legation to convince a majority of senators, the tariff pushed the resolution aside.[13]

There was a lull in the Hawaiian debate until May 22, when
James H. Kyle, of South Dakota, revived the controversy by offering
a substitute resolution proposing that no force would be used to
restore Liliuokalani or to destroy the provisional government which
should be permitted to pursue its own policy; and that intervention
by any foreign power would be considered as an act unfriendly to
the United States. Debate and maneuvering on this resolution ensued on May 24, 25, 28, and 29, indicating that there was a general
feeling that some action should be taken, but division of sentiment
remained as to the wording of the resolution. Neither Turpie's original version nor Kyle's proved acceptable. Finally, on May 31, in an
effort to express all shades of opinion, Turpie offered a compromise
draft from the Committee on Foreign Relations, which ran as follows: "That of right it belongs wholly to the people of the Hawaiian
Islands to establish and maintain their own form of government and
domestic polity; that the United States ought in no wise to interfere
therewith, and that any intervention in the political affairs of these
islands by any other government will be regarded as an act unfriendly to the United States." [14]

The vote on this substitute was 55 yeas and 0 nays, with 30 senators abstaining. Among those refusing to commit themselves were
some of the leading partisans on both sides who were dissatisfied
with the phraseology. Since the resolutions of both chambers were
not enacted in the same version, the executive was not required
either to sign or to veto them, and they were not law binding the
government. Insofar as annexation of Hawaii was impliedly condemned in this expression of majority senatorial opinion, Cleveland's
policy received an oblique approval, but disapproval of annexation

12. Thurston to Hastings, April 26, 1894.
13. James H. Kyle to Hastings, July 11, 1894. Hastings to Hatch, May 26,
1894.
14. *Cong. Record*, 53 Cong., 2 sess., pp. 5127, 5193–94, 5246, 5434–36, 5499.
Cf. Hastings to Hatch, May 26, 1894. Meanwhile Cleveland sent to the Senate
all pertinent documents. See *Sen. Ex. Docs.*, 53 Cong., 2 sess., Nos. 65, 66, 92,
103.

was omitted and no sanction was given to the President's policy of idealism or of doing justice for which he had requested power on December 18, 1893. This could hardly have been expected from the time the Senate, in the words of Lorrin Thurston, began "treating the Hawaiian question as a dog treated a bone; gnawed it a while, buried it, and gnawed it again." [15]

In spite of the obvious omission, the final compromise resolution was in a sense an approval of Cleveland's policy and partially met his wishes. He wrote to Senator William F. Vilas of Wisconsin: "The thing I care the most about is the declaration that the *people* of the islands instead of the Provisional Government should determine the policy, etc. I do not care much what is said concerning annexation . . . Can you not nail the endorsement of the Provisional Government, by putting in its place the more American and Democratic reference to the People as the source of power and control?" [16]

Passage of the separate Senate resolutions ended official United States action so far as the revolution was concerned, and clearly indicated that no steps would be taken in Washington to overturn the provisional government and restore the monarchy. The issue was settled, no doubt satisfactorily to the majority of Americans, who were tired of the Hawaiian confusion and relieved to bury the annoying question.

Although the mid-Pacific group was not annexed, the Queen not restored, and no provision made for improving communication ties with the islands through the construction of a Pacific cable, the Cleveland administration encouraged and increased Hawaii's economic dependence upon the United States through the Wilson-Gorman tariff of 1894. This act, by abolishing the sugar bounty and restoring the tariff on sugar importation, permitted Hawaii to regain her original advantageous position under the reciprocity treaty which had been nullified by the McKinley tariff.

Charles Robinson, in an article entitled "The Hawaiian Controversy in the Light of History," which appeared the same month the final resolution was passed, predicted: "When the history of the Hawaiian controversy comes to be written, after all the partisan clamor has died away, and every unpleasant incident of the passing record has been forgotten, the policy of the present administration will be fully justified at the bar of public opinion." Cleveland had

15. Thurston, *Memoirs*, p. 483.
16. Nevins, *Letters of Grover Cleveland*, p. 353.

handled "this grave and delicate question" with "unflinching integrity and courage," and in future years the American people would "honor and applaud him for having interfered that the honor of their country might not be tarnished." [17]

Uncertainty

The Hawaiian matter was officially closed so far as President Cleveland was concerned in May 1894, but the issues raised by the revolution, the arguments for and against union, the sanguine expectations of the annexationists in both the United States and Hawaii, and the forlorn hope of Liliuokalani were not interned.

Failure to secure a treaty of annexation or even a protectorate led members of the provisional government to establish a more permanent basis for their regime—that is, a "Republic of Hawaii," with a constitution similar to that of the United States, and formally established on July 4, 1894.[1] Officials of the new entity did not contemplate the long continuation of an independent status, for union with the United States was part of the fundamental law of the republic: by the second paragraph of Article 32 of the constitution, the president, with the approval of the cabinet, was "expressly authorized and empowered to make a Treaty of Political and Commercial Union between the Republic of Hawaii and the United States of America, subject to the ratification of the Senate." [2] On May 27, 1896, the Hawaiian legislature unanimously adopted a joint resolution declaring that the Republic of Hawaii "continues to be, as heretofore, firmly and steadfastly in favor of the Annexation of the Hawaiian Islands to the United States of America." [3]

H. A. Widemann, J. A. Cummins, and Samuel Parker, under instructions from Liliuokalani, journeyed to Washington in the summer of 1894 to obtain President Cleveland's answer to a single ques-

17. *American Journal of Politics*, 4 (1894), 477, 489.

1. *Laws of the Provisional Government of the Hawaiian Islands Passed by the Executive and Advisory Councils*, Act 85, An Act to Provide for the Proclamation of the Republic of Hawaii, pp. 174–76. Cf. Donald W. Rowland, "The Establishment of the Republic of Hawaii," HHS, Forty-Third *Report*, 1934 (Honolulu, 1935).

2. *Constitution of the Republic of Hawaii and Laws Passed by the Executive and Advisory Councils of the Republic* (Honolulu, 1895), p. 86.

3. *Laws Passed by the Legislature of the Republic of Hawaii at Its Session, 1896* (Honolulu, 1896), pp. 310–11. AH, Resolutions Passed by the Legislature at Its Session, 1896, p. 274.

tion: "Will the President do anything to restore the Queen to her position as the lawful Sovereign of Hawaii?" Widemann was received by Secretary Gresham on August 4, when the visitor disclosed that he and many others who favored annexation or might have favored it under different conditions, were now opposed, for they did not like the men who were managing the government. "They wear the cloak of religion, but their hearts are as black as tar . . . If the question of annexation were submitted to a vote, and only those who voted at the last election should go to the polls, the verdict would be against annexation." Gresham inquired if his caller was familiar with the President's message, and remarked: "You can hardly expect him to restore the overthrown Government."

Parker also saw the Secretary of State at the latter's residence the following morning and complained that the presence of United States warships at Honolulu and the ostentatious marching of marines through the city had been a constant moral support to the provisional government and republic. Gresham assured his caller that "our warships were sent there not to uphold the provisional government or its successor, but to afford protection to such of our own citizens as did not participate in the local strife." [4]

The agents were informed that the President would receive them at 3 P.M. on August 15. At 2:30 that day, Gresham called and handed them a letter from Cleveland, stating that he was ill. The chief executive reminded the gentlemen that after having failed in his plans, he committed the entire subject to the Congress. That body, both by its action and its failure to act, signified that nothing need be done touching American interference with the overthrow of the Queen. The recognition and the attitude of the legislators concerning Hawaiian affairs led to the absolute denial of present or future aid or encouragement on the President's part "to an effort to restore any government heretofore existing in the Hawaiian Islands." [5]

At the meeting of the Trans-Mississippi Commercial Congress, held in St. Louis, Missouri, in November 1894, Hugh Craig, delegate from San Francisco, urged annexation of the Hawaiian Islands

4. USDS, Miscellaneous Archives, Memoranda of Conversations with Secretary of State, 1893–98. Cf. *Cong. Record*, 53 Cong., 3 sess., pp. 1331–32; Liliuokalani, *Hawaii's Story*, pp. 258–59.

5. Cleveland to Widemann, Cummins, and Parker, Aug. 15, 1894, in "Unpublished Correspondence Pertaining to the Report of Queen Liliuokalani's Commissioners in 1894," pamphlet in HHS Library, pp. 61–62. This letter is not in the Cleveland Papers.

in as spread-eagle a speech as was ever delivered in the ardor of the congressional debate. After citing statistics to show why the islands would be a valuable addition to our republic, especially to the states on the Pacific coast, he asserted: "We must have Hawaii, we cannot let anybody else have it. We propose to overrun the whole of that South Pacific [sic] some day; we propose to keep that as a safety point for our people with our ships and our steamers." His ostentatious oratory was not taken seriously; his remarks about annexing "everything in sight," Australia, New Zealand, Canada, "and the 38,000,000 in dear old England," evoked only amusement. No resolution praying for annexation was passed, but the delegates resolved that the attention of Congress be called "to the imperative necessity of the immediate construction of a Submarine Cable between a point on the Pacific Coast of the United States and the Hawaiian Islands." [6]

The withdrawal of United States naval units from Hawaiian waters, which were left without a national vessel for about three months during the latter part of 1894,[7] served as an occasion for expansionist Republicans in the Senate, particularly Henry Cabot Lodge, junior senator from Massachusetts, and Nelson W. Aldrich, from Rhode Island, to attempt to embarrass the Cleveland administration and to reopen debate on the annexation proposition. The latter senator insinuated that the President had conspired with Liliuokalani's agents and her supporters to bring about her restoration by withdrawing our warships in order that the royalists, encouraged by that act and by the presence of British ships, might rise and overthrow the republic which we had recognized.[8]

More fuel was added to the fire of disputation when, on January 9, 1895, President Cleveland sent a special message to Congress concerning the lease of Necker Island to Great Britain. This small

6. *Official Proceedings of the Seventh Convention of the Trans-Mississippi Commercial Congress Held at St. Louis, Mo., November 26, 27, 28, and 30, 1894* (St. Louis, 1894), pp. 204–05; cf. pp. 197–205, 266.

7. At least one U.S. warship had been continuously in those waters since 1887. See *Sen. Reps.*, 55 Cong., 2 sess. No. 681, App. VII, p. 111, for list of national vessels stationed there, with the dates of their visits.

8. *Cong. Record*, 53 Cong., 3 sess., pp. 555, 782, 891, 1136–37. The reader, examining this insinuation, should bear in mind that Admiral Walker's mailing orders reached him on Aug. 2, 1894, or two days before Widemann conferred with Gresham, and that the Admiral left Honolulu on Aug. 12, or three days before the President's letter to the agents. Cf. New York *Times* (Jan. 7, 1895), editorial.

precipitous rock, one mile long and one-half mile broad, approximately 403 miles from Honolulu in the range of small islands and rocks extending to the northwest as far as Midway, and always claimed by Hawaii, was to be leased—not given or sold—to the Dominion of Canada with the understanding that it would be used only as a cable station, with a connection to Honolulu, and that the right to purchase or acquire the island should always remain with the United States, subject to the provisions of the lease. At the request of the Hawaiian government, the subject was laid before the Congress for its determination to modify the reciprocity treaty so as to permit the proposed lease.[9]

Some members of Congress appeared shocked and incensed. Senator Lodge found the English cable proposition—a way for British advance into islands which had always been identified with the United States—an outgrowth of a mistaken policy in regard to the Sandwich Islands. It was part of the same policy that had taken away our warships from the islands. The policy of the State Department stood "athwart the wishes of the American people in regard to what we should do about Hawaii." [10]

Arrival of the news of the abortive January 1895 royalist uprising, which aimed to overthrow the republic and restore the Queen, was seized upon by annexationists in Congress, particularly Representatives Charles A. Boutelle, Robert R. Hitt, and William C. P. Breckinridge, to undermine the President's policy of nonintervention. The last named, representing Kentucky, resolved "that it is the sense of the House that the President should enter into negotiations with the Republic of Hawaii, looking toward annexation," [11] which resolution was referred to the committee on foreign affairs.

Some senators, including James H. Kyle and Henry Cabot Lodge, were as deeply vexed as the riled representatives. The latter, in a speech of January 21, asserted that the American people intended to take the Hawaiian Islands "and they will do so just as soon as they have an Administration which will not thwart their desires in that respect." Two days earlier, he had introduced a resolution approving the dispatch of a ship of war to Hawaii, and expressing the

9. Richardson, *Messages and Papers of the Presidents* (20 vols., New York, 1917?) 13, p. 3991. *Sen. Ex. Docs.*, 53 Cong., 3 sess., No. 16, pp. 8–10. *House Ex. Docs.*, 53 Cong., 3 sess., No. 1, Pt. I, pp. 1378–79. New York *Times*, Jan. 10, 1895; *Cong. Record*, 53 Cong., 3 sess., pp. 768, 823.

10. *Cong. Record*, 53 Cong., 3 sess., pp. 1137, 1639.

11. Ibid., pp. 1158, 1164, 1200.

opinion that for the present one should be kept there; that prompt measures should be taken to construct a submarine cable from San Francisco to Honolulu, and that no part of the rights and privileges secured to the United States under the existing treaty between her and the Hawaiian government "should be abandoned or waived in order to enable any other government to secure a foothold or lease upon any part of the Hawaiian Island"; and that "immediate steps should be taken to secure possession of the Sandwich Islands by their annexation to the United States."

Not deterred by the old cry of twisting the lion's tail, Lodge was determined to uphold American interests against British interests or those of any other foreign power. He called the attention of the Senate to what Great Britain had acquired in the Pacific Ocean during the preceding six years, listing twenty-five island groups with their respective distances from the Hawaiian archipelago. This record, including the seizure of Palmyra and Johnston, claimed by Hawaii since 1854, seemed to indicate that England had been "taking every Pacific island she could reach, and that she might be persuaded to take the Sandwich Islands if they came in her way." Always coming nearer to Hawaii, she had attempted to add Necker Island to the long list of acquisitions, but she was prevented from seizing it only by the quickness of the Hawaiian government in establishing its authority over that island. She was then attempting to procure it by obtaining a modification of our treaty, which would permit her to take Hawaiian territory. This was all "a part of the conquering and aggressive policy of England." Lodge was the last to find fault in her. He believed that she was wise in her acquisitions. His criticism was that the United States did not exhibit the same spirit "in protecting American interests and advancing them everywhere at all times." [12]

Clashing arguments in the Senate clearly indicated a divergence of views of the traditionalist and expansionist senators. Donelson Caffery regretted that the President was "a target at which all the poisoned arrows of envenomed partisan malice" were leveled. George Gray asserted: "I do not believe that the policy, the traditions or true interests of this country are consistent with annexation. I believe our policy is a continental one, and that we are not called upon by anything in our past history to step off this continent in a career of colonial aggrandizement." Lodge countered that he did not "mean

12. Ibid., pp. 1133, 1136–37, 1167, 1205, 1210–12; cf. pp. 17, 117–72, 1637, 1639. New York *Times*, Jan. 22, 1895.

that we should enter on a widely extended system of colonization," but that he did "mean that we should take all outlying territories necessary to our own defense, to the protection of the Isthmian Canal, to the upbuilding of our trade and commerce and to the maintenance of our military safety elsewhere. I would take and hold the outworks as we now hold the citadels of American power." [13]

Senator William V. Allen, a Populist senator from Nebraska, who was among those who believed that the overturning of the Hawaiian government in January 1893 was "inexcusable and unlawful," nevertheless was of the opinion that "a wise and enlightened foreign policy" required that steps should be taken by this government to annex the Hawaiian Islands and in the meantime protect the personal property rights of American citizens there by the presence of sufficient naval force. He presented a resolution to this effect on January 24, which two days later was countered by one from Senator George Graham Vest of Missouri, reaffirming "the policy of absolute noninterference, unless by agreement, with the affairs of other nations," recognizing "the right of every people to adopt and maintain their own form of government unawed and uninfluenced by foreign dictation," and approving President Cleveland's policy. The amended version was agreed to by a vote of 24 to 22, with 39 abstaining.[14] Thus, within a period of less than a year, the Senate twice declared for noninterference in Hawaiian affairs and for support of the President.

Following the second official declaration of United States policy, there was a period of relative calm in Hawaiian-American relations so far as the Congress, the public, and the press were concerned. For the State Department the most serious complications arose out of efforts to protect bone fide American citizens implicated in the January conspiracy.[15]

Censorious Henry Cabot Lodge, not content to permit his "captious barking" to remain buried in the *Congressional Record*, addressed himself to "Our Blundering Foreign Policy" in the pages of the *Forum*, where he castigated President Cleveland for flinging aside our well-settled policy and established traditions in dealing

13. *Cong. Record,* 53 Cong., 3 sess., pp. 1139, 1210–11. Cf. New York *Times,* Jan. 22, 25, 1895.

14. *Cong Record,* 53 Cong., 3 sess., pp. 1329, 1335. Cf. New York *Post,* Jan. 25, 1895.

15. See *House Docs.,* 54 Cong., 1 sess., No. 1, Pt. II; *For. Rels.* (1895), pp. 820, 834–48, 850–51, 853, 856, 861–62.

with the Hawaiian Islands, so essential to us, both commercially and strategically. The Senator reviewed the course followed by the chief executive and his "paramount commissioner of no diplomatic experience" in a most uncomplimentary manner, and, in a vein similar to that pursued in the Senate chamber, pointed to Cleveland's efforts "to destroy American influence by methods which, if persisted in, can result only in throwing the Hawaiian people into the arms of England." [16]

Republicans capitalized on the Democratic fiasco in Hawaii and made annexation an issue in the presidential campaign of 1896. On considering the issues of that year, Theodore Roosevelt and William E. Russell, in addition to advocating the construction of a "first class fighting navy," asserted: "We should annex Hawaii immediately. It was a crime against the United States, it was a crime against white civilization, not to annex it two years and a half ago. The delay did damage that is perhaps irreparable; for it meant that at the critical period of the islands' growth the influx of population consisted, not of white Americans, but of low caste laborers drawn from the yellow races." [17]

The Republican platform of 1896 announced that the "Hawaiian Islands should be controlled by the United States and no foreign power should be permitted to interfere with them." Soon after, the victory of William McKinley revived hope and activity among the jubilant annexationists. As the period of the Cleveland administration drew to a close, the subject of acquiring Hawaii was again thrust upon the American public. Assertions were made in the press that the little republic was willing, that it was growing impatient of United States delay, etc. John W. Foster, returning from a six weeks' visit to Honolulu in the interest of the Pacific Cable Company, reported that Hawaii was prosperous and flourishing, and that her future was bright. The government had "the approval of a majority of the native Hawaiians," and there was no likelihood that there ever would be a restoration of the monarchy. English and German elements, nevertheless, were opposed to annexation to the United

16. *Forum*, 19 (1895), 8–17.

17. "The Issues of 1896," *Century*, 51 (1895), 71. Cf. New York *Sun*, Oct. 25, 1895. Two years before the election Roosevelt had expressed the wish that "our Republicans would go in avowedly to annex Hawaii and build an oceanic canal with the money of Uncle Sam." Roosevelt to Lodge, Oct. 27, 1894, in *Selections from the Correspondence of Theodore Roosevelt and Henry Cabot Lodge 1884–1918* (2 vols. New York and London, 1925), *1*, 139.

States, fearing interference with their contract labor. Although the government was running smoothly and successfully, there was continued anxiety that some change might occur. In Foster's opinion, annexation was the only way out of the situation.[18]

The anticipated return of a Republican to the White House led to renewed interest in acquiring overseas possessions. Whitelaw Reid, journalist and diplomat, who at the time was editor-in-chief and proprietor of the New York *Tribune*, was among the influential Americans who urged annexation. He wrote to the President-elect, predicting that someday we would have Cuba, as well as the Sandwich Islands. To this extent he believed in Manifest Destiny, and flatteringly observed: "To get both, in your administration, would put it beside Jefferson's in the popular mind and ahead of it in history."[19]

A Patriotic League of America, composed of citizens of New York organized for a broader national policy, issued an address in December 1896 to the people of the United States, which, among others, contained the following objectives: "To maintain the broadest interpretation of the Monroe doctrine as applied to this hemisphere, encourage and promote by peaceful, lawful and honorable means the independence of Canada with a view to political union with the United States, and the admission into the Republic of Hawaii and all the islands upon the east, which, as satellites to a planet, belong to the continent of North America." [20]

In an editorial on "Contemporaries and Annexation," the *Pacific Commercial Advertiser* quoted an observation of the Victoria (British Columbia) *Colonist*, to the effect that the United States had "become coy and almost half accepts proposals which she would not listen to a few months ago," and pointed up the significance of the Nicaragua Canal, which eventually would be constructed; then, it stated, "the surpassing value of Hawaii will manifest itself." Control of the islands as a coaling station would be in the future indispensable to the United States Navy and to her rehabilitated mercantile marine.[21]

The news of McKinley's election, which was received in Honolulu

18. New York *Morning Advertiser*, Dec. 1, 1896.
19. Reid to McKinley, Dec. 5, 1896, McKinley Papers, Library of Congress, Vol. 4.
20. New York *Commercial Advertiser*, Dec. 16, 1896. Cf. *Pacific Commercial Advertiser*, Jan. 8, 1897.
21. Jan. 9, 1897.

on November 16, 1896, by way of Japan, caused renewed activity and agitation in that capital, and was a welcome relief to Dole and his colleagues, for they still considered the matter of annexation of vital importance to the country. The Republican victory coincided with a growing concern in Hawaii over mounting Japanese immigration, Japanese absorption of the trade of the islands, and pressure from Tokyo to recognize the rights of Japan's nationals in the republic, as well as increasing anxiety over the possibility of the revision of the United States tariff in such a way as to jeopardize the advantages of, or to destroy completely, reciprocity. There had been fear that if the United States was not concerned enough to promote annexation, there would not be sufficient interest in Congress to continue the reciprocity treaty. If the United States let go of the islands, they would immediately become a prize for England, Japan, or Russia. Dole was convinced that without United States aid, the republic would not remain independent.[22]

Liliuokalani, who had in late October 1896 been granted full pardon and released from confinement after conviction for "misprison of treason" for her alleged involvement in the 1895 uprising, boarded a mainland steamer, quietly and almost secretly, on December 4, 1896, "for a change of scene to forget sorrow." She traveled across the country to Boston, where she was the guest of relatives of her husband and friends, and also visited Washington, D.C. The ex-Queen was reticent, declined to reveal why she had left Hawaii, refused to talk about annexation and her proposed pension, and did not see President Cleveland. Her visit puzzled Minister Hatch, whose government sent no official notice of her coming.[23]

Meanwhile the Hawaiian Women's Patriotic League prepared and had forwarded to President-elect McKinley a petition, dated December 30, 1896, which stated "that no cause can arise that will alter or change the mind of the Hawaiian people, and their desire to see the Monarchy restored, and the Throne occupied by the queen, who would never had been deposed by a handful of foreigners but for the support rendered by the U.S.S. Boston." Thus the position of native Hawaiians remained what it had been in April 1893, when they had prayed that their country might "be granted the preserva-

22. Dole to George H. Dole, Nov. 21, 1896, Letters of Sanford B. Dole.
23. Liliuokalani, *Hawaii's Story,* pp. 305 ff. Ellis Mills to Olney, Dec. 9, 1896, No. 174, USDS, Dispatches, Hawaii, 28. Mills, Secretary of U.S. legation, carried on during the fatal illness and after the death of Willis on Jan. 6, 1897.

tion of its independence and the restoration of its legitimate native monarchy under our Queen Liliuokalani." [24]

William N. Armstrong, writing from San Francisco on December 28, warned the Hawaiian planters of the danger to their sugar-cane economy from beet-sugar competition and urged them to get into the United States fold before any new questions were raised. He reported that California had turned to the sugar beet for a money crop; that Nebraska was rapidly learning how to make this sugar; that beets could be grown successfully in many Atlantic States; and that the reason they had not been planted there was that the farmers had no faith in the business. Success in California and in Nebraska would eventually have an effect in the east. Those who had put large capital into the business might at any time "raise a cry against the cane product and fire the hearts of the farmer and laborer." Hawaiian planters hardly realized the changed conditions of sugar production. The British West Indies were on the verge of bankruptcy and were clamoring for relief or annexation to the United States. The policy of the American legislators would be to protect the home production in some form; and it was doubtful that reciprocity would bring the Hawaiian Islands within that protection for any period of time. "Under these conditions, the Hawaiian planter should see the supreme need of getting into the American fold. Delay is dangerous." [25]

Thurston, Judge A. S. Hartwell, and Attorney General W. O. Smith, all in the interest of annexation, left Honolulu at the end of January and in early February 1897, for Washington, where they arrived even before the inauguration, to be on hand at an opportune moment. Meanwhile, there was planned in Honolulu, under the auspices of the National Guard, "a huge monster meeting favoring annexation," which did not materialize, as the authorities considered it inexpedient to hold such a gathering.[26] Nevertheless, there was a prevalent feeling in the Hawaiian capital that not enough was being done there to further the cause, that the republic was unprepared

24. Sen. Ex. Docs., 52 Cong., 2 sess., No. 76, pp. 491–92. Blount Report, pp. 17–18.

25. Pacific Commercial Advertiser, Jan. 8, 1897. Cf. "England and the West Indies," New York Morning Advertiser (Nov. 26, 1896), editorial. "Beet Sugar Industry," New York Commercial Advertiser (Dec. 17, 1896), editorial. "Sugar Industry Injured, England Alarmed at Condition of West India Trade," New York Times (Dec. 19, 1896), editorial.

26. Mills to Olney, Jan. 20, 22, 26, Feb. 9, 1897, Nos. 185, 186, 188, 196.

"to organize a campaign and push it with vigor." While the ministers were in agreement on annexation as a policy, they differed on matters of detail. Reportedly, President Dole, Minister King, and Attorney General Smith were willing to accept annexation in any form obtainable, while Ministers Cooper and Damon thought that the advantages Hawaii had to offer entitled her to impose certain restrictions in the event of annexation, one of these being that all federal appointments to be made by the President of the United States for the territory of Hawaii had to be from bona fide citizens of the islands.[27] W. O. Smith, in discussing the possibility of an island delegation to Washington, expressed the belief that everything possible was being done by the Hawaiian representatives abroad toward paving the way toward closer union with the United States.[28] His conviction was true.

27. Honolulu *Evening Bulletin*, Feb. 8, 1897.
28. Honolulu *Star*, Feb. 6, 1897.

SUCCESS OF THE ANNEXATIONISTS

Less than a month after the victory of the Republican party in November 1896, Henry Cabot Lodge journeyed to Canton, Ohio, where he talked with President-elect McKinley about Hawaii. Without going into details of policy, the Senator simply obtained permission to have Henry E. Cooper, Hawaiian minister of foreign affairs, who was then in Washington, stop in Canton, on his homeward trip, to see the President-elect.[1]

Back in Honolulu, Cooper optimistically reported to a large and enthusiastic meeting of the reorganized Annexation Club that he had heard much that was encouraging to the cause, and that, while the Republican party had committed itself to the policy that the United States should maintain control of the Hawaiian Islands, annexation was not made such a question as would compel its consideration as a party measure.[2]

A Second Treaty

Attorney General William O. Smith left Honolulu on February 10, 1897, for Washington, to act in conjunction with Minister Hatch in

1. Lodge to Roosevelt, Dec. 2, 1896, in *Correspondence of Theodore Roosevelt and Henry Cabot Lodge*, p. 240.
2. "Annexation with Conditions," *Pacific Commercial Advertiser*, Jan. 13, 1897.

negotiating a new treaty of annexation. Only eight days after his inauguration, William McKinley, who had a personal interest in Hawaii (his brother David had acted as United States consul at Honolulu and later served the Republic of Hawaii as consul at San Francisco), discussed with Foster and Senator William P. Frye of Maine the general features of such a treaty, a relevant message to Congress, and the question whether the subject should be initiated by treaty or by joint resolution. Finally, the latter plan was approved.[1]

Hatch, Hartwell, and Thurston, already in Washington armed with commissions and ready to act, were heartened, for they had heard reiterated the impossibility of annexation receiving any attention at the special session of Congress called to deal with the tariff. Further encouragement came from Representative Robert R. Hitt, chairman of the House Foreign Affairs Committee, who asked Smith for a copy of the joint resolution which the congressman had drafted in 1893. Moreover, the Nicaragua Canal matter, closely related to the control of Hawaii, was to be taken up where it was left when Cleveland withdrew the treaty from the Senate during his first administration. Thus there appeared to be considerable sentiment in favor of annexation.[2] Smith was nonetheless aware that if the subject were brought up in the special session, no matter how strongly the administration favored it, there would be strenuous opposition from several sources, including the sugar trust. Liliuokalani's visit had had some effect and no chances could be taken. He therefore urgently requested that Attorney William A. Kinney be dispatched to Washington to lobby with congressmen. Smith and Hatch were assured by the President as early as March 25 that he realized the necessity for early action and would give the matter full consideration; but the tariff was the real question of the hour, and he was unwilling to recommend any new subject until that was settled. After the pressure of domestic matters was relieved, he would consider sending a special message to Congress on Hawaii.

At first by-passed in this significant matter, the enfeebled and forgetful Secretary of State John Sherman was for some time unaware of pending negotiations. When Hatch called at the State Department, the Secretary frankly expressed his opposition to all acquisi-

1. Boston *Herald*, March 13, 1897.

2. Smith to Cooper, March 15, 1897, AH, Hawaiian Officials Abroad, U.S. Minister, Washington. All the following dispatches of Hawaiian officials to each other are in this file, unless otherwise indicated.

tions of territory not on the mainland. In the case of Hawaii he would not oppose a strong protectorate. His personal opinions, however, would not necessarily control his action as Secretary of State. The whole question would be referred to Congress, and there his views would have no weight. He suggested that Hatch have a private interview with McKinley on the subject.[3]

Instead of depending upon Sherman, the Hawaiian commissioners worked through key legislators, among whom the opinion prevailed that a joint resolution would be safer than a treaty of annexation.[4] Of all the senators, Marcus A. Hanna, of Ohio, was the most helpful and approached the subject in a realistic business manner, frankly stating that annexation could not be allowed to interfere with the tariff bill, but he refrained from predicting that the former could not be considered at the special session. He, more than any other man, voiced the President's views.[5]

In the meantime Thurston, as a free agent, was of the greatest value. He cautioned the planters that their personal presence in the national capital would be anything but a help to union, for "there is a feeling of hostility to them which does not extend to our community at large."[6] He further recommended that their supporters restrain Honolulu papers friendly to the government from indiscriminate attacks upon American newspapers and public men, as the censure did the cause no good and sometimes hit the friends of Hawaii.[7] Then, on April 3, the Minister laid before the Secretary of State an official communication of the desire of the Hawaiian government to renew negotiations looking toward the annexation of the Hawaiian Islands to the United States, which referred to the constitutional provision on the subject of union as well as to the related resolution passed by the legislature.

In May, William Rufus Day, an intimate Canton friend of William McKinley, assumed, out of personal loyalty and at a considerable financial sacrifice, the duties of first assistant secretary of state, a post for which he had no particular inclination or training. Nevertheless, the President came to rely upon him rather than on Sherman

3. Smith to Cooper, March 26, 1897, with encl. Memo. of Conversation of Hatch and Smith with Pres. McKinley, March 25, 1897. Hatch to Cooper, March 27, 1897.

4. Smith to Cooper, March 26, 1897.

5. Hatch to Cooper, April 2, 1897.

6. Hatch to Dole, March 27, 1897.

7. Hatch to Cooper, April 5, 24, May 1, 1897.

for the management of affairs in the State Department. Because of his inexperience in diplomacy, John W. Foster, at his request, prepared the draft of an annexation treaty, thus changing the destiny of a nation.[8] With a minimum of contention and counterproposals, the terms of a treaty were agreed upon and the document signed on June 15, 1897.

The islands were to be annexed to the United States under the name of the "Territory of Hawaii," with all rights of sovereignty and public property, including the crown lands, transferred to the United States, who assumed Hawaii's public debt in a sum not exceeding four million dollars; existing treaties were to be replaced by those made or to be made by the United States; further immigration of Chinese to the islands, "except upon such conditions as are now or may hereafter be allowed by the laws of the United States," was prohibited and no Chinese were, by reason of anything in the treaty, to be allowed to enter the United States from the Hawaiian Islands. The organic provisions of government were reserved for action of Congress. Except that the provisions of annuities to ex-Queen Liliuokalani and compensation to Princess Kaiulani were omitted, the new treaty embodied the essential features of the one of February 15, 1893.[9]

In a brief companion report Secretary Sherman explained that the Republic of Hawaii had been recognized as sovereign, and in Article 83 of its constitution, had authorized annexation. Neither a simple commercial union nor a political protectorate was practicable, for "a tributary dependence or a measure of suzerain control would be a retrograde movement toward a feudal or colonial establishment alike inexpedient and incompatible with our national policy." Annexation was the only satisfactory solution.

In his message accompanying the submission of the treaty to the Senate on June 16, McKinley indicated that the union of Hawaii to the United States represented "no new scheme," but was

the inevitable consequence of the relation steadfastly maintained with the mid-Pacific domain for three-quarters of a

8. Foster, *Diplomatic Memoirs*, 2, 172–73. Cf. L. B. Shippee and R. B. Way, "William Rufus Day," in S. F. Bemis, ed., *The American Secretaries of State and Their Diplomacy* (10 vols. New York, 1927–29), 9, 33–36. "William Rufus Day," in *Dictionary of American Biography*, 5, 164.

9. For the text of the treaty see *Sen. Reps.*, 55 Cong., 2 sess., No. 681, pp. 96–97; *Cong. Record*, 55 Cong., 2 sess., p. 2873; Liliuokalani, *Hawaii's Story*, pp. 352–54. Cf. ibid., pp. 354–57.

century. Its accomplishment, despite successive denials and postponements, has been merely a question of time. While its failure in 1893 may not be a cause of congratulations, it is certainly a proof of the disinterestedness of the United States, the delay of four years having abundantly sufficed to establish the right and the ability of the Republic of Hawaii to enter, as a sovereign contractant, upon a conventional union with the United States . . . *Under such circumstances annexation is not a change. It is a consummation.*[10]

Americanists and Strategists

The immense strategic value of the mid-Pacific group from both the naval and the commercial point of view and the fact that Americans had civilized and Christianized their people made annexation appear obligatory and urgent to Americans of the manifest destiny school. After the Republicans were returned to power, which period coincided with the spectacular growth of the Japanese navy, strategists and big navy men of the United States, less concerned than Grover Cleveland and Walter Gresham over the ethics of annexation, marshaled their forces in a determined effort to acquire strategic posture and fulcrums essential to the development and security of United States naval power. These strategists—Captain Alfred Thayer Mahan in particular—were supported by several distinguished statesmen and publicists, and especially by young Republicans who, like Whitelaw Reid, Theodore Roosevelt, and Henry Cabot Lodge, espoused the "large policy" and were convinced that we could not with impunity pass up an opportunity to acquire the Hawaiian Islands, which were in danger of seizure by either Great Britain or Japan. Not only were the white residents entitled to rule the islands, but acquisition of the group was the only policy compatible with United States interest and "the interest of the white race." [1] We had "no right to leave them to be engulfed by an Asiatic immigration." [2] Only two days after President McKinley transmitted the second treaty of annexation to the Senate, Ambassador John Hay in London

10. *Sen. Reps.*, 55 Cong., 2 sess., No. 681, p. 66.
1. Roosevelt to James Bryce, Sept. 10, 1897, in Morison, *Letters of Theodore Roosevelt*, 1, 672.
2. Lodge to Herbert Myrick, Jan. 10, 1898, quoted by Harold K. Beale, *Theodore Roosevelt and the Rise of America to World Power* (Baltimore, 1954), p. 58.

was informed by Whitelaw Reid, ambassador of the United States to Queen Victoria's Diamond Jubilee, that he had just given confidential instructions to the New York *Tribune* "to support the treaty with energy." [3] Both Roosevelt and Lodge addressed public meetings and prepared articles on the necessity for annexing Hawaii, and they, along with Mahan, whom they constantly consulted, pressed their views on doubtful senators, Secretary Sherman, and President McKinley.[4]

Roosevelt reminded New York Republicans that we had not created the Hawaiian Islands, that they had already existed:

> We merely have to face the alternative of taking them ourselves and making them the outpost for the protection of the Pacific coast or else of seeing them taken by any powerful nation with which we are at war, and at once transformed into the most dangerous possible base of operations against our Pacific cities. We cannot help Hawaii's being either a strong defense to us or a perpetual menace. We can only decide whether we will not take the islands when offered to us as a gift, or by force try to conquer them from the first powerful nation with which we may become embroiled.[5]

In an address before the National Geographic Society, on March 26, 1897, on the relations of the United States to Hawaii, attended by numerous members of Congress and the diplomatic corps, John W. Foster, who had recently returned from Honolulu as the representative of the Pacific Cable Company, expressed the opinion that if, "in view of our great and rapidly growing interests in the Pacific, it has become a political and military necessity that these Islands should not pass into the control of any other nation, and if it is manifest that such a contingency now threatens them, it is . . . the plain duty of the United States to annex them to its territory." [6]

Largely on the recommendation of his long-time intimate friend

3. Hay to McKinley, June 18, 1898, McKinley Papers, Vol. 7.

4. Morison, *Letters of Theodore Roosevelt*, 1, 607, 725–26, 728, 741.

5. Beale, *Theodore Roosevelt*, p. 58, quoting New York *Sun*, Feb. 13, 1897; clipping in T.R. Scrapbook. The article is not in the *Sun*.

6. John W. Foster, *Annexation of Hawaii* (Washington, 1897), p. 14. Cf. Foster, *Memoirs*, 2, 170. This address was ordered printed by the U.S. Senate and became *Sen. Doc.*, 55 Cong., 1 sess., No. 23. Cf. *Cong. Record*, 55 Cong., 1 sess., p. 573.

Henry Cabot Lodge, ebullient Theodore Roosevelt was appointed assistant secretary of the navy in April 1897. His accession to that post had added significance, since the expansionist-minded Benjamin Tracy had been replaced as secretary by John D. Long, who was indifferent toward both the acquisition of Hawaii and the construction of a large fleet. In correspondence with Roosevelt, whom he knew would welcome his views, Mahan urged the annexation of the Pacific group, writing: "Do nothing unrighteous, but as regards the problem, take the islands first and solve afterwards." [7] The strictly private reply in part read:

> I suppose I need not tell you that as regards Hawaii, I take your views absolutely, as indeed I do on foreign policy generally. If I had my way we would annex those islands tomorrow. If that is impossible I would establish a protectorate . . . I have been getting matters in shape on the Pacific coast just as fast as I have been allowed. My own belief is that we should act instantly before the two new Japanese warships leave England. I would send the *Oregon,* and if necessary, also the *Monterey* . . . to Hawaii, and would hoist our flag over the island, leaving all details for after action.

Roosevelt lamented: "If only we had some good man in the place of John Sherman as Secretary of State there would not be a hitch." The best that the ambitious and unctuous underling could do was to press these views on his chief and prepare some memoranda for his use in the May 4 cabinet meeting.[8]

After a time, Roosevelt became despondent over the necessity of persuading others to act on the question of annexation. This delinquency was "due to men of a by-gone age" having to deal with facts of the "present," which attitude among our educated class he considered a survivor of the Little England movement among Englishmen thirty years earlier. To him it seemed "incredible that such shortsighted folly could obtain among our public men." If we refused the Hawaiian Islands, then he honestly hoped that England

7. Mahan to Roosevelt, May 1, 1897, quoted by Beale, *Theodore Roosevelt,* p. 57. Cf. William D. Puleston, *The Life and Work of Captain Alfred Thayer Mahan* (New Haven, 1939), p. 182.

8. Roosevelt to Mahan, May 3, 1898, in Morison, *Letters of Theodore Roosevelt, 1,* 607.

would "take them, if only to bring back to our people the knowledge
of their folly." [9]

Captain Mahan, in an article entitled "A Twentieth Century Outlook," referred to Hawaii as an outpost of an isthmian canal, as
surely as Aden or Malta was of Suez.[10] Little Brown and Company
assembled and brought out in November 1897 nine of his most important articles in a small volume entitled *The Interest of America
in Sea Power, Present and Future*, which applied the Captain's broad
principles directly to the United States, enlarged his reading public,
and provided his influential supporters "both chapter and verse
with which to convert unbelievers." [11]

Complying with a request from Senator John T. Morgan for his
views, Major General John T. Schofield wrote "without reserve,"
emphasizing that the Pearl River lagoon had to be held at any cost
and expressing the opinion that it could be defended without a navy.
For twenty-five years he had regarded annexation as a public necessity. When he appeared before the House Committee on Foreign
Affairs he reiterated that Pearl Harbor was capable of absolute defense by shore batteries. A fleet, after stopping there, replenishing its
supplies and making necessary repairs, could sail away and leave
the harbor to the protection of the army. The weak Spanish flotilla
was the only one of all the powers that we could have overcome as
we did. He maintained: "We are liable at anytime to get into a war
with a nation which has a more powerful fleet than ours, and it is of
vital importance therefore, if we can, to hold the point from which
they can conduct operations against our Pacific coast. Especially is
that true until the Nicaraguan Canal is finished, because we cannot
send a fleet around from the Atlantic to the Pacific." When asked if
the United States should acquire Pearl Harbor without the islands
themselves, the General expressed the opinion that if the islands
were left free, complications would arise with foreign powers, who
would take advantage of the weakness of the republic. We would be
much stronger and able to settle any Pacific dispute if we owned the
entire group. Admiral John G. Walker, who had had long experience
as a naval officer in the Pacific and was well acquainted with the sit-

9. Roosevelt to Mahan, Dec. 9, 1897, ibid., pp. 725–26. Puleston, p. 184.
Cf. *The Works of Theodore Roosevelt*, 12 (New York, 1925), pp. 251–52.
For a similar statement of Lodge's lack of sympathy with the American counter-
part of the Little England party cf. *Cong. Record*, 53 Cong., 3 sess., p. 1211.

10. *Harper's New Monthly Magazine*, 95 (1897), 531, cf. 531–37.

11. Puleston, p. 183. See Roosevelt's review of this book in the New York
Sun, Dec. 26, 1897, and Feb. 13, 1898.

uation in Hawaii, emphatically confirmed the views of General Schofield that it would cost far less to protect the Pacific coast with the Hawaiian Islands than without them, and that we would be taking a point of vantage instead of giving it to our enemy.[12]

At the beginning of the new year, Theodore Roosevelt, writing on "The Needs of the Navy," again insisted: "We must take Hawaii just as we must continue to build a navy equal to the needs of America's greatness . . . Hawaii cannot permanently stand alone, and we have no right to expect other powers to be blind to their own interests because we are blind to ours. If Hawaii does not become American then we may as well make up our minds to see it become European or Asiatic." [13]

Captain Mahan's views on the importance of Hawaii as a military and naval stronghold and outpost were sought by Senator James H. Kyle of South Dakota, who requested an answer to the following questions: 1) Would the possession of Hawaii strengthen or weaken the United States from a military standpoint? 2) In case of war, would it take a larger navy to defend the Pacific coast with or without the possession of Hawaii? 3) Is it practical for any trans-Pacific country to attack the Pacific coast without occupying Hawaii as a base? 4) Could such an attack be made by transporting coal to colliers and transferring coal to sea? The Captain replied that, from a military point of view, American possession of the islands would strengthen, not weaken, the United States; that without the islands, a greater navy would be needed to protect the Pacific coast; that invasion of that coast would be impracticable without Hawaii as a base; and that coaling at sea was not feasible. He believed that if the United States did not hold the islands, we could not expect neutrals in war to prevent other belligerents from occupying them. Since their inhabitants were powerless to prevent such occupation, the United States would need a larger navy not only to defend our own Pacific coast during a conflict but to prevent an enemy from occupying the archipelago.[14] These opinions were given widespread publicity by the American press.

12. *Sen. Reps.*, 55 Cong., 2 sess., No. 681, App. III, pp. 2–3, 106, also printed in *Sen. Docs.*, 56 Cong., 2 sess., No. 231, Pt. VII. See pp. 285–94 for views of strategists. Cf. "Pearl Harbor Coaling Station, Imperative Necessity that the United States Take Possession," New York *Times*, Jan. 9, 1892.

13. *Gunton's Magazine of Social Economics and Political Science*, 14 (1898), 4.

14. *Sen. Reps.*, 55 Cong., 2 sess., No. 681, App. III, 98–100. Cf. New York *Journal*, Feb. 10, 1898.

General Benjamin F. Tracy also championed the annexation of Hawaii, employing arguments similar to those of Mahan and Schofield, and maintaining that the possession of that group "is vital to the protection of our coast in war and the growth of our commercial interest in peace." He criticized those who felt that the policy of acquisition by which we had grown great and powerful should cease, that the nation was large enough, and that the annexation of the islands, even with their own consent, would mark a new departure in national policy.[15]

Commodore George W. Melville, engineer in chief of the United States Navy, emphasized the necessity of Hawaiian annexation in the light of contemporary events, especially the emergence of Japan as a naval power, and expounded arguments similar to those of General Schofield on the importance of the Pearl River lagoon. That harbor was the key to the defense of our western shore, and could be made an impregnable fortress, a vantage point "from which a force may sally and under whose wing that force may supply and recruit for a fresh attack." The Commodore advocated not merely the exclusive right to acquire and administer the harbor site; he desired the United States to annex the entire Hawaiian group, his reasons being: (1) The Pacific Ocean was so broad that passage would exhaust the coal supply of a merchant war vessel, unless the Sandwich Islands were acquired as refueling points. (2) The entire chain was, in a sense, isolated since there was no land between that area and our coast line. (3) A potential enemy attacking our western shores would have to control Hawaii first or risk violating one of the cardinal principles of naval strategy and thereby invite almost sure disaster. (4) Some misconceptions as to the archipelago's value in war existed through a lack of appreciation of what steam had done in the reduction of ocean distances, measuring the latter in time spent in traversing them, instead of in miles. Captain Melville concluded that annexation would give the coming generation of the United States a firm grasp on the vast—but for us almost untouched —trade of the Pacific shores and its islands.[16]

Melville, writing on our future in the Pacific, observed that a territory linked far more with the future than with the present of the union was Alaska, whose development would afford problems

15. New York *Sun*, Feb. 13, 1898, reporting an address delivered at the Lincoln dinner of the Middlesex Club of Boston, Feb. 12, 1898.

16. *Sen. Reps.*, 55 Cong., 2 sess., No. 681, App. III, pp. 100–04. New York *Tribune*, Feb. 13, 1898.

not easy of solution. He referred to William H. Seward's prediction that the "Pacific Ocean, its shores, its islands, and the vast regions beyond will become the chief theatre of events in the world's great hereafter." As a realization of this prophecy, the Commander enumerated the recent acquisitions of Germany, France, and Great Britain in that greatest of oceans and lamented that only the United States stood aloof while other nations had acquired territory in the waters which guarded future commerce.[17]

John R. Procter, president of the United States Civil Service Commission, also pointed up the effect on the United States if this "derelict flying a flag of distress" in the mid-Pacific should fall to another power. "A cruiser or battle-ship with a coal capacity necessary to carry her 5,000 miles, steaming at ten knots an hour, will exhaust her coal in less than 1,000 miles, by doubling her speed. With a supply of coal well guarded in Pearl Harbor, our war-ships and merchantmen can cross the Pacific at maximum speed, or concentrate at distant points at high speed, thus largely increasing their efficiency," while our adversaries, being under the necessity of conserving coal or risking to run out of it away from their own ports, would have to move at much less speed, thus being placed at a great disadvantage. Mahan had well likened a modern warship without coal to a wingless bird. With Hawaii in our possession, we need fear no attack across the Pacific.

This resourceful writer argued that the United States, having annexed possessions of France, Spain, Mexico, and Russia—with their alien customs and laws—and having, with ease, incorporated them within our system, should be little concerned over a few thousand Orientals in Hawaii. With annexation, this would prove a diminishing evil; without annexation, it might become incurable.[18]

In spite of their number and the apparent validity of their arguments, the strategists and Americanists did not remain unchallenged. Carl Schurz analyzed and criticized the shibboleth of "Manifest Destiny," which now meant "not merely the incorporation in the United States of territory contiguous to our borders, but rather the acquisition of such territory, far and near, as may be useful in enlarging our commercial advantages, and in securing to our navy facilities desirable for the operations of a great naval

17. George W. Melville, "Our Future in the Pacific—What We Have There to Hold and Win," *North American Review*, 166 (1898), 281–96.
18. John R. Procter, "Hawaii and the Changing Front of the World," *Forum*, 24 (1897), 34–45.

power." He held that we could secure all sorts of commercial advantages and coaling stations which would serve us as well as if we possessed the country in which they were situated. The United States was the only one of the great powers not threatened in any of its areas by powerful neighbors. In our compact continental stronghold we were substantially unassailable. We presented no vulnerable point of importance. Hawaii, or any other outlying domain, would be our Achilles' heel. Other nations would observe it, and regard us no longer as invulnerable. If we annexed Hawaii, we would "acquire not an addition to our strength, but a dangerous element of weakness."

Schurz further observed that democratic institutions had never flourished in tropical climates. Hawaii had the characteristic population of the tropics—"a number of semi-civilized natives crowded upon by a lot of adventurers flocked together from all parts of the globe to seek their fortunes, with Chinese and Japanese making up nearly one-fourth of the aggregate." If the American people should "yield to the allurements of the tropics and embark on a career of indiscriminate aggrandizement, their 'manifest destiny' points with equal certainty to a total abandonment of their conservative traditions of policy, to a rapid deterioration in the character of the people and their political institutions and to a future of turbulence, demoralization and final decay." [19]

The strategic or defense argument for the annexation of the Hawaiian Islands both in and out of Congress received as much attention as any other, and perhaps was taken more seriously. Yet the Congress failed to act decisively on Hawaii until mid-1898, and then only as a result of the partial dismemberment of China, the outbreak of the Spanish-American War, and Dewey's victory at Manila. Prior to the conflict, the strategic argument carried little weight with American laymen generally; but the operation of Admiral Cervera's fleet caused a minor panic among the civilian population of some Atlantic coastal cities and a deeper appreciation of the strategic importance of Hawaii to the West Coast. The debates in Congress brought out clearly "that although the war

19. Carl Schurz, "Manifest Destiny," *Harper's, 87* (1897), 737–46. This was practically the identical argument of the following month's *American Federationist, 3–4* (1897), 217. Because of his opposition to imperialism, Schurz was a "prattling foreigner" in Roosevelt's opinion, and he would not read what the German-American "shrieked or prattled." (Roosevelt to Lodge, Oct. 20, 1899, in *Correspondence of Roosevelt and Lodge, 1,* 422; Morison, *Letters of Theodore Roosevelt, 2,* 1896).

had added nothing to the defense argument it had put the public in a position better to appreciate its force." [20] Actually, the one great unassailable contention in favor of annexation, from the American standpoint, was the need of possessing in the Pacific a great commercial exchange, like Hong Kong.

To and from Annexation

For over a month before the treaty was transmitted to the Senate, Attorney Kinney worked diligently among members of the Senate for both the reciprocity and the annexation treaties, having decided if the former were lost to urge the latter immediately. The lobbyist directed his efforts exclusively toward the opposition, having secured the entering wedge through the Utah delegation, and found in Senator William A. King of that state, who had prepared an annexation resolution, a willing medium to agitate actively for annexation among the Democrats. The point that Kinney emphasized in arguing for the reciprocity treaty was that annexation was going to be debated and decided one way or another within the next year; pending the decision of that question, it was manifestly improper and unwise to tinker with the commercial treaty. He also stressed that the convention was essentially a matter involving foreign relations and should not be dealt with or disposed of in a tariff measure, but should be decided by itself on its individual merits. In this he had the support of certain friends of Hawaii, Senator William B. Allison of Iowa for one, who opposed the linking of the Hawaiian question with the tariff, either for abrogation or for annexation. Kinney was convinced that if they won at all, it had to be "by patient appeal and reasoning" from the political— not the financial—standpoint, which was the weakest side of annexation.[1]

Meanwhile, Thurston worked hard to bring out an annexation handbook to present to the senators on the eve of debate.[2] The

20. Thomas A. Bailey, "The United States and Hawaii during the Spanish-American War," *American Historical Review, 36* (1931), 559. Cf. *Cong. Record*, 55 Cong., 2 sess., pp. 5775, 5795, 5839; App., pp. 560–61, 665.

1. Kinney to Dole, May 4, June 1, 1897. Cf. Hatch to Cooper, April 27, May 1, 1897; "Pearl Harbor Retreat" and "Political Argument Strong," *Pacific Commercial Advertiser*, May 11, 19, 1897; L. A. Thurston, "A Big Issue: What to Do with Pearl River?" ibid., Nov. 19, 1892.

2. Hatch to Cooper, June 2, 1897. L. A. Thurston, *Handbook on Annexation* (St. Joseph, Mich., 1897). Cf. Thurston, *Why I Am an Annexationist* (Honolulu, 1895).

appointment in April as minister to Hawaii of Harold M. Sewall, an avowed annexationist and an exponent of a dynamic Pacific policy, as his record in Samoa attests, was a distinct gain for the cause. This assignment was urged and sponsored by William P. Frye, the commissioners' most "reliable friend" in the Senate,[3] who, incidentally, was interested in a Pacific cable.

On June 23, 1897, John T. Morgan introduced Senate Bill 2263 to provide for and regulate the annexation of the Hawaiian Islands as a territory of the United States. This was read twice and referred to the Committee on Foreign Relations. Earlier, George A. Spalding, of Michigan, and William A. King introduced in the house a similar joint resolution.[4] The Dingley tariff was made inoperative with regard to Hawaii on the last day of June—that is, the exemption clause in favor of Hawaii which had been removed in the finance committee was replaced. Since duties were raised on raw sugar from elsewhere, Hawaiian planters, in the two years that had to elapse before the reciprocity treaty could be abrogated, would get double duty benefits. Hatch was certain that their "sugars would have been put on the dutiable list if the President had not come forward with annexation." [5]

In addition to the opposition from the powerful sugar trust and the rapidly growing beet-sugar industry, with both of which Claus Spreckels was then associated, other complications were immediately encountered. Only three days after the signing of the annexation treaty, Toru Hoshi, the Japanese minister in Washington, informed Secretary of State Sherman that his government had instructed him to protest against the proposed annexation on these grounds:

> First. the maintenance of the status quo of Hawaii is essential to the good understanding of the Powers that have interests in the Pacific. Second. that annexation of Hawaii would tend to endanger the residential, commercial, and industrial rights of Japanese subjects in Hawaii secured to them by treaty, the constitution and laws of that country. Third. such annexation might lead to the postponement by Hawaii of the settlement of claims and liabilities already existing in favor of Japan under treaty stipulations.

3. Hatch to Cooper, April 23, 1897.
4. *Cong. Record*, 55 Cong., 1 sess., pp. 459, 941, 1924.
5. Hatch to Cooper, July 1, 1897. Cf. Hatch to Cooper, July 7, 1898.

Hoshi further stated that Japan had no desire to embarrass the United States, nor did she have any designs upon the integrity and sovereignty of Hawaii.[6]

Although the Japanese minister disclaimed that this was a protest, calling it only an inquiry, Hatch "devotedly hoped" that Japan would make some protest in the matter and would have been "very glad to hear of some direct attempt of the British authorities to prevent annexation," for that would have had the desired effect in the Senate.[7]

The Pacific naval force was strengthened and new orders were issued to the admiral in command. However, after assurance was given that Japanese treaty rights and pending claims against Hawaii would not be prejudiced by annexation, the objection of the imperial government was not further pressed. Japan formally withdrew the protest against annexation December 22, 1897, but continued to press her claims against the Hawaiian government under a convention of 1888.[8]

The provocative attitude of Japan in 1897 toward United States acquisition of the mid-Pacific archipelago was in sharp contrast to her gracious posture four years earlier, when, on March 16, 1893, her minister to Washington, Gazo Tateno, called at the State Department and confidentially informed Secretary Gresham that since 20,000 pacific, industrious Japanese subjects were resident in the Hawaiian Islands, his government felt interested in what had recently transpired there and would "regret exceedingly to see any European Government obtain control of the Islands," but would be pleased "to see the sovereignty of the United States extended over them."[9] The change in policy, as indicated by the official inquiry, was due to the fact that in the intervening years Japan had fought and won the first Sino-Japanese War and was on the way to becoming a great power with heightened interest in the Pacific. It is highly improbable that Tokyo ever intended to resort to extreme measures. Her protest appears to Professor Thomas A. Bailey,

6. See Thomas A. Bailey, "Japan's Protest against the Annexation of Hawaii," *Journal of Modern History,* 3 (1931), 46–61, 66.

7. Hatch to Cooper, June 18, 1897. As time passed, Hatch could "ask for no better assistance" than a pronounced protest from Japan (Hatch to Cooper, Dec. 10, 1897).

8. See "Japan Talks Loudly—Pressing Its Claims against Hawaiian Republic," Washington *Post,* July 8, 1897.

9. USDS, Misc. Archives, Memoranda of Conversations with Secretary of State, 1893–98.

of Stanford University, to have been largely a political maneuver for home consumption. The Japanese government must have realized that in 1897–98 the United States would not under any circumstances tolerate interference in her program for annexing Hawaii. Assistant Secretary of the Navy Roosevelt, speaking to the Ohio naval reserves, declared that "the United States is not in a position which requires her to ask Japan or any other foreign Power what territory it shall or shall not acquire." The following week he made a similar statement to Secretary Sherman.[10]

Although no action was taken on the annexation treaty in the special session of the fifty-fifth Congress, Minister Hatch felt that since the treaty would again come up in the winter under more favorable circumstances, the wisest plan was to take no radical step in the controversy with Japan, and to make no definite agreement to arbitrate without submitting the matter to the United States government, for the treaty being signed, it was Hawaii's duty to refer all her matters of foreign relations to the State Department. The Minister assured his government that there was no occasion to yield to the nervousness of the planters or to the delay in annexation, for the President of the United States would protect Hawaii during the pendency of the treaty. Proponents of annexation in Washington—namely, Senators Cushman K. Davis, acting chairman of the Foreign Relations Committee; Lodge; and Morgan —suggested Hawaii's ratifying the treaty first, without waiting for action by the United States. Morgan was particularly anxious for this before the elections in the islands, as he apparently feared that the members of the sugar trust would transfer the fight to defeat the treaty to Hawaii.[11] He had his wish: the treaty was unanimously ratified by the Hawaiian Senate and President Dole on September 10, 1897.

When Congress reassembled on December 6, 1897, the expected support from the Populist senators was not forthcoming, thus making ratification appear impossible. Moreover, Senator Hoar asked and received consent to present and have referred to the Committee on Foreign Relations a memorial of the Patriotic League of the Hawaiian Islands, signed by its secretary and 21,269 other citizens of those islands, remonstrating against annexation.[12] The same

10. New York *Tribune*, July 27, 1897; Roosevelt to Lodge, Aug. 3, 1897, in *Correspondence of Roosevelt and Lodge*, 1, 268.

11. Hatch to Cooper, July 7, 10, 17, 21, 1897.

12. *Cong. Record*, 55 Cong., 2 sess., p. 45. *Journal of the U.S. Senate*, 55 Cong., 2 sess., p. 17.

day Minister Sewall in Honolulu reported on the popularity of Princess Kaiulani with all classes of the community and of the friendship displayed toward her by some members of the government, who did not regard with disfavor a proposition to make her queen—"certainly in the event of the rejection of the treaty." Those who overthrew the monarchy, however, "were ready to prevent this at the sacrifice of their lives," and would "do so despite the defection of any or all the members of the Government." [13]

Francis Hatch optimistically explained to the minister of foreign affairs that if the treaty failed, there was a clearly decided majority for a joint resolution in the house, where some Democratic support was expected to counterbalance considerable defection on the part of Republican mugwamps. The most disconcerting feature of the opposition was the attitude of Thomas B. Reed, speaker of the House of Representatives, who had the power to prevent a vote being taken there during the session by merely failing to give his casting vote as chairman of the Committee on Rules, to report a rule fixing a day on which the vote could be taken. Without this rule being reported, a joint resolution for annexation, if reported by the Committee on Foreign Affairs, could be easily talked to death during the two days privileged.[14]

Stephen M. White, on his arrival from California, directed his energies against the treaty, and presented a memorial of the Federated Trades Council of Sacramento, remonstrating against the annexation of the Hawaiian Islands. His colleague, George C. Perkins, brought forward on the same day, December 14, a similar one from the Chamber of Commerce of San Francisco. These were followed by analogous petitions from the Board of Trade of Los Angeles, the Commercial Club of Chicago, and various citizens of the United States. Soon, however, there occurred an apparent reaction in favor of Hawaii.[15] An effort to get Democrats and Populists in the house to declare against annexation in caucus failed; both

13. Sewall to Sherman, Dec. 9, 1897, USDS, Dispatches, Hawaii, 30.
14. Hatch to Cooper, Dec. 6, 10, 22, 1897; May 13, 1898. The rules of the House of Representatives are such that a measure that comes up in the regular order holds its place at the head of the list for two days only. If a vote has not been reached by that time, it goes to the foot of the list, which practically means defeat. Cf. Honolulu Evening Bulletin, Jan. 2, 1898.
15. Journal of the U.S. Senate, 55 Cong., 2 sess., pp. 23, 59, 70, 98, 100–02. There were, however, as many memorials favoring annexation from various interest groups, including the Republican Club of New York City. See ibid., pp. 93, 102, 133, 145, 153, 161, 171, 317, 326, 335, 378.

groups preferred to leave the subject alone. Under the circumstances, this was a distinct gain for the annexationists.[16]

James Bryce, a distinguished British jurist and author, writing at the close of the year from an American point of view—for the Hawaiian question did not occupy the British mind at all—warned the United States of the problems ahead from a break in her traditional policy. She had already

> a great and splendid mission in building up between the oceans a free, happy and prosperous nation of two hundred millions of people . . . It would be, for her, a descent from what may be called the pedestal of wise and pacific detachment on which she now stands, were she to yield to that earth-hunger which has been raging among European states, and to imitate the aggressive methods which some of them have pursued. The policy of creating great armaments and of annexing territories beyond the sea would be . . . an un-American policy, and a complete departure from the maxims—approved by long experience—of the illustrious founders of the Republic.[17]

Senator Morgan answered the renowned Englishman by examining the question of whether "a sense of national duty" compelled us to annex Hawaii. A protectorate, which Great Britain would find quite easy and natural to establish under the reign of Princess Kaiulani, "would seriously offend American sentiment, and would subject our people to self reproach for a weak desertion of a very high moral and national duty." On the other hand, if we annexed the group, we would "rapidly build up at Honolulu, in sight of Pearl Harbor, a commercial mart, like Hong Kong, protected by a fortress, easy of construction, far stronger than Gibraltar, that will stand sentinel over the surrounding ocean for thousands of miles."[18]

While native Hawaiians remained antipathetic, the American public as a whole was apathetic to annexation. Only special interest groups, concerned for either religious, commercial, or other reasons, made their views known.[19] At the close of the year, international complications in China had the effect of strengthening the case among the mercantile interests for the annexation of Hawaii, the

16. Hatch to Cooper, Dec. 22, 1897.
17. "The Policy of Annexation," *Forum*, 24 (1897), 385–95.
18. "The Duty of Annexing Hawaii," ibid., 25 (1898), 11–16.
19. See Memorial of Congregational Ministers' Union to Sherman, March 16, 1897, USDS, Misc. Letters, March 1897, Pt. II.

entrepôt of the Pacific. The influential New York *Journal of Commerce and Commercial Bulletin* came over to the cause, asserting that events in Asia "conclusively silence the objections that have hitherto been well taken against connecting the Atlantic and Pacific oceans and annexing Hawaii," and cited the action of Germany and Russia in the Far East as the reason.[20] Several editorials the last week of December pointed up the activities of those powers in China and indicated the interest of the United States in that vast country.[21] A similar New York journal, *Commercial America*, expanding on the mercantile arguments in favor of a policy of annexation, warned that the acquisition of Hawaii by England, Germany, or Japan would mean that within 2,000 miles of our Pacific coast the only available territory in the Pacific Ocean would be transformed into a huge manufacturing depot, "supplied with European capital, worked by Asiatic labor, for the supreme control of the trade of every country bordering upon the Pacific, whether in North or South America, in Asia or in Australia." [22]

The increasing uncertainty in the Senate over the ratification of the treaty, the memorial against annexation signed by an overwhelmingly large number of Hawaiian citizens, the failure of the annexationists to match it with a petition so numerously endorsed, the continued popularity of Princess Kaiulani, and the projected journey to Washington of Joseph Carter, an old and respected resident and a strong supporter of the monarchy, to help the Queen and the native Hawaiian delegates accompanying her with his advice and to use his utmost influence against the treaty, caused grave concern in Honolulu. Liliuokalani was again in the national capital not to appeal for restoration to her throne but to secure from McKinley a statement condemnatory of Minister Stevens' action in January 1893. An executive council and council of state meeting on January 5–6, 1898, voted unanimously to send President Dole thither to neutralize, if possible, the effect of the native memorial and to turn the scales in favor of annexation, the general feeling being that if he did not go and annexation should be lost, severe criticism would be engendered by the failure to use one available means to excite interest in the cause.[23] He sailed on January 8.

20. Editorial, Dec. 28, 1897.
21. Dec. 22, 28–30, 1897.
22. Jan. 7, 1898.
23. Cooper to Hatch, Jan. 6, 1898, AH, Hawaiian Legation, Washington, D.C., 1888–98, Vol. 2. *Pacific Commercial Advertiser*, Jan. 6, 1898.

Every possible courtesy was extended the visiting President. As a guest of the nation while in the capital, he was entertained extensively. His commanding mien and good judgment throughout the tour met with pleasant comment, and there was some reason to believe that he disarmed to a certain extent hostile and unkind criticism. Whether his visit won any votes for annexation no one could say, nor could it be immediately determined if any harm was done among the wavering Democrats and Populists, plain men who did "not like a great display of brass buttons." [24] Senator John M. Thurston of Nebraska, however, turned against Hawaii, and the two votes of that state were lost.

After Dole's departure on February 6, the Cuban war of liberation and the crisis attendant upon the U.S.S. *Maine* explosion of January 15 became the center of attention, necessarily forcing little Hawaii into the background. Hatch felt that if the United States should intervene in the war, the treaty would be carried "through on the jump," but in early and mid-February no one could tell what the result would be until the roll was called. There was new hope from a report that Speaker Reed had reversed his stand, had decided to support annexation by act of Congress, and was in favor of prompt action. According to the New York *Herald* and the Washington *Post*, he considered that it would be impossible to secure the two-thirds majority necessary to ratify the pending treaty, and was anxious that a vote demonstrating this fact might be speedily taken and that both houses begin consideration at once of the Morgan bill, which would require only a majority vote in each house to bring about the same result contemplated by the treaty. The *Herald* claimed that Speaker Reed wanted an early adjournment of Congress, which was not possible as long as the treaty was hanging in the balance, and that he would use Hawaiian annexation as one of the great achievements of the Republican party in the approaching congressional campaign. This report of a reversal met with a vigorous denial from the Speaker,[25] and for a time the situation remained the same in the House of Representatives.

Reaction of American Labor

From its very inception, the movement for the annexation of Hawaii might have appeared a menace to American laborers; yet appar-

24. Hatch to Cooper, Jan. 18, 28, Feb. 6, 10, 1898.
25. *Herald,* Feb. 7, 1898. *Post,* Feb. 7, 8, 1898.

ently their leaders were apathetic to the issue until 1897. The only reference involving labor that this writer found in the pro- and anti-annexation literature of 1893 was an article by T. Graham Gribble entitled "The Sugar Industry and the Labor Question as Affected by Annexation," which appeared in the March issue of the *Engineering Magazine*. Considering the Oriental element in Hawaii, the labor costs there, and the improbability of the United States extending the beet-sugar bounty to cane sugar in the islands, Gribble raised the question whether annexation would not aggravate the labor difficulty.[1]

In four years the situation changed. After the submission of a second annexation treaty to the Senate, the Hawaiian question served to bring the American labor movement to grips with the ideology of imperialism.[2] The West Coast labor organizations were the most vociferous in their opposition. The San Francisco Central Labor Union addressed to the California senators a petition which maintained that annexation jeopardized the liberties of American wage earners, while the labor councils of San Francisco, Sacramento, and Los Angeles passed resolutions against annexation, without a single voice being raised in favor of it.[3]

Opposition was also voiced in the *American Federationist* and the *Coast Seamen's Journal*, official organ of the International Seamen's Union of America. In the former, Samuel Gompers, president of the American Federation of Labor, opposed the proposed annexation of Hawaii, for in it he could detect all the evils attendant on imperialism and was certain that this group was only the first step in empire building.[4] The latter journal maintained that the acquisition of any islands lying within the tropics contained a menace to labor, that the residuum of McKinley's reasoning was "slavery, pure and simple," and that annexation was unsafe, even though confined to the Hawaiian Islands. The whole question turned upon the profits of eastern traders as against the interests of the producers.[5]

1. Condensed in *Review of Reviews*, 7 (New York, ed. 1893), 326.
2. John C. Appel, "American Labor and the Annexation of Hawaii, A Study in Logic and Economic Interest," *Pacific Historical Review*, 23 (1954), 1–18.
3. *Coast Seamen's Journal*, Dec. 29, 1897, p. 7.
4. "Should Hawaii Be Annexed?" *American Federationist*, 3–4 (1897), 217. Cf. Philip Foner, *History of the Labor Movement in the United States* (2 vols. New York, 1955), 2, 407.
5. "Annexation Argument(?)," *Coast Seamen's Journal*, Jan. 12, 1898, p. 8; cf. ibid., Dec. 15, 29, 1897, pp. 6, 7.

The American Federation of Labor, at its seventeenth annual convention, in Nashville, Tennessee, on December 15–21, 1897, declared decisively against territorial expansion by passing a seven-point resolution embodying the classic arguments against annexation,[6] and the declining Knights of Labor generally maintained a similar view.[7] Yet not all American laborers denounced the proposed annexation as a capitalist conspiracy to reintroduce into the United States the contract labor system which had been outlawed by Congress in 1885, and only a small portion feared that the acquisition of Hawaii would menace their jobs and full dinner pails. Others saw opportunities for American labor in the islands whose industrialized economy would eventually sustain a population of a million instead of a hundred thousand. Some labor unions were convinced that overseas expansion would be a boon to their crafts. In general, according to Appel, the relationship of American labor to the annexation of Hawaii "can be summarized as 'pure and simple unionism' at work."[8]

The Trans-Mississippi Commercial Congress, held in Salt Lake City in July 1897 and presided over by William Jennings Bryan, was an occasion for Edward M. Walsh, representing California, to remind the audience that Hawaii already needed workmen and that once in the union she would offer "a new field for labor and a new source of prosperity," and for Lorrin A. Thurston to emphasize that "with stability of government" in the archipelago would come "immigration, development and growth," as had taken place in other territories annexed by the United States.[9]

A feeble effort was made to voice the opposition of some of the unorganized American farmers. Herbert Myrick—president of Orange Judd Company, editor of *American Agriculturist,* of New York, *Orange Judd Farmer,* of Chicago, and *New England Homestead,* of Springfield, Massachusetts—addressed a plea to J. W. Wadsworth, chairman of the House Committee on Agriculture. In the name of nearly one million American farmers, Myrick as-

6. *Report of Proceedings of the Seventeenth Annual Convention of the American Federation of Labor, Nashville, Tennessee,* 1897 (Bloomington, Ind., 1898), pp. 36, 88–89.

7. Appel, *Pacific Historical Review,* 23, 17–18.

8. Ibid., p. 18.

9. *Official Proceedings of the Ninth Session of the Trans-Mississippi Commercial Congress Held at Salt Lake City, Utah, July 14, 15, 16, and 17, 1897* (Salt Lake City, 1897), pp. 66, 147. For Thurston's address "The Annexation of Hawaii," see pp. 61–74.

serted that it would be unfortunate "for the American farmer should Uncle Sam ever decide to embark upon an era of 'imperial coloniza-tion.' The cooly labor of these tropical colonies, directed by capable overseers, and their products manipulated by world-wide trusts, would close up every beet sugar proposition and cane sugar-mill in the United States . . . The growing and manufacture of smoking tobacco and cigars . . . would be annihilated, and the heavy leaf industry also injured." He asked that Wadsworth bring this plea promptly to the official attention of the House of Representatives before a vote on annexation was taken.[10]

Nonetheless, the opposition from American farmers was cer-tainly insignificant and ineffectual. The *American Agriculturist*, in its 1893 and 1897–98 issues conducted no organized campaign and carried no articles or letters of disapproval. Neither does the Amer-ican press for those years reflect any concerted action against the annexation of Hawaii on the part of the tillers of the soil.

Opposition of the Sugar Interests

In contrast to the passivity of the agrarian population was the active and strenuous opposition of the sugar interests, both beet and cane. Henry Oxnard, a beet-sugar producer, conducted a house to house canvass among congressmen early in May 1897 and, by claim-ing that he was friendly to Hawaii, induced the press to allow him space for statements.[1]

Determined that its monopoly should not be jeopardized, the sugar trust persisted in its opposition to annexation. The Western Sugar Refinery Company of San Francisco, owned by the Spreckels family, controlled the entire market for refined sugars in all the United States lying west of the Missouri River. This monopoly was so complete that it prevented any raw sugar from being sold by the grocers in the area. With annexation, that refinery would lose control of the Hawaiian crop: yellow sugars and washed sugars from Hawaii would at once be put on sale throughout the Pacific states. Every pound of that sugar consumed would displace an equal number of pounds of refined sugar. Consequently, the West-ern Sugar Refinery would lose its refining profit on exactly that quantity of sugar, the aggregate of which would be considerable.

10. Myrick to Wadsworth, undated, *Cong. Record*, 55 Cong., 2 sess., pp. 6270, 6643–44.
1. *Pacific Commercial Advertiser*, May 19, 1897.

With annexation there would be nothing to prevent the establishment of refineries at the Hawaiian Islands, and in this way the monopoly of the Western Sugar Refinery Company would be broken.[2]

The Beet Sugar Association of Nebraska launched a vigorous campaign against the treaty in the latter part of 1897 by flooding the country with circulars urging the people to oppose annexation and to write their congressmen to that effect. The association maintained that annexation was the only thing that threatened the success of the beet industry. Offers were made to start beet factories all over the country, which proved an effective move and one that the Hawaiian commissioners found impossible to meet.[3] Senator William Vincent Allen from Nebraska presented to the Senate, on January 5, 1898, a memorial of the American Sugar Growers Association remonstrating against the annexation of the Hawaiian Islands, which was followed by a similar one on February 7 from the Beet Sugar Association of Nebraska and another from the citizens of that state on July 9.[4]

Abandonment of the Treaty

The Senate, as in committee of the whole, proceeded to consider the Hawaiian treaty (Executive E) on January 10, 1898, and continued to do so on January 11, 13, 17, 18, 19, and 20.[1] Discussion was interrupted in the latter part of January by the silver question, which engendered considerable hard feeling in the country, after President McKinley, on January 27, addressed the National Association of Manufacturers in New York City, declaring that Congress must redeem the pledges made in the St. Louis platform and make every effort to put the currency of the country on a sound, stable basis.[2] Some of the warmest supporters of the treaty were silver men who unfortunately got into a snarl with the President at this critical time. Even Senator Morgan opposed the President on the silver issue. At the end of January there was no indication

2. "Sugar Trust and Annexation," statement of H. M. Hatch, Dec. 27, 1897, in AH, Hawaiian Officials Abroad, U.S. Minister, Washington.

3. Hatch to Cooper, Dec. 22, 1897.

4. *Journal of the U.S. Senate*, 55 Cong., 2 sess., pp. 36, 60, 90.

1. *Executive Proceedings of the Senate*, 55 Cong., 31, Pt. I, 465, 470, 474, 485, 489, 495, 500, 502.

2. New York *Times*, Jan. 28, 1898. For comments on and criticism of the President's address see ibid., Jan. 29, 30, Feb. 3, 1898.

of a vote for a long time, perhaps a month or six weeks.[3] Debate was resumed on February 7, with Senator Teller delivering an able four-hour speech advocating annexation, arguing that the acquisition of the islands was in the interest of our commerce and in line with our national policy for the previous half-century, and replying to objections to union based on the domination of native races. Even he confessed his doubt as to the prospect of obtaining the sixty votes necessary for the ratification of the treaty, and along with some other exponents of annexation, including Senator Joseph B. Foraker of Ohio, favored dropping the treaty and going ahead with the Morgan bill.[4] Discussion of the subject was continued on February 8, 14, and 16, and was resumed on March 9,[5] at which time the consensus among the members of the Foreign Relations Committee was that the necessary votes for ratification of the treaty could not be obtained.[6]

On March 16 a joint resolution (S. J. *Res.* 127) to provide for annexing the Hawaiian Islands to the United States, which was a substitute for the Senate Joint Resolution 100 and Senate Bill 2263, was read the first and second time by unanimous consent.[7] Thus the subject was brought within the reach of the legislative power of Congress, under the precedent established in the annexation of Texas.

All the traditional and hackneyed arguments for the acquisition of Hawaii were advanced by the Committee on Foreign Relations in its report accompanying the joint resolution. This official document of 119 pages described the islands, cited a long list of American statesmen who had advocated annexation of the archipelago, brought together the evidence and opinions of naval officers, and with equal emphasis indicated our moral duty to the Hawaiians, the strategic value to the United States of the "key of the Pacific," the commercial significance of the "Cross-roads of the Pacific," the menace of British interests, and the imminent dangers of Japanese infiltration and influence in the islands. The committee listed five specific reasons for acquiring Hawaii, the paramount one being to secure a vantage ground for the protection of what the United

3. Hatch to Cooper, Jan. 21, 1898.
4. Washington *Post*, Jan. 8, 1898. *Executive Proceedings of the Senate,* 55 Cong., *31*, Pt. I, p. 551.
5. *Executive Proceedings,* pp. 559, 567, 578, 628.
6. Hatch to Cooper, March 2, 3, 6, 1898. Hatch to Dole, March 6, 1898.
7. *Journal of the U.S. Senate,* 55 Cong., 2 sess., p. 164.

States already owned. The report indicated that the movement of population was already to, and not from, Hawaii; annexation would greatly accelerate this. Twenty objections to annexation were refuted, the last being that the United States had enough territory, people, and problems, and should let well enough alone.

The issue raised by the question of referring annexation to the vote of the people of Hawaii, the committee contended, "necessarily includes a denial of the sovereign power of that Government to agree to annexation until a majority of the people have given their consent. . . . Congress has never demanded a plebiscite to test the question of any annexation of territory to the United States on behalf of the people directly affected by it, nor the assent of the people of the United States to accept any people into our Union." [8]

Meanwhile, Harold Sewall, in his dispatches from Honolulu, reported rumors in early February of a native insurrection which, when investigated, proved false and revealed dissension in the ranks of the American Union party in Hawaii, the two wings of which were the Annexation Club and the American League. The long delay in ratifying the treaty, along with the continued strain of anxiety to which all classes of the community were subjected, was having the natural effect of increasing the number of those who doubted its final success and who were weary of waiting on the United States government to act. Samuel Damon, who had successfully administered the finance department, had, for one, lost faith in annexation, and there was open suspicion that he did not desire it.[9]

Annexation through Joint Resolution

In spite of the changed approach to annexation, there was considerable delay in the Senate. The District of Columbia appropriation bill had the right of way during the second week in March, and at the end of that period the report of the American court of inquiry on the *Maine* was ready to be considered. Hatch recognized

8. *Sen. Reps.*, 55 Cong., 2 sess., No. 681, "Annexation of Hawaii," sometimes called the "Davis Report" after Cushman K. Davis, chairman of the Foreign Relations Committee, pp. 8, 14, 27, 20–21, 61. (For charges directed against Great Britain see the *Times* (London), March 18; New York *Times*, Washington *Post*, and other American newspapers, March 22, 1898.)

9. Sewall to Sherman, Feb. 3, March 15, 1898, USDS, Dispatches, Hawaii, 30.

that his adopted country could well afford to wait until that matter was disposed of, for developments in Havana were sure to help the cause of Hawaii. Well aware that State Department officials were occupied and that anyone who interrupted them during the Cuban crisis would lose all power of persuasion thereafter, the Minister remained away from that office for over a fortnight.[1]

The commissioners did not, however, overlook the advantage of keeping Hawaii before the Navy Department. Early in March, Hatch presented Secretary of the Navy Long with a draft for $500 sent from Hawaii to the families of the *Maine* victims.[2] Later, Castle directed the attention of the Navy Department to the possibility of procuring the U.S.S. *China* as a naval reserve, and her superb fitness for it, which suggestion was well received and enquiries ordered. Soon thereafter he called again—the idea being Thurston's—and recommended that the Navy purchase all the available coal in Honolulu for war purposes. Theodore Roosevelt immediately dictated letters and sent off dispatches to consummate the purchases. The Hawaiian executive council, on application from the United States government, voted, on April 12, to allot to the latter four additional esplanade lots for storage purposes. This action, if not an actual breach of neutrality, was certainly a definite commitment to the side of the United States.[3]

In the meantime, Hatch recommended that his government encourage the increase of the American population of the islands, specifically through a liberalization of homestead legislation and an appropriation of a quarter of a million dollars to promote the immigration of American farmers.[4] He warned against a proclamation of neutrality in case war was declared between the United States and Spain, convinced that Hawaii should maintain silence, especially considering the fact that Congress might at any moment annex the republic. If that body adjourned without passing the joint resolution and war was declared, thus making it a matter of necessity for President McKinley to order the occupation of the islands as a naval supply depot, there was no likelihood of obstacles being placed in his way. If, however, neutrality should be proclaimed, it might be enforced against the United States by the

1. Hatch to Cooper, March 6, 1898.
2. Hatch to Dole, March 6, 1898.
3. Hatch to Cooper, March 26, 1898; Bailey, "U.S. and Hawaii," *American Historical Review, 36,* 555.
4. Hatch to Cooper, March 5, April 14, 1898.

other great powers—for instance, Japan or Great Britain. The Minister advised that Hawaii "should do nothing and say nothing, and let the President of the United States act." If he should take the step mentioned, his motive would not be merely to obtain strategic advantage for his country, but also to protect the citizens of Hawaii from financial loss in consequence of having in good faith attempted to make their country a part of the United States. The conflict on Spain's part would probably result in a privateering war. There was no place on the face of the globe where so much American property was exposed to the attacks of privateers as upon the Hawaiian Islands. Furthermore, the advice of friendly senators should not be disregarded, for if they should get the idea that Honolulu was indifferent to their suggestions, there might be disastrous effects on their zeal in pressing annexation. And that was not the worst of the situation. If annexation met defeat, the next attack would be upon the reciprocity treaty. There was already a dangerous state of indifference to annexation. Hawaii could not afford to lose the active assistance of any senator who had hitherto been favorable to its cause. The activity and the power of the interests arrayed against her should not be underrated: they adopted methods, had agents throughout the entire country, and exerted power, all of which were very difficult to counter and to overcome.

After the rupture with Spain, Hatch went even further and suggested that his government offer a battalion from the National Guard. The two paid companies of that Guard should form the nucleus which, together with volunteers, would make a battalion of 200 to 240 men that should be sent to California and there tendered to the United States.[5]

The day following the receipt of news in Honolulu of the outbreak of war, Dole authorized a telegram to the minister in Washington, requesting him to ascertain what McKinley wanted the Hawaiian government to do, and in case the latter appeared to favor such a course, to "tender to the President the support of this Government in the pending conflict," even to the extent of negotiating a treaty of alliance. As the first detachment of the United States army was about to sail for the Philippines, Hatch urged his colleagues in Honolulu to "extend every possible hospitality to the

5. Hatch to Cooper, April 14, 24, 1898. Cf. "Privateering, in War—Interest in Policy of United States and Spain," Washington *Post*, April 15, 1898.

expedition, let there be no half-way measures in the welcome of-fered. Do not discuss neutrality. Events have progressed far beyond that point. The reports of the tender of the Islands for war pur-poses have made a great impression on the public men and have done great good." [6] Nine days later the Minister reported that Hawaii was "right on top of the wave" in having Dole's offer before the public mind in connection with the situation at Manila. "You can fancy what use people here would have for Americans who could talk neutrality in Hawaii under the present conditions." He heard no one "impugn the sincerity of our motives as to suggest the possibility of our taking a stand which might embarrass the United States after having ratified the treaty." [7]

Hatch was aware by early June that if the President of the United States hoisted the flag in Honolulu and took possession under stress of war conditions, there would be absolutely no similarity whatever to the situation which existed when Stevens extended a protec-torate. Hawaiian officials could rely definitely upon the assurance that if the flag should be hoisted under the above conditions, it would never come down. [8]

Meanwhile, Thurston sought to inform and influence the Hawaiian public on the matter of neutrality and the delay in ratifying the treaty. In a letter to the editor of the Pacific Commercial Adver-tiser, dated May 22, 1898, the Commissioner asserted that "a decla-ration of neutrality by Hawaii at this stage, under present condi-tions, would be an act bordering on imbecility, for anyone who favors the annexation policy." Technically right or practically wrong, such a declaration would be looked upon in Washington "as a slap in the face; as an indication of fair weather friendship." He assured the home folks that "we are losing nothing by delay." The cause had never before been so strong in the United States. All that was necessary for success was "to allow nothing in our calendar that stands in the way of annexation; cultivate a patience that knows no weariness and a watchfulness that will take advan-tage of every opportunity. Our opportunity now is to demonstrate by deed as well as word, that we appreciate the friendly treatment

6. Cooper to Hatch, May 10, 1898; Hatch to Cooper, May 13, 1898. At the time the Hawaiian government tendered its support, Dole and Cooper had not heard of Dewey's phenomenal victory of May 1.

7. Hatch to Cooper, May 22, 1898.

8. Ibid., June 9, 1898.

and enormous financial benefits which have been conferred upon us by the American people; and that no technicalities of law will be invoked against American interests in Hawaii." [9]

The Hawaiian government's proffer of assistance, in view of the fact that it came in the face of strong local opposition and before the knowledge of Dewey's victory, not as a result of it, heightened interest in annexation in the United States and undoubtedly assisted in the passage of the joint resolution. Yet there was some delay, for although the House of Representatives began to discuss the annexation of Hawaii on March 15, even in advance of having the resolution, there was the intervening war crisis and the reluctance of the lower chamber to touch a matter until it comes from the Senate. After the outbreak of war, more money was needed to prosecute the conflict, and another tariff bill on which the parties could not agree became an obstacle in Hawaii's path. In addition, the new Secretary of State, William R. Day, appointed to the post after the resignation on April 25 of the elderly John Sherman, remained away from Washington, detained by his wife's illness. There was no man in public life who could put the case for Hawaii to the President so tellingly as Judge Day, and his help was missing when it was most needed. Once more the commissioners seemed to be at the very crisis of their fate.[10]

Soon the situation in the Philippines, especially after Dewey's spectacular victory at Manila Bay, the morning of May 1, brought home to the minds of many who had hitherto been doubtful the necessity of completing the annexation business, of "bridging the gap" in the Pacific. Only three days after the battle, Representative Francis G. Newlands of Nevada introduced a resolution (H. Res. 259) for annexing Hawaii to the United States as a territory, which in its ten paragraphs embodying the terms of a treaty stipulated the conditions that should obtain in the Hawaiian Islands until "Congress shall provide for the government of such islands." [11]

There were dissenting voices both in and out of Congress, however. Carl Schurz, for one, on May 9, 1898, wrote a letter to William McKinley, warning that if his administration took advantage of the war to press the annexation of Hawaii—"that annexation having been violently discountenanced by the public opinion of the coun-

9. AH, L. A. Thurston file.
10. Hatch to Cooper, April 28, May 4, 1898.
11. *Cong. Record,* 55 Cong., 2 sess., p. 4600. *United States Statutes at Large,* 55 Cong., *30,* 750.

try before the war began"—the confidence of the world in the unselfishness of our policy would be destroyed. "It will be in vain to say that for the purposes of the war we must have a naval station in Hawaii, for the world knows that we own Pearl Harbor, which we can use as a naval station without annexing Hawaii." Annexation "under such circumstances would therefore be an acquisition of territory by means of this war. From that time on it would be useless to protest that this is not a war of selfish ambition and conquest." [12]

In the meantime, Hawaii's complications with Japan arising out of the treatment of Japanese laborers emigrating to the islands under the Hawaiian-Japanese convention of 1888, particularly the refusal in March 1897 to admit a group of them, undoubtedly proved helpful in arousing American public opinion, and was the strongest argument in favor of union. Delaying tactics were pursued in Honolulu; Hatch, with the approval of Day, warned the minister of foreign affairs to concede nothing as far as the convention with Japan was concerned, to take ample time for full consultation before any reply was made to the Japanese claim, to "Do Nothing. Sign Nothing," and if any proposition came from Japan, to refer the whole matter to President McKinley.[13]

The United States was not invited to mediate and sought no intervention in the matter, "further than to evince its kindest disposition toward such a speedy and direct adjustment" by the two states as should "comport with equity and honor." [14] President McKinley, however, notified Japan that no compulsory measures upon Hawaii, in behalf of the Japanese government, would be tolerated by this country. It is probable that if annexation had not forced the removal of the difficulty, the United States would have become involved with Japan.[15] Judge Day eventually recommended settling the controversy, feeling that this might help the treaty through the Senate. In view of early action by Congress on the joint resolution, John Bassett Moore, assistant secretary of state, by direction of President McKinley, asked Minister Hatch to consider "whether it would not be well to make definite provision for the immediate adjustment of

12. Bancroft, *Papers of Carl Schurz*, 5, 466.
13. Hatch to Cooper, Jan. 28, Feb. 16, 1898; cf. ibid., July 7, 10, 17, 1897. *Cong. Record*, 55 Cong., 2 sess., pp. 6621–22.
14. McKinley's first annual message, Dec. 6, 1897, in Richardson, *Messages and Papers* (New York), 13, 6263.
15. Hoar, *Autobiography*, 2, 308. Bailey, "Japan's Protest," *Journal of Modern History*, 3, 60.

the claims of Japan against Hawaii, whenever the Joint Resolution shall have passed Congress." [16] Eventually, the Hawaiian government, ignoring the question of strict right and without admitting its error or responsibility, agreed to pay an indemnity of $75,000 to cover hardships to laborers returned, and Japan accepted that sum in satisfaction of her claims.

Judge Day, after his return to Washington, fully aware that this was the moment for a supreme effort, got the House Committee on Foreign Affairs to act. That body, by a vote of ten to four, on May 12, agreed on a favorable report on the Newlands resolution. Of those approving, eight were Republicans; one Democrat, Albert S. Berry, of Kentucky; and Francis G. Newlands, a member of the Silver party; of those opposing, all were Democrats.[17] Robert R. Hitt, chairman of the committee, submitted the resolution without amendment, accompanied by a report (No. 1355) to the committee of the whole house on May 17, while Hugh A. Dinsmore, of Arkansas, presented the views of the minority, accompanied by a report (No. 1355, part 2), which were similarly referred.[18] No great difficulty was anticipated in the lower house, where the resolution was expected to have the support of nearly all the Republicans, while many Democrats would join Berry in voting for it.

Hawaii's fate, nevertheless, hung by a thread. Speaker Reed's opposition became more aggressive and determined as the session drew to its close. Friends of the administration used every effort to force him to one side, but as the pressure increased, the opponents became more obstinate, with the Speaker ranged in opposition to the President. Moreover, the sugar trust interest moved "heaven and earth to get an adjournment," believing that if they could cause consideration of annexation to be deferred until the next session, they would have accomplished their purpose, for in that session, a short one expiring by limitation on March 3 or 4, ordinary routine business would occupy all the time. As late as June 9, Hatch found it "simply impossible to forecast the result." [19]

After blocking passage of the Newlands resolution for three weeks,

16. Moore to Hatch, June 29, 1898, USDS, Hawaiian Legation, Notes to, 2. AH, Hawaiian Officials Abroad, U.S. Minister, Washington.

17. New York *Herald*, May 13, 1898.

18. *Cong. Record*, 55 Cong., 2 sess., p. 4989.

19. Hatch to Cooper, May 22, 26, June 9, 1898. Lodge, too, at the end of May complained that "the opposition now comes exclusively from Reed, who is straining every nerve to beat Hawaii" (Lodge to Roosevelt, May 31, 1898, in *Correspondence of Roosevelt and Lodge*, 1, 302).

Reed finally consented to let it come up for floor debate on June 11. Hitt, who had marshaled the views of military and naval experts to support his position, and Jonathan P. Dolliver, from Iowa, restated in part the strategic arguments for the annexation of Hawaii. The most outspoken opposition was voiced by Henry U. Johnson, Republican of Indiana, who contended that the acquisition of Hawaii was not necessary as a war measure in the conflict with Spain; that annexation was not necessary in order to prevent the islands from falling into the hands of some other great power to be used by it to menace and attack our coast; and that annexation of Hawaii was of itself inherently wrong. Pearl Harbor and the immediate surrounding environs were practically all that was imperative for war operations and a coaling station. He was unconvinced that the sovereignty of Hawaii would be transferred to some other power, for the people of the islands had never "manifested the least inclination to join their fortunes with that of any other nation but ours." The issue was not simply whether we should annex Hawaii: that territory was "not the ultimatum of the annexationists." It was but "the entering wedge" which would lead to still further acquisitions of foreign territory in no wise contiguous to our soil.

Congressman De Elva S. Alexander, representing New York, met the argument that Hawaii was not contiguous by asserting: "Alaska is not contiguous; the Aleutian Islands are not contiguous; Midway Island, 1,200 miles west of Honolulu, which we annexed in 1867, and for the development of which we appropriated $50,000, is not contiguous territory. When we annexed Louisiana, it was further away from our seat of government than Hawaii is today." [20]

The house voted down a substitute resolution proposing to guarantee the independence of the Hawaiian Islands, and passed the Newlands resolution on June 15 by a vote of 209 to 91, 6 answering present, 49 not voting.[21] It was favorably reported without amendment two days later to the Senate, where the tougher struggle was anticipated, where Stephen M. White, the leader of the opposition, was prepared to consume several days in reading numerous documents into the record. That chamber proceeded to the consideration of the Newlands resolution in open executive session on June 20, and continued debating it until July. Even under the stress of war con-

20. Cong. Record, 55 Cong., 2 sess., pp. 5771–72, 5775–76, 5992, 5594–96, 6435, 6441.

21. Ibid., p. 6019. Cf. United States Statutes at Large, 55 Cong., 30, Nos. 259, 750; New York Times, July 7, 1898.

ditions, the opponents of annexation and the new imperialism fought to the utmost. Southern antagonism centered round the racial issue involved and the competition of Hawaiian sugar, while many Northern and Western senators doubted the constitutionality of the acquisition. The repetitious arguments and clichés, interrupted almost daily with roll calls to adjourn or to determine a quorum, continued even through the hot July 4. In general, the advocates of annexation, having already reiterated all possible arguments on the subject, did not consume time and refrained from debate, thus conserving their energies in the exhausting heat, but they were adamant on maintaining a quorum and on remaining in session until a vote was taken. There were involved technicalities: the fact that the Hawaiian government had not yet ceded the islands; the definition of a treaty; the power of Congress to destroy but not create one; and the question of whether annexation except by treaty was legal. Amendment after amendment was offered, but the proponents of annexation stood solidly together. Lodge, for one, devoted all his strength to the task, determined to break the filibuster and to put the resolution through before adjournment, gaining rather than losing on successive votes.[22]

Perhaps the persistence of the Americanists was in part due to the encouragement of an interested British official. Sir Cecil Spring Rice, then on the staff of the British embassy in Berlin, let drop an opinion on the necessity of acting swiftly and of annexing Hawaii before the Spanish-American war ended, at which time, if the archipelago were acquired, Germany would demand compensation. He addressed to John Hay, the United States ambassador to the Court of St. James, a letter with whose contents the former probably expected Theodore Roosevelt, a close friend of both, and his intimates to become acquainted. In it Sir Cecil dealt with Germany's attitude toward the war and pointed out that her official newspapers had stated that she would issue no declaration of neutrality "in order to keep her hands free as she did in the case of the Turco-Greek war and the Japanese war." He observed that in both cases she spent neither men nor money but reaped more advantage from the struggle than either combatant. Applying this policy to the present case, her demand would likely be Samoa or some position in the Pacific. However, "if the U.S. were to annex Hawaii *now*, Germany would not dare to object. It is most evident that she is anxious to be on the sunny side of the affections of the U.S. But if America put

22. Lodge to Roosevelt, June 24, 29, July 4, 6, 1898, in *Correspondence of Roosevelt and Lodge*, 1, 313–14, 317–18, 321.

the step off till the end of the war, Germany would immediately demand compensation—i.e. Samoa . . . So I think it worth while . . . to urge again that it is vitally important, if Hawaii is to be annexed without compensation, to annex it now." [23]

John Hay was extremely obliged for this kind letter, which "jumped so precisely" with his own ideas that he sent the substance off to Washington. The Ambassador could not "fathom the stupidity of those senators, who preserving the Cleveland tradition," still fought the annexation, but he concluded that against stupidity the gods fight in vain.[24] Before receiving a reply from his friend in London, Sir Cecil again warned: "Don't let the Americans forget what happened after the Turco-Russian war, after the Chino-Japanese war and after the Turco-Greek war. Those who profited were not those who fought." [25]

There was a genuine basis for his concern. The year before, the German ambassador in London had spoken more than once to F. H. Villiers, undersecretary of state for foreign affairs, regarding the prospective annexation of Hawaii and proposed joint action by England and Germany, for which the object was to be either to acquire from the United States a share in the dominion of Hawaii or, in case of the refusal of the former to entertain this proposal, to obtain her withdrawal from Samoa in consideration of the title to Hawaii. Her Majesty's government had no intentions of joining with Germany in such a proposition, stating formally that the reason for declining was the insuperable obstacle of the November 28, 1843, Anglo-French declaration to consider the Sandwich Islands as an independent state. Actually, officials in both the Foreign and Colonial offices doubted whether the withdrawal of the United States from the Samoan arrangement would improve matters in the Pacific so far as the British were concerned, for it would have left them "face to face with the Germans alone," and would, as one undersecretary feared, have led to their "being readily elbowed out." Under the existing arrangement they could "usually rely on American support in resisting German encroachment." [26]

23. Spring Rice to Hay, April 30, 1898, in Stephen Gwynn, ed., *The Letters and Friendships of Sir Cecil Spring Rice, A Record* (2 vols. Boston and New York, 1929), *1*, 246. Hay to Day (telegram), May 3, 1898, USDS, Dispatches, Great Britain, *192*.

24. Hay to Spring Rice, May 5, 1898, in Gwynn, *1*, 246.

25. Spring Rice to Hay, May 7, 1898, ibid., p. 248.

26. F. H. Villiers to F. Lascelles, undersecretary in the Colonial Office, Aug. 18, 1897, with minutes, CO 537/136. Cf. my "Great Britain and the Sovereignty of Hawaii," *Pacific Historical Review, 31* (1962), 345–48.

Similarly, British officials, while understanding that the protest of the Japanese government was no doubt prompted by the desire to protect the large number of Japanese subjects already in the Hawaiian group and to secure an outlet for their population in the islands, felt that they could not join Japan, as she proposed, in attempting to "maintain the *status quo* or to establish a joint protectorate, with a view to securing the right of immigration into Hawaii for the Japanese, more especially in the face of legislation with respect to alien immigration which has recently been passed in some of the Australasian Colonies." [27]

Senator Morrill spoke at length on June 20 to show why the annexation of the Hawaiian Islands in time of war was "more inopportune than in time of peace," and to point out that if the islands ever came under the United States flag and Constitution, the provisions of the latter relating to citizenship, aliens, suffrage, and homesteads "would be likely to get badly tangled." To the argument for the need of a coaling station in the Pacific, he maintained that we had "such a harbor as an irrevocable grant." John Mitchell also attacked the dogma of the strategists, observing in the event of war Hawaii "would have to be defended by fortifications and guarded by a fleet." [28]

Richard Pettigrew deplored manifest destiny, which was "simply the cry of the strong in justification of their plunder of the weak." He contended that the acquisition of territory "not contiguous to our own, and inhabited by an inferior race of people" was contrary to the American theory of government, customs, and precedents as a people.[29] Senator McEnery objected to annexation of Hawaii for several reasons, the most important being that there had never been a proposition coming from the great body of the people of Hawaii to be annexed to the United States. "It would be a spoliation"— "a piece of unblushing larceny"—on the part of our government to take possession of the islands.[30] Senator Caffery of Texas could not

27. J. Branston, for Joseph Chamberlain, to the Earl of Ranfurly, Governor General of New Zealand, Sept. 6, 1897, CO 537/136. National Archives of New Zealand, Governor General's Archives, G/2, No. 289/97. Richard J. Seddon Papers, Archives of N.Z., fol. 84. Cf. my "Australasian Interest in the Commerce and the Sovereignty of Hawaii," Australia and New Zealand *Historical Studies, 11* (1965), 500–13.

28. *Cong. Record,* 55 Cong., 2 sess., pp. 6141, 6145, 6229–31. Cf. New York *Times* and Washington *Post,* June 21, 1898, and successive dates through July 7, 1898.

29. *Cong. Record,* 55 Cong., 2 sess., pp. 6191, 6258, 6262, 6267.

30. Ibid., p. 6306.

see how we could defend our frontiers by extending them. "The more you increase your frontier the more force is required to protect it." He and Senator Clay were convinced that the Monroe Doctrine was "shelter enough for these little islands to hover under, protected by the enormous strength and resources of the United States." [31]

Senator Hoar, a critic and foe of McKinley and an avowed anti-imperialist who was emphatically opposed to the acquisition of the Philippines, considered unique the case of Hawaii—2,100 miles from our shores—a group with which we had "a sustained and peculiar relation." Yet he warned and pleaded:

> If this be the first step in the acquisition of dominion over barbarous archipelagoes in distant seas; if we are to enter into competition with the great powers of Europe in the plundering of China, in the division of Africa; if we are to quit our own to stand on foreign lands . . . or worse still, if we are to govern subjects and vassal States, trampling as we do it on our own great Charter which recognizes alike the liberty and dignity of individual manhood, then let us resist this thing in the beginning, and let us resist it to the death.[32]

Notwithstanding this plea, the joint resolution to annex Hawaii to the United States as a territory was carried in the Senate on July 6, 1898, according to Lodge, "very handsomely," with a vote of 42 yeas and 21 nays, 26 not voting.[33] Morrill was the only Republican who voted against the resolutions, although Thurston, of Nebraska, and John C. Spooner, of Wisconsin, were paired against it. Six Democrats voted in favor of annexation.[34] Obviously, if 22 of the 26 doubting, silent senators had cast their ballots in the negative, the course of Hawaii's history would have been quite different.

Some members of Congress voted for the joint resolution, hoping that Hawaii would be the last step in territorial expansion. But they were soon asked: "What good will Hawaii do us if we are not to

31. Ibid., pp. 6454, 6482, 6487.

32. Hoar, Autobiography, 2, 307. Cong. Record, 55 Cong., 2 sess., p. 6661. Cf. New York Times, July 6, 1898.

33. Lodge to Roosevelt, July 12(?), 1898, in Correspondence of Roosevelt and Lodge, 1, 323.

34. Cong. Record, 55 Cong., 2 sess., p. 6712. New York Times, July 7, 1898.

35. Carl Schurz, "Our Future Foreign Policy," address at Saratoga, N.Y., Aug. 19, 1898, in Bancroft, Papers of Carl Schurz, 5, 485. Cf. Cong. Record, 55 Cong., 2 sess., p. 5994.

go beyond?"[35] President McKinley spoke of the action as "a step in a policy,"[36] and approved the resolution on July 7.[37] News of the Senate action was received in Honolulu on July 13.

Hawaiians were not as enthusiastic over the union as were Lodge and Spring Rice. Many native inhabitants viewed with indignation the prospect of the Hawaiian flag being lowered on the old Iolani Palace. Queen Liliuokalani, apparently suffering from nervous prostration, returned home on August 2, welcomed with much state by her numerous adherents—white, as well as native. The Hawaiian nationalist societies, six days before the scheduled flag raising ceremony, presented to President Dole and to Minister Sewall a joint and final protest against the annexation of their country to the United States.[38]

Formal Transfer of Sovereignty

Transfer of the sovereignty of the Republic of Hawaii to the United States took place in an unostentatious but impressive and dignified ceremony on August 12, 1898. Minister Sewall, addressing President Dole, formally communicated to him the text of the joint resolution of Congress, annexing the Hawaiian Islands to the United States. Next, Dole tendered the sovereignty of the islands to the United States, through her representative, who accepted it in the name of his government. Then followed the ceremony of exchanging flags, which began by the Hawaiian band playing "Hawaii Ponoi," the national anthem. Colors were sounded, and a twenty-one-gun salute was fired by the shore battery and the U.S.S. *Philadelphia* and *Mohican,* after which the Hawaiian flag was slowly lowered from the staff above the executive building, formerly the royal palace. Following the hoisting of the United States ensign, during which the "Star-Spangled Banner" was played, and the repetition of the twenty-one-gun salute, Sewall delivered a short address and communicated the directions of President McKinley, continuing the government officials in office until Congress should provide a form of government for the islands. Sanford Ballard Dole was then sworn in by Chief Justice Albert Francis Judd, followed by the members of the cabinet, after which the battalion from the two battleships and the local troops marched to the drill grounds, where the military officers

36. Lodge to Roosevelt, July 23, 1898, p. 330.
37. *United States Statutes at Large,* 55 Cong., 30, No. 50, 750–51.
38. Kenny to Salisbury, Aug. 4, 6, 1898, Nos. 25, 26, FO 58/319.

were sworn in before the battalion returned to the ships, escorted to the landing by the local troops.[1]

The day was not one of great triumph and universal rejoicing. There was no jubilation, and except for the annexationists and those in the employ of the government, there was scant enthusiasm. The audience at the ceremony was composed mainly of Americans, Asians, and Portuguese laborers. Very few Hawaiians attended, and many of the leading families—white as well as native Hawaiian—absented themselves from the city during the day, going to other parts of Oahu, where they could not see the Hawaiian flag lowered and hear "Hawaii Ponoi," composed by King Kalakaua, played for the last time as the national anthem. The British minister noticed, at the time the Hawaiian ensign was being lowered, that some members of the Cabinet and of the legislature "showed signs of being sorrowfully affected."[2] All the Hawaiian members of the band excused themselves, and the Hawaiian members of the National Guard, who had to be present as a matter of discipline, covered their faces or stared at the ground with tears in their eyes.[3]

In Washington, as well as among the oligarchy in Honolulu, there were doubts as to the fitness of the native Hawaiian and Oriental population for the degree of self-government that statehood would confer. For two years, while Congress debated as to what disposition should be made of the islands, President Dole and his cabinet carried on the Hawaiian government as a republic within a republic, under the authority of the United States.

Eventually, an act of Congress made Hawaii a territory, effective as of midnight, June 13–14, 1900. On June 14, Flag Day, Sanford Ballard Dole, first and only president of the republic, was sworn in as the first governor of the "United States Territory of Hawaii." In spite of Senator John T. Morgan's assertion of February 26, 1894, that "Hawaii is an American state, and is embraced in the American commercial and military system,"[4] over fifty-nine years elapsed after Flag Day before the "Paradise of the Pacific" was admitted to statehood on August 21, 1959.

1. *House Docs.*, 55 Cong., 2 sess., No. 3, *Annual Report of the Navy Department for the Year 1898*, App. to the Report of the Chief of the Bureau of Navigation, pp. 145–47.
2. Kenny to Salisbury, Aug. 17, 1898, No. 31, FO 58/319.
3. Clifford Gessler, *Tropic Landfall: The Port of Honolulu* (New York, 1942), p. 221.
4. *Morgan Report*, p. 364.

SUMMARY AND CONCLUSION

No event in history has been more thoroughly documented than the Hawaiian Revolution of 1893, yet reports of the same incidents differed markedly, as they were colored by the opinions and prejudices of those who witnessed or participated in them. There could be little objectivity concerning the extirpation of the monarchy, as the residents and inhabitants of the islands were sharply divided into annexationists and royalists, and their description or explanation of occurrences was either intentionally or unintentionally presented from a myopic point of view. Descendants of the participants, especially the sons and grandsons of the Sandwich Islands missionaries, have perpetuated certain myths. Only now are meticulous historians, unrelated to the partisans—like Ralph S. Kuykendall and William Adam Russ, Jr.—presenting objective studies of the twilight and eclipse of the Hawaiian monarchy.

This particular survey might appropriately bear the subtitle "An Economic Interpretation of the Hawaiian Revolution," for it shows that the underlying cause of the *coup d'état* was the determination of the propertied class—to a large extent American and Hawaiian-born American—to direct or control governmental policy. The misjoinder of the producing with the expending power, a natural concomitant of the rise and expansion of the plantation sugar industry, and related commercial activities incident to reciprocity caused dissatisfaction, among the white residents of substance, with the constitutional arrangements.

Governmental impotence, political tyranny, and royal immorality were avowed and reiterated reasons for overthrowing the monarchy, but they were arguments employed to cloak ulterior and more basic causes. At times the annexationists themselves disclosed their true motives. W. C. Wilder, one of the commissioners dispatched to Washington in January 1893, informed San Francisco newspapermen that the revolution was "the desperate and determined effort of the foreign residents, with possibly half a dozen exceptions, to free themselves from tyranny and protect the capital they have honestly invested on the islands from being wrested out of their hands."[1] Yet only two months earlier, T. T. Williams, editor of the San Francisco *Examiner*, who conducted an extensive five weeks' investigation of the annexation agitation in Hawaii, found much of the talk about the need for a stronger government insincere. Although some capital may have been frightened out by the rumors of revolutions, no man could point to an instance where he had lost any property because of the inability of the government to protect his rights. Nor could anyone indicate to the editor in what way Queen Liliuokalani leaned toward the British, advanced their interests, and impaired those of the United States.[2] Minister Rollin M. Daggett, reporting to Secretary of State Frelinghuysen nearly a decade before the revolution, observed: "taxation is light; the laws are well administered; life and property are as secure here as in any part of the civilized world; and with the advantages of the reciprocity treaty the general business of the island is fairly prosperous." The two million loan of 1882, the entire amount of which was to be devoted to the encouragement of immigration, to agriculture, to the construction of railways, to public buildings, and to internal improvements generally, had something like a claim upon public approval. There could be little question, however, that this loan was authorized by a native legislature with the incentive and full knowledge that the burden of its payment would fall largely upon American and other foreign property owners in the kingdom.[3]

A number of resident American planters, merchants, and professional men who had accepted the hospitality of the friendly Pacific kingdom and had invested capital there, together with some Hawaiian-born Americans, became determined by the 1880s to con-

1. San Francisco *Morning Call*, Jan. 30, 1893.
2. San Francisco *Examiner*, Nov. 21, 1892.
3. Daggett to Frelinghuysen, Sept. 20, 1882, No. 11, USDS, Dispatches, Hawaii, 20, printed in *For. Rels.* (1882), pp. 347–48.

trol the government and thus guarantee peace, stability, the security of their investments, and the promotion of "legitimate" business, rather than see their tax money expended on "wild" financial welfare-state schemes for the salutary and economic benefit of the tragically desperate, decaying, and disappearing Polynesians. This intelligent, law-abiding, property-owning portion of the community took positive action in 1887, backed by the threat of force, and obtained from King Kalakaua the dismissal from office of Walter Murray Gibson, an unorthodox and unethical American leader with unbridled ambition and unbounded influence, and the so-called Bayonet Constitution, which was intended to secure for them the control of governmental policy while retaining the institution of monarchy. Their persistent agitation, desultory, delaying legislative tactics, clandestine intrigue, and potent propaganda, reinforced and supported by the complotting diplomatic and naval representatives of the United States in Honolulu, patiently prepared a confused climate favorable for revolutionary activity. Later the cogent arguments of able strategists and vociferous expansionists in the United States created official and unofficial interest in the "key to the Pacific," the coign of vantage for the Orient, which could be satisfied only by annexation. While the United States government up to 1892 consistently supported the authority of the royal house of Hawaii, our influence as a people "pulled directly the other way." [4]

Simultaneously with the growth of the annexationist movement in Hawaii, in which economic motives, revolving around sugar and large shipping and mercantile interests, were the strongest elements, there emerged an influential group in the United States advocating the acquisition of outlying possessions. Thomas F. Bayard, in a conversation with H. A. P. Carter, four years before the revolution and almost a decade prior to annexation, mentioned that there was "evidently in the United States a growing consciousness of the possession of large material resources—superabundant population, a great deal of money, and a disposition to extend themselves beyond their present boundaries." The Secretary referred to the interest in a Panama canal, the Nicaraguan treaty, and Senator Edmund's pet idea of acquiring political control of Central America, and thought all these things should be considered in respect to the conduct of affairs in the Sandwich Islands.[5] Thus the annexation of Hawaii

4. New York *Tribune*, Nov. 28, 1892.

5. Memo. written after Conversation with Carter, Jan. 5, 1889, Bayard Papers, Vol. 125.

fitted in with that "large policy" of a big navy, an isthmian canal, a two-ocean fleet, with appropriate bases for it, espoused by Americanists and others in the United States at the close of the nineteenth century. The strategic or defense argument for the annexation of Hawaii perhaps received more attention than any other, but prior to the Spanish-American war, it carried little weight with the American public. Perhaps if that war had not come when it did, Hawaii might not have been annexed for years.

The sophistical method of those who campaigned for annexation by arguing that unless the United States hastened to acquire the islands, Great Britain, Japan, or Germany would seize them, was a puerile practice, an indiscreet indirection, for an insuperable obstacle to British annexation was the November 28, 1845, Anglo-French declaration to consider the Sandwich Islands as an independent state. There was no danger of the sovereignty of Hawaii being transferred to some other power, for the Hawaiians had never manifested the least inclination to join their fortunes permanently with those of any other nation than their big neighbor. The United States government made no official propositions looking to annexation before 1854, but it was determined to resist strenuously any attempt on the part of Great Britain or France to obtain possession of the islands, and refused to enter with the governments of those countries into a tripartite agreement guaranteeing the independence of Hawaii. A laboriously negotiated annexation treaty of that year, considered by the Privy Council for nearly three months, was never signed and ratified by the King, Crown Prince, and chiefs. Even if it had been, its statehood provision would have made it unacceptable to the President of the United States. Thereafter, numerous unofficial suggestions for annexation emanated from various sources, but never from the Hawaiian sovereigns.

The moral interpretation of the Hawaiian revolution appears untenable, and "the moral argument more emotional than practical." [6] According to testimony collected by James H. Blount from relatively unbiased sources, the attacks upon the Queen's character and faith were unjustifiable, and at the time of the *émeute* the Hawaiian monarch was still the philanthropic, gracious, Christian lady described by the Reverend Sereno E. Bishop a year and a half earlier. Of the eye witnesses examined by the commissioner, only one credited the charges against Liliuokalani's personal morals. His

6. Bailey, "U.S. and Hawaii," *American Historical Review*, 36 (1931), 560.

evidence was purely circumstantial and hearsay, and his own character was not such as to give weight to his opinion. Others who had known her well and had associated with her intimately, women who had had entree to her apartments, maintained that not an impure word nor the suspicion of a concealed action had ever met their notice, that Liliuokalani was the most upright Christian woman in the city.[7] Nothing in the public or private life of the Queen known to Davies, Joseph Carter, and other respectable men of substance in the community could justify the charges of immorality.[8]

Chances are that the opium and lottery bills signed by Liliuokalani as one of the final acts of her reign won over to the side of the annexationists the vacillating missionaries, and perhaps helped to increase the discontent in the islands. But the latter legislation was supported by retail merchants, grocers, clothiers, professional men—in fact, many of the middle class, including some of the most "righteous" elements in the community, to say nothing of the native Hawaiians—for when the lower classes of Hawaiians and part-Hawaiians prospered, business was good for the entire community. The advantages to be reaped from chartering a lottery would immediately become apparent, because the income spent on much needed public works would bring some little prosperity to the poorer people to compensate for that enjoyed by foreigners under the reciprocity treaty. Great Britain had earlier adopted license of lotteries instead of prohibition, and the Hawaiian statute was drawn from one in use in British colonies.[9] The opium and lottery measures, which could have been repealed in a constitutional manner, did not require a revolution; neither did the unsuccessful attempt to promulgate a new constitution, later retracted, justify the overthrow of the monarchy. This coup had been determined upon months in advance of the overt act, and a situation had been covertly and carefully created so as to entice the Queen to commit the deed which could be used to justify in Washington a revolution in Honolulu.

An almost bloodless *coup d'état* was engineered and executed by the firm and determined action of an efficient, forward-looking, un-

7. Julius A. Palmer, *Memories of Hawaii and Hawaiian Correspondence* (Boston, 1894), pp. 110–12.

8. See Blount's Interview with J. O. Carter, May 13, 1893, *For. Rels.* (1894), App. II, pp. 735–36. Cf. Sir Edwin Arnold's article "East and West —The Happy Isles," London *Daily Telegraph*, Feb. 4, 1893. Sermon of Rev. E. G. Beckwith on the accession of the Queen, *Pacific Commercial Advertiser*, Feb. 17, 1893.

9. Liliuokalani, *Hawaii's Story*, pp. 239–40.

compromising nucleus of clever and audacious leaders within the Reform party who, by the spring of 1892, and certainly by August 23,[10] were convinced that union with the United States was the best means to secure a stable government and ensure protection to the thirty to forty million dollars worth of "American" property in Hawaii. Directly implicated in the design was Minister John L. Stevens, whose official and private correspondence and conduct for months preceding and during the revolution, as well as the facts assembled in the evidence presented to Commissioner James H. Blount, established beyond question his connivance with the junto in achieving his paramount objective. Captain Wiltse was an efficient helpmate.

Commissioner Blount concluded that United States troops "were doubtless so located to suggest to the Queen and her counselors that they were in cooperation with the insurrectionary movement, and would when the emergency arose manifest it by active support." [11] That the success of the *émeute* depended upon the presence near the seat of the government of American marines was contended by one side and denied by the other. The royalists and the Cleveland administration asserted that the insurgents had not relied upon their own strength to carry the revolution into effect, and cited as proof the request of the committee of safety to the United States minister to lend assistance. Even Lorrin A. Thurston, Peter C. Jones, and William D. Alexander recognized and admitted that the presence of troops on shore had a "moral effect" on native Hawaiians and "was a strong feature in preventing the irresponsible and lawless elements of all nationalities from outbreak, but it was not asked, nor used for the purpose of dethroning the queen nor establishing the provisional government." [12] The revolutionists maintained that Minister Stevens, although sympathetic to their cause, informed the committee of safety that he would not assist them against the monarchy, and he gave specific assurance that troops would be landed for the exclusive purpose of protecting American lives and property. Nevertheless, the committee members knew that the royalists believed that American marines would be used to overthrow the monarchy, but it was not the duty of the former to apprise their op-

10. Declaration and pledge signed Aug. 23, 1892, Thurston Papers.

11. Blount to Gresham, July 17, 1893, USDS, Dispatches, Hawaii, 25, printed in *For. Rels.* (1894), App. II. p. 585.

12. Committee of Safety, 1893, Jan. 16, 1893, Thurston Papers. Alexander and Jones Statements, *Morgan Report*, pp. 202, 308.

ponents that their impression was erroneous. Royalists harbored an exaggerated idea of Thurston's influence, particularly his control over United States forces. This misapprehension probably contributed to their subsequent supine submission to the committee of safety.

The annexationists insisted that they had to depend entirely on their own strength for the success of the movement to abrogate the monarchy. Knowing precisely what they wanted, they proceeded with intelligent deliberation, thoroughness, and confidence to adopt a bold course—one that had been successful on several previous occasions. The royalists, on the other hand, lacking the assistance—moral or actual—of any outside force, had neither the character nor the ability to resist; they had the disintegrating consciousness that the tenuous and questionable course which their Queen was seeking to pursue had been defeated several times, "and they were disposed to quail before the determined, progressive attitude of the revolutionists." In the words of Chief Justice A. F. Judd, "men are not eager to risk their lives in a bad cause." [13] The Queen's government was demoralized before it was properly organized; her ministers were inexperienced as a cabinet, having been in office only four days, all of which were tumultuous; they and her other advisers were divided in purpose and fearful of precipitating bloodshed. Under the great difference in leadership and support on both sides, the natural consequence of the clash of the two opposing forces was success for the revolutionists and submission by the royalists.

In the midst of the 1898 Senate debate on acquiring Hawaii, Grover Cleveland, delivering the annual Founders' Day address of the commencement exercises of the Lawrenceville School in New Jersey, expostulated on the "Dangers of Today" in the territorial expansion idea, and again maintained that this alluring temptation would be "a dangerous perversion of our national mission." [14] Two days after the joint resolution passed the Senate, the ex-President wrote Richard Olney, lamenting, "Hawaii is ours. As I look back upon the first step in this miserable business and as I contemplate the means used to complete the outrage, I am ashamed of the whole affair." [15]

Ashamed Cleveland might be, but his sensibilities could not stem the force of vibrant economic and nationalist impulses that

13. Judd Statement, ibid., p. 444.
14. New York *Times*, June 22, 1898. Cleveland Papers, 2d ser., Vol. 352.
15. Cleveland to Olney, July 8, 1898, ibid. Olney Papers, Vol. 83.

were pressing for overseas expansion. His Hawaiian policy, commendable as it was, sharply conflicted with the expansionist tendencies of Secretaries Blaine, Foster, and Day, of the strategists and
Americanists, and of President McKinley, who was very firm about
the matter and intended to annex the islands. After the outbreak of
the Spanish-American War and Dewey's victory at Manila, the
whole policy of annexation grew "rapidly under the irresistible
pressure of events." [16] The contention that Hawaii was indispensable
for the prosecution of the war was fallacious; but "the defense argument so far as the Pacific Coast was concerned, was relatively sound."
This argument had been employed since the 1850s, "and although
the war added nothing to its validity, it added much to its comprehensiveness and force." [17] The Hawaiian controversy was more
than a partisan issue; it actually initiated the great debate in American history over the merits of imperialism.

Furthermore, although not clearly recognized at the time, the
annexation of Hawaii without a single protest from Great Britain—
despite considerable twisting of the lion's tail, proposals to Her
Majesty's government from both Japan and Germany for concerted
action, and persistent remonstrances from Richard J. Seddon, premier of New Zealand—illustrated the growing identity of interests
between her and the United States, and served as the first symbol of
Anglo-American understanding or rapprochement, which was to
become a significant factor in international relations at the close of
the nineteenth century.[18] In fact, annexation was promoted by the
growing Anglo-American cordiality. The rapprochement and the
mutual distrust of the great powers prevented any organized action
to check the United States in her designs on Hawaii. In general
and on the surface, however, there was no diplomatic opposition to

16. Lodge to Roosevelt, June 15, 1898, in *Correspondence of Roosevelt and
Lodge*, 1, 311.

17. Bailey, "U.S. and Hawaii," *American Historical Review*, 36, 560.

18. See Villiers to Lascelles, Aug. 18, 31, 1897, with minutes, and J.
Branston (for Joseph Chamberlain) to Earl of Ranfurly, Sept. 6, 1897, CO
537/136. Seddon to Chamberlain, June 23, July 12, 30, 1897, ibid., also in
National Archives of New Zealand, Governor General's Archives, G/2, No.
287/97, and in Seddon Papers, fol. 84. Cf. the editorial "England and Amer-
ica in Polynesia," London *Speaker*, Feb. 4, 1893; editorials, ibid., March 18,
April 1, 1897; Beale, *Theodore Roosevelt*, p. 148; my "Great Britain and the
Sovereignty of Hawaii," *Pacific Historical Review*, 31 (1962), 344–48; my
"Australasian Interest in the Commerce and the Sovereignty of Hawaii,"
Australia and New Zealand *Historical Studies*, 11 (1965), 500–13.

the proposed union. Only two days after the treaty had been transmitted to the Senate, John Hay reported from London that he had
heard of no objection to annexation from any quarter. "All diplo-
matists here as at Washington four years ago—seem to regard it as
a matter lying 'wholly within the sphere of our influence.' " [19]

Recognition on the part of some Englishmen of an identity of
interest with the United States is found in the correspondence of Sir
Cecil Spring Rice. After the joint resolution had passed the Senate,
he wrote from Berlin as follows to Henry Cabot Lodge: "I can't
tell you what pleasure I see that Hawaii is at length to be annexed."
Sir Cecil believed that there was an intention to depose English
civilization—American as well as British—from the Pacific, and reflected: "we have the right and duty to defend what we most certainly have fairly won on the American, Australasian and Chinese
coasts. I don't believe that England, the island, is strong enough,
or will remain comparatively strong enough to defend English
civilization alone . . . And I welcome any step which America
takes outside her continent because it tends to the increase of the
common good." [20] Lodge, for his part, was delighted with this letter,
as similar thoughts and feeling had been in his mind for a long
time. He believed the annexation of Hawaii "to be a good thing not
only for the United States but for the world." He felt as Spring
Rice did "about the fate of the civilization of the English-speaking
people." One of the general results of the war had been their coming together, and he was enough of an optimist to believe that it was
going to last.[21]

    19. Hay to McKinley, June 18, 1897, McKinley Papers, Vol. 7.
    20. Spring Rice to Lodge, June 8, 1898, in Gwynn, ed. *Letters and Friend-*
ships, 1, 249.
    21. Lodge to Spring Rice, Aug. 12, 1898, ibid., p. 250. Cf. Alfred T.
Mahan and Charles Beresford, "Possibilities of an Anglo-American Reunion,"
North American Review, 159 (1894), 551–73. See my "Hawaii: A Symbol of
Anglo-American Rapprochement," *Political Science Quarterly*, 79 (1964), 555–
75.

APPENDIX I: BIOGRAPHICAL NOTES

ALEXANDER, William DeWitt, son of the Rev. William P. Alexander, was one of the most brilliant Hawaiian-born Americans. A historian and government official, he, as surveyor general, became acquainted with the details of Hawaiian land tenure, and as privy councillor and a member of the Board of Education, was able to familiarize himself with government policy under King Kalakaua and Queen Liliuokalani. He was an avid advocate of annexation.

ALEXANDER, William P., member of the Sandwich Islands Mission, taught at the Mission Seminary at Lahainaluna, and helped survey and arrange the sale of land under the *Mahele*—the division of lands between king and chiefs.

ALLEN, Elisha Hunt, born in Massachusetts, was a practicing lawyer until, as a delegate to the Whig convention of 1848, he nominated Zachary Taylor, and as a reward received the consulate in Honolulu. When that assignment was terminated, Kamehameha III appointed Allen as minister of finance, which post he retained until 1858. He was commissioned as an envoy extraordinary to the United States in 1856 to secure the ratification of the Lee-Marcy convention, which mission was the first of his several efforts extending over two decades on behalf of reciprocity. His journey with Henry A. P. Carter to Washington in 1874–75 resulted in the negotiation of a reciprocity treaty that was finally ratified by the Senate and went into effect in 1876. As Hawaii's minister resident in the national capital, he worked diligently for the renewal of the treaty until his death at a White House reception on New Year's Day, 1883.

ALLEN, William F., son of Elisha H. Allen, was graduated from Williams College, and in 1893 had resided thirty-two years in the islands, and over twenty of these had served as collector general of the customs for Honolulu and enjoyed an extensive trustee and investment business.

ARMSTRONG, Richard, an American of Scotch-Irish extraction, served as a surveyor and teacher in Pennsylvania before going to

Hawaii in 1832. He spent ten months—from July 2, 1833, to May 12, 1834—on Washington Island in the Marquesas as a missionary from the Sandwich Islands Mission. He served the mission for seventeen years in a variety of ways, before officially entering into the duties of minister of public instruction for the kingdom.

ARMSTRONG, Samuel C., son of Richard Armstrong, served as director of the Freedmen's Bureau and later as principal of Hampton Institute. He was widely known in Presbyterian and Congregational circles, and had close connections with the American Board of Commissioners for Foreign Missions.

ARMSTRONG, William N., son of Richard Armstrong, served as attorney general, as well as minister of interior *ad interim* and commissioner of immigration during the reign of King Kalakaua, and accompanied that sovereign on a tour abroad to secure a supply of labor. Later he practiced law in New York City, and assisted the agent of the Annexation Club in 1892 and the Hawaiian commissioners in 1893 in their efforts to achieve annexation.

ASHFORD, Clarence W., a Canadian, who practiced law in Honolulu for six years before he was named attorney general in the Reform ministry of 1887.

AUSTIN, Jonathan, a native of New York, an attorney who had followed his profession in Hawaii for about ten years before his appointment as minister of foreign affairs in the Reform cabinet, on December 28, 1887, succeeding Godfrey Brown.

BELKNAP, Rear Admiral George E., an unyielding annexationist, was well acquainted with the Hawaiian Islands area. In 1873 he was ordered to the U.S.S. *Tuscarora* to make deep-sea soundings in the North Pacific with a view to a submarine cable and was the senior officer in Honolulu at the time of the disturbances incident to the election of King Kalakaua. Belknap's discoveries concerning the topography of the ocean, recorded in his *Concerning Deep Sea Soundings*, read before the Asiatic Society of Japan, May 13, 1874 (Transactions, 2, 1873–74) were recognized and accepted by the leading scientists in Europe and the Americas.

BISHOP, Charles Reed, of New York, set off with William Little Lee on a journey to the Oregon territory in February 1846. At their stopover in Honolulu the young men were prevailed upon to remain at the islands. In due time Bishop was named collector of customs and introduced many useful and efficient reforms in the customs service. He married the "rarely beautiful" and accomplished high chiefess, the Princess Bernice Pauahi Paki, a descendant of the Kamehameha line, who broke her engagement—made in her infancy by her parents—to Prince Lot Kamehameha to marry the American. Meanwhile, Bishop became associated with William Arnold Aldrich in the small firm of Aldrich and Bishop, which conducted a mercantile business. The men soon came to the conclusion that a bank would be superior to their firm in serving the needs of Honolulu and returning a profit to themselves. Accordingly, the two formed a partnership for the purpose of transacting a general banking business. Bishop and Co., which opened on August 17, 1858, was a success from its first day and continues to operate. Bishop was interested in and assisted, through the advancement of loans, the development of the islands' sugar industry, and favored closer economic and political ties with the United States. He was named a member of the House of Nobles in 1860 for "so long as he shall live." Thus his personal interests were cemented with those larger ones of the growing kingdom, and he enjoyed the admiration, respect, and esteem of many before his appointment as minister of foreign affairs during the brief reign of King Lunalilo. Bishop served the Hawaiian government on the Privy Council and as president of the Board of Education during the reign of King Kalakaua. The banker happened to be on a business trip to California in January–February 1893, and assisted the Hawaiian commissioners in their mission to have the islands annexed to the United States. His are the only American remains resting in the Royal Cemetery in Honolulu.

BISHOP, Rev. Sereno E., son of the Rev. Artemas, of the second band of American missionaries to the Sandwich Islands, was an avid and rabid annexationist, whose pen proved mightier than a sword for the cause.

BOND, Edward P., was one of the most esteemed of Hawaii's former residents. Having gone to the islands for his health in 1851, he was soon appointed circuit judge of Kauai and, subsequently, from 1856–61, served as district attorney of Maui, after which he returned to West Newton, Mass., to become the founder of the Union Safe Deposit Co. of Boston, in which he served until his death in 1893. He worked through the Boston Board of Trade and the Hawaiian Club of Boston for reciprocity, and lobbied in Washington for the 1867 reciprocity treaty.

BOND, Lawrence, son of Edward P. Bond, was Hawaiian consul

at Boston in 1893. Having been commissioned by the government of Queen Liliuokalani, who was still a claimant to power after the revolution, he remained a neutral party, doing nothing for or against the provisional government, and thereby lost his commission.

BROWN, Admiral George, was commander of the Pacific squadron and of the flagship U.S.S. *Charleston,* which transported King Kalakaua to San Francisco in December 1890 and returned the royal remains to Honolulu in January 1891. Brown favored annexation.

BROWN, Godfrey, was born in England, brought to New York at the age of three, educated there, and remained in the United States until 1876. He then went to Hawaii, where he acquired considerable property. Brown served as minister of finance in the Reform ministry and in the same position in the compromise ministry of 1890.

BUSH (sometimes spelled Buch), John Edward, a part-Hawaiian, served as tax collector of the district of Honolulu, governor of Kauai, foreman of the government press, and second clerk of the Interior Department. As the editor of *Ka Leo,* a nationalist newspaper, he repeatedly emphasized the necessity of Kalakaua's obtaining the primacy of Polynesia, and reportedly infected the King with that idea. Bush held the post of minister of finance in the transitory Moreno cabinet, and after the resignation of the Italian adventurer, filled the premiership ad interim. J. E. Bush again served as minister of finance under W. M. Gibson before the Premier appointed him to head a diplomatic mission to Samoa.

CARLISLE, John Griffith, after a period as lieutenant governor of Kentucky, served that state as congressman and was an outstanding tariff reformer. As a member of the House Ways and Means Committee, he played an active part in formulating the various Democratic bills.

CARTER, Charles L., was born in Hawaii of second generation Americans. At only twenty-eight, in 1893, he was the youngest member of the Hawaiian commission.

CARTER, Henry Alpheus Peirce, was born in Hawaii in 1837 of American parents. His formal education was limited. An employee of C. Brewer and Co., specializing in ships' provisions, his business sagacity was soon recognized and he was taken into partnership at the age of twenty-five. Until his death he retained large and lucrative interests in this firm, as well as outside properties. He was among the first to realize that Hawaii's future prosperity lay not in whaling but in sugar production, and thus began to take the Brewer capital out of whaling in order to reinvest it in the rising sugar industry, furnishing the plantations with supplies and the service of marketing their product. His career coincides and is interwoven with Hawaii's transition from chiefly a refreshment station to a favored area of sugar cultivation. Henry Carter's marriage, on February 27, 1862, to Sybil Augusta, daughter of Dr. Gerrit P. Judd, led to a keen and sustained interest in government affairs and tied him to the "missionary party." On a visit to the mainland that same year, he served as a bearer of letters from the minister of foreign affairs to the State Department. He toured the United States and Europe in 1866 and again in 1871 in the interest of a reciprocity treaty, which he actively and publicly supported, but privately he foresaw annexation as the final outcome. He was named commissioner to the United States in October 1874 to negotiate a treaty of reciprocity in conjunction with Judge Elisha H. Allen, who had been sent there on three previous occasions. Tireless labor on the part of both men finally resulted in the treaty of 1875. Most of the remaining years of Carter's life were spent in the service of the Hawaiian kingdom in foreign lands. He served as King Kalakaua's special envoy to Great Britain, France, Germany, Belgium, and Denmark to mollify their governments, who maintained that the "most favored nation" clauses in their treaties with Hawaii were violated by the special privileges granted the United States in the treaty. Returning to Honolulu in 1879 to resume his business activities, he was the following year invited to fill the position of minister of the interior in the William L. Green cabinet, which office he held for almost two years. He traveled to Lisbon in 1882 to negotiate a treaty with Portugal to facilitate the immigration of Portuguese peasants to the islands in order to relieve the acute labor shortage which had developed with the rapid expansion of sugar plantations and the decline of the Hawaiian population. He succeeded Elisha Allen in 1883 as minister plenipotentiary and envoy extraordinary to the United States, where throughout the mid-1880s Carter had to meet and repel the many attacks upon the reciprocity treaty and to fight for its extension, which was secured in 1887, but with the Pearl Harbor amendment. After the passage of the McKinley tariff bill—specifically, throughout 1890–91—he labored to negotiate with Secretary of State James G. Blaine a commercial treaty of complete reciprocity. H. A. P. Carter was one of the most capable and popular representatives that the Hawaiian kingdom had ever sent to Washington, and he remained there as minister resident until his untimely death on November 1, 1891, at the age of fifty-four.

CARTER, Joseph O., an elder brother of H. A. P. Carter, was a successful Honolulu businessman and a supporter of the Queen at the time of and after the revolution of 1893. He opposed the contract labor system.

CASTLE, Samuel N., a citizen of New York, went to Honolulu in 1837, in the seventh reinforcement of missionaries, as assistant secular superintendent of the Sandwich Islands Mission, and in that capacity was one of the founders of Oahu College and its treasurer from its inception in 1840 until 1881. He was appointed to the Privy Council on the death of Kamehameha III, membership in which he retained under two succeeding sovereigns. He was elected to the legislature in 1864, after which he actively and publicly advocated reciprocity with the cession of Pearl Harbor to the United States as a *quid pro quo*, or if this did not procure the desired commercial convention, then annexation. A similar course was subsequently followed when he became a member of the House of Nobles. Castle was a founder and senior member of Castle and Cooke, Ltd., importers and retailers of merchandise, who later acted "as agents, factors or trustees for estates, plantations, factories, persons and companies." He was one of the incorporators of the Kohala Sugar Co. and of the Kaiku Sugar Co., and a charter and influential member of the Royal Hawaiian Agricultural Society, serving as its first treasurer and on its board of managers. He was also one of the incorporators, and for a time president, of the Honolulu Chamber of Commerce, a dominating figure in the Hawaiian Immigration Society, organized under the auspices of the chamber of commerce, and a charter member of the Planters' Labor and Supply Company, whose organ was the *Planters' Monthly*.

CASTLE, William R., the son of Samuel N. Castle, was born at the islands. A capable lawyer trained in the United States, he was called home to serve as attorney general in King Kalakaua's reign, sat in five sessions of the legislature, worked hand in hand with attorney Lorrin A. Thurston to anathematize the Hawaiian monarchy in January 1893, and was appointed one of the five commissioners sent to Washington to negotiate a treaty of annexation.

CLEGHORN, Archibald Scott, husband of Princess Likelike, Liliuokalani's only sister, and father of Princess Victoria Kaiulani, was an Englishman who came to Hawaii after considerable residence in

New Zealand. He served as collector of customs, an important and influential office, until he replaced the deceased John O. Dominis as governor of Oahu.

COOKE, Amos Starr, pioneer missionary teacher who, along with Mrs. Cooke, became keeper of the Royal School. With Samuel N. Castle, he founded the Honolulu firm of Castle and Cooke, Ltd.

COOKE, Charles, of Hawaiian birth and American parentage, was the son of Amos Starr Cooke. When appointed to the advisory council of the provisional government in January 1893, he was managing partner in the firm of Lewers and Cooke, the leading importers and dealers in lumber and building material, and owned ships and sugar plantations to the amount of $700,000. He was a member of the board of directors of several large corporations, a trustee of the Bishop estate, and was known in the islands and in California as a most conservative and careful man.

COOPER, Henry E., was an American lawyer who, in 1893, had resided in Honolulu for only four years, during which time he organized and became president and manager of the Hawaiian Title Abstract Co. Cooper suggested to Thurston the idea of an annexation club. He was a member of the Advisory Council of the provisional government and minister of foreign affairs in the Republic of Hawaii.

CUMMINS, John A., a successful half-Hawaiian sugar planter, minister of foreign affairs in the compromise ministry of 1890.

DAMON, Samuel M., son of the Rev. Samuel C. Damon, who served for forty years as chaplain of the Honolulu Seamen's Bethel (Chapel) and also edited the *Temperance Advocate and Seamen's Friend*, later called the *Friend*, claiming to be "the oldest newspaper west of the Rockies." Starting as a clerk to Charles R. Bishop, Damon became the managing partner of the banking house of Bishop and Co., a concern approximating two million dollars in capital; one of the managing trustees of the Bernice Pauahi Bishop estate, valued at one million dollars; a director of several corporations; and an owner of large cattle ranches. He was a great and trusted friend of native Hawaiians, who sought him whenever they got into trouble. Damon acted as minister of finance for a period under Kalakaua and in the same post for an even shorter time under Liliuokalani.

DILLINGHAM, Benjamin F., an American interested in railway and colonization undertakings on the island of Oahu, in the neighborhood of Ewa. He constructed the Oahu Railroad around the island, acquired title to a considerable part of the west side of Honolulu Harbor, and interested himself in dredging slips and constructing wharfs in the harbor. He became one of the wealthiest residents of Hawaii.

DOLE, Sanford Ballard, son of the Rev. and Mrs. Daniel Dole who directed Punahou school, was educated there and at Williams College, after which he studied law under William Brigham in Boston and was admitted to the Massachusetts bar in 1869. Shortly thereafter, he returned to Honolulu where he became a leading attorney. Initially, he was a member of the executive council of the Hawaiian League, but resigned because he did not approve some of the proposed radical action, particularly that of V. V. Ashford, who seemed anxious to inaugurate a reign of terror to overthrow the monarchy. Dole was a writer, a member of the Honolulu Social Science Club and of the Hawaiian Historical Society, a trustee of the Honolulu Public Library, one of the founders of the YMCA, and a member of the Congregational Church.

DOMINIS, John O., an Italian-American, husband of Liliuokalani and, therefore, brother-in-law of Prince, and later King, David Kalakaua. Dominis exercised a stabilizing and democratic influence over the Princess Liliuokalani during the first half year of her reign as Queen, until his death on August 27, 1891. He served as governor of Oahu.

GIBSON, Walter Murray, a son of English emigrants, lived for a while in the backwoods of South Carolina among the Indians, taught in a small school, married, and at the age of twenty-one was widowed with three children. Leaving them in the care of a relative, Gibson began a roving career. After several adventures abroad, he proceeded to study Mormonism, was baptized into the faith on January 15, 1860, and was then assigned to go on a mission to the eastern United States. Subsequently commissioned as a roving missionary to the Pacific, he arrived in Honolulu on July 4, 1861. There he permitted himself to be publicized as a traveler for "scientific purposes connected with the ethnology of the Malaysian and Polynesian races," and his several lectures in the capital were well received.

Without disclosing his connection with the Church of the Latter Day Saints, Gibson quietly investigated the Mormon situation in the archipelago. To the native Hawaiian Saints he introduced himself as "Chief President of the Islands of the Sea and of the Hawaiian Islands, for the Church of the Latter Day Saints," and soon took over the direction of the mission affairs. Under his prompting, substantial amounts of money were collected for the support of the church, which the "Chief President" augmented by selling church offices at a scale of prices ranging from $150 down to 50 cents. With the funds thus collected, be bought the lands of Palawai on Lanai, rehabilitated the settlement, stocked the holdings with livestock and poultry, planted crops of various kinds, and made it his headquarters and residence. At a later time, he wrote that his "temporary connection" with the Mormon community was "for a political object," but failed to indicate what the object was.

After a year or so, some of the Hawaiian Mormons doubted Gibson's true connection and requested President Brigham Young to send an investigatory commission. The deputation, after inquiry, excommunicated him on April 7, 1864. The investigation revealed that he held in his own name the deeds to the lands of Palawai and the contribution of the Saints, which he had supposedly secured for the church. Lanai had become a stronghold of Gibsonism rather than of Mormonism. Following the recommendation of the Utah deputation, most of the Saints who had come to Lanai left that island, but a few remained with their leader. Gibson declined to give up the title to the land and Palawai, which remained his private estate and was developed primarily as a sheep ranch. The Mormon mission, however, was reorganized under the direction of American elders sent from Utah, and a new settlement was made at Laie, on Oahu, on land bought for the purpose in January 1867.

The occasion which brought Walter Murray Gibson again into public attention was his advocacy, in 1868, of Malaysia as a region from which immigrants might be secured as agricultural laborers for the Hawaiian Islands. His rise to power through the editorship of *Nuhou Hawaii*, which campaigned against the cession of Pearl Harbor, the *Wednesday Press* or *Elele Poakolu*, and the *Pacific Commercial Advertiser*, which flattered the King and royal family and advocated "Hawaii for Hawaiians," can be attributed to his unbridled ambition, boundless energy, brilliant abilities, genial personality, unique resourcefulness, uncanny shrewdness, and perpetual optimism; but his "unstable romantic imagination," which made him too impractical to be a successful statesman, contributed to his downfall. This human dynamo was objurgated by foreigners of substance, who united in a common cause to overthrow his regime on June 30, 1887. He died of tuberculosis in San Francisco on January

21, 1888, less than seven months after he was forced to leave the kingdom.

GILMAN, Gorham D., who amassed a fortune in ocean business between San Francisco and Honolulu, established the firm of Gilman and Co. in Lahaina, for sometime resided at the islands, and was twice decorated by King Kalakaua, before returning home to Boston to become a wholesale druggist. An ardent annexationist, Gilman was appointed Hawaiian consul at Boston on September 13, 1893, displacing Lawrence Bond.

GODKIN, Edwin L., editor of the *New York Evening Post* at the time of the Hawaiian Revolution and the annexation period, went to the *Post* when he became editor of the *Nation*, and carried with him a high reputation as an independent commentator on political and social affairs. One of the leading features of his editorship in the period under consideration was his strong support of Cleveland, which he always had, except in connection with the Venezuelan incident.

GREEN, William Lowthan, born in London, went to seek his fortune in China, but having no money, he shipped before the mast on a vessel bound to the Orient. When this ship called at Honolulu in 1856, young William, well supplied with letters of introduction to prominent residents in the capital, was given employment with Starkey, Janion and Co., a leading business house, in which he became a partner and an active manager, and which thus became known as Janion, Green and Co., the predecessor of Theo. H. Davies and Co. Green was not a politician, not an office seeker, but a merchant, geologist, and entrepreneur, who assisted in the development of several industries in the kingdom. Hawaiians are indebted to him, in a measure, for interisland steam navigation, and especially for the establishment of the Honolulu Iron Works, an indispensable enterprise without which all the leading industries would have suffered. He held the premiership twice under King Kalakaua, edited the *Pacific Commercial Advertiser*, served briefly as acting British commissioner and consul general, and as president of the Honolulu Chamber of Commerce for fifteen years. Outside of the Hawaiian Islands, William L. Green is best known as a geologist, having made a special study of volcanic phenomena and written *Vestiges of the Molten Globe* (London, 1875–78), which publication established his name in scientific circles round the world.

GRESHAM, Walter Quintin, a soldier, jurist, and statesman, was appointed brigadier general and placed in command of the Natchez district during the Civil War. On September 25, 1884, on the death of Charles J. Folger, he accepted a stop-gap appointment as secretary of the Treasury until October 28, when he was appointed circuit judge of the 7th judicial district. His fearlessness in decisions was well illustrated in the celebrated Wabash case, when he ordered the removal of one of Jay Gould's friends from the receivership of the railroad. His name was considered at the Republican national convention of 1884 in Chicago, but no votes were cast for him. Four years later at that party's convention, he received 107 votes on the first ballot, John Sherman leading with 229. Benjamin Harrison, fourth on the first, was finally nominated on the eighth ballot.

Gresham's hostility to a protective tariff became pronounced; after the passage of the McKinley bill in 1890, he and others announced their opposition. He was unofficially tendered the presidential nomination by the Populist party in 1892, but declined, went over to the Democrats entirely and voted for Cleveland, who offered him the post of secretary of state. At first Gresham demurred, but he was finally prevailed upon to accept and entered the State Department on March 7, 1893. He died in office on May 28, 1895.

GULICK, Charles T., one of the seven sons of the Rev. P. J. Gulick, missionary to the Sandwich Islands, served as finance minister under W. M. Gibson and in the same capacity in the short-lived Macfarlane ministry under Queen Liliuokalani.

HALL, Edwin O., a printer who served in a secular capacity as overseer of the mission printing establishment from 1835 to 1850, was appointed director of the Hawaiian government press and editor of the *Polynesian*, a weekly organ of that government. During the absence of Dr. G. P. Judd from the kingdom in 1849–50, Hall administered the Department of Finance. In the latter year he was released from the mission. Five years later he was replaced as government printer by Charles Gordon Hopkins, an Englishman, after which the American engaged in mercantile business and established the hardware firm of E. O. Hall and Son, which operated into the twentieth century. King Lunalilo recalled Hall to the government by appointing him minister of finance as well as president of the Board of Education, which appointments terminated with the brief reign of the King.

HALL, W. W., son of Edwin O., served in the revolution by administering the commissary of the provisional government.

HARRIS, Charles Coffin, was a native of New Hampshire who resided and practiced law in the islands for several years before entering government service. During the annexation crisis of 1853, Harris, then police justice, took a public stand against the agitators, intimating that an idea of treason or revolution was involved in the proceedings. Kamehameha IV appointed the lawyer to the office of attorney general, but without portfolio. Kamehameha V reappointed him to the same position, with membership in the cabinet. He was named minister of finance in 1865.

HARTWELL, Alfred S., of Massachusetts, rose from the rank of a petty officer to that of brigadier general in the Civil War and sat in the Massachusetts legislature before taking up residence in the Hawaiian Islands in 1870. He served as a justice on the Supreme Court, before his appointment as attorney general in 1876, and later returned to the bench.

JONES, Peter Cushman, son of a Boston merchant of the same name, was born in 1837 of old Puritan and Revolutionary stock. The lure of business drew him to Honolulu, where he landed, on October 2, 1857, with 16 cents in his pocket. He worked in several companies, but in 1866 formed a partnership with C. L. Richards in the ship chandlers business, in which he remained until 1871, when he became a partner with H. A. P. Carter in C. Brewer and Co. Meanwhile, he married a "mission girl," Cornelia Hall, daughter of Edwin O. Hall. In 1883 Jones became president and manager, as well as one of the principal owners, of the above-named corporation, which was one of the largest importing-exporting houses and sugar plantation agencies in the islands, owning property in 1893 valued at one million dollars. He was then also engaged with his son in the business known as the Hawaiian Safe Deposit and Investment Co. He was recognized as one of the ablest financiers in Hawaii and as a leader in the business community, possessing alike the confidence of government officials, capitalists, and the working classes of all nationalities—a Robert Morris, so to speak. Jones was a deacon of Central Union (Congregational) Church, president of the board of the Hawaiian Evangelical Association, and director of the YMCA. With Mrs. Jones, he contributed money for the establishment of the Portuguese Mission, and built the Palama Chapel, out of which grew Palama Settlement, a social welfare center.

JUDD, Albert Francis, son of Gerrit P. Judd, served as attorney general during the reign of King Lunalilo, as a justice on the Supreme Court of Hawaii under Kalakaua and Liliuokalani, and as chief justice during the period of the provisional government and of the Republic of Hawaii.

JUDD, Charles, son of Dr. Gerrit P. Judd, served as adjutant general during the reign of King Lunalilo. His alleged unfair treatment of the Household Troops in the matter of clothes was reportedly one of the causes of the mutiny of September 7–10, 1873.

KAAHUMANU, a female high chief, was the wife of Kamehameha I, the mother of Liholiho and Kauikeaouli (Kamehameha II and III), and the rival of Chief Boki, governor of Oahu. She served as *kuhina-nui* and regent from 1823 to June 1832, a period when the teachings of the missionaries spread their influence and were felt in the measures adopted by the rulers. Of autocratic temper, she governed her people, according to a contemporary, "with a rod of iron." Next to Kamehameha I, Kaahumanu was the most impressive and powerful of the native rulers of Hawaii.

KAAI, Simon K., was considered the ablest Hawaiian of pure unmixed blood in the kingdom in the 1870s. He was a leader of Walter Murray Gibson's "Young Hawaiian" party, and was friendly to the English. As a manager of Princess Ruth's estate, he no doubt helped engineer the Maui land deal. He served in the ministries of finance and interior, but this inveterate inebriate resigned from the latter department and drank himself to death.

KAPIOLANI, Chiefess, daughter of Chief Keawe, was a great niece of the celebrated Chiefess Kapiolani, who broke the idolatrous taboos by defying *Pele*, goddess of the volcano, and was immortalized in verse by Tennyson.

KEKUANAOA, Mataio, chief and governor of Oahu, while not himself of royal blood, was father of both Alexander Liholiho and Lot Kamehameha, Kamehameha IV and V, and held several positions of government trust, including that of president of the Board of Education after the death of Armstrong.

KING, J. A., a Scotsman by birth, was for many years a sea captain by profession. He resided in the islands for twenty-five years and was superintendent of the Wilder Steamship Co.

KINNEY, William A., born in Hawaii, resided there for many years before the revolution, and for a period, was Lorrin A. Thurston's law partner. Later he practiced his profession in Salt Lake City and lobbied for annexation during the period of the first annexation treaty in 1893 and the pendency of the second, 1897–98. He was rewarded for his 1893 service to the Hawaiian commission by appointment to office in the islands. Without military experience, he was commissioned captain and afterward was charged with the responsibility of judge advocate in trying Liliuokalani.

LEE, William Little, commenced the practice of law in Troy, New York, but symptoms of tuberculosis determined him to seek a more salubrious climate in the distant Oregon Territory. The brig *Henry*, carrying him thither, reached Honolulu after a tempestuous voyage of 231 days, on October 12, 1846. During the delay incident to the vessel being laid up for extensive repairs, Hawaiian officials became interested in Lee's legal training and urged him to abandon his Oregon project and to remain in the kingdom to head the prospective judicial system. After strong persuasion from Attorney General Ricord, long hesitation, and thorough consultation with his traveling companion, Charles R. Bishop, Lee—in fact both men—decided to cast their lot with the islands. In the fine climate all symptoms of his pulmonary disease disappeared for a time and he proceeded to become one of the most influential and powerful personages in the kingdom—a true builder of Hawaii.

LIKELIKE (pronounced Lik-e-lik), Princess, the sister of David Kalakaua and Liliuokalani, married Archibald Scott Cleghorn, an Englishman who came to Hawaii after a considerable residence in New Zealand.

Low, Frederick Ferdinand, governor, diplomat, and banker, was a Maine lad apprenticed at the age of fifteen to the East India firm of Russell, Sturgis and Co., Boston, and learned much about California and the Far East, where the firm operated. The expiration of his apprenticeship coincided with the exciting news from California in 1849. Arriving there in June, he panned some gold, but later began a successful career as a merchant, first in San Francisco and then in Marysville, where he established a banking business. After serving part of a term in Congress, he was persuaded by Secretary of the Treasury S. P. Chase to accept the post of collector of the port of San Francisco, but this position was soon terminated by his election as the ninth governor of California. Low founded the University of California and preserved from land grabbers the site of San Francisco Golden Gate Park. He was appointed minister to China in 1869 and made an unsuccessful attempt in 1870 to open treaty negotiations with Korea. Returning to San Francisco after the expiration of his four-year term (1870–74), he accepted the position of joint manager of the Anglo-California Bank (1874–91), the second in size on the Pacific coast. Thus worldly-wise, experienced in banking, and familiar with the methods of lobbyists, F. F. Low brought Spreckels' bank bill to Honolulu.

LUNALILO, Prince William Charles, a pure Hawaiian chief representing the ancient line of kings, was the grandson of a brother of Kamehameha I and traced his rank as a chief from his mother, Her Royal Highness Miriama Kekaulouhi, *kuhina-nui* of the kingdom who succeeded Kinau. He was a Congregationalist, was partial to American residents and missionaries, and looked upon them as his best and most sincere friends. *Ke alli lokomaikai,* "the kind chief," was idolized by the Hawaiian populace, who watched his every action and movement for what bearing they might have on the alienation of his country's sovereignty.

MACFARLANE, E. C., royal chamberlain to King Kalakaua and premier in a short-lived ministry of Queen Liliuokalani, accompanied Paul Neumann and Prince David Kawananakoa to Washington in February 1893 to lay the Queen's case before the United States government.

McGREW, Dr. John S., an ardent annexationist, was known as the "Father of Annexation," His mansion in Honolulu was renowned for its hospitality.

MARSDEN, Joseph, an Englishman, was an engineer by profession who came to the islands in 1869. He entered the sugar plantation business in 1876—the year that the reciprocity treaty was ratified—achieved success, and became one of the principal owners of the Honokaa Sugar Co. He represented the Planters' Labor and Supply Co., composed of men interested in sugar, at the New Orleans Exposition, and was sent by the same company to study the labor situation in Japan, China, India, and Java. He was elected a noble to the legislature of 1890 and re-elected for a term of six years in 1892. Marsden was considered one of the most representative and influential Englishmen in the islands and for that reason was included in the commission dispatched to Washington to negotiate a treaty of annexation.

MORENO, Caesar Celso (or Celso Caesar), a big six foot, burly lobbyist, was well known in Sacramento and Washington before he arrived in Honolulu on November 14, 1879, to secure for the China Merchants' Steam Navigation Co. a subsidy for a line of trans-Pacific steamers, which would have been destructive of American interests. He adroitly manipulated the plastic material of the palace and government house with "astounding success," and soon gained more influence with the sovereign than his constitutional ministers had.

MOTT SMITH, Dr. John, an American dentist of considerable residence in Honolulu, who was appointed chargé d'affaires of the Hawaiian legation in Washington in late 1868. He labored for reciprocity through the change of administration from Andrew Johnson to Ulysses S. Grant, until the special session of Congress adjourned in April 1869, shortly after the Senate voted down the motion to take up the Hawaiian reciprocity treaty. Returning to Hawaii, his stay was brief, for he joined Elisha Allen in Washington in the latter part of 1869 and again lobbied for reciprocity through the early months of 1870. In that year he succeeded C. C. Harris as minister of finance, and during his tenure of office carried through the project of constructing the Hawaiian Hotel, which had the backing of his predecessor and the support of Kamehameha V. Mott Smith served as King Kalakaua's minister of the interior and premier from December 1876 to July 1878. Later he was appointed Hawaii's minister to Washington, which post he held at the time of the January 1893 revolution and until May of that year, when he was replaced by Lorrin A. Thurston. Dr. Mott Smith was supported by the conservative older mercantile men of Honolulu, but did not possess the confidence of those interested in the annexation movement.

NAHAOLELUA, P., was one of the oldest and most influential native nobles who served under Kalakaua's three predecessors as governor of Maui. He was related by birth and marriage to the family of the late Governor Young, of which Queen Emma was the most renowned representative. Nahaolelua was appointed minister of finance in 1874 to satisfy the frequently expressed native demand for a Hawaiian in the cabinet. He seemed to be the most deserving and the best qualified person for that department, for he was known for his strictness in compelling accounts to be promptly rendered and he allowed no person under him to remain delinquent in performing his official duties.

NEUMANN, Paul, once an attorney for Claus Spreckels, served as attorney general under W. M. Gibson. Although Neumann was recognized as "bright," he was criticized by his opponents as "unscrupulous—a Bohemian, and with it a bonhomie" which pleased the people of the lower classes. He was a royalist who served as

Queen Liliuokalani's attorney and special agent to Washington in February 1893.

OLESON, William B., an American resident of the Hawaiian Islands for fifteen years, served as the principal of the largest school on Hawaii and later in the same capacity at the Kamehameha Manual Labor School in Honolulu. After his return to New England, he was influential with the editors of eastern metropolitan newspapers and with the American Board of Commissioners for Foreign Missions. An avid annexationist, he assisted the cause by contributing to the New York *Independent* and, in collaboration with John L. Stevens, brought out, in 1900, *Riches and Marvels of Hawaii*, a description of Hawaii's history, people, geography, "corrupt monarchy, revolution, provisional government and annexation" from the annexationist point of view.

OLNEY, Richard, was elected to the Massachusetts state legislature in 1873. He was hardly known to the people when, in 1895, he was selected by President Cleveland as attorney general to represent New England in the cabinet. Following the death of Gresham on May 28, 1895, Olney, on June 8, was commissioned secretary of state.

OXNARD, Henry T., was one of three Oxnard brothers, all of whom were sugar magnates. Exceedingly industrious and considered by his enemies as unscrupulous, he diligently organized the sugar-beet interests in many states and furthered his interests in several publications. In May 1897 he conducted a "house to house canvass" among congressmen against annexation, and by claiming that he was friendly to Hawaii, induced the press to allow him space for statements.

PARKER, Samuel, was a grandson of John Parker, of New England stock, who served as a lieutenant of the conquering Kamehameha I. From his maternal grandmother and mother, who were Hawaiian chieftesses, he inherited large landed estates on Hawaii, where he was a rancher. He was one of the most capable Hawaiians of mixed blood, and popular with both foreigners and natives. At the time of his appointment as minister of foreign affairs in 1891, he was about forty years old and the most prominent native Hawaiian in public life.

PETERSON, A. P., a barrister from Massachusetts, served as attorney general in the compromise cabinet appointed by King Kalakaua on June 17, 1890, after the fall of the Reform Cabinet.

PHILLIPS, Stephen H., a lawyer of Massachusetts, was invited to Honolulu in 1866 to fill the post of attorney general, which he held throughout the remainder of Kamehameha V's reign. While in office, Phillips was apparently opposed to Hawaii's losing her sovereignty, but on March 11, 1873, he not only publicly declared for annexation but abjured his Hawaiian citizenship.

PRESTON, Edward, an Englishman of unknown antecedents, came to Honolulu from Botany Bay, and no one knew how he got there. This roving British subject served the Hawaiian kingdom well as attorney general in Kalakaua's third cabinet, in Gibson's ministry, and later as a justice of the Supreme Court.

PROCTER, John Robert, a distinguished geologist who participated in the Harvard geological survey of Kentucky. His reports and studies appeared in the *Geological Survey of Kentucky*, 1880–92. On the recommendation of Theodore Roosevelt, Procter was appointed by President Cleveland, in December 1893, to the United States Civil Service Commission and soon thereafter became president of the commission, which position he held for ten years.

RICORD, John, although English by birth, received his legal training in New York and had brief professional experience in the states, [Florida, Louisiana, Texas, Arizona, and Oregon] before sailing to Honolulu, where he was appointed attorney general of the kingdom on March 9, 1844. He was the first American layman with legal background to enter the service of the Hawaiian government, which he left in the autumn of 1847, dejected and apparently jilted by Miss Elizabeth Judd.

ROBERTSON, Judge George M., filled the vacancy as associate justice on the Supreme Court created in 1854 by the appointment of Lorrin Andrews to the new probate court. He assisted in the preparation of the Constitution of 1864 and served as attorney general of the kingdom under Kamehameha IV and V.

SCHURZ, Carl, a naturalized American, by his ability as an orator, his services as a general in the Civil War, his editorship of the *Westliche Post* in St. Louis, his position as secretary of interior in President Rutherford B. Hayes' cabinet, and his editorship of the *Nation* and *Evening Post*, before turning to editorial writing for *Harper's Weekly*, became the most distinguished German-American in the United States. He was editor of the last named weekly from 1894 to 1898.

SMITH, William O., was born in Hawaii of American parents, Dr.

and Mrs. James William Smith, and attended the Rev. Daniel Dole's school at Kolea, later Punahou, in Honolulu, and finally the Massachusetts Agricultural College at Amherst. He acted as sheriff of the Islands of Kauai and Maui for two years each, before reading law in the office of Judge A. S. Hartwell. In addition to practicing his legal profession, Smith conducted a large trust and investment business which administered some thirty or more estates, served as a director of about a half dozen corporations, was managing trustee of the estate of King Lunalilo, and was an extensive owner of sugar plantation stock. He was married to a woman of Irish birth and was a member of the Congregational Church.

SPENCER, Charles N., an American of long residence in the kingdom, served as minister of the interior in the latter part of King Kalakaua's reign and was reappointed by Queen Liliuokalani to the same post.

SPRECKELS, Claus, *una miliona,* the millionaire, as he was commonly known in Hawaii, was the largest, most conspicuous, and notorious of the late nineteenth-century Hawaiian sugar planters, processors, shippers, and agents. Born in Lamstedt, Hanover, in 1828, of impecunious parents, Claus migrated to the United States in 1846. Within a few years he achieved a series of successes in the grocery business in Charleston, in New York City, and on the Pacific coast with the lucky miners. When he had increased his capital to $50,-000, he invested in a brewery which, along with his grocery, sold in a few years for $100,000. With his brother and brother-in-law, Claus Mangels, he founded in 1863, the Bay Sugar Refinery, which proved a lucrative business and grew rapidly. Anxious to expand further than the hesitant directors, and determined to learn every angle and trick in the sugar business, Spreckels sold his business at an enormous profit and returned to his native Germany. In the course of a couple of months, working as a laborer in a refinery at Magdeburg, he learned every step of processing refined sugar. Returning to San Francisco, he organized, in 1868, the California Sugar Refinery Co., and invented a process by which the time for making hard sugar was reduced from three weeks to less than twenty-four hours. He incidentally introduced cube and crushed sugars to Americans.

Originally an opponent of reciprocity because of his plans for creating a large beet-sugar industry in California and the fear of competition from Hawaii's high grade sugars, Claus Spreckels, after the reciprocity treaty was ratified by the Senate, decided that the agreement could be made to inure to his benefit. On an 1876 visit to the islands, the early bird bought up half the estimated 14,000–ton sugar crop for 1877, before the full price rise caused by the news that the necessary legislation for implementing the reciprocity convention could take effect. At the same time, he envisaged expanding his operations by securing the source of his own raw material through the establishment of his own plantations in Hawaii. On a second visit in 1878 the entrepreneur purchased a half interest in 16,000 acres on the Waikapu Commons, located on the barren central coastal plains of Maui, and leased 24,000 acres of adjoining crown lands for thirty years at $1,000 per annum, upon which he developed a sugar plantation called Spreckelsville and incorporated the new ten million dollar Hawaiian Commercial Co. Since 800 pounds of water is required to produce one pound of sugar, the California refiner endeavored to secure from King Kalakaua and cabinet a thirty-year lease on all the surplus water in certain streams of Maui, but Attorney General Hartwell and Minister of the Interior John Mott Smith, the Premier, refused to grant these rights on the terms offered. A large loan to Kalakaua induced him to request unceremoniously the resignation of these ministers and to appoint others more amenable, who granted the requested rights for thirty years at the nominal price of $500 annually. Spreckels then had constructed a mammoth irrigation project, at an estimated cost of $500,-000, which, on completion, delivered 50 million gallons of water daily, enough to produce 50,000 tons of sugar annually. On the land thus made arable was founded the Hawaiian Commercial and Sugar Co., which took over the assets of Spreckels' privately owned Hawaiian Commercial Co., but in which, as a majority stockholder, he retained control. Under his ingenious management, the company developed into the largest sugar plantation in Hawaii and the most modern in the world, with the optimum utilization of manpower, irrigation water, agricultural machinery, and technological processes in the harvesting and milling of cane, including the islands' first intraplantation railroad system, with both permanent and portable tracks. The entire plantation and milling system at Spreckelsville was so efficiently managed that, according to reports, the California magnate was eventually able to realize profits of 50 per cent or better each year on his investment.

To facilitate the marketing of his product as well as to gain control of a large portion of the output of other planters, Claus Spreckels, in 1880, became the sole partner of William G. Irwin and Co., a sugar agency founded in 1874. The partnership became pre-eminent among the agencies, holding a grip on other plantations with loans which at one time amounted to about $2,500,000, and by 1893 controlled plantations which produced 50,000 tons of sugar annually, more than one-third of the total production of the islands, and provided agency service for an additional 20,000 tons. This was transported to the Pacific coast in vessels of the Oceanic Steamship Line, founded by the elder Spreckels and his son, John D., and which in 1883 started a semimonthly de luxe steamer service between San Francisco and Honolulu, with Irwin and Co. serving as the Honolulu agents of the line. A few years later the service was extended to Australia. Although the mainland interloper failed to secure a franchise from the Hawaiian legislature of 1884 for a National Banking Corporation with power to issue notes receivable as legal tender for taxes and customs and to serve as a government depository and fiscal agent, he continued the efficient operation of his private bank of Claus Spreckels and Co., which opened on January 14, 1884. Through his Spreckelsville plantation, his partnership with William G. Irwin, the Oceanic Steamship Co., and the California Sugar Refinery, "Spreckels controlled Hawaiian sugar more completely than any man before or since his time."

SPRING RICE, Sir Cecil, devoted years of service to the British Foreign Office, first in London, then in the British legation in Washington during the later 1880s when warm and genuine friendships were made with John Hay, Henry Adams, Henry Cabot Lodge, and Theodore Roosevelt, and finally in Berlin and Tokyo. After thirty years of diplomatic service, Sir Cecil was promoted to the post of British ambassador at Washington, and served in that capacity during World War I.

STIRLING, Robert, a Scotsman who served as minister of finance for a few months under Kamehameha V, was appointed to the same office by King Lunalilo, as well as to the Board of Education. Stirling opposed the cession of Pearl Harbor in exchange for a treaty of reciprocity.

THURSTON, Lorrin Andrews, was a second-generation Hawaiian by birth: his paternal grandfather, the Rev. Asa Thurston, was a member of Hiram Bingham's pioneer band of missionaries who arrived in 1820; his mother was Sarah Andrews Thurston, daughter of Lorrin Andrews, of Connecticut, who came to Hawaii in 1828 and remained to serve the Hawaiian kingdom in several capacities, including that of justice of the Superior Court. Lorrin was educated at

Punahou (Oahu) College and Columbia University Law School. In addition to practicing as an attorney, he engaged in considerable extraprofessional activity. He edited the Honolulu *Daily Bulletin* in 1884. The funds he accumulated as attorney for Claus Spreckels he invested in the sugar industry, in cattle ranches, and in fruit companies. Thurston was the secretary, director, and one of the principal owners of the Halakala Ranch Co., incorporated for $225,000, as well as secretary and director of the Maui Cattle Co., the Hawaiian Fruit and Packing Co., the Eleele Plantation Co., and the Kilauea Volcano House Co. He was an organizer and secretary of the Hawaiian Bureau of Information, predecessor of the Hawaiian Tourist Bureau, was appointed special commissioner to Chicago to arrange for the Hawaiian exhibit at the World Columbia Exposition, and headed a syndicate which produced the Kilauea Cyclorama, a representation of the volcano in full action on the fair grounds.

WIDEMANN, Hermann A., a German of long residence in the islands, had large private interests there. A royalist through marriage to a native Hawaiian, he served as associate justice of the Supreme Court, on the Board of Education under King Kalakaua, and as minister of interior in Queen Liliuokalani's first cabinet. He remained loyal to her during and after the revolution of 1893, and served as her agent on a trip to Washington in her interests.

WILCOX, Albert S., wealthy sugar planter and annexationist was the son of early missionaries, and the brother of George N. Wilcox.

WILCOX, George N., served as minister of the interior and premier for a couple of months before the revolution of 1893. This wealthy planter and industrialist, one of the older native sons of Hawaii, was born at Hilo, his parents having come to the islands in 1837 as missionaries and for years conducted a manual labor school at Waioli, Kauai. He was educated at Punahou and attended the Sheffield Scientific School, Yale University, during 1861–62. Upon his return to Hawaii, Wilcox became a pioneer in sugar planting at Hanalei, Kauai, developed Grove Farm, Lihue, and eventually became the sole owner of the estate which finally included about 12,-000 acres. He was president of Kekaha Sugar Co., the Waianae Co., and the Pacific Guano and Fertilizer Co., and a director of Lihue Plantation Co. and the Inter-Island Steam Navigation Co. Wilcox served as representative from Kauai to the legislature of 1880, and after 1887, sat in the House of Nobles.

WILDER, Samuel G., represented the mid-nineteenth-century American spirit of the westward march of progress. Although born in Massachusetts in 1831, he lived as a boy and youth first in Canada, then in New York and Illinois, before heading across the plains to California in 1852. Four years later he was in Hawaii, where he married Miss Elizabeth Kinau Judd, thus firmly planting himself in the islands with the established missionary party. He returned to the mainland, chartered the clipper ship *White Swallow* for his first business enterprise of shipping guano from the Pacific Islands. After two years in that business, he had acquired enough capital to engage in the cultivation of rice and sugar. As agent, he managed efficiently the government steamer *Kilauea*, later organized the Wilder Steamship Co., and distinguished himself in the development and expansion of interisland navigation. Wilder served as agent of the board of immigration on an 1870 mission to China to secure contract laborers. He was appointed noble of the kingdom by King Lunalilo, supported the candidacy of David Kalakaua on the death of the former, and continued as a member of the House of Nobles. Wilder's demonstrated ability and energy as premier (1878–80) entitled him to be considered one of the ablest administrators the Hawaiian kingdom ever had.

WUNDENBURG, F. W., an annexationist closely identified with the revolution, was placed in charge of the police station at a time when everything depended upon reliable leadership. As a reward for his services, he was named collector general of customs, a position for which he was qualified by long business experience.

WYLLIE, Robert C., a Scotsman who served as Hawaiian minister of foreign affairs for twenty years, from 1845 to 1865, was one of the most loyal and distinguished servants of the kingdom, and a leading architect of the constitutional monarchy.

YOUNG, Alexander, a Scotsman by birth, was fifty-two years old and had spent thirty of those years in Hawaii when, in 1893, he was named to the advisory council of the provisional government. He was manager and principal owner of the Pepeekeo Sugar Co. and the Kahuku Plantation Co., incorporated for $750,000 and $500,000 respectively, and a director and principal owner of the Waiakea Sugar Co. He was elected as a noble to the legislatures of 1887, 1888, and 1892, was a trustee of the Congregational Church, and was among the most active and progressive businessmen of the islands.

APPENDIX II: TAXATION, 1881

The following table indicates the proportion of taxes paid by native Hawaiians and other nationalities in 1881, and illustrates the taxation burden that some 1,243 American taxpayers bore.[1]

Of the total of "other nationalities," $1,916.00 was paid by 389 Norwegians; $1,878.80 by 376 South Sea Islanders; and $1,244.94 by 252, nationality scattered or unknown.

1. Compiled by me from tables Nos. 1–9 of "Analysis of the Taxation of the Hawaiian Kingdom for the Year 1881 Showing the Proportion of Taxes Paid by Hawaiians and Other Nationalities," compiled and tabulated by Fred H. Hayselden, assessor of the District of Makawao, by order of the Hawaiian Legislative Assembly, 1882, encl. in Daggett to Frelinghuysen, Nov. 18, 1882, No. 29, USDS, Dispatches, Hawaii, 20. Note: The statistics are actually for the most populous and developed islands of Oahu, Hawaii, Maui, and Kauai, not for the entire kingdom.

Nationality	Number	Real Estate	Personal	School, Road, Dog Poll, Horse, etc.	Total
Hawaiians	15,769	$34,133.63	$13,561.55	$76,386.25	$124,081.43
Americans	1,243	44,241.89	50,764.99	6,857.00	101,863.88
	886 375N²				
British	952	18,375.83	27,166.99	6,188.75	41,731.57
	721 231N				
Germans	409	8,066.12	18,636.71	2,755.50	29,458.23
	328 81N				
Chinese	10,894	3,780.18	12,901.45	53,720.00	70,401.63
Portuguese	677	1,276.68	1,245.95	3,641.25	6,163.88
Others	1,088	4,759.89	5,000.70	6,187.50	15,948.09
	1,017 71N				
	31,032	114,634.22	129,278.34	155,736.25	389,648.81

2. Naturalized, over two-thirds of whom were born in the kingdom.

APPENDIX III: NATIVE MONARCHS OF HAWAII

Name	Birth	Accession	Death
Kamehameha I	c. 1758	1795	May 8, 1819
Kamehameha II (Liholiho)	1797	May 20, 1819	July 14, 1824
Kamehameha III (Kauikeaouli)	March 17, 1814	June 6, 1825	Dec. 15, 1854
Kamehameha IV (Alexander Liholiho)	Feb. 9, 1834	Dec. 15, 1854	Nov. 30, 1863
Kamehameha V (Lot Kamehameha)	Dec. 11, 1830	Nov. 30, 1863	Dec. 11, 1872
William C. Lunalilo	Jan. 31, 1835	Jan. 8, 1873	Feb. 3, 1874
David Kalakaua	Nov. 16, 1836	Feb. 12, 1874	Jan. 20, 1891
Liliuokalani	Sept. 2, 1838	Jan. 29, 1891 *	Nov. 11, 1917

* Liliuokalani was deposed and the Hawaiian Kingdom came to an end on January 17, 1893.

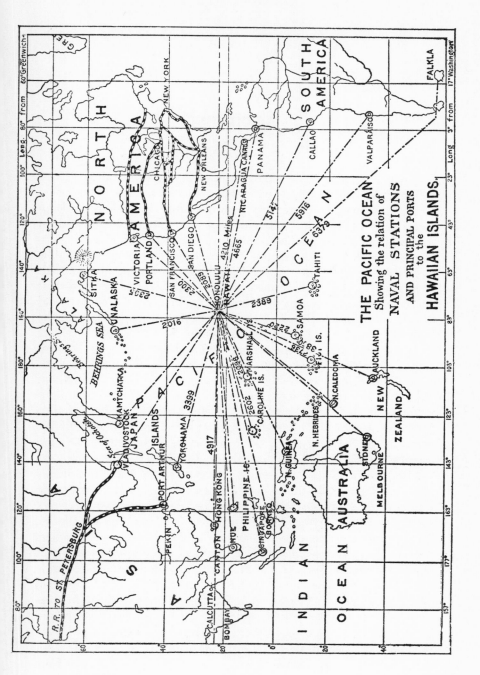

THE PACIFIC OCEAN
Showing the relation of
NAVAL STATIONS
AND PRINCIPAL PORTS
to the
HAWAIIAN ISLANDS

SOURCES

The major portion of the material used in the preparation of this volume and contemporary with the events described therein was archival. Naturally, the principal sources were collections of documents available only in the Archives of the United States (National Archives) and the Public Archives of the State of Hawaii. Supplementing these were printed government documents, the public and private papers, correspondence, diaries, memoirs, and journals of individuals—often statesmen—and the archives of organizations housed in the manuscript divisions of the Library of Congress and the Harvard College Library, and in the Mission-Historical and the University of Hawaii Libraries in Honolulu.

The diplomatic correspondence of the Department of State is contained in two sets of volumes which may be designated department file and legation archives. The most frequently consulted and quoted of the former were: (1) *Dispatches, Hawaii*, a thirty-four volume series (1843–1900). These consist of the original letters from the American diplomatic representative in Honolulu to the Secretary of State, together with enclosures. Some dispatches are of considerable length and many are confidential. The enclosures are frequently voluminous, containing copies of private and official correspondence with ministers of foreign relations and others, trade statistics, newspapers cuttings, printed copies of addresses delivered, annual reports of the cabinet ministers to the Hawaiian legislature, etc. The first two volumes are marked "Sandwich Islands," the others "Hawaii." (2) *Instructions*, which consist of three volumes of copies of letters from the Secretary of State to the United States diplomatic representative in Honolulu. The first volume, for 1843–47, is entitled *Special Missions*, I. Volumes 1 and 2 are entitled *Hawaii Instructions*. These do not contain enclosures sent with the instructions. The original instructions received in Honolulu, together with enclosures, are bound in the Legation Archives. (3) *Notes*, four volumes, consisting of communications to the Secretary of State from the Hawaiian diplomatic agent in Washington, from the Hawaiian consul general residing in New York, and from the Hawaiian minister of foreign relations, and including some memoranda of interviews between the Secretary of State and the Hawaiian minister in Washington, letters from private individuals, and a few miscellaneous documents relating to Hawaiian affairs. (4) *Notes to,* in one volume, which are copies of communications from the Secretary of State to the Hawaiian diplomatic representative in the United States. (5) *Miscellaneous Letters,* numerous volumes of unofficial correspondence received by the State Department but often relating to official matters, bound according to the date received. (6) *Miscellaneous Archives, Memoranda of Conversation with the Secretary of State, 1893–1898.* (7) *Protocol First Conference between Hawaiian Commissioners and Secretary of State, February 4, 1893.* This volume, incorrectly titled, contains the protocols of all seven conferences, February 4–14, 1893, as well as the stenographic notes of the same.

The Legation Archives most extensively used were Volumes 1 and 2 of the three-volume series *Private and Official Interviews,* "memorandum of facts, events, and conversation," prepared in the form of a diary, partly in pursuance of instructions, and partly to afford convenience in the preparation of official dispatches. Most of the facts, but not absolutely all, are embodied in dispatches to the Secretary of State. Volume 2, of 131 pages, covering the period of David L. Gregg's term as commissioner but more detailed for 1854–55, in which the record parallels in many but not in every respect his private diaries, is most helpful to the research scholar. Also consulted were the nine volumes of *Miscellaneous Letters Received,* which contain all the correspondence received, except instructions from the Secretary of State and notes from the Hawaiian government.

In the Navy Department archives the most valuable sources proved to be Outgoing Letters, Flag Officers, especially those of Secretary Gideon Welles, Commanders' Letters, Captains' Letters, and Letters Received from the Pacific Squadron, and the VP series on the protection of life and property.

In the Public Archives of Hawaii the "Foreign Office and Executive" files were most frequently used. These are classified and labeled in various ways: "Local Officials," "Hawaiian Officials Abroad, United States, Minister to Washington," which contains the instructions of the Hawaiian foreign office under the monarchy to its minister to the United States, and the dispatches of the Hawaiian minister at Washington to the foreign minister at Honolulu; "United States, Ministers and Commissioners to Washington," and "United States, Ministers and Envoys to Washington," in both of which is preserved the same type of instructions and dispatches under the provisional government; and "United States, Minister at Washington," a similar file for the period of the Republic of Hawaii. Other invaluable sources were the Foreign Office Letter Books, the Privy Council Records, Minutes of Cabinet Council Meetings, Journal of the Legislature, Resolutions of the Legislative Assembly, Naturalization Books, British Commissioners' Letter Book, and the Papers of Sanford B. Dole, as well as those of Lorrin A. Thurston.

Not in the Archives of Hawaii but in the Collection of the Robert E. Van Dyke Foundation, Honolulu, are the Letters of Sanford B. Dole to George H. Dole 1859–1912, MSS, which reveal some of the innermost convictions of the former brother.

A considerable correspondence addressed to the Foreign Office in London by the British consul generals in Hawaii, communications sent to the Admiralty by commanders of the British Pacific fleet, and remonstrances directed to the Colonial Office by Richard Seddon, premier of New Zealand, concerning annexation, were read in the British Public Record Office. Especially helpful were the Foreign Office volumes 58/136, 58/241, 58/270, 58/279, 58/319, and Colonial Office volume 537/136.

In the Manuscript Division of the Library of Congress pertinent information of significance was secured from the papers of the following officials: William L. Marcy, Hamilton Fish (including his diary), Frederick T. Frelinghuysen, Chester A. Arthur, Grover Cleveland, Thomas F. Bayard, James G. Blaine, John Sherman, Benjamin Harrison, Richard Olney, Walter Q. Gresham, and William McKinley.

The manuscript division of the Harvard College Library now houses the archives of the American Board of Commissioners for Foreign Missions, formerly deposited at Mission House, Boston; the Hawaiian Club of Boston papers, including minutes of meetings and letter books; the correspondence of Edward P. Bond, who was a member and officer of both the Hawaiian Club and the Boston Board of Trade; the correspondence of Charles Sumner, and the larger portion of the James Hunnewell Papers, the remainder being in the Baker Library of the Harvard University Graduate School of Business Administration, as are also the tariff papers of Justin S. Morrill.

In the Hawaiian collection of the University of Hawaii Library are the transcript copies of the Gregg Collection, which contains David L. Gregg's dispatches, without enclosures, his private letters in two parts, and the eight extant volumes of his diaries, together with some miscellaneous papers. The diaries are a rich storehouse of observations on mid-nineteenth-century life and society in Honolulu, as well as a revelation of Gregg's innermost convictions and intentions. A transcript copy of William Castle's diary was useful for the narration of events on the journey to Washington and the efforts there of the five commissioners appointed by the provisional government in January 1893 to negotiate an annexation treaty. Several master of arts theses of the University of Hawaii in the field of history led to further investigation of certain aspects of United States-Hawaiian relations.

The printed sources used in the preparation of this study, far too numerous and varied to be listed, included government documents, especially those entitled *Papers Relating to the Foreign Relations of the United States* from the first date of publication up to 1898. Mention should be made of United States *House of Representatives Executive Documents,* 53 Congress, 3 session, no. 1, part 1, *Foreign Relations of the United States,* 1894, Appendix II, "Affairs in Hawaii." This volume of 1437 pages comprises various Senate and House documents, with some duplications, dealing with Hawaii. Other comprehensive volumes frequently consulted were United States *Senate Reports,* 53 Congress, 2 session, no. 227, often referred to as the *Morgan Report; House Executive Documents,* 53 Congress, 2 session, no. 47, *Report of Commissioner to the Hawaiian Islands,* otherwise known as the *Blount Report; Senate Executive Documents,* 52 Congress, 2 session, nos. 76 and 77, the first of which is entitled "Hawaiian Islands"; the second is correspondence respecting relations between the United States and Hawaiian kingdom from September 1820 to January 1893, together with a report upon the official relations of the United States with the islands from the first appointment of a consular officer there by this government. *Senate Reports,* 55 Congress, 2 session, no. 681, also printed in *Senate Documents,* 56 Congress, 2 session, no. 231, part 7, contains arguments from many sources, including those of strategists, for the annexation of the mid-Pacific archipelago. United States relations with Hawaii prior to union are discussed in John Bassett Moore, *A Digest of International Law* (8 vols. Washington, D.C., 1906), *1,* 475–520. Also valuable were the *Reports of the Minister of Foreign Relations* (Honolulu) for the applicable years; the *Report of the Historical Commission of the Territory of Hawaii . . . December 21, 1924,* and the one for December 31, 1926; the *Journal of the Executive Proceedings of the Senate of the United States;* the *Congressional Record;* and James D. Richardson, ed., *A Compilation of the Messages and Papers of the Presidents (1789–97)* (10 vols. Washington, D.C., 1896–99; 20 vols. New York, 1917?).

Of the general histories covering part of the period, Ralph S. Kuykendall, *The Hawaiian Kingdom 1778–1854: Foundation and Transformation* and *The Hawaiian Kingdom 1854–1874: Twenty Critical Years* (Honolulu, 1947, 1953) are, and perhaps will remain for all time, the most comprehensive and scholarly treatment. William DeWitt Alexander, *History of the Later Years of the Hawaiian Monarchy and the Revolution of 1893* (Honolulu, 1896), and Lorrin A. Thurston, *Memoirs of the Hawaiian Revolution* (Honolulu, 1936), are definitely slanted in favor of the annexationists. Sanford Ballard Dole, *Memoirs of the Hawaiian Revolution* (Honolulu, 1936), though slightly more objective, is less comprehensive. Liliuokalani's position is stated in her *Hawaii's Story by Hawaii's Queen* (Boston, 1898), while John W. Foster, *Diplomatic Memoirs* (2 vols. Boston and New York, 1909), Vol. 2, proved revealing of that statesman's attitude.

Mention can be made of only a few of the most frequently consulted periodicals. The *Pacific Commercial Advertiser* (at times in opposition to and at other periods controlled by the minister of foreign relations), the *Hawaiian Gazette,* the Honolulu *Daily Bulletin,* and the *Hawaiian Star,* organ of the annexationists, were informative. For the earlier period of the study the *Polynesian,* the *Sandwich Island Gazette,* and the *Weekly Argus,* later called the *New Era,* were consulted. The San Francisco *Alta California,* the San Francisco *Herald,* the San Francisco *Morning Call,* the New York *Times,* the New York *Herald,* the Washington *Post,* and the Boston *Evening Transcript* were the most frequently used American newspapers; the *Times* (London) and the London *Post* proved superior for England; while the *North American Review, Nineteenth Century Review, Nation, Forum, Pacific Historical Review, Journal of Modern History, American Historical Review, Review of Reviews* (American edition), and certain state historical society papers, like those of the Massachusetts Historical Society, provided scholarly articles on special topics of Hawaiian-American relations.

INDEX

Act of Union (Great Britain), 158 f.
Adams (N.S.S.): sojourns in Hawaiian waters, 91; landing of troops from, 89, 98 f.
Adams, Charles Francis, quoted on Cleveland's policy, 239
Adams, Samuel, 164
Aden, fortified, 224, 276
Adler, Jacob, 71
Advisory council of provision gov., 186, 323, 339
Aholo, L., 54, 72
Alameda (ship), 180, 192, 194
Alaska, 301
Albany *Times Union*, 205; quoted, 207
Aldrich, Arnold, 319
Aldrich, Nelson W., attacks Cleveland's policy, 260
Aldrich and Bishop (firm), 319
Aleutian Islands, 301
Alexander, De Elva S., 301
Alexander, William De Witt, 50, 51; quoted on Kalakaua's influence, 81; quoted on constitution of *1887*, 93; writings, 225; moral effect of landing marines, 313; sketch of, 317
Alexander, Rev. William P., 9; sketch of, 317

Alioolani Hale, 183 f., 187 f., 190. *See also* Government building
Allen, Elisha H., 16, 18, 20, 32, 39
Allen, Frederick, 116
Allen, William F., 317
Allen, William V., 292; resolution quoted, 263
Alli (king and high chiefs), 26, 116; decline of, 48; reduced to figurehead, 93
Alliance (U.S.S.), 141
Allison, William B., 281
Almy, Rear Admiral John J., 38 f.
Aloha Oe, song composed by Liliuokalani, 112
Alvensleben, H. von, on Hawaiian–Samoan Confederation, 79 f.
American Agriculturist, 290 f.
American Board of Commissioners for Foreign Missions (ABCFM), 4, 8 ff., 221, 318, 333
American business and professional interests: concern for invested capital and political power, 58 f.; desire for security, 119, 140, 309 f., 313, 341
American farmers, and annexation, 290 f.
American Federationist, opposed an-

nexation, 280 n., 289
American labor: and annexation, 288 ff.; A. F. of L., 289; Knights of Labor, 290
American League in Hawaii, 294
American press and annexation, 137 f., 195, 199 n., 205 ff.
Americanists and strategists, 273 ff., 279, 302; criticized, 279 f.
Americans, in Hawaii, 44; concern for diminishing political power, 58, 63, 119; status under constitution of 1887, 91 f., 94 f.; taxes paid, 341
Andrews, Lorrin, 12 ff.; sketch of, 337
Anglican Church, 21, 22, 25
Anglo-American contest, 2, 105 f., 137, 143, 149, 217
Anglo–American rapprochement, 315 f.; Lodge quoted, 316; Spring Rice quoted, 316
Anglo–California Bank of San Francisco, 68
Anglo–French Declaration on independence of the Sandwich Islands (1843), 303, 311
Anglo–German partition of non-Dutch New Guinea, 77
Annexation Club (1892): Cooper suggests, 115 n.; sends Thurston to Washington, 116 ff.; receives promise of support, 129, 154, 166 ff.; contacts State Dept., 146, 153; becomes committee of public safety, 154, 163; members as officials of provisional government, 185; W. N. Armstrong assists, 318, 323
Annexation Club (1893): organized by Dr. John C. McGrew, 226; reactivated in 1897, 269; monster meeting planned, 284
Annexation of Hawaii to the U.S.: Peirce on, 32 f.; missionaries, planters, and merchants for, 32; Fish on, 33; movement for, 114; letter of Thurston to Blaine, 117 ff.; foreigners in Hawaii on, 119; Senate For. Rels. Com. discusses, 121, 138; preparing for, 135 ff.; reaction of American press, 137 f., 195, 199 n.,

205 f.; opinion in Hawaii on, 142 f.; problems involved in, 147 ff.; Stevens presses hard for, 149 ff.; objective of provisional government, 185, 220, 246; propaganda for, 195 f., 218, 231, 308; official reaction to, 196 ff.; opposed by anti-imperialists, 198, 252, 262, 304 f.; petitions for, 198, 285 n.; object of the Republic of Hawaii, 258; urged by Americanists and strategists, 273 ff., 279, 301 f., 311; petitions against, 285; opposed by American labor, 288 ff.; opposed by sugar interests, 291 f.; Spanish–American war hastens, 298, 311; southern antagonism to, 302; Spring Rice urges, 302 f.; joint res. of Congress, 305 ff.
Annexation treaties of 1854, 1893, 1897. See Treaty of Annexation, of 1854, 1893, 1897
Anti-imperialists, 198, 252; quoted, 262, 301 f., 304 f.
Anti-missionary parties, 19
Apia, Samoa, district and municipal government of, 76, 78, 81
Appel, John C., on U.S. labor and annexation, 290
Arion Hall, 179 n., 184
Armstrong, Rev. Richard, 13, 17, 18; sketch of, 317 f.
Armstrong, Gen. Samuel C., letter to N.Y. Post quoted, 220 ff.; sketch of, 318
Armstrong, William N., 116, 121, 146; warns sugar planters, 267; sketch of, 318
Ashford, Clarence W., 84, 96; deserts colleagues, 101 f.; sketch of, 318
Ashford, Volney V., 84 f.; arrests Gibson, 88; commands military, 97; helps organize Equal Rights League, 114 f.
Asia, Asian system, and Asians, 45, 307. See also China; Japan
Astor, John Jacob and Son, 2
Atherton, Joseph B., 178
Auckland, New Zealand, 180, 192
Austin, Jonathan, 101; sketch of, 318

Australasian Monroe Doctrine, 75
Australia (S.S.), arrives in Honolulu, *June 28, 1887*, 86, 203
Australia, Australian Colonies, and Australasians, 38; and Hawaiian sugar, 40; rivalry in the Pacific, 75, 224

Bailey, Thomas A.: on Japanese interference in Hawaii, 283 f.; quoted on annexation, 315
Baker, Hoapili: manifesto, 52, 57; authors *A Reply to the Ministerial Utterances,* 53
Balanea (whaler), 3
Baldwin, Henry P., 87
Ballieu, Dr. M., 37
Bank of California, 74
Bank of England, 72
Bay Sugar Refinery, 335
Bayard, Thomas F., 71; Hawaii's program of primacy in the Pacific, 76 ff.; quoted on Pacific annexations, 77; disapproves German annexation of Samoa, 78; quoted on Hawaiian revolution of *1887,* 89 f.; on interference in Hawaii, 90; on status of Americans under Constitution of *1887,* 94 f.; on British protectorate over Hawaii, 106; differentiates between Samoa and Hawaii, 107; policy toward Hawaii, 220; quoted on Gresham's policy, 238 f.
"Bayonet Constitution." *See* Constitution of *1887*
Behring (Bering) Sea Controversy and Commission, 137, 218
Belknap, George E., 36; quoted on annexation of Hawaii, 225 f.; on pulling down flag, 233; sketch of, 318
Benicia (U.S.S.), 31, 38 f.
Berlin Conference (*1884–85*), 80; (*1889*), 107
Bermuda fortified, 207 f., 224
Berry, Albert S., 300
Bible, 6, 12
Bingham, Rev. Hiram, 4; sketch of, 337

Bishop, Artemas, 9, 319
Bishop, Charles R.: favors independence, 32; requests troop landings (*1874*), 37; and Revolution of *1887,* 87; assists commissioners in San Francisco, 220; for annexation, 220; sketch of, 318 f., 323, 330
Bishop, Mrs. Charles R. *See* Pauahi, Bernice
Bishop, Sereno E.: quoted on missionary influence, 9; appraisal of Liliuokalani and her kingdom, 112 f.; 311; threatens Queen, 142; maligns Queen, 222 f., 246; sketch of, 319
Bishop Bank (Bishop and Co.), 115, 171, 173, 319, 323
Blaine, James G.: on preserving Hawaii for U.S., 45 f.; sees Thurston, 117; death of, 117 n.; expects revolution in Hawaii, 138; Pacific scheme, 142; expansionists, 315
Blaine–Carter convention, 100 ff.; opposition to, 101 f., 122; Pearl Harbor and troop landing under, 122
"Bloodless Revolution." *See* Hawaiian Revolution of *1887*
Blount, James H., 116 f.; and Treaty of Annexation (*1893*), 152 f.; appointment and instructions, 229, 232, 234; ends protectorate, 232 f.; criticism of appointment, 234; method of procedure, 235 f.; report, 235 f., 241, 243; criticized and cleared, 251 ff.; finds attacks on Queen unjustifiable, 311
Bluejackets and marines, 99, 178; presence in Honolulu (*1893*), 313. *See also* Troop landings
Bolte, C., 164, 180 f., 189
Bond, Edward P., 319
Bond, Lawrence, 222, 319 f.
Boston, Liliuokalani visits, *Dec. 1896–Jan. 1897,* 266
Boston (U.S.S.): departs Honolulu on *Jan. 4, 1893,* 39 n., 129 f.; expected support from, 141, 166, 168; com. of public safety requests troops from,

175; Stevens confers with officers on landing, 175 f.; Wiltse decisions, 176, 178, 180, 187, 196, 198, 202, 206, 210, 215; marines from, reembarked, 233, 253; bluejackets from, 266, 313

Boston *Advertiser*, 205

Boston Bank, 115

Boston Board of Trade, 40, 319

Boston *Evening Transcript*, 138, 205, 233

Boston Hawaiian Club, 40

Boston *Herald*, quoted, 137, 205, 208, 225 f.

Botany Bay (Australia), 334

Bounty. *See* Sugar bounty

Boutelle, Charles A., 261

Boyd, Robert, 98

Breckinridge, William C. P., 261

Brewer, C., and Co., 86, 178, 320, 328

Bribery in Hawaiian legislature (*1892*), 133

British Columbia, 224; Esquimalt fortified, 207 f.

British Guinea, fortified, 208

British Honduras, fortified, 208

British West Indies, 267

Brooklyn *Citizen*, 205

Brown, Andrew, 165

Brown, Cecil, 126

Brown, Rear Admiral George, 107, 109; quoted on troop landings, 139; sketch of, 320

Brown, Godfrey, 96; sketch of, 320

Brown Island, German protectorate over, 77

Bryan, William Jennings, 290

Bryce, James, 286

Buffalo Lilliputian (Cleveland), 233

Bull, John, holds back protest, 217

Bush, John Edward: appointed minister of finance, 62; heads mission to Samoa, 78 ff.; recalled from Apia, 81; helps organize Equal Rights League, 115; encouraged primacy in Polynesia, 120; introduces vote in Wilcox-Jones cabinet, 129; supports lottery bill, 133; sketch of, 320

Bush-Wilcox faction, 136

Butler, Matthew C., 255 n.

Cable, Pacific: Merrill quoted on, 105 f.; L. A. Kimberly quoted on, 106; franchises, 143; Stevens quoted on, 150; British, 150, 260 f.; Foster on, 199, 257, 259; necessity of, 260; Pacific Cable Co., 264, 274; Frye's interest in, 282

Caffery, Donelson, on Continental policy, 262, 304 f.

California, 9, 38; Hawaii an outlying district of, 45; annexation petitions from, in *1893*, 198; opposes annexation, *1897–98*, 285

California business interests, 195; sugar refiners, 41, 335

California press, general, 195

Camp Boston, 178, 181, 190

Canada, Dominion of, 101 f., 105; anxiety over Hawaii, 107 f.; Stevens on Canada's interest in Hawaii, 149 f., 152; possible lease of Necker Island, 260 f.; Patriotic League of America (N.Y.) on Canadian independence, 265

Canadian Pacific Railway, 102, 105, 150

Cantacuzena, Prince, 232

Canton, China, 1, 4

Canton, Ohio, Lodge and Cooper see McKinley at, 269

Caribbean, 224

Carlisle, John G., 213, 239, 320

Caroline Islands, dispute arbitrated by Vatican, 77

Carpet baggers in Hawaii, fear of, 148, 268

Carter, Charles L.: aids committee of public safety, 185; Commissioner to Washington, 192; confers with Foster, 199 ff.; lectures for the cause, 219; sees Cleveland's friends, 230; sketch of, 320

Carter, Henry A. P.: negotiates treaty of reciprocity (*1875*), 39 f., 317; appointed minister for foreign af-

fairs, 49; concerned over renewal of
reciprocity treaty, 67; misrepresents
London loan, 72 f.; on South Sea
islands independence, 75 ff.; urges
Bayard to support Honolulu Reform,
89; supports combined protectorate,
free trade treaty, 106 f., 321; opposes lease of Pearl Harbor, 108 f.;
quoted on reciprocity, 109; sketch of,
320 ff.; envoy to European countries, 321; untimely death, 322

Carter, Joseph: with Queen during
Willis' second interview, 244; mission to Washington, 281; on character of Queen, 312

Carter–Blaine Treaty or Convention.
See Blaine–Carter Convention

Castle, Henry N., 221

Castle, Samuel M., 9; on annexation in
certain circumstances, 32

Castle, William R.: relations with
Stevens and Wiltse, 129; on Wilcox–
Jones ministry, 134; on radical
change of Hawaiian monarchy, 135,
164; acts with committee of public
safety, 170; appeals to Stevens for
troops, 175; incapacitated, 183 n.;
journeys to Washington, 192; confers with Foster, 199 ff.; quoted on
sugar and the revolution, 207; influences American press and public,
219, 221; confers with Gresham,
231 f.; sketch of, 322

Castle and Cooke, 178, 322

Cervera, Spanish Admiral, 280

Charleston (U.S.S.): conveys Kalakaua to California, 107; returns his
remains, 109, 320

Charlton, Richard, 11

Charlton's Wharf, 178

Chase, S. P., 330

Chicago Commercial Club, 285

Chicago Herald, quoted, 205, 219, 238

Chicago Inter-Ocean, 231

Chicago Tribune, 205

Chicago Union League, Thurston lectures at, 219

China and Chinese, 1; in population,
44, 47, 150, 280; alliance with, 45;

and opium trade, 56; immigration,
66 f., 148, 220 ff., 272; excluded
from the franchise by Constitution
of 1887, 92, 120; contract labor,
111, 148, 265, 287, 291, 322; U.S.
exclusion laws and, 200; prostitution
and, 223; international complications, 286; labor situation in studies,
331; and taxes, 341

China Merchants' Steam Navigation
Co., subsidy for, 52, 56

Chipman, J. Logan, 199

Cincinnati Journal and Messenger, 206

Citizenship of Hawaiians omitted from
treaty of 1893, 202

Civil War, 19

Claudine (steamer), 192 f., 194 n.,
203; conveys commissioners to San
Francisco, 194

Clay, Alexander S., quoted on Monroe
Doctrine, 305

Cleghorn, Archibald, Governor of
Oahu, father of Princess Kaiulani,
118, 136; pleads for Kaiulani, 172;
protests landing of troops, 179, 180,
184; sketch of, 322 f., 330

Cleveland, Grover, 129; first administration, 141; probable policy of, 153;
Queen's letter to, 192 f., 213; Lakewood, N.J., Conference and results,
213 f.; receives Kaiulani and Davies,
216; Hawaiian policy, withdraws
annexation treaty, 228 ff.; favors reciprocity, 229 n., 230; on annexation,
231; reaction to policy of, 238 ff.;
message to Congress, Dec. 4, 1893,
244; special message, Dec. 18, 1893,
246 ff.; on "national mission," 250,
314; policy criticized, 254; policy
approved, 256 f.; letter to Queen's
agents, 259; message on Necker Island, 260 f.; tradition of, 303; on
presence of marines in Honolulu,
313

Coast Seamen's Journal, 289

Codes, civil and criminal, 15; penal,
11 f.

Colburn, John F.: knows of new constitution, 156, 159; declines to join

com. of public safety, 167, 169, 179;
airs Queen's story, 206

Columbia (ship), 1

Comly, James M.: gives moral support
to ministers, 35; on Hawaiian polity
and decay, 45 ff., 52 ff.; receives
memorials, 56; advises Kalakaua, 57;
warns State Dept., 57

Commercial Club of Chicago. *See* Chicago Commercial Club

Committee of public safety, 154; selected from Annexation Club, 163;
mass meeting, 169; requests troops,
170, 175; determines on abrogation
of the monarchy, 172, 174; prepares
and reads proclamation, 183 f.; ten
members become officials of provisional government, 186

Committee of Thirteen, 57, 62

Congregational   Church   (Central
Union) of Honolulu, 324, 328, 335,
339

Constitution, new, requested during
Kalakaua's reign, 100, 103 f.

Constitution of *1840*, 18, 22

Constitution of *1852*, 22 ff.

Constitution of *1864*: provisions of,
25 ff.; amended, 25; Americans wish
to abrogate, 35; sovereign must be
alli, 48; denizenship under, 91 n.;
desire to restore, 101; parts incorporated in Constitution of *1893*,
156 f., 335

Constitution of *1887* ("Bayonet Constitution"): provisions of, 91 ff.;
oath under, 94 f.; status of Americans under, 94 f.; Article 78 on veto,
96; provision for amendment, 104;
heavy property qualification under,
105

Constitution of *1893* (new): proposals
and petitions for, 122 f., 155 f.;
warnings of, 134; provisions of, 155;
knowledge of, 156; advocated by S.
Parker, 156; criticism of, 157 ff.; destroyed, 157 n.; Queen's attempt to
promulgate revolution, 174

Constitution of the United States, 309

Constitutional   convention,   requests

and petitions for, 103 f., 122 f., 155,
173

Daggett, Rollin M., 67; on Hawaiian
appropriation bill, *1884*, 69; on taxation, security to life and property,
309

Dalziel, agent of the *Times*, 138

Damon, Rev. Samuel C., 323

Damon, Samuel M., 98, 101; cooperates with provisional government,
183 f., 186, 189 f.; proposes surrender, 189; favors conditional annexation, 268; loses faith in annexation, 294

Daniel, John W., 255 n.

Dare, John T., 71; amends bank bill,
81

Davies, Theophilus (Theo.) H.: on
diminution of U.S. influence, 32, 34;
on Revolution and Constitution of
1887, 93; opposes cession of Pearl
Harbor, 151; visits New York and
Washington with Kaiulani, 215 f.;
on Queen's character, 222, 302

Davis, Cushman K., 116, 254 n., 284

Davis, William Heath, 1

Day, William Rufus, 271, 298 f., 315

De Wolf, "Nor'west John," 2

De Young, M. D., 195

Declaration of Independence (U.S.),
12, 93

Declaration of rights, 12

Decline: of Hawaiian nation, 43 ff., 62,
310; of chiefs, 48, 310

De facto government and recognition,
169, 171, 188 f., 190 f., 196, 248

De jure government and recognition,
191, 248

Democrats, 196 f., 288, 300

Denizenship under Constitution of
1864, 91 n.

Dewey's victory at Manila, 280, 298,
315

Diamond Head, 109

Dillingham, Benjamin F.: declares
Queen responsible for revolution,
220; interest in railroads, 323 f.

Dimond, William H., 50, 116; assists commissioners, 121, 195, 220

Dingley tariff, 282

Dinsmore, Hugh A., 300

Diplomatic corps (in Honolulu), 88; confers with cabinet, *July 30, 1889,* 98; interviews cabinet, *Jan. 14, 1893,* 160; at palace, 162; consults cabinet, *Jan. 16, 1893,* 172; supports Queen's government, 173; recognizes de facto provisional government, 191, 192 n.

District of Columbia, territorial type government, 120

Dole, Daniel, 9, 324, 335

Dole, Sanford Ballard: supports Prince W. C. Lunalilo, 31; resigns from Hawaiian League, 82, 84; participates in Revolution of *1887,* prepares constitution, 86, 91; criticizes Constitution of *1893,* 158; prorogation ceremony, 160; suggests regency, 180 f.; accepts presidency, 182, 185 f.; regrets course of revolution, 195; restricts troop drill landings, 243; refuses to relinquish authority, 245; President of Republic of Hawaii, 258, 307; considers annexation, 266, 268; journeys to Washington (*1898*), 287 f.; supports U.S. in war, 296; receives petitions against annexation, 306; tenders sovereignty of Hawaii, 306; first Governor of Territory of Hawaii, 307; sketch of, 424

Dolliver, Jonathan, 301

Dolphe, Joseph N.: amendment proposal, 141; interest in annexation, 197 f., 199; critical of Cleveland's policy, 254 n., 255

Dominis, John O., 323; declines to vote for Prince William, 31; requests Peirce to land troops, 37; travels to U.S., 39; sketch of, 324

Drei Hundert, description of, 85; commanded by Capt. C. W. Ziegler, 85; participates in Revolution of *1893,* 120, 186

Dutch sugar standard, No. 16, 114

Ebbets, John, 2

Edmunds, George F., 107

Egypt, 224, 226

Elele Poakolu or *Wednesday Press,* 62, 325

Emerson, Rev. Oliver P., 170 f.

Émeute, Mott Smith on action of U.S. in case of, 139 n.

Émeute of Jan. 14–17, 1893, 155 ff., 311; success of, 313

Emma, Queen, 21, 33 f., 36 ff., 48. *See also* Queen Emma's party

Emmeluth, John, 165

Engineering Magazine, on labor and annexation of Hawaii, 289

Episcopal Church, Anglican Church, or Church of England, 21 f., 25

Equal Rights League: organization of, 114 f.; fails, 115

Esquimalt (British Columbia), fortified, 207 f.

Evangelist (New York), S. N. Castle advocates annexation in, 32

Executive council of provisional government, 183 f., 186, 188

Fiji, desired by New Zealand, 75

Filibuster, on Newlands resolution, 302

Fish, Hamilton: on good offices of U.S. in Hawaii, 30; quoted on U.S. annexation policy, 33; negotiates reciprocity treaty of *1875,* 39

Fitch, Dr. George L., on infectious diseases in Hawaii, 46

Flag, Hawaiian: origin and design of, 2; retention as local emblem, 201 f.; lowered for last time, 306

Flag, United States: partially copied by Hawaiians, 2; hoisted in Honolulu, 210; hauled down, 232 f.; opinions on pulling down, 233 f.; Dole unperturbed, 234; raised over Iolani Palace, *Aug. 12, 1898,* 306

Flag Day, *June 14, 1900,* 307

Folger, Charles J., 327

Foraker, George B., 293

Forum, Lodge attacks Cleveland in, 363 f.

Foster, John W.: favors annexation,
152 f.; recommends delay on annexation, 153; approves Stevens' recognition of de facto government, 196;
submits to Senate unratified annexation treaty of *1854*, 198; negotiates
treaty of *1893*, 199 ff.; letter to Harrison, 203 f., 247; disavows protectorate, 204, 211, 254; sees Queen's
agent, 214; resigns, 216; recommends annexation of Hawaii, 264 f.;
interest in a Pacific cable, 264, 274;
prepares draft of the annexation
treaty of *1897*, 272; on growing
American interests in the Pacific,
274
France and the French: in population
of Hawaii, 20, 41, 44; acquisitions
and ambitions of in the Pacific, 75,
279, 311; U.S. annexed territory of,
279
Frankfort Assembly, 165
Free Dispensary in Honolulu, 46
Freedmen's Bureau, 317
Frelinghuysen, Frederick T., 46, 67;
on Hawaii's program of primacy in
the Pacific, 75, 309
French Constituent Assembly of *1848*,
165
Frye, William P., 152; on Hawaiian
affairs, 251; and Morgan report,
254 n.; interest in Pacific cable, 282

Gantz, J. H., letter of Colburn to, 260
Garfield, James, 41
Garner, George W., 2
Gatling guns, 98, 168, 178
George, James Z., defends Blount,
255 n.
Germany and Germans: in population
of Hawaii, 44, 120; sugar plantations, 47; influence in the Pacific,
75 ff., 279; interest in Samoa and
Apia, 76, 78; Anglo–German partition of New Guinea, 77; retain original citizenship and privileges under Constitution of *1887*, 92, 120;
defensive system of, 226; attitude

during Spanish–American War, 302;
proposes joint action with Great Britain, 303; taxes paid, 341
Gibraltar, fortress, 224, 286
Gibson, Walter Murray: on decline of
Hawaiian nation, 44 ff.; rise to
power, 45, 50, 52; elected to legislature, 57; program, 57, 60 ff.; influences royalty and masses, 61, 325;
opposes cession of Pearl Harbor, 62,
325; power weakened, 71, 81; program of primacy in Polynesia, 74 ff.;
cabinet crisis, *June 28, 1887*, 85 ff.;
dismissed, 86, 88, 310; death, 88;
sketch of, 324 ff., 329, 332
Gilbert Islands, 78, 150
Gilman, Gorham D.: appointed consul
at Boston, 222 f.; sketch of, 326
Girvin, Jack W., supports commissioners, 220
Glade, H. F., German consul in
Hawaii, 163, 166
Globe (whaler), of Nantucket, 2
Godkin, Edwin L., 209, 219; sketch of,
326
Gold law, "Act to Regulate the Cur-
rency," 69
Golden age of whaling, 3
Golden Era, a prospectus on the opium
license, 131 f., 162, 164
Golden Gate, 194
Gompers, Samuel, opposes annexation,
289
Good, Captain John, 184, 187 n.
Gould, Jay, 327
Government building (Aliiolani Hale),
179 f., 183 ff.; occupation of, 187 f.;
189
Grand Cross of the Royal Order of the
Star of Oceania, awarded to Malie-
toa, 79
"Grand Dominion" (of Pacific is-
lands), Vogel's scheme for, 40
Grant, Ulysses S., 42, 332
Gray, George, 255 n.
Gray, Captain Robert, 1
Great Britain and the British: early
influence in Sandwich Islands, 2, 13;
possibility of acquiring an island or

protectorate, 32, 41, 106, 150, 152, 260 f., 311; in population of Hawaii, 44, 120; propertied class, 47, 58; American concern over British influence in Hawaii, 72 ff., 106, 137, 145 f., 149 ff.; interest in Samoa, 78, 86; retain original citizenship and benefits under Constitution of *1887*, 92, 120; and sovereignty of Hawaii, 108 n., 303; and Pearl Harbor, 137 n.; interest in Necker Island and Pacific cable, 150, 260 f.; delays de facto recognition of provi-government, 191 f.; strategic posture in Atlantic, Caribbean, and Pacific, 207 f., 224; indifferent to U.S. annexation of Hawaii, 216 f., 315; attacked by H. C. Lodge, 262; "Little England" movement in, 275; acquisitions in the Pacific, 279, 282; declines joint action with Germany, 304; declines Japanese proposal for a joint protectorate, 305; makes no protest, 315; rapprochement with U.S., 315 f.; taxes paid, 341. *See also* Australia; British West Indies; Canada; New Zealand

Green, William L.: first cabinet passes treaty of reciprocity, 49; second cabinet forced on Kalakaua, 57; resigns, 60; fails to cede Pearl Harbor, 60 f.; Reform cabinet forced on King, 86; program and efficiency of, 96 ff.; opposition to, 97 f.; fall of, 100 ff.; author of *Vestiges of the Molten Globe*, 326; sketch of, 326

Gregg, David L., negotiates treaty of annexation (*1854*), 20, 198, 311

Gresham, Walter Quintin: appointed and present at Lakewood, N.J., conference, 213; advises withdrawal of Hawaiian treaty, 229; policy evolves 237 ff., 243; N.Y. *Times* quoted on, 239; grudge against Republicans, 239; receives Queen's agents, 259; receives Japanese minister's opinion on annexation, 283; sketch of, 326 f.

Gribble, Graham, 289

Grinbaum and Company, M. G., 164

Grove Farm, Lihue., 338

Guillou, Dr. Charles F., on need for hospitals in Hawaii, 53

Gulick, Charles T., 65; sketch of, 327

Gulick, Rev. Peter, 327

Habeas, corpus, writ of: suspended in Hawaii, 188; restored, 211

Hackfeld and Company, 163, 165

Halifax, fortified, 207 f., 224

Hall and Son, E. O. (Hardware), 169, 184, 187, 327

Hall, Edwin O.: Editor of the *Polynesian*, 20; minister of interior, 32, 169; sketch of, 327

Hall, W. W., 169, 327 f.

Hampton Institute, 318

Hanna, Marcus A., 271

Harper's Weekly, 206; quoted 213, 231, 334

Harris, Charles C., 30, 36, 332; sketch of, 328

Harrison, Benjamin: sees Sec. of Navy Tracy on annexation, 127; proposal by, 146; Queen's letter to, 192 f.; approves annexation, 196; accepts Foster's letter, 203, 247; message transmitting treaty of *1893*, 204; views on restoration of Queen or protectorate, 204

Hartwell, Alfred S., 30, 36; in Kalakaua's first cabinet, 49; sent to Washington to act on annexation, 267, 270, 328; sketch of, 335

Hasting, Frank P., 188, 256

Hatch, Francis M., 255 n., 266; in Washington, 269 ff.; hoped for Japanese and British protest, 283; cooperates with U.S., 294 ff.; to entice American farmers to Hawaii, 295; on Hawaiian neutrality effort, 296 f.; on offer of battalion from Hawaiian National Guard, 296

Hawaii, sovereignty of: London loan and, 73; British and Canadian anxiety over, 203; Anglo–French declaration (*1843*), 303; proposals to guarantee, 304, 311; U.S. refuses to guarantee, 306 f., 311

"Hawaii for the Hawaiians," 52, 61, 100, 325
Hawaiian Board of Health, *Kahunas* organized into, 64
Hawaiian Club of Boston, 40, 319
Hawaiian Evangelical Association, 10, 326
Hawaiian flag. *See* Flag, Hawaiian
Hawaiian Fruit and Packing Co., 165
Hawaiian Gazette, correspondence on Pearl Harbor, 128
Hawaiian Homestead Act and American colonization, 46, 295
Hawaiian–Japanese controversy on labor immigration, 299
Hawaiian League: suggested by Dr. S. G. Tucker, 82; preliminary meeting, 82; constitution of, 82; membership, 83 f.; Dole and P. C. Jones resign, 84; Honolulu Rifles revitalized, 85; *Drie Hundert* promises support, 85; precipitates crisis *June 28, 1887,* 86; mass meeting presents demands to King Kalakaua, 86 f.; Reform ministry, 86
Hawaiian monarchy: decline of alli, 48; abolished or abrogated, 135, 149, 165, 171 f., 174, 185, 322; criticized and maligned, 150, 191, 222, 228, 246, 311; attempts to restore, 192 f., 214 f., 258 f., 261; abolition not promoted by U.S. government, 204; petitions to restore, 266 f., 306; table of, 342
Hawaiian National Guard, 267; Hatch proposes battalion for U.S., 296, 307
Hawaiian Planters' Monthly, 322
Hawaiian Political Association. See *Hui Kalaiaina*
"Hawaii Ponoi," national anthem, 306 f.
Hawaiian Railway Company, 164
Hawaiian Revolution of *1887* ("Bloodless"), 85 ff., 170, 310
Hawaiian Revolution of *1893,* 155 ff., 308 ff.
Hawaiian–Samoan Confederation, 76 ff.
Hawaiian Spectator, quoted, 12

Hawaiian Star, 43; quoted, 226
Hawaiian Women's Patriotic League, petitions McKinley, 266 f.
Hawaii's business leaders, 7. *See also* Honolulu Chamber of Commerce; Planters' Association; Propertied class
Hay, John, 273 f., 303; Spring Rice correspondence, 302 f.; no objection to annexation, 316
Hayes, Rutherford B., 334
Heligoland, McGrew compares to Hawaii, 226
Henry, Patrick, 164
Hilo, Hawaii, 3
Hitt, Robert R., 153; resolution, partial victory for Cleveland, 251, 261, 270; submits Newlands resolution, 300; marshals strategist views, 301
Hoar, George Frisbie: on Liliuokalani, 223 f., 251 f., 255; presents memorial, 284; on acquisition of Hawaii, 305
Hong Kong, Honolulu compared to, 281, 286
Honolulu: early commerce, 2 ff.; becomes capital, 2; favorite port, 3; a yankee outpost, 4; District of, 51 f.; leaders of, 115; prosperity envisioned under lottery license, 131; map of, 177
Honolulu *Bulletin,* 142
Honolulu Chamber of Commerce, urges reciprocity, 69, 322, 326
Honolulu Harbor: marine railroad in, 54; improvement of, 73; improvement proposed under lottery license, 132
Honolulu Iron Works and Foundry, 165, 326
Honolulu Lyceum, 53; meeting in *June, 1884,* 87
Honolulu Public Library, 324
Honolulu Rifles, 84; armed for Revolution of *1887,* 85; status of members under Constitution of *1887,* 95; assist in suppressing insurrection of *July 30, 1889,* 98 f.; dissolved and under cover as Knights of Phythias,

121 f., 170; revived, 170 f.; prepare for action on *Jan. 17, 1893*, 183

Honolulu Rifles Armory ("Armory of the Rifles"): public meeting *June 30, 1887*, 86 f.; mass meeting of *Jan. 16, 1893*, 169, 173 f.

Honolulu Seamen's Bethel (Chapel), 323

Honolulu Social Science Club, 219, 324

Honolulu YMCA, 324, 328

Hopkins, Archibald, 146, 148, 153 f.

Hopkins, Charles Gordon, editor of the *Polynesian*, 20, 327

Hopkins, Charles L., 189

Hoshi Toru, protests annexation, 282 ff.

House Committee on Agriculture, 290

House Committee on Foreign Affairs, 138, 269, 276, 285, 300

House Committee on Rules, 285 n.

House of Nobles, 24, 48; attitude on annexation, 143 f., 322

House of Representatives (Hawaiian), 22

House of Representatives (U.S.): views on annexation, 198; passes Newlands resolution, 301

Household Troops (Royal Guards): mutiny of, 33, 98; disbanded, 193

Hudson's Bay Company, 4

Hui Kalaiaina (Hawaiian Political Association), Petitions for new constitution, 123, 155, 162

Hula-hula, 112, 223

Hunnewell, James, 2

Ii, John, 16

Illinois, annexation petitions from, 198

Immigration, encouraged (in Hawaii), 73

Imperialism (new) and imperialists: Schurz criticizes, 231, 279 f.; J. Bryce warns U.S. against, 286; H. U. Johnson opposed to, 301; G. F. Hoar on, 289, 302, 305, 315. *See also* Americanists; Anti-imperialists

Independent. *See* New York *Independent*

Independents, 65 ff., 70 f.

India, 224; labor situation in, 331

Indians (American), 205

Infectious diseases in Hawaii, 47

Influence of Sea Power on History, 1660–1783, The, 224

Insurrection of *1888*, 98; of *1899*, 98 f.; Royalist, of *1895*, 261

International Seamen's Union of America, opposes annexation, 289

Iolani Palace, 37, 171, 178 f., 183, 189, 223, 306

Irwin, Rear Admiral John, 237

Irwin, William G., 337

Isenberg, Paul, Sr., 87

Isthmus and Panama Canal, Lodge on, 236, 246 n., 310 f. *See also* Nicaraguan Canal

Jamaica, fortified, 208, 224

Janion, Green and Co., 326

Japan and Japanese, 38; in population of Hawaii, 44, 150, 280, 304; excluded from benefits of Constitution of *1887*, 92, 120; contract labor in Hawaii, 148, 210, 299; delays recognition of provisional government, 191; Hawaiian anxiety over, 266, 311; protests annexation in *1897*, 282 f.; Hawaiian–Japanese convention of *1888*, 299; labor complications with Hawaii, 299, 304; proposal for tripartite protectorate, 304; labor situation in, 331

Java, labor situation in, 331

Johnson, Andrew, 332

Johnson, Henry U., opposes annexation and imperialism, 301

Johnson Island, 150, 262

Johore, W. D. Alexander, on despotism of, 82

Jones, John C., 2

Jones, Peter Cushman, 31; on evils of Hawaiian government, 83; resigns from Hawaiian League, 84; in Wilcox-Jones ministry, 126; end of tenure, 134; pressed to join provisional government, 182 f.; testimony in *Morgan Report*, 252; on "moral effect" of troops, 313; sketch of, 328

Judd, Albert Francis: prepares Constitution of *1887*, 91; on Constitution of *1864* and Revolution of *1887*, 93; appeals to Queen against new constitution on *Jan. 14, 1893*, 161; seizes Queen's private papers, 243 n.; swears in Governor Dole, 306; on weakness of Queen's government, 314; sketch of, 328 f.

Judd, Charles, sketch of, 329

Judd, Dr. Gerrit P., adviser and minister of Kamehameha III, 13, 18 f., 51, 62, 321, 328

Ka Leo (nationalist newspaper), 136, 320

Kaahumanu, a female chief, favorite wife of Kamehameha I, *kuhina-nui* and regent, 11; sketch of, 329

Kaai, Simon K.: appointed and described, 50, 62; leads "Young Hawaiian" party, 329

Kahulii Railway Company, 164

Kahunas (sorcerers), organized into Hawaiian Board of Health, 64, 112; disapproved by Liliuokalani, 112

Kaimiloa (ship), armed for Samoan mission, 80

Kaiulani (Victoria Kaiulani), Princess and heir to the throne, 48 n., 136; under British influence, 151; Cleghorn pleads for rights of, 172; Dole suggests regency for, 181; visits New York and Washington, 215 f.; popular in Hawaii, 285, 287

Kalakaua, David, Prince and King: election of *Jan. 8, 1873*, 30 f.; described, 34; and succession, 34 ff.; recognized as King, 37; popular, 37, 42; journeys to U.S., 39 f.; ratifies convention, 41; first cabinet, 49; controls government *1882–87*, 63; and primacy in Polynesia, 74 ff.; alliance with Malietoa, 80; Merrill advises on political situation, 85; and Hawaiian League demands, 87 f.; accepts new constitution, 91;

struggle with Reform ministry, 96 f.; veto power, 96, 100; and conspiracies, 98 f.; opposes Blaine–Carter treaty, 101 f.; endorses movement for a new constitution, 103; visits California, 107 ff.; dies, 109; debts repudiated, 114

Kalakaua family: not recognized as high chief blood, 48; Davies on, 113; Thurston's determination to end rule, 171 f., 181

Kalanianaole, Jonah Kuhio, heir to the throne under Constitution of *1893*, 157

Kaleleonalani, 34. *See also* Emma, Queen

Kalua, J. W., 103

Kamehameha I, 2, 21; statue of, 63, 329, 333

Kamehameha II (Liholiho), 11, 329

Kamehameha III (Kauikeaouli), 3, 11, 16, 19 ff., 322, 329; dominated by missionaries, 51; fails to ratify annexation treaty of *1854*, 311

Kamehameha IV (Alexander Liholiho), 16, 19 ff., 328 f., 334; fails to ratify annexation treaty of *1854*, 20; marriage, loss of son, death, 21; antimissionary policy of, 21

Kamehameha V (Lot), 20 f., 328 f., 334; antimissionary policy, 21; proclaimed king without taking oath, 23 f.; provides Constitution of *1864* (coup d'etat), 24 ff.; died without naming successor, 29, 34; licenses *kahunas*, 64, 112

Kamehameha Manual Labor School, 333

Kanakas, 45 n., 47 f.

Kapaakea, 111

Kapahu, John W., 133

Kapena, John M.: visited U.S. with King, *1874–75*, 39; becomes minister of finance, foreign affairs, and interior, 49 f., 62

Kapiolani (chiefess and wife of Kalakaua), 34, 38, 136, 329

Kauai Island, 3, 335, 338

Kauikeaouli. *See* Kamehameha III

Kawaiahea Seminary, 112

Kawanakoa, David, Prince: named heir to throne in Constitution of *1893*, 147; assists provisional government, 188; member of Queen's first mission to Washington, 193 n.

Keaulouhi, Miriama (Royal Highness), 331

Keawe, Chief, 329

Keelikolani, Ruth, Princess Luka, 48, 64 n., 329

Kekuanaoa, Mataio, Governor of Oahu, 16, 23; sketch of, 329

Kennebec Journal, 153, 205, 207, 212

Keohokalole, 111

Key to the North Pacific (Hawaiian Islands), 225, 227, 293, 310

Kilauea (steamer), 339

Kilauea Cyclorama, 338

Kilauea Volcano House Company, 338

Kimberly, Rear Admiral Lewis A., 106

Kinau (a female chief, *kuhina-nui*), 331

King, J. A., 183; sketch of, 329

King, William A., 281 f.

Kinney, William, 70; member of Hawaiian League, 82; lobbies for annexation and reciprocity in *1897*, 270, 281, 329; sketch of, 329 f.

Knights of Labor, general opposition to annexation in *1897–98*, 290

Knights of Pythias, Honolulu Rifles in disguise, 170

Knutsford, Lord, 108

Korea, 330

Kuykendall, Ralph S., 308

Kyle, James H.: annexation resolution, 256, 261; marshals strategist views, 277

La Le o Ka Lahui, publishes Queen's proclamation, 173

Lackawanna (U.S.S.), in Hawaiian waters, 29, 38, 51

Lahaina, Maui, 3, 62, 326

Lahainaluna (Upper Lahaina) and Mission Seminary, 7, 13, 317

Lakewood (N.J.) Conference and results, 213 f.

Lanai Island, stronghold of Gibsonism, 325

Land bill, 64 f.

Land division (*Mahale*), 18, 317

Lansing, Theodore F., 165

"Large policy" of a big navy and isthmian canal, 311. *See also* Strategists

Lauterback, Edward, 67

Lease, Mrs., 205

Lee, William Little, 14 ff., 18, 21, 318; sketch of, 330

Lee-Marcy Convention (*1856*), 317

Legislatures of Hawaii: changing complexion of, 43, 51; bribery and "wild" financial proposals, 52 f., 57, 310; session of *1880*, 55 f.; of *1882*, 57 f.; corruption, 60, 123, 133 f.; session of *1884*, 69 f.; of *1886*, 70; special session, *1887*, 96 f.; *1888*, 97 ff.; *1890*, 103 ff.

Leleialoha, only casualty of the Revolution of *1893*, 184, 187 n.

Leleiohoku Kalahoolewa (William Pitt), Chief, Kalakaua's brother and heir, 35, 37, 42

Leper Settlement on Molokai, 46

Lewers and Cooke (firm), 323

Liberal party, 118, 122 ff.; joins National Reform or Palace party, 130 f.; requests constitutional convention, 155

Lihue Plantation Co., 338

Likelike, Princess, 48, 322, 330

Lilikalani, and manifesto (*1882*), 57

Liliuokalani (Lydia Kamakaeha or Mrs. John O. Dominis), Princess and Queen of Hawaii, 15; heir to the throne, 42; childless, 48; ability and character, 110 ff., 232 f., 311 f.; supports Constitution of *1887*, 110 f., 253; alleged involvement in conspiracies of *1888, 1889,* 112 f., 162; wins a new cabinet, 113; reaction to new ministry, 113 f.; economic depression, 114, 128, 133, 151; dissatisfied with constitution, 115; native Hawaiians's attitude toward, 119, 155 f.; struggles with Reform-Liberal coalition, 122–130 passim; regains control, 130 ff.; lottery and opium license bills pass, 134; selects new cabinet, 135; opponents prepare for annexation, 136–152 passim; dies, 137 n.; warned of overthrow and troop landings, 141 f.; confers with Wodehouse, 142; prepares new constitution, 155 f.; prorogues legislature, 159 f.; constitution delayed, 160 ff.; issues proclamation to abide by the Constitution of 1887, 173 f.; mass meeting condemns action of, 174; attempts to inform world of her plight, 180; cabinet demoralized, 187, 314; declines to abdicate, 189; surrenders to U.S. under protest, 189 f.; retires to Washington Place, 191; deprived of Household Guards and royal standard, 191; appeals to Queen Victoria, 191 f.; appeals to Harrison and Cleveland, 192 f.; envoy denied passage on *Claudine*, 192, 203; sends delegation to Washington to negotiate restoration, 193 n.; annuities to, 201 f., 229, 272; Commissioners reply to Queen's protest, 202 f.; restoration of monarchy undesirable, 202; maligned, 220 f., 222 f., 246, 311; Willis interviews, 241 ff.; position on rebels, 242 n., 244 f.; Cleveland on her surrender, 248 f.; not restored, 257, 258; sends agents to Washington, 258; no prospect of aid from Cleveland, 259; convicted and pardoned, 266; visits Boston and Washington, 266; seeks to condemn Stevens, 287; returns home, 306

Little England attitude, Roosevelt on, 275 f.

Loan acts: ten million loan, 52 f.; public works under, 52, 58; national loan, 65; two million loan, 65, 71, 73 f. *See also* London loan

Lodge, Henry Cabot, 284, 306, 337; attacks Cleveland's policy, 260; on English cable proposition, 261; resolution on warship, 261 f.; on British aggression in the Pacific, 262; on securing U.S. interests, cable, and defenses, 262 f.; quoted in *Forum*, 263 f.; on "large policy," 273 ff.; supports joint resolution for annexation, 302; on acquisition of Hawaii, Anglo–American rapprochement, 316

London, 71

London loan (*1886*) and Dare amendment, 69, 71 ff., 81, 106, 125; attitude of Bayard toward, 72 ff., 106

Long, John D., 275

Los Angeles, visited by Kalakaua, 109

Los Angeles Board of Trade: petitions against annexation in *1897*, 285; labor councils pass resolutions, 289

Lottery license bill: pigeoned-holed and revived, 131; opinions on bill, 131 f.; *The Golden Era* (a prospectus) quoted on, 131; provisions of, 132; public works under, 132; propertied class concern, 132 f.; Queen favors, 132; W. White railroads legislature through, 133; support, 133; Queen signs, 135; copied from British colonies, 312

Louisiana, lottery of, 132; penal code, 15

Louisiana Purchase, 201, 226

Louisiana Territory, 301

Louisville *Courier Journal*, 238

Low, Frederick F., 68, 330 f.

Luka, Princess. *See* Keelikolani, Ruth

Lunalilo, William Charles, Prince and King, 30 f., 34 ff., 44, 319, 328, 335, 337; dies, 35; sketch of, 331

McBride, James, 27 f.

McCandles, John A., 165

McCarthy, Charles J., 185

McChesney, F. W., 165

McChesney and Sons, 165

McCook, Edward M., 30

McCreary, James B., 153; supports Cleveland and Blount, 251

McEnery, Samuel D., 304

Macfarlane, E. C.: accompanied Kalakaua to California, 109; Hawaiian–American relations, 109; policies considered unfriendly to U.S., 125; Queen's agent to Washington, 193 n.

McGrew, Dr. John C.: founded Annexation Club (1893), 226; compares Hawaii to Heligoland, 226; sketch of, 331

McKinley, David, 270

McKinley, William, 287, 289, 292; elected, 265 f.; petition from Hawaiian Patriotic League to restore monarchy, 266; sees H. E. Cooper, Foster, and Frye on new treaty, 269 f.; annexation treaty message, 272 f.; warns Japan against interference in Hawaii, 299; views on acquisition of Hawaii, 306

McKinley tariff (Oct. 1, 1890), 206, 321, 327, 331; depression in Hawaii under, 114, 118, 128, 133, 151 f., 257

Mahan, Captain Alfred Thayer: letter to the N.Y. Times, 224 f.; on "large policy," 273 ff.; writings, 276 f.

Mahele (division of land), 18, 317

Maine (U.S.S.): crisis, 288; report on, 294 f.; Hawaiian aid to victims of, 295

Malaysians, 324 f.

Malietoa, King of Samoa, 64, 79 f.; alliance with Kalakaua, 80

Malta, fortified, 224, 276

Mangels, Claus, 335

Manifest Destiny: W. Reid quoted, 265; Schurz quoted, 279 f.; R. Pettigrew deplores, 304

Manila, Dewey's victory at, 280, 298, 315

Man-of-war in Hawaiian waters, 122, 261 f. See also Warships in Hawaiian waters

Marcy, William L.: negotiates reciprocity convention with W. L. Lee, 16; furthers annexation treaty of 1854, 151 f.; Senate receives treaty and correspondence of 1854–55, 198

Marquesas Islands, 318

Marsden, Joseph: suggests Queen abdicate, 184; Commissioner to Washington, 192; sketch of, 331

Marshall and Wilds (firm), 2

Marshall Islands, occupied by Germany, 77

Martial law: proclaimed in Hawaii, 188; rescinded, 211

Mass meetings in Rifles Armory, Honolulu: June 30, 1887, 86; Jan. 16, 1893, 169, 173 f.

Massachusetts' penal code, 15

Maui Cattle Company, 338

Maui Island, 7, 12; water rights leased to Spreckels, 50 f., 55, 336

Mauritius, compared to Hawaii, 53

Melanesia, 73 n.

Melville, Commodore George W., 278 f.

Merrill, George W.: on London loan, 71 f.; receives memorial of grievances from Americans, 83 f.; advises Kalakaua, 85, 100; authorized to land forces, 89; consults captains of U.S.S. Adams and Vandalia on troop landing, 91; instructed on American rights under Constitution of 1887, 94; on warships in port, 97; arranges for troop landings from Adams, 99; on Americans and revolutionary outbreaks, 100; on growing British influence in Hawaii, 105 f.; on Pacific cable, 106, 209; prefers protectorate, 209

Micronesia, 73 n.

Midway Island, 261, 301

Miller, William, 21

Minneapolis Times, 208

Misjoinder of producing with the expending power, 43, 52 ff., 58 f., 341

"Mission boys," 81 f., 84, 171, 190, 252

"Mission girl," Cornelia Hall, 328

Missionaries: achievements and influence, 4 ff.; schools, 8 f.; homeward current of, 9; decline of, 18 f.

Missionary party, political influence, 10 ff., 61, 122

Missouri Compromise, 21

Mitchell, John, 304

Mohigan (U.S.S.), 211; in flag raising ceremony, 306

Molokai, 12; leper settlement on, 46

Monroe Doctrine: in House of Representatives, 198; Patriotic League of America on, 265; Senator Clay on, 305

Montclair, N.J., Thurston lectures at, 219

Monterey (U.S.S.), Roosevelt would send to Hawaii, 275

Moore, John Bassett, 299

Moreno, Caesar Celso, 55 f., 320; sketch of, 331 f.

Morgan, John T.: Pearl Harbor amendment to reciprocity treaty, 70 n., 152; favors annexation, 197; presents report, 252 f.; requests views of Schofield, 276; introduces Senate Bill 2263, 282; suggests Hawaii ratify annexation treaty first, 286; opposes McKinley on silver issue, 292; on Hawaiian statehood, 307

Morgan Bill, Senate Bill 2263, 282; S. J. Res. 127, substituted for, 293

Morgan Report, 252 ff.; N.Y. *Times* on, 252; W. D. Alexander's writings in, 252; procedural methods of For. Rels. Com., 252; berates Queen, 253; exonerates Blount, 253; criticizes Cleveland, 254; clears Stevens, 254; Republican views, 254 n.; Democratic views, 255 n.

Mormons and Mormonism in Hawaii, 324 f.; settlement at Laie, 325

Morrill, Justin S., 304 f.

Mott Smith, Dr. John, 49, 116, 137 ff., 146; on U.S. support of *émeute,* 139 n.; favors large annuities and compensation to Queen and Kaiulani, 201; sketch of, 331

Myric, Herbert, 290 f.

Mystic Shrine, San Francisco, Kalakaua entertained at, 109

Nahaolelua, Paul, Governor of Maui, 29, 49; sketch of, 332

"Nancy Hanks Cabinet" (W. H. Cornwell's), in office two and a half hours, 125

Nantucket, 2 f.

Nation, The, 326, 334; quoted, 207, 217, 219

National Association of Manufacturers, addressed by McKinley, 292

National bank bill (Spreckels' and Low's), 68 f.

National Banking Corporation, 337

National Geographic Society: C. L. Carter addresses, 219; Foster addresses, 274

National Loan Act, 65. *See also* Loan acts

National Reform party (Palace party) 97, 103, 122, 130

Navy Department: neglect of Pearl Harbor, 128

Navy War College, 224

Necker Island: Cleveland's special message on British lease of, 260 f.; Lodge on, 261; Hawaii extends sovereignty over, 261

Negroes (American): a possible labor force for Hawaii, 48 n.; Chicago *Herald* on, 205

Netherlands, 78

Neumann, Paul, 65, 162, 169, 189, 193; leads Queen's mission to Washington, 192 n., 214 f.; presents Queen's protest, 214 f., 215, 216 n.

Neutrality of Hawaii during the Spanish American War, 295 ff.

Nevins, Allan, on Cleveland's policy, 250

New Bedford, 2

New constitution, requests for under Kalakaua, 103 f.; requests for under Liliuokalani, 155. *See also* Constitution of *1893*

New England Homestead, 290

New Guinea (non-Dutch), Queensland annexes, 75; Anglo–German partition of, 77

New Hebrides, 75

New Orleans Exposition, 311

New York, petition from legislature of, 198

New York *Christian at Work,* 205

New York City, petition from Republican Club of, 285 n.

New York *Commercial Advertiser,* 205; on hauling down "Old Glory," 233

New York *Commercial America,* 287

New York *Daily Tribune,* 144, 153, 205; quoted, 206, 208, 212, 231, 265, 274

New York *Evangelist,* S. N. Castles advocates conditional annexation, 32

New York *Evening Post,* 205, 276; quoted, 207, 213, 217, 219, 326, 334

New York *Herald,* 33; quoted, 205, 207, 238, 288

New York *Independent* (Congregational weekly), 205, 221; Queen maligned in, 222 f.

New York *Journal of Commerce and Commercial Bulletin,* quoted, 287

New York *Mail and Express,* 137 f., 205

New York *Morning Advertiser,* 205

New York *Morning Sun,* 146, 153; quoted, 238

New York *Observer,* 205

New York *Press,* quoted, 208, 231

New York *Times,* quoted, 138, 145, 205 f., 213, 218, 224, 230, 233, 238, 239, 252

New York *World,* 138, 205; quoted, 206, 209, 212 f., 215, 219, 238

New Zealand and Hawaiian sugar and loan, 40, 180, 224, 315, 323; designs of in the South Pacific, 75

Newlands, Francis G., 298

Newlands resolution (H. Res. 259), 298, 300 f.; Reed opposes, 300 f.; passes, 301

Nicaraguan Canal and treaty, 107, 197, 229 n., 265, 270, 276, 310. *See also* Isthmian canal

North American Review, quoted, 219

North Pacific, 75, 224. *See also* Pacific Ocean

North Pacific squadron (U.S.), 30, 38 f.

Northwest Coast. *See* Pacific Northwest Coast

Northwestern Railway, conveys Commissioners toward Washington, 195

Norwalk Club (Conn.), Thurston lectures before, 219

Norwegians: in population of Hawaii, 44, 47; retain original citizenship under Constitution of *1887,* 92; and taxes, 340

Nor'west John (De Wolfe), 2

Nowlein, Sam, Commander of Household Guards, 98

Nuhou Hawaii and Pearl Harbor, 62, 325

Oahu College, 7, 18, 322, 338

Oahu Island, 3, 14

Oahu Mission press, 7

Oahu Prison, 190

Oceanic Steamship Company (Spreckels'), 66 ff., 337

"Off-shore Ground" (whaling), 2

Old armory in Honolulu, not available for marines from the *Boston,* 178

Old Glory, N.Y. *Commercial Advertiser* on hauling down, 233. *See also* Flag, United States

Oleson, William B.: influences American press, 221, 333; author of *Riches and Marvels of Hawaii,* 333; sketch of, 333

Olney, Richard: letter to Gresham on restoration of the Queen, 239 ff.; prepares special message (*Dec. 18, 1893*) for Cleveland, 246 f.

Opera House, Honolulu, 98, 178, 184, 188

Opium law of *1886:* bribery scandal, 85; immediate cause of Revolution of *1887,* 85, 88

Opium license bill (*1893*) and Chinese traffic, 56, 85, 88; pigeoned-holed and revived, 131; provisions of, 131; W. White railroads through legisla-

ture, 133; intended to check cor-
ruption in smuggling, 133; Cornwell
defends, 133; Queen signs, 135; not
cause for a revolution, 312
Orange Judd Company, 290
Orange Judd *Farmer*, 290
Oregon (U.S.S.), 275
Oregon territory and state, 9, 138, 318,
330; petition from, 198
Oregonian. See Portland *Oregonian*
Orient and Orientals, 279, 307, 310,
314, *See also* China; Japan
Overland Express, 195
Oxnard, Henry T., 291, 323; sketch of,
333

Pacific Cable Company, Foster representative of, 264, 274
Pacific Commercial Advertiser, quoted,
58, 62, 125, 128, 136, 191, 265, 297,
325 f.
Pacific Mail Steamship Company, 50,
66 ff.
Pacific Northwest Coast, 1, 4, 38; and
reciprocity, 40; labor organizations
oppose annexation, 289
Pacific Ocean, annexations and rivalry
in, 24 ff., 90, 224, 279; U.S. influ-
ence in, 196, 221; U.S. defense in,
207 f.; trade in, 208
Pacific Quano and Fertilizer Company,
338
Pacific squadron, 107, 176
Pacific whaling grounds, 2 f.
Page, Walter Hines, requests Mahan's
views, 224
Pago Pago, Tutuila, Samoa, 145
Paki, Chief, father of Bernice Pauahi,
48
Palace party. *See* National Reform
party
Palace Square, 63; meeting in summer
1890, 103 f.; meeting in *Jan. 16,
1893*, 172, 188
Palace Walk, 98
Palace wall, removed, 99
Palama, Queen's residence at, 98, 113
Palama Chapel, 328

Palama Settlement, 328
Palawai (Gibson's estate on Lanai),
325
Palmyra Island, 262
Panama Canal, 310. *See also* Isthmus
Paradise of the Pacific, 307
Parker, John, 333
Parker, Samuel: in Liliuokalani's cabinet, 113, 135; for lottery and opium
license bills, 135; supports new constitution, 156, 160 f.; discusses troop
landings, 169; seeks to avert revolution, 172 f.; protests landing of
troops, 179; threatened by Stevens,
184; seeks refuge in police station,
187; his cabinet demoralized, 188,
314; Queen's agent to Washington
(*1894*), 258 f.
Patriotic League of America, objectives of *1896*, 265
Patriotic League of the Hawaiian Islands, memorial against annexation,
284
Pau, Samuel K. Noble: quoted on lottery, 132; on McKinley tariff, 143
Pauahi, Bernice (Mrs. Charles R.
Bishop, high chiefess), 319; declines
crown, 29
Pauncefote, Sir Julian, 191; unperturbed over proposed annexation
(*1893*), 217 n.
Pearl Harbor: J. M. Schofield and
B. S. Alexander probe, 31; Davies
reflects on British, 32; Peirce recommends cession of, with reciprocity,
33; W. L. Green's cabinet stays, 61;
Nihou Hawaii campaigns against
cession, 62; renewal of reciprocity
treaty (*1886*), 70 n.; described,
70 n.; Wodehouse apprehensive,
108 n.; H. L. P. Carter opposed to
long term lease of, 108 f.; exclusive
and permanent control provided in
Blaine–Carter treaty, 122; map of,
127; Hawaiian concern over U.S.
failure to develop, 128; committee
plans trip to Washington, 128; epistolary battle over, 128; British opposition to cession of, 137 n.; appro-

priation for naval station, 140 f.;
Schofield-Alexander report, 141;
land and cable speculation, 143;
Washington *Post* on, 145; N.Y.
Times on, 145; U.S. Navy neglect
of, 145; Stevens on, 150; Schofield
opinion of, 276; Melville agrees,
278; Procter on, 279; Morgan compares to Gibraltar, 286; Schurz on,
299; H. U. Johnson, 301; R. Stirling
opposes cession, 337

Peirce, Henry A.: on annexation, 29 f.,
32 f.; urges dispatch of war vessel,
30; on reciprocity with cession of
Pearl Harbor, 33; believes reciprocity will lead to annexation, 33; re-
veals Vogel's alleged designs on
Hawaii, 40 n.; on decadence of
Hawaiian nation, 43

Penal code of Hawaii, 11 f., 21

Pennock, Admiral A. M., 30, 33

Pennsylvania, annexation petition from,
198

Pensacola (U.S.S.), 38

Perkins, George C., 285

Peterson, Arthur P.: fails to form a
cabinet, 124; supports lottery, 133;
knowledge of new constitution, 155,
160 f., 172 f.; refuses to join in overthrowing Queen, 167; declines to
sanction arrest of committee of
safety, 168 f.; discusses troop landings, 169; informed by Stevens, 184;
takes refuge, 187; demoralized, 188,
314; sketch of, 333

Petitions and memorials (in Hawaii):
for a lottery license, 131; for a new
constitution, 103, 123, 155, 162; for
restoration of the monarchy, 266 f.,
306; opposing annexation, 284, 306

Petitions and memorials (in the U.S.):
for annexation, 198, 285 n.; against,
285, 292

Pettigrew, Richard, 304

Phelps, E. J., 153

Philadelphia (U.S.S.), 306

Philadelphia *Inquirer*, 205

Philadelphia *Press*, quoted, 208

Philadelphia *Record*, quoted, 252

Philippines, 296, 298

Phillips, Stephen H., 30

Pierce, Franklin, 21

Pilipo, G. W., 64

Pitt, William. *See* Leleiohoku Kalahoolewa

Planters' Association, 60 f., 63. *See also*
Sugar planters

Planters' Labor and Supply Company,
322, 331

Platt, Orville, 197, 218

Police station (Honolulu): refuge for
Parker's cabinet, 169, 187; committee of safety meets, 171, 188 f.

Political Economy party, 101

Polygenetic cabinet, 50 f.

Polynesia, 74 n.; Kalakaua's and Gibson's program of primacy in, 74 ff.,
320

Polynesian, the (Honolulu), 20, 327

Polynesian Confederacy, 45

Polynesians, disappearance of, 310. *See
also* Decline, of Hawaiian nation

Population: of Hawaii, 44; decline of
natives, 44 ff.; foreigners in, 44; and
taxes, 341

Populist party: vote on quorum, 251;
senators and annexation, 263, 284,
288, 327

Portland, Oregon, Chamber of Commerce, 198

Portland *Oregonian*, 145 f.

Portsmouth (U.S.S.), 33, 38

Portugal and Portuguese: in population of Hawaii, 44; imported for
labor, 47; privileges, franchise under
Constitution of *1887*, 92, 120, 307,
321; and taxes, 341

Portuguese Mission, 328

Presidential campaign and election of
1896: issue in Republican platform,
264, 292; election of McKinley,
265 f.; effects of, 269

Presidential election of *1892*, 129

Press opinion (American): on annexation, 195, 205 ff., 219, 221 ff., 265;
on protectorate and pulling down
the flag, 209, 212 f., 233; on Cleveland's and Gresham's policy, 230 ff.,

238. *See also* individual newspapers, infra

Preston, Edward, 50, 62; prepares Constitution of *1887*, 91; sketch of, 334

Prince of Hawaii, 21

Printing, early (in Hawaii), 6 f.

Privateers, 296

Privy Council, 13, 20, 311, 319, 322

Proclamation of martial law, 158

Proclamations, of the Queen and ministers, 172; of the committee of public safety, 185

Procter, John R., 279; sketch of, 334

Propertied interests and capital class in Hawaii: disaffection of, 52 ff., 58 f., 63, 119; under Constitution of *1887*, 92, 120; desires free trade treaty, 122; on lottery license, 132 f.; under Constitution of *1893*, 158; desire for stable regime, Annexation Club quoted on, 140. *See also* Stable government and security in Hawaii

Prosperity, 3, 58, 152, 266; incident to reciprocity, 49, 58, 152, 266, 308

Protectorate: or annexation, 149; Harrison on, 204; public opinion and press divided on, 208 f.; Merrill on, 209; Godkin on, 209; no enthusiasm for protectorate, 209; protectorate proclaimed, 210; disavowed by Foster, 211, 254; Belknap on, 226; N.Y. *Times* on, 230; Morgan on, 286; joint protectorate declined, 304

Providence Island, 77

Provisional government, 185; organization of, 185 f.; functions until Republic declared, 186–258 passim; threatened, 241; defense of, 245 f.

Public buildings (all), surrender, 191

Public works (in Hawaii): under Wilder cabinet, 51, 54; under ten million loan, 52; Moreno's cable company proposal, 55 f.; under London loan, 73; under lottery license bill, 132. *See also* Railroads

Pula: defined, 40 n.; seeds, admitted duty free to U.S., 40

Pulitizer, Joseph, 206

Punahou School and Oahu College, 7, 9, 18, 322, 335, 338

Puritans, 6 ff., 6, 19, 61, 328. *See also* Missionaries; Sandwich Islands Mission

Putnam, J. H., 94 f.

Quadripartite treaty, 15

Queen Emma's party ("Queenites"), 51, 332

Queen's (Liliuokalani's) party, or Palace party, 115

Queensland, Australia, 75

Race issue and slavery in Hawaii: "bleeding Kansas" and Civil War, 19; unratified annexation treaty of *1854*, 19, 21 n.; in elections of *1882*, *1887*, 52, 96; and southern antagonism to annexation in *1897*, 302. *See also* "Hawaii for the Hawaiians"

Railroads (Hawaiian): S. G. Wilder's interest in, 51, 54; under ten million loan, 52; in Honolulu Harbor, 54; under lottery bill, 132; on Hawaii, 132; on Oahu, 132, 323; Dillingham's interest in, 220, 323

Ralik Islands, 77

Ramage printing presses, 6, 8

Reciprocity, movement for and treaties: first proposed, 15 f.; Peirce urges reciprocity and lease of Pearl Harbor, 33; consummated, 39 ff.; provisions of *1875* treaty, 39 f.; opposition to, 41; ratified in Hawaii and by Senate, 41; prosperity under, 49, 58, 152, 266, 308; threatened, 70; renewed in *1886*, 70 n.; Bayard quoted on, 73; amendment, 145; nullified, 257; Kinney on renewal, 281; treaty of *1886* threatened, 296. *See also* Pearl Harbor

Reply to the Ministerial Utterances, A, by Hoapoli Baker, 53

Review of Reviews, 112, 219

Revolution of *1887*. See Hawaiian Revolution of *1887*

Revolution of *1893*. *See* Hawaiian Revolution of *1893*

Revolutionists and annexationists, 313 f.
Rhode Island, 2
Rhodes, Godfrey, 63
Rice and rice culture, 43, 46; alleged fraudulent export of, 42 f.
Richards, C. L., 328
Richards, Rev. William, 12, 13, 17 f.
Ricord, John, 13 f., 18, 333; sketch of, 334
Rifles. *See* Honolulu Rifles
Rifles Armory or "Armory of Rifles," mass meeting in *June 30, 1887,* 68 f.; on *Jan. 16, 1893,* 169, 173
Robertson, George M., 25, 334
Robinson, Charles, 257 f.
Rooke, Emma. *See* Emma, Queen
Rooke, Dr. T. C. B., 21
Roosevelt, Theodore, 302, 334, 337; on "Issues of 1896," 264; on annexation of Hawaii, 264 n., 274 f., 277; on "large policy," 273 ff., 277; on Carl Schurz, 280 n.; on Japanese intervention, 284; buys up coal in Hawaii, 295
Rosebery, Lord, 144, 192 n.
Royal Cemetery, 219
Royal Guard. *See* Household Troops
Royal Hawaiian Agricultural Society, 322
Royal Hotel, 98
Royal School, 7, 323
Royalists: uprising (*Jan. 1895*), 261; fear presence of marines, 313; weak and demoralized, 314
Russ, William Adam, 250
Russell, William E., 264

Sackville-West, Sir Lionel, 76 f., 80
Sacramento Federated Trades Council, 285
Sacramento labor council, 289
Saint Louis *Republican*, 205, 207
Saint Lucia (British West Indies), 207, 224
Salt Lake City, Utah, 290, 329
Samoa and the Samoan embroglio, 226, 320; Kalakaua–Malietoa alliance, 64; Bayard on Samoa and islands of Polynesia, 64 f.; German interest in, 76, 78 f., 302; Hawaiian–Samoan confederation, 78 ff.; British interest in, 78; Bayard on Hawaiian–Samoan confederation, 79; Washington Conference on Samoa, 80 f.; recall of Bush, 81
San Diego, California: cable from to Honolulu, 150; Kalakaua visits, 109
San Francisco (Bay City): Kalakaua visits, 109; possible cable to Honolulu or Hilo, 150; Commissioners in Washington, 195
San Francisco (U.S.S.), 139
San Francisco Board of Trade, 198
San Francisco *Bulletin*, 142, 195, 205
San Francisco Central Labor Union, 289
San Francisco Chamber of Commerce: petitions for annexation (*1893*), 198, 220; opposes annexation (*1897*), 285
San Francisco *Chronicle*, 195
San Francisco *Examiner*, 136, 139, 142 ff., 195, 309
San Francisco Golden Gate Park, 330
San Francisco labor council, 289
San Francisco *Morning Call*, 41, 145, 195, 205
San Francisco *Newsletter*, 195, 206
San Francisco *Post*, 195
San Francisco *Record*, 195
Sandalwood trade, 1 ff.
Sandwich Islands Mission, 4, 6 ff.; schools, 7 f.; predominating white influence in Hawaii, 9; object of, 10, 18 f., 322. *See also* Missionaries
Saranac (U.S.S.), 33
Schofield, Maj. Gen. John M.: at Pearl Harbor, 31 n.; Schofield–Alexander report on Pearl Harbor, 141, 145; on defense of Pearl Harbor, 276 ff.
Schurz, Carl: condemns protectorate, 231; on hauling down the flag, 233; on Cleveland's administration, 250; on manifest destiny, 279 f., 299 f.; Roosevelt's opinion of, 280 n.; letter to McKinley, 298 f.; sketch of, 334

Scout (H.B.M.S.), 39
Seddon, Richard, 315
Select schools, 7
Senate, Hawaiian: debate in, 255 ff.; approves Cleveland's policy, 256 f.; and noninterference in Hawaii, 263; Sen. Bill *2262*, 282; J. Res. *127*, substituted, 293
Senate Committee on Foreign Relations: hears Peirce's report on New Zealand, 40; Thurston's visit, 138; discusses annexation, 141; favors annexation, 197, 200, 218, 251 f.; *Morgan Report* of, 252 ff., 256, 284; *Davis Report* of, 293 f.
Sewall, Harold M., 282, 285, 294, 306
Sheffield Scientific School, Yale University, 338
Sherman, John T., 152, 254 n., 269 ff., 282, 284; resigns, 298, 327
Silver issue, 300; delays annexation, 292
Simpson, Jerry, 205
Sino–Japanese war (first), 283, 303
Skerrett, J. S., Admiral: mutiny of Household Troops, 33; on location of American troops, 179; takes charge of protectorate, 211; hauls down flag, 232 f.; troop landings, 243; on provisional government, 326
Slavery: prohibited in Hawaii, 15; deters annexation in *1854–55*, 19, 21 n.; slavery controversy, 19
Smith, William O.: reports on Pearl Harbor committee, 128 f., 133; Annexation Club, committee of public safety, 159, 161 f., 164, 169, 183; named to executive council of provisional government, 186; sent to Washington (*1897*), 267; for annexation in any form, 268, 270; sketch of, 334 f.
"Snap-shot diplomacy," 213
Solomon Islands, 75
Soper, John, 102, 169; commands provisional government forces, 180
South Pacific, 76, 259. *See also* Australia; Melanesia; New Zealand; Polynesia

South Pacific whaling grounds, 2
South Sea Company, 41
South Sea islands and islanders, 47; sovereignty of, 90; taxes paid, 340. *See also* Melanesia; Polynesia
Southern (U.S.) antagonism to annexation, 302
Southern Pacific Railway, 115
Southern states' situation compared to Hawaii, 119
Spain, acquires Caroline Islands, 77
Spalding, George A., 282
Spalding, Col. Z. S., 252
Spanish–American War: delays debate on treaty of annexation, 280; hastens annexation, 296 f.
Spencer, Charles N., 113; sketch of, 335
Spooner, John S., 305
Spreckels, Claus: profits from reciprocity, 41, 335 f.; secures water rights on Maui, 50 f., 55; assists Kalakaua and Gibson, 63; operates Oceanic Steamship Company, 66; fails to secure franchise for national bank, 68 f.; operates private bank, 337; interference and reciprocity, 70; and sugar-beet industry, 97; cooperated with Thurston, 195; blamed for revolution, 207; pressure removed from, 220, 222; monopolizes market west of the Missouri, 291; opposes annexation, 282; sketch of, 335 ff.; develops Spreckelsville, 336; operates private bank, 337
Spreckels, Gus S., 195
Spreckels, John D., 66, 195, 337
Spreckelsville, 64 n., 336
Spring Rice, Sir Cecil: urges annexation, 302 f., 306; on Anglo–American solidarity, 316; sketch of, 337
Stable government and security in Hawaii: *Pacific Commercial Advertiser* on, 58; Thurston on, 86, 117; Steven on, 122; Annexation Club on, 140; A. F. Judd quoted, 158; W. Castle on, 164; Daggett on, 309 f.; Thurston on, 290; Annexation Club seeks union with U.S., 313

Stevens, John L.: counsels Kalakaua, 104; member of Annexation Club, 117, 129, 147, 313; warships in Hawaiian waters, 121 f., 134; leaves Honolulu, 134; fosters Blaine's scheme, 141 f.; criticizes Hawaiian monarchy, 141, 150, 223; presses annexation, 149 ff.; on Pearl Harbor and cable, 150 f.; complains of British influence, 150 f.; sugar loss under McKinley tariff, 151; uses *Kennebec Journal* as mouthpiece, 153, 205, 207, 212; on support for provisional government, 159, 166, 168; confers with cabinet, 160; on de facto recognition, 166, 169; requests troops, 175 f.; confers with Thurston and Castle, 175 f.; de facto recognition of provisional government, 189; establishes protectorate, 210 f., 211; maligns Queen, 223; Cleveland excoriates, 244, 248; Queen seeks condemnation, 287; protection of American lives and property, 313; author of *Riches and Marvels of Hawaii*, 333

Stirling, Robert, 337

Strategists, strategic arguments for annexation, 207 f., 273–79; criticized, 279, 304; public alerted to, 280 f. (*1897*), 301, 315. *See also* Americanists

Suez Canal, 276

Sugar bounties: possible lease of Pearl Harbor in exchange for, 108; annexation and, 152; eliminated from treaty of *1893*, 200, 229; abolished by Wilson–Gorman tariff (*1894*), Hawaii regains original advantage under reciprocity, 257; beet-sugar bounty, 289

Sugar interests, 207; oppose annexation, 282, 284, 291 f., 300

Sugar planters, 47; U.S. only market for, 40 n., 220; prosper under reciprocity, 49, 58, 152, 266, 308; depressed under McKinley tariff, 114, 206, 257, 321; desire free trade treaty, 122; blamed for revolution,

207, 219; pressure removed from, 220, 222; warned by W. N. Armstrong, 267; cautioned by Thurston, 271; work for reciprocity and annexation, 281 f.

Suhr, Ed., 163, 165

Supreme Court (Hawaiian): created, 15; advisory opinions, 15, 96, 100, 113; remodeled, 22 f.

Swinburne, Lt. Com. W. F.: commands shore forces, 178; protects American property, 181; in *Morgan Report*, 252

Sydney, Australia, 180

Sydney Intercolonial Conference (*1883*), 75 f.

Synge, William W. F., 22, 28

Tamasese, 78 f.

Tasmania, 165

Tateno, Gazo, 283

Taxation: American concern over, 52 ff., 59; destroys capital, 57; by nationalities in Hawaii, 341

Taylor, Zachary, 317

Teller, Henry M., 293

Temperance Advocate and Seamen's Friend, 323

Tenedos (H.B.M.S.), 36 f.

Texas, annexation of, 226

Thurston, Asa, 9, 337

Thurston, John M., 288, 305

Thurston, Lorrin A., 82; leads mass meeting of *June 30, 1887*, 86; on Constitution of *1887*, 93; Minister of Interior, 96; warns Kalakaua of losing throne, 101; approves secret Annexation Club, 115 f.; journeys to Washington, 116 f., 146; discussion with Claus Spreckels, 116, 195; sends Blaine memo, 117 ff.; relations with Stevens and Wiltse, 117, 129, 141, 147; proposes line of action, 120 f.; objectionable to the Queen, 124; opposes lottery license bill, 133; warns of Queen's determination to change constitution, 134; proposal considered by Senate Foreign Relations Committee, 141; encouraged by Annexation Club, 146, 153 f.; on Queen's authority to abrogate constitution, 158; advises Colburn to resist Queen, 159; assumes leadership of Annexation Club, 163, 164; seeks assistance from Stevens, 166, 169; attempts to have Colburn and Peterson abrogate monarchy, 167; cautions planters, 171; seeks extirpation of monarchy, 171 f., 174; leads mass meeting, *Jan. 16, 1893*, 174; on troop landing, 175, 313; prepares proclamation abrogating monarchy, 183; bedridden, 183 n.; leads commission to Washington, 192; negotiates treaty of annexation, 199 ff.; reports on "citizens of Hawaii," 201 f.; on protectorate, 209; prefers small annuity and compensation, 210; reports effect of Kaiulani's and Neumann's visit, 216 n.; influences press and public opinion, 218 f., 297 f.; on "Advantages of Annexation," in *North American Review*, 219; admits Hawaii has no market except U.S., 220; on withdrawing treaty, 229; initial approach to Gresham, 231 f.; recalled, 255 n.; returns to Washington (*1897*), 267; lobbies in capital, 270 f.; prepares *Handbook on the Annexation of Hawaii*, 281; on prospects for immigration and growth, 290; suggests U.S. purchase all Hawaiian coal, 295; sketch of, 337 f.

Thurston, Sarah Andrews, 337

Times (London), on the annexation of Hawaii, 138

Tonga: desired by New Zealand, 75; Hawaii's plans for treaty with, 79

Tracy, Benjamin F.: sees President Harrison, 127; replaced by John D. Long, 275; champions annexation, 278

Trans-Mississippi Commercial Congress: declares for Pacific cable, 259, 278; Thurston addresses, 290

Treaty of annexation (*1854*), unratified, 20 f., 198

Treaty of annexation (*1893*): provisions of, 199 ff.; withheld from Senate, 203; submitted, 203 f.; Harrison on, 204 f.; U.S. press reaction to, 205 ff.; action on delayed, 213 ff.; withdrawn from Senate by Cleveland, 229

Treaty of annexation (*1897*): discussed with McKinley, 270; Foster's draft, 272; McKinley on, 272 f.; ratified by Hawaii, 284; Senate action on delayed, 284 ff., 292; opposition to, 288 ff.; abandoned, 293

Trenton, N.J., Thurston lectures at, 219

Troop landings: requested by Hawaiian officials, 36 f.; from *Adams*, 89; Merrill arranges for, 89, 99; under Blaine–Carter treaty, 102; Adm. George Brown's plans, 139; Wodehouse on general permission granted for, 139; usual procedure, 140 n.; requested by committee of safety, and accomplished, 141, 166, 168, 175 ff.; Admiral Skerritt on, 179; Cleghorn, Parker, Colburn protest, 179 f.; Liliuokalani on, 190; Washington *Evening Post* on, 217; Dole prohibits for drill purposes, 243; Cleveland on, 247 f.; "moral effect" on native Hawaiians of, 313

Tropics, acquisitions in: Schurz on, 280; dangerous for the U.S., 289; *Coast Seamen's Journal* on, 289

Trousseau, Dr. George, 136 f.

Truman, Harry S., 8 f.

Tucker, Dr. G. S., 82

Turco–Greek war, 303

Turco–Russian war, 303

Turpie, David: on resolution, 252; tariff pushes resolution aside, 255 f.; signs *Morgan Report*, 255 n.

Tuscarora (U.S.S.), 36 f., 38, 318

Union, with U.S.: forms of, 120; objective of the provisional government, 185, 220, 246; objective of the Republic of Hawaii, 258, 313

Union League of Chicago, Thurston speaks before, 219

Union party (American) in Hawaii, 294

United States Constitution, and implications of annexation, 304

United States flag, 304. *See also* Flag, United States

United States Navy, neglects Pearl Harbor, 128, 145

United States Territory of Hawaii, 307

Utah deputation to Hawaii, 325

Vancouver, Captain George, 2

Vandalia (U.S.S.), 91

Vatican, arbitrates Caroline Islands dispute, 77

Vest, George Graham, 263

Vestiges of the Molten Globe, by W. L. Green, 326

Veto provision, in Constitution of *1887,* 72, 96

Victoria (British Columbia) *Colonist,* 265

Victoria, Princess Kaiulani. *See* Kaiulani

Victoria, Princess Kamamalu, 23; designated heir to the throne in Constitution of *1864,* 25; proposed by American as successor of Kamehameha V, 28; death of, 29

Victoria, Queen, 21, 112; returns Liliuokalani's letter to foreign office unanswered, 191 n., 274

Vilas, William F., 257, 303

Villiers, F. H., 303

Vogel, Sir Julius, 40

Wabash Case, Gresham in, 327

Wadsworth, J. W., 290

Waikapu Commons, Maui, 336

Waikiki, Oahu, 2, 181, 191

Waimae, Kauai, 3

Waioli, Kauai, Manual Labor School at, 328

Walker, Admiral John S., 260 n.; on annexation, 276 f.

Walsh, Edward M., 290

War of 1812, and eclipse of British pelagic whaling, 2

Warships in Hawaiian waters: protracted sojourn of *Lackawana,* 29; Pierce urges dispatch of, 30; *Portsmouth* remains during *Sept. 1873,* 33; *Saranac* appears in *Oct. 1873,* 33; U.S.S. *Portsmouth, Tuscarora, Benicia, Pensacola,* and *Lackawana* frequent port, 38; *Benicia* and *Boston* test political situation, 39 n., 130 n.; Peirce recommends retention of *Lackawana,* 51; *Adams* stays until *Vandalia* arrives, 91; Thurston comments, 120; Stevens claims presence secured order, 122; Queen deterred from coup d'etat, 125, 134; Wodehouse claims two unnecessary, 144; Rosebery declines to send British, 192 n.; Lodge resolution on, 261

Washington Conference on Samoa (*1887*), 81

Washington *Evening News,* 199, 205 f.

Washington Island, in the Marquesas, 318

Washington Place (Liliuokalani's private residence), 191

Washington *Post,* 137, 145, 205, 212, 218

Water rights on Maui, 50 f., 55, 336

Waterhouse, Henry T., 164, 170

Waterhouse, John T., 165

Wednesday Press or *Elele Poakolu,* 62, 325

Western Sugar Refinery Company, 291 f.

Westliche Post (St. Louis), 334

Whaley, Captain, 113

Whaling industry, 3

White, Stephen M., 197, 215, 285, 301

White, William: introduces bill for constitutional convention, 123; railroads lottery and opium license bills through legislature, 133, 162

Whitney, William A., 113

Whitney, William C., 106

Widemann, Hermann A., 113; Queen's agent to Washington, 258 f., 260 n.; sketch of, 338

Wilcox, George, 126, 129 ff., 134, 141; withdraws from committee of public safety, returns to Kauai, 163; sketch of, 338

Wilcox, Robert W., 93, 98; organizes Equal Rights League, 98, 114 f.; supports lottery bill, 133

Wilder, William C., 50; cabinet opposes foreign loans, 54 f.; interest in railroads, 54, 164; member of committee of public safety, 164; seeks cooperation of Stevens, 166; commissioner to Washington, 192; on protection of capital, 309; sketch of, 339

Wilder Steamship Company, 164, 192, 194, 329, 339

Wilhelm II, Kaiser, 226

William G. Irwin and Company, 336 f.

Williams, T. T., 142 ff., 309

Willis, Albert S.: appointment and instructions, 241; mission and interviews with Liliuokalani, 242 ff.; requests Dole to relinquish authority, 245

Wilson, Charles B.: leads insurrection of 1888, 98; appointed marshal, 113; organizes Equal Rights League, 115, 125, 162; proposes arrest of emeute ringleaders, 169, 171; plans to guard government building, 184; surrenders government property, 190; maligned by Stevens, 223 n.

Wilson–Gorman tariff: abolishes sugar bounties, restores tariff, 257; possibility of revision, 266

Wiltse, Captain G. C.: cooperates with Stevens and Annexation Club, 125, 129, 144 f., 166, 313; warns Washington on constitutional changes, 134; decides to land troops, 170, 176; instructs officers, 176; declines de facto recognition, 188 f.; removal and death, 238 n.; criticized by Cleveland, 248

Winship, Captain Jonathan, 1

Winship, Captain Nathan, 1

Wodehouse, James H.: advises Kalakaua, 100, 104; concerned over Pearl Harbor, 108 n., 118; on Wilcox–Jones ministry, 126 f.; motives scored, 136; denies rumors of Queen's ill health, 137; advises Queen, 139 f., 142; on misrepresentation of Hawaiian situation, 144 f.; meets with cabinet, 160; sends Queen's statement to Auckland, 180; transmits Queen's letter to Queen Victoria, 191; delays recognition of provisional government, 191; affords de facto recognition pending instructions from London, 192 f.; sees no need for a protectorate, 211; Pauncefote's appraisal of, 217

Women's Board of Missions, 112

Woodward, Commander Edwin T., 98 f.

Wormley Hotel, Washington, 196

Wundenberg, F. W., 170, 339

Wyllie, Robert Crichton, 13, 18, 20 ff., 51; sketch of, 339

Yankee traders and Yankee trader-merchant class, 1 f., 61

Yankees, antipathy toward, 19

Yellow Peril, 45

Young, Alexander, 339

Young, Brigham, 325

Young, John, or Keoni Ana, 21, 337

Young, Lieutenant Lucien: describes prorogation ceremony, 160 n.; on decision to land forces, 176; lands accouterment, 178; serves as messenger, 188; in Morgan Report, 252

"Young Hawaiian" party, opposed to foreign influence, 62 f., 329

Ziegler, Captain Charles W.: commands the Drie Hundert, 85; promises support to Hawaiian League, 85; to committee of public safety, 170; arrives first at government building, 186

Zollverein, 45